The Great
Halifax Explosion

The Great Halifax Explosion

A World War I Story of Treachery, Tragedy, and Extraordinary Heroism

John U. Bacon

HARPER LUXE

An Imprint of HarperCollinsPublishers

HarperCollins
PUBLISHERS
Since 1817

FIRST HARPERLUXE EDITION

ISBN: 978-0-06-268699-2

HarperLuxe™ is a trademark of HarperCollins Publishers.

Library of Congress Cataloging-in-Publication Data is available upon request.

17 18 19 20 21   ID/LSC   10 9 8 7 6 5 4 3 2 1

To the memory of Wally and Helen Graham,
my beloved Canadian grandparents, who first told me
this remarkable story, and the good people of Halifax

Contents

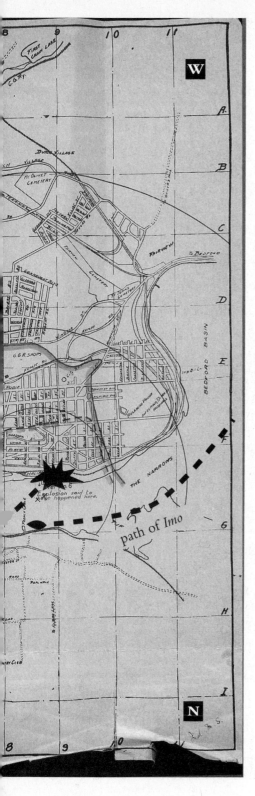

This map was produced by the Royal Society of Canada as part of their detailed scientific report on the Halifax Explosion. *Mont-Blanc* sailed toward the Narrows, while *Imo* traveled in the opposite direction, veering toward the left (port) side. When the ships collided, *Mont-Blanc*'s crew abandoned ship, and the smoking vessel drifted west into Pier 6, where it exploded. Note: the map's orientation is such that the bottom-right corner points north. *(Royal Society of Canada)*

The Great
Halifax Explosion

PART I

A Forgotten Story

Chapter 1
A Century of Gratitude

On Thursday, December 1, 2016, the people of Boston slogged through a drizzly day with temperatures in the 40s—neither fall nor winter, the kind of cold that gets deep in your bones and stays there.

At 8:00 p.m., 15,000 hearty souls left their warm, dry offices and homes to crowd around the stage in the center of Boston Common, the nation's oldest city park, dating back to 1634. They were waiting for the mayor of Boston, the premier of Nova Scotia, the Canadian Mounted Police, and Santa Claus himself to turn on the 15,000 lights draped on a forty-seven-foot white spruce Christmas tree, a perfect specimen, and brighten the dark, foggy gloom. When the crowd finished counting down, the people backstage flipped the switch and set off fireworks, and the crowd cheering as though relief had been delivered.

Every year the Nova Scotia Department of Natural Resources sends scouts across the province to locate the best tree. They found the 2016 winner in Sydney, Nova Scotia, but it was unusual because it came from public lands, instead of being donated by private citizens who compete for the honor of having their tree selected. After a tree-cutting ceremony, they load it onto a big flatbed truck, strap it down, and ship it to Halifax for a send-off parade. There they pin a provincial flag on both sides so fellow travelers along the three-day, 660-mile journey to Boston know where it came from. The tree even comes with a band of dignitaries, including an official town crier and its own Facebook fan page, and twitter account, @TreeforBoston.

All this costs the citizens of Halifax about $180,000 to continue a tradition that started in 1918—and they do it enthusiastically. As one Nova Scotian said, "Why do we have to stop saying 'Thank you!'?"

What did Boston's ancestors do to inspire contemporary Haligonians to keep thanking them a century later?

The answer to that question harkens back to World War I, which introduced submarines, tanks, and airplanes; ended empires in Russia, Turkey, Austria, and

Germany; and created a new world order. It lies in a forgotten disaster that occurred on Thursday, December 6, 1917, in Halifax—the most destructive man-made explosion until Hiroshima, one that blew out windows 50 miles away, rendered 25,000 people homeless in an instant, wounded 9,000 more, often horrifically, and killed 2,000, most of them in a flash. It lies in hundreds of Bostonians rushing to help before the people of Halifax even asked—a response so overwhelming that it helped transform these two countries from adversaries to allies.

Ultimately, it lies in a split second that brought out the best of both nations.

Chapter 2
Under Cover of Darkness

On November 9, 1917, with the Great War building to its horrendous crescendo, the French freighter *Mont-Blanc* docked at Gravesend Bay in Brooklyn, New York. Although the United States had joined the Allied forces a few months before, American troops were only just starting to fill the trenches of France, while Vladimir Lenin's Bolshevik Revolution had toppled the Russian government two days earlier. The next day Lenin had promised his countrymen they would soon be dropping out of the most destructive war the world had ever seen. This presented Germany with its best chance to break the grueling three-year standoff on the Western Front, and it was therefore of paramount importance that the Allied powers send munitions and men in greater numbers than ever before to prevent the Germans from breaking through.

The United States had remained neutral until April 6, 1917, but American manufacturers, shipping companies, and ports had been doing brisk business since the war broke out in 1914, selling the British, French, and other Allied powers supplies, weapons, and explosives. Tons of exports poured out every day from Gravesend Bay, squeezed in between Bensonhurst and Coney Island.

Mont-Blanc, built in 1899, was not among the most impressive vessels crossing the sea. She measured 320 feet long and 47 feet wide, fairly standard for a transatlantic vessel, and she wasn't the oldest ship on the seas, but her best days were definitely behind her. She was slow, with a top speed of about 12 miles per hour—roughly one-third the speed of *Lusitania*—with a long history of bare-minimum maintenance. Sensing opportunity when the war started, the French Line bought her in 1915, fixed her up enough to transport supplies from North America to Europe, and turned her into a moneymaker.

But she would be asked to do more. In 1917, German U-boats had been sinking military and merchant ships by the hundreds each month, forcing the Allied Powers to use any ships still afloat on increasingly dangerous missions.

The previous month, the French Line put *Mont-Blanc* in the hands of Captain Aimé Joseph Marie Le Médec, thirty-eight. At five foot three and 125 pounds, Le Médec was not physically imposing, but he knew how to carry himself like a captain, an impression buttressed by his regal bearing and carefully groomed jet-black beard. His highly disciplined, "by the book" approach was not initially well received by his thirty-six-man crew and four officers on their first transatlantic journey, but by the time they reached New York, he had earned their respect and trust.

When *Mont-Blanc* pulled into Gravesend Bay, Le Médec and his crew had no idea what cargo they might be picking up. During the Great War it could be almost anything, and the premium on security precluded advance notice. But they started getting hints before the cargo could be loaded onto the creaky *Mont-Blanc*. Shipwrights at Gravesend Bay attached custom-made wooden linings and magazines to the inside of the steel hull to keep the cargo as tightly packed, hermetically sealed, and immobile as possible, because high explosives are so sensitive that a good jolt can set them off. The shipwrights worked around the clock for two days to secure the partitions with copper nails because copper doesn't spark when struck. They were told a single spark could send them all skyward.

Finally, on November 25, 1917, the stevedores started loading the cargo under the protection of local police surrounding the ship. The stevedores so feared accidentally blowing up the volatile cargo—and the ship, the docks, and themselves with it—that they fastened canvas covers over their boots to keep their soles from sparking against the steel deck.

When a French government agent finally told Captain Le Médec what they were loading on his ship, it was a most unpleasant surprise: *Mont-Blanc* would be carrying almost nothing but high explosives back to Bordeaux, France. Le Médec normally exuded the calm confidence expected of a captain, but his face belied his alarm. If the U-boats' success forced the Allies to squeeze more from their remaining ships, it had the same effect on the Allies' captains. Le Médec had earned a record as a competent helmsman, but he'd never captained a ship as big as *Mont-Blanc*, nor had he ever carried high explosives. But in the conflict's fourth year, the normal rules no longer applied. The French government had directed its New York agent to buy munitions and explosives in such unprecedented quantities that they needed forty to fifty ships every two weeks to deliver the ammunition overseas. That required using ships that would ordinarily be too unwieldy, beat up, or slow for such a mission—and captains unfamiliar with the cargo to ship them.

Le Médec and *Mont-Blanc* were being asked to carry one of the largest caches of high explosives ever loaded onto a ship: 62 tons of gun cotton, similar to dynamite; 246 tons of a new and particularly combustible airplane fuel called benzol, packed in 494 thin steel drums and stacked three and four barrels high; 250 tons of TNT; and 2,366 tons of picric acid, a notoriously unstable and poisonous chemical more powerful than its cousin, TNT, which was used to make shells, the Great War's principle weapon. They had unwittingly brought together the perfect mixture of catalysts to get a fire started, plenty of fuel to keep it going, and a massive load of high explosives, most invented since the American Civil War, to finish the job. Fully loaded, the touchy cargo alone weighed almost 3,000 tons, or 6 million pounds—about thirteen times the weight of the Statue of Liberty. This was the Great War's version of the Arsenal of Democracy, packed barrel to barrel and crate to crate, with slabs of plywood between them. The total value of the cargo was $3 million, or about $72 million in current U.S. dollars. Whatever the flaws in their plan, the authorities who concocted *Mont-Blanc's* mission could not be accused of playing small.

Before leaving Gravesend Bay, Captain Le Médec met with the British Admiralty's senior naval officer, Commander Coates, whose office had jurisdiction over Allied shipping. He didn't expect Le Médec to like his mission, and probably didn't care if he didn't. In the course of the Great War, how many soldiers and sailors were thrilled to receive their assignments? Captain Le Médec had no authority to which he could appeal, and the cargo waiting for him in Gravesend Bay wouldn't do anyone any good sitting on the docks—except per- haps an observant German submarine captain looking to make a name for himself by blowing up a sizable swath of Brooklyn.

By the time Commander Coates met with Captain Le Médec in late November 1917, 70 million military personnel were entering their fourth year of demor- alizing trench warfare, a form of combat designed for defense. This created stalemates, which produced endless slaughter. Multiplying the misery, technology had advanced unevenly, creating efficient new ways to tear men apart but not to put them back together. The Great War had already claimed 9 million soldiers and 7 million civilians, with no end in sight. *Mont-Blanc*'s cargo was part of the desperate attempt to prevent the Germans from exploiting their long-awaited chance to break the stalemate, and win the war. The fearful absurdity of the ship's freight was matched by the insanity of the war it was intended to support.

It was now up to *Mont-Blanc*'s captain and crew to deliver all this to Bordeaux, France, where it would be weaponized to kill as many German soldiers as possible. All French ships during the war prohibited alcohol on board, but Captain Le Médec added a ban on smoking, or even carrying a single match in a shirt pocket, a policy reinforced by posters displayed throughout the ship, to leave nothing to chance.

If they could get *Mont-Blanc* safely out of Gravesend Bay without a mistake and avoid underwater mines, they would face even greater dangers: the notoriously rough North Atlantic, and German U-boats. These little submarines were far cheaper and quicker to build than destroyers and required only twenty-five to fifty men to operate, allowing the Germans to put 360 on the high seas during the Great War. They excelled at their job: sneaking up on big Allied ships and literally blowing them out of the water. There were enough of them out there, hunting thousands of vessels, to become a force of fear throughout the Atlantic—even for opulent civilian ocean liners like *Lusitania*, which a U-boat sank in 1915, killing 1,198 of the 1,959 aboard, including 128 Americans, a fact that almost drew the United States into the war in its second year.

Lusitania was only one of a few thousand ships the U-boats claimed during the Great War, including a few within sight of New York City, a campaign that cost some 15,000 Allied lives. The Germans sunk almost half of those ships in 1917 alone, costing some 15,000 lives.

The British realized they could not keep sending their ships across the sea just to watch the U-boats send them to the ocean's floor. They would lose the war if they did. After trying a handful of failed strategies, they went to their last resort: a convoy, which they feared was a foolhardy scheme that would only make it that much easier for the U-boats to pick off a cluster of ships at once.

They anxiously sent their first convoy on July 10, 1917, out of Halifax Harbour. When the entire convoy made it safely to Europe, the British figured out why: in the vast expanse of the ocean, a close-knit convoy of ships was almost as difficult for a U-boat to find as a single ship, yet each successful convoy delivered a few dozen more ships safely to shore. Throw in the convoy's ability to counterattack U-boats, and the game changed almost overnight. The British quickly adopted the practice for most of their major transatlantic trips, with great success.

Convoys typically consisted of a dozen or more merchant ships and a troopship or two carrying arms and soldiers in the middle of the circle, protected by a cruiser, six destroyers, armed trawlers, and torpedo boats that could detect submarines moving underwater—all designed to exploit the U-boats' weakness: they were surprisingly slow. If a convoy spotted a U-boat, it had a decent chance of getting the German crew in its crosshairs and doing to them what they were doing to Allied ships. The convoys became even more effective when the Allies started using airplanes to spot the subs. In just a few months, the convoys made the U-boats as scared of the big ships as the big ships were of the U-boats and dramatically reduced the advantage the U-boats had given the Germans.

But the convoys worked only if you could join one. When the *Mont-Blanc* approached her December 1 departure date, Captain Le Médec met again with Commander Coates to discuss *Mont-Blanc*'s route to France. Coates asked Captain Le Médec if the freighter could make 200 miles a day, or an average of 7.25 knots (about 8 mph), which would put the ship into Bordeaux in about eighteen days. Le Médec answered honestly that, having never carried such a heavy load before, he wasn't sure, but he thought perhaps they could in fine weather. Both of them knew, however, that no ship was likely to see fine weather on the treacherous North Atlantic for eighteen straight days.

Commander Coates then gave Captain Le Médec more bad news, as calmly as a blackjack dealer sweeps up your cards after you've busted: Le Médec's ship was too slow to keep up with the convoys Coates had leaving New York, so he ordered Captain Le Médec to sail some 700 miles up the East Coast to Halifax, Nova Scotia, the biggest natural port in North America, and the center of Allied shipping on the western side of the Atlantic. There, Coates said, Captain Le Médec might be able to join a convoy sailing to Bordeaux. Once in Halifax, Le Médec would also receive a sealed envelope. If he fell behind the convoy to Europe, Le Médec was instructed to open the envelope to reveal his secret route to Bordeaux—a route *Mont-Blanc* would have to navigate by herself.

To give *Mont-Blanc* a fighting chance against the U-boats, the French Line had equipped her with a 90mm cannon (or "gun") pointing forward, and a 95mm gun in the stern. But the comfort those offered was nothing compared to the protection a convoy of Allied ships would provide.

Mont-Blanc pulled out of Gravesend Bay for Halifax an hour before midnight on Saturday, December 1,

1917—the same night the British cruiser HMS (His Majesty's Ship) *Highflyer*, one of the most famous ships in the British fleet, sailed into Halifax Harbour to a hero's welcome. Just days after the war started in 1914, *Highflyer* had captured a ship carrying German soldiers and £500,000 of gold, then followed that up a few weeks later by sinking an armed German merchant cruiser off the coast of Africa. The British government awarded *Highflyer*'s crew £2,680—or almost a quarter million in today's U.S. dollars. The British boys on board suddenly had fame, wealth, and health, a rare combination during the Great War. *Highflyer*'s success made news across the ocean, giving a needed boost to morale after some early setbacks. *Highflyer* updated her fame by leading the Allies' first convoy that summer out of Halifax, a great success that dramatically shifted the balance of power on the seas. It seemed *Highflyer* could do it all, and her crew was celebrated accordingly.

While *Highflyer* and her crew were being cheered by crowds on both sides of Halifax Harbour from the moment she was sighted, *Mont-Blanc* slipped out of Gravesend Bay as quietly as she could, under cover of darkness, to make her perilous trek up the East Coast. If all went well, *Mont-Blanc*'s captain and crew would be received in Halifax in complete silence, leave Halifax as anonymously as they had arrived, and repeat that reception in Bordeaux three weeks later.

Their plans went awry from the start. A few hours out of Brooklyn, a wicked snowstorm off the Maine coast brought heavy winds and high waves. Nothing unusual by the standards of the North Atlantic, but it was enough to send the crew repeatedly belowdeck to make sure the barrels and boxes of high explosives were not shifting, toppling over, or colliding with one another. The storm also forced Captain Le Médec to run closer to the coast. Reducing one risk, however, increased another: the shallower coastline was more likely to be patrolled by German U-boats, which often left mines in front of major ports for Allied ships to find. The crew's collective paranoia was well supported by the facts.

For four harrowing days, the floating powder keg bobbed up the Eastern seaboard, with the anxious crew scanning the horizon for U-boats and Halifax Harbour's 158-year-old Sambro Island Lighthouse, oldest in the Americas. On Wednesday, December 5, it finally came into view, promising an end to the rough seas and the fear of shifting cargo.

When Captain Le Médec slowly turned *Mont-Blanc* toward Halifax Harbour, the weary crew was rewarded with a view of one of the world's prettiest ports. The harbor opens like a funnel to the sea, with almost no development on the outer edges of either side—just a thick cover of pine trees on gentle slopes. After *Mont-Blanc* entered the calm waters, she sailed to McNab's Island in the middle of the channel. If all went well, *Mont-Blanc* would be permitted to continue the remaining 10 miles past George's Island, then through the neck of the harbor, known as the Narrows—a mere 1,000 feet across—followed by the wide expanse of Bedford Basin at the end, which measured almost 3 miles in diameter, where *Mont-Blanc* would anchor to refuel and wait for the next convoy to leave for Europe, her safety assured until she headed out again.

But when Captain Le Médec checked in at McNab's Island, he saw a line of steel buoys, each about four feet in diameter, spanning from McNab's Island to the shore. Their path was blocked.

While the *Mont-Blanc*'s crewmen basked in the apparent conclusion of their nerve-fraying trip up the East Coast, their destination port hummed with a confidence it hadn't felt since its glory days had ended a half century ago.

The Great War had multiplied Halifax's shipping eightfold, fueling unprecedented wealth and status as North America's most important port. When men, munitions, or medical supplies were going from North America to Europe, they were probably passing through Halifax. That was good news for its fourteen harbor pilots, who boarded the bigger ships to guide them in and out of the harbor safely. At a time when the average Canadian made about $70 a month, a harbor pilot could earn an astounding $1,000. Nova Scotia native Francis Mackey, forty-five, a short, thick, bald man known for his natty attire and precisely groomed mustache, was one of the fortunate harbor pilots, and among the best. In his twenty-four years piloting ships in Halifax Harbour, he could still boast a spotless record, with nary an accident against his name.

When they said Mackey "knew every rock and bend of land around the harbor," he replied, "Well, some of the pebbles I might not know." Captain Le Médec had never been to Halifax before, so he was lucky to get an experienced pilot like Francis Mackey on board *Mont-Blanc* that day.

With Halifax Harbour's traffic expanding exponentially, the captains and harbor pilots had grown increasingly lax about nautical conventions and communications. This was a particular problem for the harbor's chief examining officer (CXO), F. Evan Wyatt. Noticing the disorder and confusion among the sea captains growing daily, Wyatt wrote to his superiors, "It is not possible to regulate the traffic in the harbor, and it is submitted that I cannot in this regard accept the responsibility for any accident occurring."

But Wyatt's commanders apparently weren't worried about Halifax Harbour's rush-hour traffic. Winning a war required accepting risks, after all. Wyatt's warnings went unheeded.

Back at McNab's Island, Captain Le Médec learned those steel buoys spanning the harbor were holding up a metal gate that ran from McNab's Island to the western shore, and that was anchored to the harbor floor by three-ton concrete weights. They had installed the gate to keep the U-boats out, lest the submarines sneak in and decimate a dozen sitting ducks, or leave mines behind for all the rest. Just a couple nautical miles beyond that first gate, the authorities had stretched another fence from George's Island to both shores, just to be sure. They worked: not one U-boat had yet made a strike inside McNab's Island.

Mont-Blanc reached McNab's Island just a few minutes after Wyatt had decided to pull both gates across the channel that day at 4:30 p.m. Captain Le Médec, his crew, and Harbour Pilot Mackey would have to spend a sleepless night atop their floating bomb, exposed to any U-boat that was bold enough to come so close and lucky enough to stumble upon one of the most dangerous and defenseless ships the Allies had ever commissioned.

While *Mont-Blanc* was anxious to get inside Halifax Harbour, the Norwegian ship *Imo* was just as eager to get out and go in the opposite direction to New York. There it would load relief supplies intended to alleviate the desperate situation of the civilians in German-occupied Belgium.

Imo's captain, Haakon From, forty-seven, was an experienced skipper who had already sailed *Imo* into Halifax twice without incident. Usually self-possessed, he also had a violent temper that could erupt at odd times. Captain From's latest assignment, however, looked simple—until the coal he had ordered for the trip arrived late, leaving his ship on the wrong side of the harbor when CXO Wyatt ordered the gates closed for the day.

No one on shore knew anything about the concerns of Captain Le Médec, Captain From, or Chief Examining Officer F. Evan Wyatt, and they might not have cared. They were busy making money and having a good time.

Halifax's population had grown from 47,000 in 1910 to an estimated 60,000 during wartime, which that didn't include the thousands of transient sailors, soldiers, and workers passing through—not to mention the bootleggers and prostitutes who arrived from all over Canada to support the troops, in their way. They seemed to work with impunity throughout downtown, with taxi drivers often serving as rum runners.

A beautiful port city, Halifax's Victorian homes and sloping terrain resembled a miniature San Francisco, while its population, dominated by English, Irish, a stew of immigrants, and generations of sailors, suggested a smaller Boston. The town had been founded at the midpoint of the 18-mile-long harbor and then expanded south, where wealthy residents like the Cunards of cruise- line fame built their mansions. Then the town expanded up the coastline, where the working class in the North End neighborhood of Richmond earned solid livings in the dockyards, railyards, and factories that framed their district.

Few in Richmond were doing better than the Orrs, who lived, worked, studied, and prayed in the middle of the growing neighborhood. Samuel Orr Jr. had founded Richmond Printing Company, which supported forty-plus employees, including his father and brother. Samuel Jr. and his wife, Annie, had recently moved into a handsome new home with their six children a few blocks from the printing plant; the Richmond School, which their children attended; and Grove Presbyterian, where they worshipped.

Their oldest child, Barbara, fourteen, helped raise her five siblings while still finding time for dancing and ice skating. Ian Orr, just two years younger, spent so much time studying the warships in the harbor that his parents gave him books on modern ships and a pair of binoculars to watch them from their bay window.

"You'd be of great value to German spies, Ian," their father joked. "You must know more about these convoys than any of them."

Like most Haligonians, the Orrs saw the war only from a distance, largely unaware of the carnage occurring daily in the trenches. Not so Joseph Ernest Barss, who had returned from the Western Front a changed man. The great-grandson of Canada's greatest privateer, Joseph Barss Jr., who had captured, burned, or sunk dozens of American ships in the War of 1812, Ernest had inherited more than a little anti-American sentiment. But in 1917 that was true of most Canadians, who resented the Americans' persistent threats to annex their land from the time the United States was born to as recently as 1911.

Standing five-eight, Barss had starred on the baseball, football, and hockey teams of his hometown Acadia University, graduating cum laude in 1912. Three years later, when he learned Germans had gassed a famed Canadian unit, he signed up to fight. A year later, a German shell found Barss, launching him into something hard and knocking him out. The blast seriously injured his back and his foot, and left him with shell shock, insomnia, nervousness, and hand tremors, but he knew he had beaten the odds just by surviving. Back in Nova Scotia, Barss forced himself to relearn to walk with a cane, a very painful process, to prove the doctors who said he'd never walk normally again wrong. But beyond recovering, he still didn't know what he wanted to do with his life. At twenty-five, with no money and shaky health—in an era when forty-seven was the average life span—he felt time was slipping away.

That Wednesday night Haligonians were rewarded with a warm, calm, and dark evening, due partly to the strictly enforced blackout regulations, which required the lights on Halifax's streets, businesses, and homes to be turned off to prevent the Germans from identifying a target-rich environment. Instead of spending the beautiful night sitting behind drawn curtains, however, they took advantage by strolling the sidewalks, visiting the town's many parks, and talking about the famed

Ringling Brothers Circus, which had just arrived in town.

In Richmond, the Orrs's neighbors attended a special midweek event at Grove Presbyterian to celebrate paying off the construction loan to build the church. As of that night, the congregation owned its beloved building free and clear.

Ernest Barss was still struggling with his health, his finances, and his future, but he was home from the Great War, and he was safe. He knew it could be worse.

With fresh troops due to depart for Europe the next morning, Halifax buzzed with anxious energy. The darkness inspired many of the bolder sailors and soldiers to take their girlfriends and dates—hired and otherwise—to the Citadel's sweeping "Garrison Hill," which was so dark passersby walking below on Brunswick Street couldn't detect couples having sex on the sloping grass just a hundred feet away.

Nineteen-year-old Ethel Mitchell, a budding pianist who had been studying for the Halifax Conservatory of Music entrance exams, took a break to get ready for a big night out. She was one of five lucky young ladies to be invited to meet five officers from the celebrated HMS *Highflyer* at a local home, a common practice in Halifax during the war. Mitchell wore her finest: a rose-pink evening dress and matching satin slippers.

The night was such a success that after dinner the officers invited Ethel and her friends aboard *Highflyer*—a clear violation of rules prohibiting civilians on board during wartime. The women, sworn to secrecy, were enjoying cookies and wine in the Captain's Quarters when a small dance party kicked up, and they joined in.

In the wee hours, *Highflyer's* Lieutenant Commander Percy Ingram escorted Miss Mitchell to the door of her parents' home, where they said good night. After climbing the stairs to her room, happily spent, the normally fastidious Ethel made an exception that night and draped her best dress over a chair, crawled into bed, and fell asleep with her fluffy white cat, Buttons, nestled at her feet.

The next morning, Thursday, December 6, Captain Le Médec and his crew woke early to make sure *Mont-Blanc* would be one of the first ships to slip into the safety of Halifax Harbour. At the other end of the harbor, in Bedford Basin, Captain From and his crew did the same, to ensure the *Imo* would be the first to leave Halifax Harbour for the open sea.

PART II

O Canada

Chapter 3
"Why Aren't We Americans?"

1497–1865

Halifax came to life as a military base, and quickly made itself invaluable by supplying just about everything nations needed to wage war.

Europeans first set foot on what is now Nova Scotia in 1497, and soon recognized the land's strategic importance. Nova Scotia was not only the gateway to the St. Lawrence River, which provides access to present day Montreal, Toronto, Detroit, Chicago, and Duluth, as well as the vast lands west, but it was also the last stop for European ships sailing to New England. Thus, when the French set up a base called Louisbourg on Nova Scotia's northern island of Cape Breton in 1713,

New Englanders feared the French would cut the colonists' shipping lifeline with England. At the colonists' urging, England countered by appointing Edward Cornwallis the first Governor of Nova Scotia, Latin for "New Scotland," on June 21, 1749. The first structure Cornwallis built was a humble log palisade, right by the Narrows, but daunting fortresses would follow.

Cornwallis picked his spot very well. Halifax is the world's second-biggest natural harbor, behind only Sydney, Australia, and is almost ideally formed. The late Halifax lawyer and writer Donald Kerr described the shape of the harbor as that of a wine bottle standing upright on a table with a basketball balanced on top. In Kerr's model, the table represents the Atlantic Ocean, and the fat part of the bottle is the body of Halifax Harbour, 5 miles long and a 1 wide, with the city of Halifax on the west side and Dartmouth on the east. The neck of the bottle is the Narrows, which runs 1.5 miles long but a mere 1,000 feet across. Once a ship gets beyond the Narrows, she is rewarded with the vast expanse of Bedford Basin, the basketball in Kerr's model, which stretches 2.5 miles by 3.5 miles, a naturally sheltered deepwater anchorage—so big and safe that entire fleets of Allied warships gathered there during both world wars.

Halifax Harbour is sheltered from wind by granite

slopes covered by trees and later homes, factories, and offices, and the water almost never freezes. Cornwallis also found Halifax Harbour very easy to defend against intruders, who have to travel 18 miles from Chebucto Head (satisfyingly pronounced "She-BUCK-toe," a bastardized version of the native Mi'kmaq term for "big harbor"), which marks the entrance from the North Atlantic. The British later built forts at Chebucto Head and York Redoubt, four more on McNab's Island alone, plus more garrisons on Fort Ogilvie, George's Island, Citadel Hill, and Fort Needham, which sits near the top of the Richmond neighborhood, directly above the Narrows. The odds of running that gauntlet are so slim that no invading ship has ever attempted it.

Halifax's climate is much more temperate than most would guess. The city sits at 44.69 degrees latitude, which places it south of Grenoble, France; Bangor, Maine; Champlain, New York; Minneapolis, Minnesota; and the entire states of North Dakota and Washington. Halifax's winters are typically not as cold as those at the same latitude, thanks to the Atlantic's warming effect.

Less than a month after founding the town, Cornwallis granted a license for the town's first bar, predating its first churches by a year, and that first bar, the Split Crow, is still thriving today. Halifax's identity quickly fell into place: a military base that likes its beer, with more pubs per capita than any city in Canada. Of course, the English weren't paying their men in Halifax to drink but to defeat the French up the coast.

After a twenty-two-year-old lieutenant colonel named George Washington ambushed a thirty-five-man French patrol near present-day Pittsburgh in 1754, the French and Indian War was under way, a conflict that would shape the future of the continent. Halifax cemented its central role in the New World on a moonless night in July 1758, when four hundred ships sheltered in Halifax Harbour sailed up the coast and mounted a surprise attack on the French in Louisbourg. The English quickly boarded France's meager fleet of five ships, burning one and capturing another, then brought it back to Halifax with her crew intact. The British owned the gateway to the continent, and Halifax became its most patriotic city.

While young Halifax was becoming one of Great Britain's most important ports, Boston was already a full-fledged international capital.

Settled by Puritans in 1630, it quickly became New England's economic, political, and intellectual hub, starting with the nation's first university, Harvard, which opened in Boston's sixth year. All that power came to bear on December 16, 1773, when Boston's "Sons of Liberty" protested "taxation without representation" by dressing like Mohawks, dumping dozens of boxes of tea—which were lined with lead to keep it dry, and weighed 300 pounds each—and destroying $1.5 million of East India Company property. The Tea Party erased any doubt that Boston was the center of colonial resistance.

After the American Revolution sparked the continent's first civil war, the newly minted Americans were not above abusing their neighbors who remained loyal to the Crown, often branding, tarring and feathering or simply killing United Empire Loyalists. Not surprisingly, some 60,000 United Empire Loyalists became refugees, with half of them heading north to what is now New Brunswick and Nova Scotia, often leaving their property behind for the Americans to take without compensation. In North America's first civil war, the southern rebels won. The Nova Scotians' misgivings about the American government started the day the United States was born.

No sooner had the Rebels kicked the British Loyalists out then they started eyeing the Loyalists' new land, too. In fact, the Americans' ambition to annex the land to the north is baked into the Articles of Confederation, Article XI: "Canada acceding to the confederation, and adjoining in the measures of the United States, shall be admitted into, and entitled to all the advantages of this Union."

Canadians understood a threat when they heard one—no matter how courteously phrased. Their worst suspicions would be confirmed in just a few decades.

On June 18, 1812, President James Madison, responding to real and perceived British threats, sent his "War Message to Congress," accusing Great Britain of "a series of acts, hostile to the United States as an independent and neutral nation." The United States, now 7.5 million citizens strong, entered the rematch confident of victory. Thomas Jefferson, who had never seen combat, boasted that beating the British again would be "a mere matter of marching."

Early on the Americans earned upset victories against the world's greatest naval force, on both the Great Lakes and the Atlantic. They boldly attacked Fort York, now called Toronto, where they burned public buildings and private homes. But the British turned things around when the HMS *Shannon* blasted away at the USS *Chesapeake* off Boston, then boarded her. In just thirteen minutes, 252 men were wounded or killed before *Chesapeake* surrendered. The *Shannon* then towed the *Chesapeake* to Halifax Harbour, where the townspeople ran to the docks to cheer.

Haligonians were fiercely loyal British subjects, but they were also shrewd businesspeople. During the War of 1812, Halifax port receipts tripled, from £31,041 in 1812 to £93,759 in 1814. Halifax celebrated the British naval and army officers with lavish parties, while offering its many pubs and taverns to the lower-ranking sailors and soldiers, who stumbled about the city streets at all hours.

Halifax historian Thomas Akins was a young boy during the War of 1812, and recalled that "the upper streets were full of brothels; grog-shops and dancing houses were to be seen in almost every part of town. The upper street along the base of Citadel Hill between the north and south barracks was known as 'Knock Him Down Street,' in consequence of the number of affrays and even murders committed there."

One theory goes that the term "Haligonian" was coined as a play on Haligoonian. If so, we know where it started. (Ditto the nickname Bluenosers, given to the sailors for their cold noses and their blue-dyed wool mittens, which deepened the color when their owners wiped their noses.) But if Halifax wasn't exactly a monastery, it knew its strengths: supplying wars, and all that went with them. Halifax proved exceedingly good at all of it.

A few Halifax residents found a way to profit more directly from the war: privateering. A privateer is exactly like a pirate, except the privateer is licensed by his government to attack enemy ships and capture, sink, or burn them. When Nova Scotia's privateers captured an American ship, they would bring it back for auction at the Privateers' Warehouse, a three-story stone building right next to the docks (now a popular college pub), and split the proceeds with the government.

It sounds like a lark, but it was an extremely dangerous business, usually starting with the privateers catching up to a boat and firing a shot across the bow. If the other ship's captain didn't surrender, the privateers fired their cannons at the ship, which returned fire. The ship whose guns did the most damage usually won, but if that didn't settle things, one crew would invade the other's ship and start punching, strangling, and stabbing with knives and bayonets—all of them more reliable than rudimentary firearms. If the ship started to sink, the sailors were often doomed to drown no matter how close to shore, since many of them couldn't swim. As they said, swimming just prolonged the agony.

All this explains why outgunned ships typically tried

to run away, and if they couldn't, they simply surrendered. The winning crew would board the losing ship, put their own crewmen in charge, and steer the prize back to their home harbor.

It wasn't easy to make a living out of it either. During the War of 1812, a third of Nova Scotia's privateers never seized a single American ship, only half could capture more than two for all their troubles, and a quarter Nova Scotia's privateering ships were captured, burned, or lost.

But if you were good at it, you could become rich and famous—and Joseph Barss Jr. was the best. When Barss's father, Joseph Barss Esq., was just eleven his widowed mother left Barnstable, Massachusetts, in 1765, for Liverpool, Nova Scotia, where her son grew up to become a noted privateer against the Americans in the Revolutionary War. His son, Joseph Jr., inherited his seamanship and antipathy for Americans.

When Joseph Barss Jr., and his business partners sensed war with the United States was coming, they spent a mere £440 to buy a tiny, putrid-smelling former Spanish slave ship called the *Black Joke*. They fumigated her with a concoction of vinegar, tar, and brimstone; rechristened her the *Liverpool Packet*; and installed five rusty cannons.

Barss, a hale and hearty thirty-six-year-old with

flowing black hair, headed straight for Massachu-setts Bay, where he took eleven American vessels in one week, and followed that up by taking nine fish-ing schooners—in one day. While the American press howled for his capture, Barss and crew kept it up until Christmas 1812, when they returned to Halifax to bask in their bounty: more than $100,000 in prize money, or $3 million today. When they returned to sea in the dead of winter, the hardest season for privateering, they took thirty-three more ships in two months.

Barss finally met his match on June 11, 1813, when an American privateer in a bigger boat with more fire-power spotted the infamous *Liverpool Packet* off the coast of Maine and gave chase. After six hours, Cap-tain Barss had to concede the inevitable, and struck his colors. But the Americans were not going to let a little thing like surrender keep them from storming the highly coveted *Liverpool Packet*, with sailors on both sides dying in the fight before the two captains ended it.

The Americans towed Captain Barss and crew to Portsmouth, New Hampshire, where local authorities shackled them in irons, marched them through Ports-mouth, and then tossed them in jail, where Barss re-ceived "especially severe treatment." They kept him in shackles and fed him only hardtack, crackers as tough and dry as plywood, designed to last months at sea. Several months later Joseph Barss's captors paroled him, on one condition: that he never engage in privateering against American ships again.

Barss retired to a farm in Nova Scotia, but not before establishing himself as the greatest privateer on the continent, catching somewhere near a hundred American vessels in less than a year. We don't have Barss's journals, but it stands to reason that capturing a few dozen American ships indicates you want to be rich. Capturing, burning, or sinking six or seven American ships suggests you don't like Americans very much.

By the end of the war, few citizens of the British Commonwealth would disagree, including the ones who burned the United States's Presidential Mansion in retaliation for the Americans' torching their homes in Fort York. They didn't finish the job, but the smoke damage forced the Americans to whitewash it, which inspiring a new name: the White House. The man behind that attack, Major General Robert Ross, was killed days later, and is buried in Halifax's central cemetery, with signs leading you to his gravestone. He died a hero.

These combatants passed their anti-American sentiment down through the generations, including to

Joseph Barss Jr.'s great-grandson Ernest, who would fight valiantly in the Great War while grumbling about Americans staying on the sidelines.

When the War of 1812 ended three years after it started, Haligonians focused on cementing their city as the banking capital of British North America—and its shipping capital, too, with an effort led by Samuel Cunard. During the last year of the War of 1812, Cunard expanded into steamships, sending one across the Atlantic in 1840 to Liverpool and then back to Boston, establishing a popular route for Cunard's standing as a leader in the cruise industry.

In its first sixty-five years, Halifax learned that war could pay, but only if it prepared for the next one, and kept a vigilant eye on the Americans.

After the War of 1812, the Duke of Wellington ordered that Halifax's Citadel be rebuilt to keep out the French, the Spanish, and any other attackers, but mainly the Americans, who'd already shown an appetite for Canadian land. They started rebuilding the massive structure in 1828 and finished it in 1858—just in time.

When the American Civil War broke out in 1861, British North America was conflicted, and Halifax even more so. Haligonians still had many family and commercial ties with Boston, one of their biggest shipping partners, but they were also doing a lot of business with Southern cotton growers, too. In fact, Halifax's Richmond neighborhood had been named for Richmond, Virginia, because that Southern city shipped cotton to Halifax, where it was processed and shipped around the world. This divide explains why both the Union and the Confederates attracted hundreds of Haligonians to fight for their side.

Haligonians also feared war-hungry Americans might instigate border skirmishes, or worse. Canadian politician D'Arcy McGee was the first to recognize the danger of the Civil War to British North America. If Americans were willing to kill each other over a principle, he reasoned they would also be willing to attack Canadians for their land—something the Yanks had been considering since 1776. When large Union armies gathered on the Maine–New Brunswick border, older Loyalists remembered 1812. When Union forces finally got the upper hand against the Confederates after Gettysburg, Northern newspapers urged the Union to keep going until they'd driven the British out of Canada.

This was no mere rumor. In April 1861, Secretary of State William Seward proposed to President Lincoln that they attack British North America, and offered to start the war himself. Nova Scotians knew it wouldn't take much of a spark to set the Yankee brush-fire headed their way, yet they still took chances that could strike one.

During a remarkable ten-day run in August of 1864, the Confederate State Ship (CSS) *Tallahassee*, captained by the skilled and daring helmsmen John Taylor Wood, grandson of U.S. president Zachary Taylor and nephew of Confederate president Jefferson Davis, destroyed twenty-six Union ships and captured seven more off the coast of New England. It was a streak worthy of Joseph Barss Jr. himself—and one that earned Wood the enmity of every Union general.

But as Barss himself could tell Wood, they eventually catch up to you. On August 18, when two Union ships chased the CSS *Tallahassee* up the Eastern seaboard, Captain Wood sailed into Halifax Harbour, ostensibly to re-coal before returning South. With the two Union ships blocking the harbor, however, it seemed that Wood and his crew were doomed. Under British neutrality laws, the *Tallahassee* had exactly forty-eight hours to refuel, repair any damages, and return to sea.

While one of Halifax's many Confederate sympathizers, the highly respected Dr. Almon, distracted a Union officer who'd been ordered to keep an eye on *Tallahassee* by punching him in the face, Captain Wood brought aboard local helmsman Jock Fleming, "who knew the rivers as well as the fish who swam in them." Fleming waited until dark on a moonless night to sneak *Tallahassee* around the narrow side of McNab's Island, a passage normally too shallow to get a large ship through. But not, Fleming knew, at high tide, when it offered an additional seven feet of water, enough for him to gingerly guide *Tallahassee* through the small, dangerous strait, out of sight of the Union ships, and out to sea.

Once the Union captains realized they'd been duped, they were furious with the Haligonians. If the Yankees needed an excuse to open fire on Nova Scotia, Dr. Almon and Jock Fleming had given it to them. But once again President Lincoln kept his cool, keeping his soldiers squarely on the American side of the border.

Captain Wood never forgot the Haligonians' help, nor their beautiful town. After the Civil War ended, he and some Confederate leaders returned to Halifax to raise their families. Wood's neighbors "long remembered the upright figure, the quiet courtesy, the broad hat, the white hair and trim goatee of a typical Southern gentleman of the old school," wrote Halifax historian Thomas H. Raddall, who was born the year before Wood died and knew many of his Halifax friends. Wood's oldest son would graduate from the Royal Military College of Canada, and was the first Canadian officer to fall during the Boer War in 1899.

Wood's grandson, S. T. Wood, joined the Royal Canadian Mounted Police and would rise to commissioner, one of the best to lead that revered unit.

The affection was returned. In 1992, Dartmouth, Nova Scotia, which has since been absorbed by Halifax, opened a grade school named for the CSS *Tallahassee.*

Chapter 4
Waking Up Just in Time

1865–1914

From Halifax's birth in 1749 through 1865, Haligonians had ridden a wonderful wave of wealth by supplying materials, people, and transport for wars around the world, mass migrations, and even the California Gold Rush. But after the American Civil War, Halifax struggled, and the Americans were none too eager to help the people who had helped the Confederates. Instead, talk resumed in New England papers of annexing British North America.

This perpetual fear of an American invasion pushed British North America to set up a central government among Nova Scotia, New Brunswick, and the "Province of Canada," present-day Quebec and Ontario, in 1867. Voting against its own economic self-interest, Nova Scotia approved "Confederation," and to this day Canadians consider July 1, 1867, their birthday. To replace the unwieldy "British North America," everyone agreed that "Canada," a Huron-Iroquois word meaning "village" or "settlement," was a fine name, and that was that. To celebrate the Dominion of Canada's first birthday on July 1, 1868, the Citadel fired its cannons in salute, but one of them fired prematurely, killing two artillerymen. Things didn't go much better for Nova Scotia afterward.

Confederation brought Canada its own Intercolonial Railway, which was supposed to help Halifax sell its products in the West, but instead it boosted Toronto and Montreal at the expense of Halifax, whose population dropped from fourth highest to eleventh, behind former backwaters like Winnipeg, Calgary, and Edmonton. Halifax was no longer a rowdy town of privateers and entrepreneurs but a quiet haven for retirees who valued a rich lifestyle over mere riches. Without a war to work for, Halifax went into hibernation.

One thing everyone could agree on: if Halifax didn't do something soon, it would fall hopelessly behind the rest of the world, which was spinning faster than ever before. The turn of the century saw women fighting for the right to vote, workers earning the right to unionize, and Ford employees in Detroit soon earning five bucks a day. With that kind of money, they could afford to buy the Model Ts rolling off their assembly lines, or to travel to their growing cities by train, and once there get about by streetcar or subway. A few years later, airmail would carry their letters.

These sweeping political and social changes accompanied an equally dramatic wave of innovation, which brought this brave new world telephones, toasters, instant coffee, tea bags, and Kellogg's Cornflakes in the 1910s alone.

Canada could claim full credit for at least one modern creation: the sport of hockey. The Mi'kmaq invented the game while manufacturers in Halifax and Dartmouth produced the first clamp-on skate; the first popular hockey stick, which they called the Micmac; and the Halifax Rules of Hockey. While Americans were consumed with baseball, boxing, and college football, Canadians formed the National Hockey Association in 1909, which became the National Hockey League in 1917. But the NHL's first teams were based in the booming cities of Montreal, Ottawa, and Toronto, with none in Nova Scotia—a harsh slap in the face of the sport's creators.

But the spirit of reform introduced by American

progressives soon hit Halifax. In March 1911, the city organized a campaign called Halifax Uplift, a kind of religious revival to push Halifax to throw off its sleepy past and join the future.

In Canada's 1911 national election, still considered the most important in Canadian history, citizens voted on a proposal called "Reciprocity," which was intended to reduce trade tariffs with the United States—the NAFTA of its time.

In a reversal of modern roles, Canada's Liberal Party, led by its famously charismatic prime minister Wilfrid Laurier, sixty-nine, from Quebec, pushed to pass Reciprocity so Western Canadian farmers could sell their produce to the United States. Canada's Conservative Party, led by Halifax's fifty-seven-year-old Robert Borden, who had already lost two elections for Prime Minister to Laurier, opposed the deal, because Conservatives feared it would weaken Canada's ties to Great Britain and leave its economy and national identity in the hands of the Americans. (A small example: Canadians still drove on the left side of the road, British style.) While Liberals tried to argue that the Americans were Canada's partners, not predators, the Conservatives warned of the worst sort of behavior from their southern neighbors.

The Americans gave them plenty to fear when the United States Congress's speaker of the House, Missouri Democrat Champ Clark, took the floor to openly express an American ambition that went back to the nation's founding: annexing Canada. "I look forward to the time," he declared, "when the American flag will fly over every square foot of British North America up to the North Pole. The people of Canada are of our blood and language." He went on to describe the trade agreement as just the first step toward taking over Canada.

The *Congressional Record* reported that Clark's speech received "prolonged applause." The American press took note. "Evidently, then," the *Washington Post* reported, "the Democrats generally approved of Mr. Clark's annexation sentiments and voted for the reciprocity bill because, among other things, it improves the prospect of annexation."

The United States had already gained most of its territory by buying, annexing, or fighting for land from the English, French, Spanish, Mexicans, and Russians. To Clark and his compatriots, weaned on Manifest Destiny, annexing Canada seemed like the next logical step—and to the Canadians, an entirely rational fear. New York Republican William M. Bennett, who opposed Reciprocity, sought to sabotage the bill by introducing a resolution asking President William Howard Taft's administration to begin negotiating the annexation of Canada with Great Britain.

Predictably, the congressman's actions "roused the opponents of reciprocity in and out of [Canada's] Parliament to the highest pitch of excitement they have yet reached," the *Washington Post* reported. The Canadian Conservatives who opposed Reciprocity shrewdly reproduced the American politicians' speeches in thousands of pamphlets and distributed them across the country, which had exactly the effect the Conservatives had hoped for: alerting Canadians to the American threat.

The beneficiary of this turmoil was Halifax's own Robert Borden, who hoped to unseat Prime Minister Wilfrid Laurier in the 1911 election. Borden warned that Reciprocity would "Americanize" Canada, even claiming that Taft's administration had a secret plan to annex the country.

"It is beyond doubt," Borden said in a widely published speech, "that the leading public men of the United States, its leading press, and the mass of its people believe annexation of the Dominion [of Canada] to be the ultimate, inevitable, and desirable result of this proposition, and for that reason support it."

Hyperbolic, to be sure, but the Americans had provided him with all the ammunition he needed.

Reciprocity was finished off by none other than the Nobel Prize–winning British poet and novelist Rudyard Kipling, much loved on both sides of the border, who'd been asked by his publishing friend Max Aitken to write something for the *Montreal Star* about the upcoming vote. On September 7, 1911, two weeks before the election, Aitken published Kipling's comments.

"It is her own soul that Canada risks today," Kipling wrote. "Once that soul is pawned for any consideration, Canada must inevitably conform to the commercial, legal, financial, social and ethical standards which will be imposed on her by the sheer admitted weight of the United States." Kipling's essay ran in every English-language newspaper in Canada.

On September 21, 1911, the Reciprocity agreement, Prime Minister Wilfrid Laurier, and the Liberal government all went down in flames. In his third try, Halifax's Robert Borden became the nation's new prime minister. All this raised a lot of questions while providing at least one clear outcome: in 1911, many Canadians, including the new premier, concluded they should not count on the American government in a crisis. But Nova Scotia, at least, felt safer with its native son in power.

While Halifax was dropping out of the list of Canada's ten biggest towns, Boston was approaching its fourth century as one of North America's most important cities—and one of only three U.S. cities to appear in the top seven of every census since 1790, along with New York and Philadelphia. And the best, it seemed, was yet to come.

In 1901, Boston had 600,000 residents and a new ball club, the Red Sox. By 1912 Boston had grown to 700,000, tying St. Louis as the nation's fifth biggest city, with a thriving economy. When Red Sox owner John I. Taylor went looking for an architect to design a new ballpark for his team in 1911, he picked James Earnest McLaughlin, a thirty-seven-year-old Halifax native who had risen to become one of Boston's leading architects. McLaughlin didn't need to dazzle Red Sox fans with fancy features, but he did give them one architectural advancement: pedestrian ramps for fans to exit the grandstands. Many of McLaughlin's childhood friends from Halifax would try out McLaughlin's ramps for themselves during their visits to Boston, the closest big city to Halifax, to cheer for their adopted major league team.

Booming Boston could afford luxuries like Fenway Park and "America's First Subway," which celebrated its inaugural run in 1897, but Halifax was hustling just to get back in the game with publicly funded projects to upgrade the docks and rail service. Without a war to pay for its projects, Halifax relied on taxes, tourism, and shipping. In the homegrown cruise industry, the White Star Line raced to catch up to Cunard, with tragic consequences. In 1873 White Star's flagship, *Atlantic*, crashed into the coast off Halifax, killing 562, the world's worst civilian maritime disaster at the time, followed by the line's *Naronic* going down in 1893 and *Republic* in 1909. After J. P. Morgan bought White Star from the Ismays in 1902, the company came out swinging with three gleaming, new state-of-the-art ships: *Olympic*, to be launched in 1911, borrowing the name of the popular new athletic event; *Titanic* in 1912; and *Britannic* in 1914—each of them designed to set a new standard for the largest and most luxurious ships ever built.

Titanic left Southampton, England, on April 10, 1912, under the command of Captain Edward J. Smith. He had years of experience on the seas, but with boats half the size of the behemoth he had taken over. Four days later *Titanic* scraped past an iceberg on her starboard side, gouging a hole in her hull below the waterline. Four hundred miles off the coast of Newfoundland, the grand ship started sinking. To keep the passengers calm, a small band of musicians kept playing instead of seeking safety for themselves. When the great ship finally cracked in half and dropped beneath the Atlantic's freezing waters on April 15, 1912, at 2:20 a.m., she took 1,503 victims with her, including most of the crew, the captain, and the musicians.

Harold Cottam, the radio operator on *Carpathia*, a Cunard ship also heading to New York, was scheduled to end his shift at midnight. But he had kept working at his desk until 12:20 or so, and had just started taking off his boots at 12:25 a.m. when he received *Titanic*'s plea for help. Thanks to him, help was coming.

Most accounts of *Titanic* end with the rescue of the passengers and the court cases that followed, but the dangerous, difficult, and grisly tasks of recovering the floating bodies, identifying, and burying them fell to the Haligonians. The search-and-recovery missions were conducted out of Halifax, starting with *Mackay-Bennett*, a ship built to lay and repair cable under the sea. It went out to find the victims with a chaplain to administer last rights and enough embalming fluid, coffins, and canvas bags for a hundred victims, plus weights to bury about seventy bodies at sea.

It took *Mackay-Bennett* four days to reach the field of debris floating in the sea. The crew saw chairs, tables, and decomposing bodies bobbing in the frigid waters "as far as the eye could see," one crewman said. Many bodies had been attacked by birds and fish; some victims had clearly been wounded or killed by long falls during *Titanic*'s descent into the ocean. The *Mackay-Bennett* sent crewmen out in smaller skiffs to recover the bodies.

The *Mackay-Bennett* crew soon realized they had greatly underestimated the number of victims they might find, so Captain Frederick H. Larnder ordered his men to embalm first-class victims on deck and perform burials at sea for second- and third-class casualties. When colleagues on shore sent out another ship with more supplies, including embalming fluid, the crew was able to bring the rest of the victims back to Halifax.

In all, the *Mackay-Bennett* retrieved 306 bodies, while two other ships brought back 22 more; 116 were buried at sea. The crew did not attempt to identify the victims, but one casualty they would never forget: a nineteen-month-old boy floating face-up, his arms folded across his chest.

"I honestly hope I shall never have to come on another expedition like this," crewman Francis Dyke said. "The doctor and I are sleeping in the middle of fourteen coffins."

St. John's, Newfoundland, is closer to the *Titanic* site than Halifax, but thanks to Canada's transcontinental railway, created by Halifax's Sandford Fleming, Halifax's North Street Station could access the rest of the continent within two days. Because time was of the essence when dealing with decomposing bodies, Halifax became the recovery's base of operations. After thirteen days at sea, the *Mackay-Bennett* approached Halifax on April 30, 1912, eighteen days after *Titanic* went down. The announcement went out: "The death ship will arrive at noon." When *Mackay-Bennett* came into view, church bells rang.

To handle the sheer volume of corpses, a Halifax doctor named John Henry Barnstead devised the first system for identifying, numbering, and cataloguing mass casualties. He also pioneered the use of mortuary bags to hold the body, unattached body parts, and the victim's clothing and effects for later identification, and the use of toe tags, which listed the victim's name and any descriptive information rescuers could provide.

Of the first-class deceased, fifty-nine would be sent to their homes at their family's request. Most second-class passengers and almost all third-class passengers were interred in Halifax. The crew, haunted by all they had seen, felt compelled to carry the unnamed infant boy to his grave themselves, and paid for his granite tombstone. The Halifax police chief, who had been instructed to burn all the victims' clothes to avoid disease and memorabilia mongers, completed the task with one exception: he couldn't bring himself to destroy the baby's shoes, which he kept in the bottom drawer of his desk for years.

The missing included Halifax's own beloved George Wright. Thanks to his revised will, his fortune helped Halifax build a new YMCA downtown, and supported a group that would help Canadian women secure the vote in 1918.

They stored the bodies on the ice at the curling rink, then performed two dozen funerals a day for a week. Forty undertakers buried 148 victims in three cemeteries: 119 in Fairview Cemetery, for Protestants; 19 in the Catholic cemetery, where the victims were identified by rosaries or crucifixes; and 10 in the Jewish cemetery, all male, eight identified as Jewish based on circumcision, the other two because their names "sounded Jewish," although it was later discovered that one was Anglican and the other was Catholic.

The Fairview Cemetery plots are all marked by simple, elegant cubes of black granite, set on a small slope. They are arranged in three graceful arcs, although the third line has only a few headstones because it was assumed many more victims would eventually be found, though none were. The number on each gravestone indicates the order in which the bodies were found, and they are arranged not alphabetically but in the order they were removed from the curling rink. Their names are chiseled on the front cube faces, all legacies of Dr. Barnstead's carefully detailed work.

The mystery of the nineteen-month-old boy, however, was not solved until 2009. With the help of the pair of baby shoes the police chief had passed down to his relatives, it was determined that he was Sidney Leslie Goodwin. Almost a century after he was born on September 9, 1910, Sidney had his name engraved on his tombstone.

No city was touched by *Titanic*'s sinking more than Halifax, whose Maritime Museum of the Atlantic holds the world's largest collection of *Titanic* artifacts, and whose cemeteries hold the most victims. What the people of Halifax, from the recovery crews to the wagon drivers, storage workers, coroners, undertakers, and clergy performing dozens of funerals every day, could not know in 1912, was that this effort was a mere rehearsal for a much bigger task ahead.

PART III
The Great War

Chapter 5
As Near to Hell

R ight when Halifax was catching up with the rest of the world, a century of peace in Europe and Canada would be shattered on a single day thousands of miles from Halifax. On June 28, 1914, Archduke Franz Ferdinand of Austria, heir to the Austro-Hungarian throne, and his wife, Duchess Sophie, were celebrating their fourteenth wedding anniversary in Sarajevo. But before they arrived, a small secret society that called itself the Black Hand, outraged by Austria's annexation of Bosnia, was plotting to assassinate the Archduke. As the Archduke and the Duchess rode in the back of a convertible car, a nineteen-year-old man named Gavrilo Princip shot the Archduke and accidentally hit the Duchess as well. The Archduke bravely declared

"It is nothing!" but he and his wife both died from their wounds.

In a tinderbox of a continent, which had been preparing for war for a decade, this tiny spark was enough to ignite the world leaders' pent-up desire for war. On July 24, 1914, Austria-Hungary declared war on Serbia, and the fire of war quickly spread across Europe. While the Central Powers of Germany, Austria-Hungary, and the Ottoman Empire were the primary catalysts of the war, the Allied powers were just as eager to fight back, especially the British and their colonies, which sent almost 9 million men into battle.

No Canadian city supported the war more thoroughly than Halifax. Whenever a regiment of Bluenosers boarded the transport ships in Halifax, the entire city went to the waterfront to cheer them as they waved from their ships.

Britain's enthusiasm for the war was shared by virtually every major power except one: the United States, which seemed determined to stay out of Europe's wars—an option the Dominion of Canada, still under British rule, didn't have. In the U.S., antiwar sentiment swept the nation from President Woodrow Wilson on down.

As is almost always the case when a major conflict breaks out, the politicians, generals, and soldiers going to war were not only convinced that their side would win but that it would do so easily and quickly—and that was the problem. One side had to be wrong, and it turned out both were. Even five months into the conflict, few believed they would still be fighting a year later. When the war's first Christmas approached in 1914, Pope Benedict XV asked for a one-day truce. The leaders refused, but on Christmas Eve, German and British troops sang Christmas carols to each other from their trenches. The next day, some brave German soldiers climbed out of their holes and walked across no-man's-land, unarmed, announcing "Merry Christmas!" in English and French. Seeing that the Germans were unarmed, the Allied soldiers also emerged, and they were soon exchanging cigarettes and food, singing carols, and playing a friendly game of soccer.

The next day they climbed back into their trenches and resumed killing each other. Before the war's first New Year, the positions of both sides were essentially fixed, forming a line of trenches 475 miles long, stretching from Belgium to Switzerland, that barely wiggled for almost four years. With so little movement along the line, transportation took a backseat to munitions, which the Great War consumed like no other. In just one thirty-five-minute segment of the battle at Neuve-Chapelle in northeastern France in March 1915, the

British army fired more shells than it had during the entire Boer War, which lasted some thirty-two months. By May of 1915, just two months later, Britain had burned through its shell supply so quickly that it had to restrict its guns to just four shells a day, a shortage that threatened to cost them the war in its first year.

To prevent this disastrous outcome, the Allies made a bold move for the era: employing women in munitions factories. France alone recruited almost half a million women to make shells so that the men could fight in the fields, fully armed. Soon, Great Britain was manufacturing 50 million shells a year, and France even more, to the Germans' 36 million. While German U-boats had closed the gap on the seas, the Allies' factory women prevented them from being overpowered in the fields.

They called it the Great War because it was far bigger than any war the world had seen, and there was not yet any need to qualify which world war was being referring to. It was the first major conflict to make effective use of airplanes, tanks (originally called landships), machine guns, razor wire, flamethrowers, gas warfare, and submarines—most famously the German U-boats, whose effectiveness initially surprised even the Germans, and allowed them to hold off the Allies despite falling behind in the munitions race.

The Great War didn't invent high explosives, but it

expanded their use to volumes no one could have imagined in 1914. Before the Great War, military power was measured in horses, ships, and soldiers. Afterward, it was calculated by the capacity to bomb the enemy— and the arms race was on.

While the science of warfare was advancing by leaps and bounds, medical science was struggling to catch up. It was only at the turn of the century that doctors had come around to the consensus that germs were real, contagious, and had to be countered by vigorous hand washing between operations. When Dr. Oliver Wendell Holmes Sr., father of the Supreme Court Justice, first promoted the practice in two papers published in the mid-nineteenth century, the more established Charles D. Meigs fired back that washing hands was unnecessary because doctors were gentlemen, and "gentlemen's hands are clean."

Fortunately, Dr. Holmes's position found proponents overseas, where Scottish doctor Joseph Lister picked up on Louis Pasteur's advances in microbiology to champion antiseptic surgery, using carbonic acid to clean surgeons' hands and tools. When survival rates soared, he worked to overcome resistance from doctors like Charles D. Meigs to spread the practice.

One of Lister's protégés, Dr. Joseph Lawrence, was so impressed by his mentor that, after Lawrence perfected his cure for halitosis, he named it after the pioneering doctor: Listerine. A native Nova Scotian named John Stewart studied under Lister in Edinburgh, where the legendary doctor took a shine to him before Stewart returned to Nova Scotia as an apostle of antiseptic surgery. He rose to become the dean of Dalhousie University's medical school and president of the Canadian Medical Association, working tirelessly to teach others what he'd learned from Dr. Lister.

Despite the essential advances promoted by Pasteur, Lister, and Stewart, Sir Alexander Fleming didn't discover penicillin, for which he won the Nobel Prize, until 1928, and it wasn't mass produced for two more decades. Halifax was fortunate to have Stewart and his students in town, but the science of healing still lagged behind the practice of killing.

The Great War also popularized the tactic of trench warfare, which dramatically increased the death rate. A strategy emphasizing defense over offense, trench warfare was highly effective in preventing the advancing force from getting very far very fast, which created a stubborn stalemate, costing thousands upon thousands of lives just to gain small patches of land.

By the second week of October 1914, in the Flemish region of Belgium commonly called Flanders near the ancient walled city of Ypres, the gap between the trenches of the two sides had been reduced to a narrow corridor. It is one of the dreariest landscapes in Western Europe, a vast, sodden, gray pasture with few signs of life. The water table is so high that a hole dug just a few feet down rapidly fills with water, followed quickly by water rats, making the already ghastly business of trench warfare that much more miserable.

The First Battle of Ypres cost the Allied forces some 150,000 dead and wounded in exchange for a grand total of 500 yards of worthless land. The Second Battle of Ypres, in April 1915, turned even worse after the Germans introduced gas warfare. By mid-April 1915, the Germans had delivered 6,000 cylinders containing 160 tons of chlorine, which, when inhaled, stimulates overproduction of fluid in the lungs and leads to drowning, even while its victim is standing on dry land.

April 22, 1915, was a sunny day with a light breeze running from east to west—perfect conditions for the Germans to test their new weapon. They selected as their first guinea pigs a few French and Algerian divisions, who were dug in near the Canadian Expeditionary Force, which included the Princess Patricia's Canadian Light Infantry (PPCLI), the first Imperial division to reach the Western Front. The Germans roused the Allies with a barrage of traditional artillery fire at 5:00 p.m. When the Allies peered over the tops of their trenches, they saw grayish-green clouds of chlorine drifting from the middle of the battlefield toward their lines. Having no idea what this strangely colored air was, or how to protect themselves from its devastating effects, they inhaled deeply. Within seconds, thousands of Allied soldiers were stumbling about, coughing, clutching their throats, and turning blue in the face before falling in the muddy fields and trenches, dead.

The Canadians, just far enough away to avoid the brunt of the gas attack, took over the French and Algerian positions to mount a dogged defense. Their efforts kept the Germans from advancing, but modern warfare had changed forever that day.

The results were perhaps best described two years later by a twenty-five-year-old British soldier named Wilfred Owen in his poem "Dulce et Decorum Est" ("It is sweet and fitting to die for one's country"), a line that comes from the great Roman poet Horace. In his poem, Owen invites the reader to walk behind the wagon into which they flung the gas victims "And watch the white eyes writhing in his face, / His hanging face, like a devil's sick of sin," and "hear at every jolt, the blood / Come gargling from the froth-corrupted lungs"; the reader then might not so eagerly tell the young, "Dulce et decorum est."

As historian John Keegan writes, the second battle at Ypres "must have been as near to hell as this earth can show."

Soldiers quickly learned that if they couldn't get to their gas masks in time, they could urinate onto handkerchiefs and cover their noses with them. This worked surprisingly well, and was certainly preferable to inhaling the deadly gas.

Despite the Germans' great success with their new weapon, more than two weeks after its introduction, the Canadian line still held—but even that was a mixed blessing. Major John McCrae, a forty-one-year-old physician, artist, and poet from Guelph, Ontario, wrote to his mother, "For seventeen days and seventeen nights none of us have had our clothes off, nor our boots even, except occasionally. In all that time while I was awake, gunfire and rifle fire never ceased for sixty seconds. . . . And behind it all was the constant background of the sights of the dead, the wounded, the maimed, and a terrible anxiety lest the line should give way."

On May 2, 1915, ten days after the Germans fired the first gas shells, they killed McCrae's good friend Alexis

Helmer. When McCrae buried Helmer, he noticed how quickly the poppies came up around Helmer's grave, and those of others of his countrymen. While sitting in the back of an ambulance the next day, McCrae composed one of the world's best-known war poems, "In Flanders Fields."

> *In Flanders fields the poppies blow*
> *Between the crosses, row on row*
> *. . .*
> *We are the Dead; short days ago*
> *We lived, felt dawn, saw sunset glow,*
> *Loved and were loved, and now we lie*
> *In Flanders fields.*

But where Wilfred Owen wrote his poem to deter the next wave of recruits, McCrae wrote his final stanza to rally them.

> *Take up our quarrel with the foe!*
> *To you from failing hands we throw*
> *The torch; be yours to hold it high!*
> *If ye break faith with us who die*
> *We shall not sleep, though poppies grow*
> *In Flanders fields.*

McCrae was not satisfied with it, but a friend convinced him to send it out to the *Spectator*, which turned it down, and then *Punch*, which picked it up. The last stanza was quickly employed in Allied campaigns for war bonds, recruiting posters, and pro-war political candidates, right up to Canada's crucial election of 1917.

The Germans' use of lethal gas in the Second Battle of Ypres so outraged Winston Churchill, then Britain's secretary of war, that he countered by authorizing the production of British gas shells. When the Red Cross protested that the strategy was inhumane, Churchill coolly replied, "So is the rest of war."

Gas warfare was a horrible business, but the people back in Halifax didn't have much sense of it. The German U-boats, however, put fear into their hearts, because even civilians were fair game. This fear peaked on May 7, 1915, just two weeks after the first Allied troops had been gassed, when a German U-boat sank the *Lusitania*. The Great War seemed to be creeping closer to home each month.

Joseph Ernest Barss, the great-grandson of Nova Scotia's greatest privateer, Joseph Barss Jr., didn't have to wait for a clever recruitment poster to enlist.

Barss was born in India in 1892 to Baptist missionaries. His mother, Libby, almost died in childbirth, and would have no more children. Libby and her husband, John Howard Barss, who went by Howard, named their son Joseph after the famed privateer, and Ernest in honor of his uncle, Ernest DeWitt Burton, who had mentored Howard at Newton Theological Institution near Boston and would become the third president of the University of Chicago.

When Libby was healthy enough to travel after giving birth, the family returned to Wolfville, Nova Scotia, a picturesque town about 60 miles across the province from Halifax and just 16 miles from Windsor, the birthplace of hockey. In Wolfville, the Barss name went a long way. After Howard's father, the son of the privateer, had made his fortune as a shipbuilder and banker, he built a big house for his growing family and served as superintendent for both the town's Baptist church and Acadia University, which was quickly becoming one of Canada's top undergraduate colleges. Most remarkable for a family living in rural Nova Scotia in the mid-1800s, when only a small percentage of North Americans graduated from high school, Barss's sons all earned college degrees, including Howard, who ministered to Wolfville's Baptist congregation while running a grocery store and fish market on Main Street.

Howard called his son by his middle name, Ernest,

and taught him how to read newspaper headlines when he was just four years old. The precocious Ernest soon became the store's best salesman, going door-to-door to take orders. Because Howard was no sportsman, Ernest learned to play hockey, football, and baseball and how to box from others, including a former Canadian champion boxer. Ernest starred in all four sports at Acadia University, despite standing only five foot eight.

"He was sort of a stocky fella, big thighs, who carried himself very straight," recalled his son, Dr. Joseph Andrew Barss, in a 1999 interview. "A tough guy. His ankles were so strong, he didn't have to lace up his skates."

Ernest graduated cum laude in 1912 at the ripe age of nineteen, and accepted a position in Montreal with the Canadian Railroad supplying dining cars. It paid a handsome $45 a month, with free transportation and a week's vacation for his twenty-first birthday—practically unheard of back then—but he soon jumped at an offer from the Imperial Oil Company for $65 a month. When the Great War broke out in 1914, the district manager transferred, so the twenty-two-year-old Barss took his position at $1,500 a year, a great salary for someone so young, with the promise of more promotions and raises ahead.

In Montreal, Barss led quite an active social life,

squiring a few women around town each week, with a knack for dating women who would help him learn foreign languages, music, and other subjects. After several dates with his French tutor, Marie, a petite French-Canadian girl "of good family," her father answered the door the next time Barss called and directed him to sit down in his library for a private conversation.

"I notice you have been here several times," her father said. "What are your intentions concerning my daughter?"

"Strictly honorable," Ernest replied, "but not matrimonial."

"Then I'll thank you not to call again. You are wasting my daughter's time."

Life was good for Barss in just about every way we typically measure for a young man: career, finances, and fun. Someone who could read headlines at four, become a skilled salesman by twelve, graduate cum laude from college with a handful of varsity letters in multiple sports at nineteen, and then leave his small town to embark on a rising career in the country's biggest city is not a person who lacks ambition, talent, or charisma. But Barss's letters give the unmistakable sense that his current lifestyle, appealing as it was, did not leave him fulfilled. He came from a line of people who had something else in spades: a profound sense of purpose. His direct ancestors attacked enemy ships on the high seas, built fortunes in business, started universities, and went on missionary trips to India. And that essential piece was something the good life Ernest Barss was living in Montreal did not provide.

Every Saturday in warm weather, Barss and three friends met at their Montreal rowing club on the St. Lawrence River to pull a four-man shell, then retired to the boathouse for a smoke, a few beers, a card game, and some casual conversation. But on one spring Saturday in 1915, a crewmate opened the paper to see a story about the Second Battle of Ypres, including an account of the Germans' gas attack on the Princess Patricia's Canadian Light Infantry. When he read out loud some of the PPCLI's 461 names on the casualty list—out of an original company of 1,068—including many friends of theirs from Montreal, the group was "filled with indignation." The four young men decided to enlist right then and there.

When Barss blithely wrote his parents about his spontaneous decision, they immediately made plans to travel to Montreal to talk him out of it. He was their only child, after all, for whom they had sacrificed much; but they could not get to Montreal in time. On April 28, 1915, two days before Ernest was officially inducted, he wrote:

"Dear Father and Mother:

"Well, this is probably the last letter you will receive from here. It is all settled and I am to report Friday morning for duty."

Barss would start two weeks of training at Niagara-on-the-Lake, getting paid $1.10 a day, a fraction of what he had been making in Montreal. He mentioned a series of dates with women named Bertha, Eileen, and Marie (suggesting that he hadn't listened to her father's admonition) and visits with various buddies. "I didn't know how many friends I had till I said I was going away," he wrote. "It certainly feels good to know it though."

He asked his parents to send him some nice underwear and undershirts with long sleeves to make his wool uniform more comfortable to wear, then closed by saying, "I think of you a great deal. . . . So long. Much love to you both. —Ernest."

On Friday, April 30, just eight days after the Germans hit the PPCLI with gas, Ernest Barss officially joined the famed Canadian unit himself, which had earned a reputation for valiant fighting and heavy losses. In Ernest's next letter to his parents, dated Monday night, May 13, 1915, he brags about this fact, clearly unaware of how it would be received by two aging parents terrified that their only child was marching toward his death.

The reason the PPCLI was in such need of reinforcements, he explained, was because "there are only 53 left out of 1500. So we have some reputation to keep up. I suppose you have read of the fine work done by the Canadians at St. Julien & Ypres. I tell you we can certainly make good when called upon. Of course, as you have probably noted, I am full of this thing. So are the other fellows."

He later added, "I suppose you have read by this time that the 13th & 14th battalions, both from Montreal, have been wiped out. The result is that the 1st McGill [University] company, which I was just too late to join, is going across on the 17th. I almost wish I was going with them for all my friends are in that unit."

He finished by describing their days, which started with reveille at 6:00 a.m. and could go as late as 11:30 p.m. with night maneuvers. "I passed my physical exam in fine shape," he told them. "The doctor said I was in perfect physical condition. I will let you know at once if we get sudden orders for a move. Much love to both of you. —Ernest."

Between that letter and his next, written three months later, Ernest's parents visited him in Montreal, then went home to Wolfville to worry that they'd never see their only child again. Nova Scotians knew more about war than most. They listened to the sailors and soldiers tell their stories in the taverns, cheered their ships going off to fight Britain's far-flung battles, and saw thousands of them come back maimed, traumatized, or dead. But their knowledge was still secondhand, their view from a distance. Aside from the occasional neighbor's son who was serving, they got most of their information from the newspapers like everyone else in North America, including dispatches Barss would send back to the Wolfville paper, but these naturally left most of the worst news out.

But in Barss's letters we can see a surprisingly candid account of his journey, including his bravado. On Tuesday, August 18, 1915, Barss sent his first letter from the Shorncliffe Camp in England. He mentioned that he'd taken the examination to become a machine gunner, one of the most dangerous jobs the Great War offered. While the position provided a bit of distance behind the front lines, and the ability to mete out punishment instead of just absorbing it, for this reason the machine gunner was a very appealing target for the Germans, and plenty close enough for their skilled snipers to hit. This position earned Barss a patch on his shoulder emblazoned with "MG," for machine gunner, which was also known as a "suicide patch," because if the Germans saw it on a captured soldier, they were much more likely to shoot him than to imprison him.

On Sunday night, August 23, 1915, Barss gave his parents an update, with his brio still in full bloom. His unit had just gotten word that they'd be leaving camp at 2:00 a.m. for France, joining a flotilla of 12,000 Allied troops. Having just heard the chaplain general of the British Forces deliver a sermon on the Kingdom of Heaven, Barss sounded both philosophical and fearless.

"Strange to say," he wrote, "I am perfectly content to take whatever fortune has in store for me with a brave heart and to do whatever lies before me in the way of duty as well as I can no matter the cost. . . . May God bless us all and find it in his mercy to bring us all together again safe & well is my earnest prayer. If he sees fit to do otherwise whatever he does is Right. With lots and lots of love to you both. —Ernest."

Barss's bravery and equanimity would soon be tested when the prospect of being killed in the trenches shifted from a far-off hypothetical to a cold reality he would face every day. But no one could claim his new life lacked purpose.

Chapter 6
Halifax at War

Halifax sent 6,000 sons to the Great War, roughly a quarter of its male population. It seemed almost every home had sent a brother, a husband, a father, or a son. The Great War drained the town of its able-bodied young men and left behind women, boys, girls, and men too old or infirm to fight.

Hospital ships brought wounded soldiers to Halifax weekly, where they were set up in the Pine Hill Military Convalescent Home, or in the newly finished Camp Hill Hospital with 240 beds for war casualties, built right next to the Citadel. The locals had sent the soldiers off with bands blasting and crowds cheering, but they returned to silence. Halifax's five daily newspapers printed lists titled "KILLED IN ACTION." Black armbands and patches were common sights on the streets of Halifax, and black-edged writing paper, black-bordered handkerchiefs, and black clothing, all indicating their owners had lost a son overseas, sold well.

Halifax's citizens were eager to contribute to the cause just about any way they could. Schoolgirls knitted balaclava helmets and slipped notes of encouragement inside them. They signed up to become Junior Red Cross members, learned first aid, and rolled thousands of bandages for the medics overseas. Adults joined the Red Cross and the Imperial Order of Daughters of the Empire. People from the upper class, who had relied on hired help for most of their domestic needs, volunteered to serve tea and cook in the canteens.

The medical school at Halifax's Dalhousie University had been whittled down to ten doctors-in-training, including a pioneering woman named Florence J. Murray. Born in 1894 and raised in rural Nova Scotia, she recalled, "The only careers I knew of open to girls were teaching, nursing, and stenography, none of which appealed to me. I wanted to do something different."

When she decided to become a doctor, she had to overcome a few obstacles, including her rudimentary education in a one-room schoolhouse that served students in ten grades at once. Her father, a Presbyterian minister, supported a wife and four children on $750 a year, and the medical profession wasn't eagerly welcoming women, with McGill University in Montreal, one of the nation's best, openly refusing to admit women to its medical school. With hard work and her family's support, however, Murray got into the medical school at Dalhousie University, which had been founded a few years after the War of 1812 as a progressive institution. She enrolled in 1914 only to watch her classmates and instructors, including Dr. John Stewart, Lister's protege, join her two brothers in the European theater.

"We students felt that since our brothers, cousins, and classmates were fighting and dying in the trenches in France," she wrote, "this was no time for dances or other fun. Most spare time was given to Red Cross work, making and folding dressings and bandages and preparing and sending socks, food, and chocolate to the boys overseas."

When Halifax needed her, Florence J. Murray would contribute more than chocolates.

Most Haligonians thought less about the trenches overseas than the daily bustle of their resurgent town. Halifax's renaissance had started a few years before the

Great War with more funding for public works, progress on women's suffrage and workman's compensation, and a general move toward modernization. But once Great Britain declared war, Halifax roared liked the old days.

The city's population surged by a third, to an estimated 60,000—and even that figure was probably low, because thousands of workers, soldiers, sailors, and spouses came into the city every day without being recorded. On Barrington Street in Richmond, just above the busy piers and the Acadia Sugar Refinery, young wives with young children from across Canada moved into newly built low-rent row houses, waiting for their husbands to return.

Halifax was not only Canada's war base but also one of the busiest ports in the world. It served as the conduit for meat and grain from the prairies, lumber from the mountains, and men from the West Indies, Canada, Australia, New Zealand, and, eventually, the United States. Halifax was the British Empire's lifeline for virtually all the supplies it needed to win, and that included explosives, which arrived from plants across New England in unmarked ships and trains.

Haligonians could watch all these resources run through their railyards to the ports and out to sea from Fort Needham, which had been converted to a park atop the slope of Richmond; from the Richmond's neighborhood homes, which often featured bay windows overlooking the Narrows; or from Citadel Hill, which lorded over the entire harbor. From those vantage points, locals could watch food, clothing, munitions, and thousands of men come in by train and leave by ship every day, while casualties were quietly brought into the city at night so as not to alarm the locals with the horrible toll the war was actually taking.

Although Halifax had always profited from war, the Great War was particularly good for business. In 1913, Halifax shipped a total of 2 million tons of goods. By 1917 that figure had multiplied more than eight times, to a stunning 17 million tons. From 1915 to 1916 alone, exports quadrupled, and they almost doubled again the next year. This was all the more impressive because during the Great War, Halifax Harbour opened every morning and closed early every evening, when the two large metal gates were drawn across the harbor, limiting shipping activity to about ten hours a day.

Halifax was more than a spigot for goods going overseas. As the area grew, so did its farming and manufacturing sectors, with local merchants fielding orders for a thousand dozen eggs, locally made flame-throwers, and the iconic "Doughboy" helmet, which looked something like a lampshade. There was a reason for that: Halifax's Willis & Bates specialized in stamping metal to make lamps, one of which looked just like the helmet they mass-produced for the Allies. The economy's sudden acceleration brought everything to life, even smaller, quieter Dartmouth across the harbor, whose businesses produced rope, iron, steel, sugar, oil, and, of course, beer in unprecedented quantities that still barely kept up with the spike in demand, both from the ships and the city.

Add it all up, and the area's exports skyrocketed from $19 million in 1916 to $142 million in 1917. Life was good in Halifax.

Before the war, Halifax already had neighborhoods of Irish Catholics in Richmond, blacks just a few blocks north in Africville, and the Mi'kmaw people across the Narrows in Turtle Grove, but the harbor was still a largely white, English-speaking area. By 1917, however, Halifax teemed with European and North American soldiers and workers of virtually every stripe. Those who couldn't be readily identified by their uniforms could be distinguished by their accents, if they could speak English at all.

Neighborhoods of Italians, Galicians from northwestern Spain, Russians hired by railway contractors, Greek fruit sellers, and everyone else who thought they could do better in Halifax during the war quickly formed. The town's small Jewish community experienced a sudden influx, while Chinese laundries and restaurants gave rise to Halifax's Chinese Quarter on Granville Street.

The war might have been fought thousands of miles away, but its impact on Halifax was obvious to everyone who lived there. The wartime prosperity created a dramatic increase in automobiles on the streets, naturally led by the military. In 1914, local troops were transported entirely by horse. Four years later, the stables had been completely replaced by "motors," as people called them. Likewise, civilian cars were a rarity in 1914, but by 1918 they had begun crowding the town's narrow streets. The potentially dangerous mix of horses and motors on a grid laid out for horse and buggy traffic more than a century ago required the creation of a new position: the traffic cop.

If you weren't heading to the trenches or worried about someone who was, it was a golden time to live and work in Halifax. When workers arrived from all over the world, they often spent a bit of their income on the town before sending the rest back home. In the pubs and speakeasies, women's skirts rose higher by the year, and "the lavish use of powder, rouge, and lip paint," wrote historian Thomas H. Raddall, who grew up in Halifax during the Great War, "hitherto confined to ladies of the demi-monde, actresses, and society girls in search of publicity, became the preoccupation of every typist and shop girl in the city."

When fresh recruits got to Halifax, they frequently made a beeline for any place that sold alcohol, where they met soldiers who had been recently discharged, were on leave, or were about to head back to the trenches. They told the recruits stories so horrifying that they might have been tempted to think they were exaggerating. The experienced soldiers knew the average infantryman lasted only three months before getting wounded or killed, so they were determined to make the most of their time on the safe side of the Atlantic. Their hard-earned fatalism fostered a devil-may-care disposition and all the elements that came with it, including scores of prostitutes from across Canada and bootleggers so fearless that they set up shop in the downtown YMCA—which was probably not what the YMCA's benefactor, Titanic victim George Wright, had had in mind when he wrote his will. During the war years, Halifax experienced a spike in venereal disease and out-of-wedlock births. Local orphanages had to expand.

Despite the daily dread that the ships bringing back the wounded and the dead would include a loved one,

Halifax remained a fiercely patriotic town, riding a wartime economy and convinced that its best years were still ahead. The Haligonians were also largely unaware of what was really happening in the trenches of Europe.

So, too, was Ernest Barss. But that was about to change.

Chapter 7
Life and Death
on the Western Front

1915–1916

On September 16, 1915, Ernest Barss wrote his first
letter to his parents from France, though we're not certain where he was at the time because censors redacted
it. He scratched it out underneath a tree behind an old
chateau where they had been billeted, and he had not
seen combat yet, but he suspected he would soon. After
finishing a 15-mile march the day before, his tone
started to shift subtly from the unbridled enthusiasm of
the fresh recruit training in England.

"I tell you it was no joke either," he wrote them. "I
didn't know whether I should be able to stick it out or

not. However, I did and brought my entire section in with me."

They were still well behind the front lines, hearing only the "occasional boom from one of the big guns. We haven't the slightest idea where we are going from here."

After wishing "Lots and lots of love to you both," he added this postscript: "Don't forget to send me a couple of pairs of socks. Also some cigarettes as they are very hard to obtain out here. Oh yes, also some foot powder as well."

Nine days later, on September 25, 1915, Barss wrote his parents again, but this note was rushed and sloppy. He told them his unit was about to make its first trip to the trenches, taking over a section from the French troops on the far right of the long line. After a 5-mile march and an overnight trip on a train with no seats, they settled in for their first breakfast of "bully beef"—tinned meat—tea, and hardtack, the same sort of industrial-strength crackers his privateering great-grandfather had to choke down while serving a few months in the Portsmouth, New Hampshire, prison, 104 years earlier. After marching for 15 more miles, Barss's unit had set up camp in the middle of nowhere, where supplies of just about everything were running low.

He also mentions, rather casually, that his unit suffered its first casualties when a German shell "blew up their kitchen spilling all their dinner, killing four men, and their major who was standing nearby, and wounding twelve."

And this is where his tone changes. "I will simply say this about the situation here. It is far more serious than anyone can imagine or almost conceive, and we need every able bodied man we can get out here."

When his fellow soldiers from Canada's western provinces bragged about how many men their hometowns had sent to the Western Front, Barss felt "absolutely ashamed" of Wolfville, "where I know there are so many husky fellows hanging around content to let someone else go and do the work which they ought to feel it their duty and privilege to do. They are all needed now not later. It may be too late then. And I can tell you that if they keep on hanging back and anything big is started I fear greatly for the outcome. —Ernest

"P.S. Please write Eileen often & keep in touch with her. I know she is anxious to do so but feels a little shy."

Eileen Clarke was one of three women Barss had mentioned in an earlier letter, and she appears in a photo with his family in Montreal taken before Barss shipped overseas. Exactly what their relationship was isn't clear, but Barss clearly valued her correspondence, and sent $15 of his $33 a month to her. He never says why, and it could simply be that he wanted her to deposit it in his Montreal account. But it could also be that they were trying to save for their future, or that he wanted her to have the money if he didn't make it back.

On the lighter side, one day the Prince of Wales, who would become King Edward VIII before abdicating the throne to marry the American divorcée Wallis Simpson, made one of his frequent trips to visit the troops. He picked the Princess Patricia's Canadian Light Infantry, one of his favorites, and drove himself there in his own Rolls-Royce. While the senior officers met behind the lines to discuss strategy, the Prince remained with the men at the front, which was his preference. When it was Barss's turn to patrol the area by "walking the boards" that they'd placed around the shell holes created by German bombs, the Prince of Wales decided to join him.

Barss was flattered, but felt compelled to warn him that "It is very dangerous and slippery," but the prince insisted. Not long after they started their tour, Barss heard a big splash behind him and turned back to see the Prince of Wales standing in a shell hole up to his waist in muddy water. Barss pulled him out and took him back to get dry clothes, putting a uniform together from whatever scraps his colleagues could spare.

When the senior officers returned to see the Prince wearing a wildly mismatched uniform, they were aghast. The captain asked Barss why he had allowed the Prince to walk among the shell holes when it was obviously a dangerous area.

"What is all this?" his officer snapped. "Do you not know this is the next King of England?"

"Yes sir," Barss replied. "But he outranked me."

Barss wrote his next letter right after he'd returned from four days in the trenches, his first tour. He gave his letter to a friend going on leave, so the censors never got their markers on it. His handwriting appears even more hurried and cramped than in his previous letter, with uncharacteristic grammatical and spelling errors.

"You can bet I was glad to get back," he said, discarding his earlier bravado for a moment. "It rained continually & mud was over our boot tops and two nights I was out all night with working parties."

One of those nights he joined a group digging a secret tunnel about sixty yards long, which extended directly under the German trenches where they could hear the Germans talking above them "very plainly."

The next morning, the Germans bombarded the Canadian position with rifle grenades and trench mortars, which broke "quite a number" of holes in their front line, "killing five and wounding 14 others" of the King's Royal Rifles. Barss's group repaired the trenches damaged by German shells, rolled out barbed wire in front of them, and lengthened the tunnels. For four days, Barss got little sleep and couldn't get a bath or change his soaked socks, all while working within 25 yards of the German trenches.

"They can hear us and their snipers are always on the lookout for a head above the parapet," he told his parents. "The bullets don't bother us but the grenades and bombs make an awful commotion and get on our nerves after a while."

Barss then reported the tunnel they had spent many dangerous days digging beneath the German trenches was finally finished—and blown up by the Germans an hour later. He joked in passing about a German sniper's bullet that whizzed "about an inch from my head," but said it was not so bad in the trenches because they got plenty to eat—making a modern reader wonder if Barss was in denial about the danger he faced, and what effect being immersed in it day and night was having on his psyche.

"I guess the hospitals are pretty full now as I hear

that the British and Canadians had 40,000 casualties in the last 5 days," he continued. "They will probably have some more after our attack. Here's hoping I am not one of them. However I am here for better or worse and if anything does happen it won't be anything to be ashamed of."

By this time Barss had already seen enough comrades die to contemplate his own death and the risk he had assumed by volunteering. He still fervently believed in the cause, and his religious faith never left him, but he was now openly hoping he would not be among the casualties, a noted switch from his early willingness—bordering on eagerness—to die for his country.

Barss was always conscientious about giving thanks for the care packages sent by his parents, aunts, and others. But in this letter, for the first time, the gifts trigger a bit of homesickness, and some sense of the anguish his decision is causing them.

"I just long & long for a sight of you again and I have lots of times [missed] you too, especially on such occasions as this. In fact I don't think you are ever out of my thoughts. My how I look forward to getting home again and seeing you again. I just have a kind of ache inside sometimes when I think of you and wonder what you are doing just then. I tell you I fully appreciate what wonderful parents I have." He adds that he's now

aware of "the terrible worry that I know I am causing you," perhaps because he was becoming genuinely
worried, too.

Twelve days later, Barss's unit crawled out of the
trenches again. It was their custom that bagpipers escort the men into the trenches, and bagpipers lead them
out, whether the soldiers were walking behind them,
being carried on stretchers, or being hauled away atop
a stack of dead men on hand wagons. The music stayed
with the survivors long after they returned.

Barss managed to lay his hands on a typewriter, which
spared his parents his ever-worsening handwriting.
He had also shed the swagger of his earlier letters, now
freely expressing unvarnished weariness and gratitude
for getting out alive. The letter, which he wrote from
"Dug out, 'Saint's Rest', The firing line," was dated
October 12, 1915.

"Dearest Father and Mother:

"I am writing tonight under rather trying circumstances," after a three-day stint in the trenches. He had
been on patrol, and because everyone expected "something to happen," they all had to " 'stand to' all night
every night." As a result, Barss got about three hours of
sleep during his seventy-two-hour shift. On the night
he got out, he had to lead a party to the front of their

line to dig a new line of trenches right in front of their own line, about 80 yards from the Germans.

"I tell you it was ticklish work. They could hear us but couldn't tell just where we were. So they kept sending up flairs [sic] every few minutes and when they would go up we would have to drop flat in the grass. However we got out without a casualty which I consider extraordinary." It was. The night before, the men of the King's Royal Riflemen (KRRC) had lost twenty men.

They were no longer just numbers to Barss. After the Germans finished dropping sixty-four-pound mortars filled with "a very high explosive" nearby, Barss's group went up to inspect the damage and found nothing but piles of debris where the trench had been.

"Poor Johnston was literally blown to pieces. Most of him was buried but his head and part of his shoulders were on top of the heap. . . . Oh it made me feel sick. He was a good boy and we all liked him so much. I have been upset all day from it. He is the first from our bunch to go. I wonder who will be the next?"

Barss was learning something they didn't teach in boot camp: modern warfare, efficient as it was, killed without warning and often without logic. Being brave, smart, or devoted didn't seem to matter much. That being the case, daydreaming of home was as good a way to pass the time as any. After closing his letter with love, Barss added this postscript: "I thought of it being [Canadian] Thanksgiving Day yesterday & wondered what & who you would be having for dinner."

The next time Ernest Barss's parents heard from him, on November 11, 1915, he sounded much better. His unit had marched a full day to a billet in a fairly large town so far back from the trenches that they couldn't hear the big guns, and had enough free time to play some bridge. They even had heat, hot water, and baths, "so that it is the most like home that I have experienced since leaving Canada."

His sense of humor had resurfaced, too, though with a darker edge, as manifest in his description of the "rather novel way in which the Germans provided a couple of fine meals for our artillery." The Germans had launched a shell intended for them but hit a canal instead, killing about a hundred fish. When they floated to the surface, the "Tommies" dived in to pick them up, and a feast of fresh fish followed.

If Barss's humor was returning, his anger toward the unenlisted back home was growing. "I can tell you the army is surely a place for straight talk and when you write of such fellows as Brent Eagles and others who are such lazy slackers I just wish I could have about ten minutes talk with them and if I wouldn't make their ears burn I'd be mighty surprised. However I didn't expect much better of him. He always impressed me as being decidedly superficial."

Given Barss's views of those who remained at home, it's not surprising he thought even less of the Americans' decision to remain neutral, an entire nation of able-bodied men all sitting out the Great War.

Sergeant Barss spent Christmas, 1915, in the trenches. There would be no "Christmas truce" with carols and soccer matches that year, but he did find time to get a letter off shortly into the new year, January 3, 1916. He composed this on small sheets of Bank of Montreal letterhead, almost illegibly, and some pages are missing. But perhaps all of that can be explained by its address: Ypres, site of some of the worst carnage the world had ever seen.

After listing some of the gifts they received for Christmas, including plum puddings, cigarettes, and extra rum rations, plus a parcel from Eileen, the girlfriend who seems to have outlasted all the others, Barss added that they were now "very near Ypres." He reported that "the Germans are still shelling that place [but] I don't know why, for it is now about deserted and pretty well a mass of ruins. I was up there one day with Lyster, and we got there just as they started shelling and had to go down into a cellar until it was over. My what a place and what stories. . . ."

When some fellows from Nova Scotia tracked him down, Barss wrote, "You ought to have heard what those boys had to say about Brent Eagles and all the other husky fit good for nothings hanging around home.

"It was almost worth while coming out here to find how many friends I have."

He was wise to savor these moments.

By January 1916, the endless butchery, and the daily fear that accompanied it, had started to wear on him. On January 25, 1916, his commanding officer demoted him from sergeant to "the permanent grade of Corporal for Neglect of Duty whilst NCO [Non-Commissioned Officer] on watch." It's not clear why, though his family guesses that Barss, a skilled boxer, might have gotten into a scrap.

If Barss's morale had been slipping before, getting demoted was not likely to improve his disposition.

Chapter 8
Halifax Harbour

Halifax Harbour had been strategically important since the day Cornwallis claimed it for the Crown, but never more so than during the Great War. Getting food and medical and military supplies to the civilians and soldiers around the world all depended on Halifax's 1,000-foot-wide channel—the world's bottleneck—being managed efficiently, carefully, and safely.

But no one could foresee that in 1905, nine years before Archduke Ferdinand took his fateful ride through Sarajevo. To cut costs, the British withdrew their army garrison and abandoned the Royal Navy Dockyard in Halifax. To a town founded as a military base, this was a kick in the gut. Not only did Halifax lose the panache of the fancy uniforms and grand balls that came with host-

ing the Royal Navy but it also lost the big military contracts that came with it—contracts that had fueled the
city's growth since the American Revolutionary War.

The withdrawal also threw Canada into a national
debate: should the country establish its own navy?
Most English Canadians thought they should so that
they could focus on protecting Canadian fishing boats
and fishing rights off the coast. Those were not high
priorities for the Royal Navy, which had more pressing
responsibilities around the globe. But many French-
Canadians feared forming their own navy would leave
them obligated to support Great Britain's wars around
the world. How much would building Canada's own
navy cost, and would it be worth it?

After a few years of hand-wringing, Canada decided
to take another small step toward independence and
create the Royal Canadian Navy (RCN) in 1910. The
good news is that it didn't cost much, but that was due
to the bad news: it wasn't worth much either. At its
inception, the RCN consisted of a ragtag fleet of fishing boats and two beat-up cruisers from the Royal
Navy. (Even their prefix, His Majesty's Canadian Ship
(HMCS), reflected Canada's murky status somewhere
between colony and sovereign nation.) The HMCS
Rainbow was already nineteen years old and would be
turned into scrap by 1920, and the HMCS *Niobe*, built

in 1898, would run aground off Cape Sable, Nova Scotia, in 1911, which robbed her of her seaworthiness.

Instead of scrapping *Niobe*, however, the RCN permanently moored her on the Halifax side of the Narrows, where she officially served as a depot ship, and unofficially as the 450-foot "Hotel Niobe," big enough to house and feed a thousand sailors and conduct training classes and communications. *Niobe* was undeniably useful, but nobody confused her with HMS *Highflyer*. Throw in the RCN's lack of officers, which required the RCN to fill positions with retired Royal Navy personnel, and it's easy to understand why the RCN was called the "Tin-Pot Navy."

But after Great Britain declared war on Germany, things changed in Halifax in ways both intended and not.

A Canadian merchant mariner named Francis R. Rudolf had served ably as Halifax's harbormaster, but when the Great War started, his authority was soon challenged. Shortly after war broke out, the British Royal Naval Reserve called up 30,000 officers, including Francis Evan Wyatt, who went by Evan. Wyatt received orders to report to Halifax Harbour, where he served on HMCS *Niobe*.

Born on September 23, 1877, in Southsea, England, a resort town at the southern tip of the Isle, at age thirteen Evan Wyatt enrolled as a Queen's Scholar at the fabled Westminster School. Founded in 1179, the school has produced Ben Jonson, John Locke, Christopher Wren, and seven British prime ministers. Young Wyatt knew he didn't want to pursue a career in letters or laws, so before turning seventeen he joined the Royal Naval Reserve (RNR). He rose steadily through the ranks until 1907, when he retired from the RNR to work for the United Fruit Company, parent company of Chiquita Banana, where he directed the company's large fleet of ships to South America to pick up the fruit, then around the world to sell it.

Wyatt's stint in the private sector ended as soon as the Great War began. Just four months into his tenure on *Niobe*, he was promoted to lieutenant-commander. Eager for more, he sent a letter to the Royal Canadian Navy's vice admiral Charles Edmund Kingsmill in Ottawa, listing his qualifications as "Master of Mail and Passenger steamers since 1904, expert Navigator and Pilot, thorough business man and fluent French scholar." Such self-promotion was uncommon in 1915, but it had the desired effect.

On September 15, 1915, the Admiralty appointed Wyatt the chief examining officer (CXO) of Halifax Harbour, a position far more important than it might sound. The CXO worked out of an office on *Niobe*, which included the RCN's Examination Service. When a ship wanted to enter Halifax Harbour, she stopped first at McNab's Island near the mouth of the harbor, where examiners on small boats would board the ship, confirm her identity, cargo, and purpose, and then send the information to the CXO's office on *Niobe*. If everything checked out, the ship would be allowed past the antisubmarine gates, and the examiner would tell the ship's captain where to anchor, usually in Bedford Basin.

Thus, during the war, the CXO's office essentially served as the gatekeeper for Halifax Harbour, supplanting the role of harbormaster. To make Harbourmaster Francis Rudolf's superfluousness obvious to all, the navy refused to supply him with as much as a boat. From that point forward, all meaningful responsibility for the harbor's smooth functioning ultimately came to rest on the shoulders of CXO F. Evan Wyatt.

Wyatt, who stood a strapping five eleven and weighed a lean 180 pounds, performed so well in his role as CXO that by January 1916, now Admiral Kingsmill wrote the secretary of the Admiralty in London that Wyatt "has carried out his duties in a zealous and able manner" and recommended Wyatt be promoted to commander.

The promotion came through. At age thirty-six, Wyatt was the commander and CXO of one of the Allies' most important bases.

Wyatt focused on ensuring the safe, civilized flow of boat traffic by enforcing conventional nautical laws and regulations, but that wasn't easy during the Great War, which frequently rendered the unreasonable reasonable. Risks that would be unacceptable in pursuit of commerce suddenly became tolerable when placed against daily casualty lists, which could run into five figures on a given day.

Before the Great War, for example, Harbourmaster Rudolf ordered all ships carrying munitions or explosives to anchor at George's Island, just outside the harbor, where the second antisubmarine gate was located. There they were to unload their dangerous cargo during daylight hours only onto smaller ships, which carried the cargo to shore in a series of safer loads. Any ship carrying munitions had to fly a red munitions flag, and while it was in motion all other ships in the harbor were required to stop moving.

But what seems wise in peacetime often looks foolish under the exigencies of war. With German U-boats likely lurking outside Halifax Harbour, raising a red munitions flag over an Allied ship's explosive cargo could be tantamount to suicide. Eliminating the red flag requirement, however, effectively rendered pointless the rule ordering other ships in the harbor to a dead stop while the munitions ship was in motion, since only a few people in the harbor would know if a ship was carrying dangerous cargo without a red flag in the first place. It was often necessary in wartime to permit more of one risk to reduce another, greater one, and this seemed a rational trade-off, with the overwhelming demand for men and materials overseas set against the spotless record of Halifax Harbour during war and peace.

The British Admiralty kept some of Harbourmaster Rudolf's rules, however, including the edict that all oceangoing vessels be assigned a harbor pilot at McNab's Island to steer through the harbor safely. Wyatt's bosses were pleased to see more ships, filled with more cargo, munitions, and soldiers, heading out of Halifax Harbour to Europe than ever before.

All of these changes put a greater burden on Wyatt to ensure the harbor's safety. His exposure was compounded by the lack of enough local licensed harbor pilots who could guide the ships through the tricky Narrows. Given the eightfold increase of cargo during the war, the need to increase the number of harbor pilots was obvious. But by 1917 the harbor still had only fourteen pilots on duty, partly because the pilots liked it that way. The pilots' coveted civil-servant posts were the products of local patronage, not merit or military rank. They could earn as much as $1,000 a month, extraordinary money when soldiers like Ernest Barss were earning $33 a month to risk their lives overseas. When the RCN proposed greatly expanding the number of licensed harbor pilots, the current pilots forcefully rejected the plan because they were none too eager to see their windfall diluted.

The Royal Canadian Navy in Ottawa ultimately didn't feel it was worth the hassle to interfere with the local patronage system, partly because Halifax had never suffered any serious accidents. But this left CXO Wyatt in a vulnerable position, ostensibly in charge of a band of pilots who had little incentive to listen to him. Thus, due to the RCN's decision to overlook risk to avoid controversy, Halifax Harbour suffered from a cloudy chain of command among the Royal Canadian Navy, the British Royal Navy, and the harbor pilots.

Wyatt was stuck with what he had: often insubordinate harbor pilots who did not feel compelled to communicate their ships' cargo and movements, creating a dysfunctional system. When spring arrived in 1917,

Wyatt discovered another problem: the crucial task of communicating these daily ship movements by telephone by the Pilotage Office to his Examination Office had been left in the hands of a fifteen-year-old clerk, Edward Beazley.

Wyatt tried to rectify the situation by clearly restating the requirement that all pilots report all ship movements to his office. A few weeks later, Beazley complained that his orders to the CXO's office were not being recorded, and worse, the people answering were in the habit of laughing at him. Beazley soon stopped calling in his reports of ship movements to the CXO's office altogether—but failed to tell the pilotage secretary of this fact.

While all wars require assuming more risk, this constituted one clear case where the rewards could not be justified. Given the increasingly dangerous conditions in Halifax Harbour, starting with the spotty communications from the harbor pilots, Wyatt felt compelled to warn his superiors in three letters to his commanding officer, Captain Superintendent E. H. Martin.

In his third letter, Wyatt wrote, "It is not possible to regulate the traffic in the harbor, and it is submitted that I cannot in this regard accept the responsibility for any accident occurring."

Wyatt's superior officers had bigger things to worry about than the troubles of rush-hour traffic in Halifax Harbour, which were relegated to the bottom of the world's mounting problems.

Wyatt's warnings went unheeded.

Chapter 9
"It Can't Be Any Worse"

1916

After more than half a year on the front lines, Ernest Barss was straining to maintain his original confidence and conviction. In three letters to his parents from mid-February to March 1, 1916, the long hours, lack of sleep, and demoralizing trench warfare were all starting to take their toll.

On February 15, 1916, Barss wrote, "We are going in again after four days so-called rest in huts right up close to the line and have been so busy on fatigue parties every day that I haven't had a minute to write. . . . Then when we come out I expect to go on leave. I tell you it hasn't come any too soon for I must confess that I have been feeling rather off color lately and fed up with everything. But I think that my eight days in England will put new 'pep' into me."

He noted that his twenty-fourth birthday, on February 27, 1916, should fall during his leave in England.

Barss wrote again, this time from Lacne, Belgium. His long-awaited leave had already been pushed back, but he wrote that he hoped to go on leave a week later, the following Sunday, "and you can't absolutely imagine how I am looking forward to it."

After his descriptions of lousy winter weather and sleepless nights, he mentioned the latest casualties with about the same level of ennui. "The only real worry was their snipers who were certainly active and extremely accurate. They started out by getting our brigadier who certainly was a fine old chap. They shot him twice. Once in the shoulder and once in the arm. Then they picked off our machine gun officer and then killed five of the men. They were all shot in the head."

While Barss was surprisingly candid with his parents, perhaps to a fault, he left a few things out of his correspondence. On February 21, 1916, Barss had guard duty, which put him in charge of sixty soldiers assigned to guard sixteen Allied soldiers who had committed minor infractions like insubordination and returning late from leave. Barss's problem wasn't the prisoners but the guards, a group of fellow Canadians who liked to hang out at the quarterhouse before their shifts began, drinking smuggled liquor and starting fights.

Knowing this, the officer of the day, a stickler no one seemed to like, warned Barss that he would return to inspect the guards at 1:00 a.m. As the witching hour approached, Barss ordered the sixteen drunkest guards to swap uniforms and places with the sixteen prisoners. When the officer of the day returned for his 1:00 a.m. inspection, he was initially impressed by the quiet, professional decorum of the guards, until he figured out what Barss had done. Two days later, on February 23, 1916, Barss was "Severely Reprimanded for Slackness whilst N.C.O. i/c [in charge] of the Quarter-Guard in the field." Perhaps for this reason, his long-sought leave was not just postponed but canceled.

Barss wrote his parents again on March 1, two days after his twenty-fourth birthday. He does his best to remain positive for his parents, yet probably belies more of his fears than he intended, all but saying good-bye to them and Eileen for good.

March 1, 1916

Dear Father & Mother: -
This is a very different letter from that I intended writing you tonight. We are all packed up ready to move out at a moment's notice and although I don't think we will be called out for an hour or two yet we are sure to go up I think. The artillery has been going at it furiously all day and doesn't show any signs of abating and I guess it's the real thing this time.

If nothing happens I will send a card at once so you wouldn't have any worry. If anything should happen I just wanted to tell you both once more how much I love you and want you to remember that you are very near my heart tonight.

I guess that's about all. Please give my love to the other relatives.

Oh yes, in case you should get any news please wire Eileen & let her know. But I don't really think anything will & want you to think that too. My heart is full of love for you both. —Ernest.

p.s. I am enclosing some little flowers I picked in a garden of a ruined house & thought of you so I picked them.
J.E.B.

While Halifax was pumping all it had into the British war effort, few of its consequences were coming back to the Haligonians, except those who received letters from the front lines or casualties quietly returned on ships.

Barss's superiors canceled his leave the next week, too, and the next, and the next, while the fighting in Ypres got hotter and hotter. Because "matters were getting so lively," he started to worry that he "should not get away at all," and would die in Belgium shortly after his twenty-fourth birthday.

Finally, on Sunday, May 7, 1916, three months after he was initially granted leave, Barss climbed out of the trenches at 5:30 p.m. and began his long journey to London. But even that would require him to haul a handcart straight through Ypres, diving each time the shells hit; haggling with the paymaster at 3:00 a.m. for his money; taking a nine-hour train ride with other sweaty servicemen, followed by a turbulent channel crossing next to a chap "who shot his lunch all over me and so set me going"; and a three-hour train to London, where he finally got "thoroughly clean" and "rolled in between clean sheets and fell asleep the moment my head touched the pillow."

Increasingly aware that his continued survival was

dependent less on his early courage than dumb luck, he did something in London that would have been unthinkable when he passed through England almost a year earlier, on his way to the front. "Incidentally," Barss told his parents, he visited a military office to see if he could transfer to England for the remainder of the war—one more sign that he'd had enough of the mud, the relentless tension, and the bagpipes that led them into and out of the battle zone. The man Barss met "was awfully kind but said that when a man is at the front they can't take him away for anything except a commission. So I have to go back [to the front] and wait there for it to come through."

A friend of Barss's, Colonel Sherman Borden, urged Barss to let him know if the administration gave him anything definite to go on, "and he'll see that it goes through without delay. You can't tell how I'm looking forward to getting it and to hearing some favorable news."

This is a striking change of heart from the man who originally was praying *not* to be stuck in England as a machine gun instructor while everyone else was going into the trenches to fight the Germans. Not anymore. By May 1916, Barss was eager to sit behind a desk in England. He had done enough for God and country to satisfy his considerable patriotism, and could still shame the boys who stayed back home if he wanted to. If he was lucky enough to get a post filling out forms in a London office, he knew he would survive, compared to the increasing odds of dying in a sodden field in France or Belgium.

Barss often dropped some artwork or flowers in his envelopes, an indication that his humanity had not died in combat. His missive from England was no exception: "I'm enclosing some violets I picked just outside Ypres [before leave] and hope you'll like them. And now I must say Good night! Lots & lots of love to both of you

"Your affectionate son Ernest."

By May 18, six days after his previous letter, London was behind him. As he wrote to his parents, "Well, I'm back again to it all. And altho' I had a perfectly lovely time of it I can tell you it's no joke coming back again to it all."

The ever-darkening calculus of war confronted him as soon as he returned. "We only have eleven left in our platoon out of 33 so you can imagine that there has been something doing with us up here . . . Ralph Donaldson was wounded while I was away. How I envy him. He got one right through the arm as well as pretty badly shaken up but will be all right again soon and I doubt if he will make 'Blighty' on it," Barss wrote, using a slang reference for a wound serious enough to be sent home, but not so serious as to leave its victim permanently handicapped. "However, he will be sure of several weeks of rest at a bad time so we look on it as a bit of luck than otherwise."

A year before he thought missing the action would be a punishment. Now it was his goal. If his friend Colonel Borden couldn't come through with an officer's commission for Barss, he hoped he could suffer a "million dollar wound" like his lucky friend Ralph Donaldson.

Thirteen days later, on May 31, 1916, Barss wrote again to his parents from Belgium, almost certainly in or near Ypres. He told them the Princess Patricias were going "into the line" that night for eight days, which he hoped would be their last trip. "I think we are all heartily sick of the whole show." But, he said, after this they needn't worry about what's next, because "it can't be any worse."

By May 1916 Ernest Barss harbored no romantic notions of war, just a clear-eyed realization that he sat every day on the razor's edge of life and death. The side bet of getting a commission, which he had initially explored on a whim, he now clung to as his greatest hope to get out alive. Another reason for hope: Eileen, to whom he continued to send his pay for deposit in his Montreal account.

To his parents, Barss wrote, "In my last letter from Eileen she said she had received a very nice letter from father, [and] thought he was a 'dear.' I tell you she is a wonderful girl. She has never missed a mail writing to me and she always writes such bright cheerful letters and tells me all the news and then she sends me little things from time to time and is always asking if she can't do more. Of course I haven't changed my opinion of her in the slightest and consider myself a mighty lucky boy to have so much to look forward to and to work for."

The next day, Thursday, June 1, 1916, the Patricias installed four companies near Mont Sorrel, less than 2 miles east of Ypres, with orders to hold their line from an expected attack of three German regiments no more than 100 yards away. The first three Patricia companies set up in a semicircle trench in Sanctuary Wood, with the fourth company—Barss's—right behind. If the Germans could break through the Canadian defenses, Ypres could finally be theirs. After almost two years of endless fighting in and around Ypres that had already cost more than 100,000 lives, capturing the ancient walled city would send a signal around the world that the Germans had broken the stalemate.

The Canadians saw plenty of signs that the Germans were preparing a massive attack, but none that indicated when. The Germans surprised them at dawn on Friday, June 2, when they unleashed a nonstop, four-hour bombardment that shattered the forward trenches so completely that the Germans felt entirely safe climbing out of their trenches and walking toward the Patricias' first company laughing and singing, so certain were they that no enemy soldiers could have survived the onslaught. Yet six men in the PPCLI's first company had survived, and kept fighting until the end—the Patricias' trademark—which came when German flamethrowers snuck up on them from the side.

The pattern repeated with the Patricias' no. 2 and no. 3 companies, which were pounded relentlessly by German shells until the few survivors who remained tried to take down as many Germans as they could before their time came. The list of casualties included seven of the Patricias' eight top-ranking officers, three dead and four wounded. The Germans secured their gains by digging new trenches, but failed to capitalize on their success by advancing.

That left the Patricias' no. 4 company, which had

seen each successive PPCLI unit fight, fail, and fall. Instead of running, which was the most rational decision for self-preservation, they held their posts, waiting for the German onslaught they knew was coming, in the hopes of preventing a complete collapse of the line.

Barss was in the middle of it all, manning his machine gun, the Germans' favorite target. The Germans seemed content to keep blasting away at the PPCLI no. 4 company from afar with their big guns, but that was enough to take out scores of Barss's trenchmates. The clash would cost 14,000 lives, most of them Allied.

With communications and supply lines cut off on the first day, the no. 4 company kept fighting without food or water for days. On the second day of the battle, June 3, a high-explosive trench mortar soared over Sanctuary Wood and landed right next to Barss, sending him flying against something made of steel—we're not sure what—and knocking him out cold for two hours. His back had been injured and his left foot seriously damaged, but no one could tell how badly he'd been hurt while they were still under fire. A day later, his comrades felt they could risk running him back on a stretcher to the dressing station.

That day, June 4, 1916, a military administrator in France sent a form postcard addressed to Mr. and Mrs. J. Howard Barss, Wolfville, Nova Scotia, Canada.

The postcard was as coldly efficient as the war itself. When Barss's parents turned it over, they saw the following boxes checked:

I have been admitted into hospital
Wounded
I have received your letter
Letter follows at first opportunity

Signed: Ernest
Date: June 4th

This could mean anything. The Great War killed 18 million civilians and military personnel and wounded 23 million more, including several hundred thousand counted as "grand mutiles," those who lost arms, legs, or eyes. The war also created a special class of victims who suffered wounds to their genitalia, a group Ernest Hemingway observed while driving an Italian ambulance and depicted in *The Sun Also Rises*—"You have given more than your life"—and another class of men whose faces were so badly disfigured by shells, shrapnel, bullets, and bayonets that the French government would create secluded rural resorts for them after the war where they could vacation together without stares or comments.

All Barss's parents knew was that their only son was not dead, or lost. Since more than half of those killed on the Western Front were lost on the battlefield, which inspired the Allied Forces to honor them in the Tomb of the Unknown Soldier in Westminster Abbey and in the Arc de Triomphe, the stark postcard Barss's parents received provided at least some comfort, though they also knew that soldiers wounded in the Great War often became dead soldiers weeks or months later.

Libby and Howard Barss would not find out more about their wounded son for several long days.

Chapter 10
"The City's Newer Part"

The Great War flooded Halifax with money, people, and energy. The rising tide lifted all boats, but none higher than the North End, also known as Richmond.

Halifax had grown from the center out, with the taverns, privateers' auction houses, and finest homes downtown. When Halifax's wealthiest residents—like Samuel Cunard; Sir Sandford Fleming, the railroad magnate who created Canada's Intercontinental Railway and implemented time zones to ensure it ran properly; and Enos Collins, who backed Joseph Barss Jr.'s *Liverpool Packet* before becoming a banker and Canada's richest man—all moved to the quieter South End to build new mansions, which became the town's most opulent area, and remains so.

That left Halifax's North End as the peninsula's next frontier. Richmond started as a separate, largely rural village, which got its first boost in 1858 when the Nova Scotia government built the North Street Station, with two train lines reaching west to the rest of the nation starting at the base of its grid of streets. Where Richmond's rails ended its docks began, allowing an easy hand-off for produce, raw materials, and finished products going to and from the rest of the continent and Europe. By the end of the nineteenth century, Halifax had absorbed Richmond.

"Richmond with land to spare knew no overcrowding and was spared the greater city's problems," observed the Reverend Charles Crowdis, Minister of Richmond's Grove Presbyterian Church. "Here dwelt the artisan, the railroad man, the independent man of moderate means, the home maker, the man of enterprise building the city's newer part."

When the Great War broke out, Richmond was already home to the Acadia Sugar Refinery, Hill & Sons Foundry, and the Richmond Printing Company, to name just a few of the manufacturers and mills within blocks of the railyard and docks. During the Great War, every company in Richmond that made or moved almost anything was running three shifts around the clock, with fathers and sons often working side by side.

When they finished their shifts, they would walk a few blocks up the slope of Richmond to their homes. At just about any hour of the day or night, you could see workers walking down the hill to work or back up the hill for a hot meal and some well-earned sleep.

Richmond consisted of a grid of about ten blocks across by fifteen blocks rising up from the shore, often quite steeply. Before the Great War, few of Richmond's roads were paved—and why should they be? Few Richmond residents owned cars, and those who did wouldn't dare drive them over the snowy, icy inclines, which were hard on the primitive autos' delicate clutches. Horses, wagons, and sleighs did a better job of handling whatever the weather brought, including rivers of water running down the muddy roads each spring.

Richmond homes were typically solid, two-story wooden structures, with a bay window to watch the ships gliding by in the harbor down below and often a backyard to keep a hen, a pig, or milking cow. The produce helped feed the big families common in that era, and any surplus could be sold at the farmers' markets on the outskirts of Richmond. The neighborhood also featured a number of rental flats and boarding rooms for the migrant workers and transient military families who came to Halifax during the war, including young mothers whose husbands had boarded the ships down the hill to take them to the fighting fields of Europe.

Near the turn of the century, Samuel Orr Jr. started Richmond Printing Company and, with the help of his father, Samuel Sr., and brothers William and David, built it into one of the neighborhood's bigger businesses. Their two-story granite building sat right beside the railroad tracks, one of the first buildings visitors might see getting off a train or a ship in Halifax.

Samuel Jr. and his wife, Annie, had built a beautiful new home for their six children right in the middle of Richmond. The plant, the Richmond School, and Grove Presbyterian were all short walks from their new home, which featured white shingles made of asbestos, a revolutionary new material heralded as fireproof, and a big bay window looking out on the harbor. The carpenters finished the home in November 1917, just in time for the Orrs to celebrate Christmas there.

Fourteen-year-old Barbara was the oldest of their six children, and helped her mother with the younger ones. Her favorite, Ian, just two years younger, was fascinated by the Great War and loved to watch the daily procession of soldiers and sailors getting on and off the trains and ships right in front of their home. Ian and his buddies could identify the uniforms from Canada, Australia, the United States, and more, and often the soldiers' accents, too. Halifax didn't have a major league baseball team, so most Haligonians pulled for the Boston Red Sox and their talented young pitcher, Babe Ruth. But the world's biggest competition was the Great War, and to Ian and his classmates these military men were the real major leaguers. It made them feel special that Halifax was home to it all. Just like the boys in Boston collected baseball cards and caps, the kids in Halifax collected souvenirs from the sailors and soldiers: coat buttons, shoulder patches, gloves, and the occasional hat.

For Ian's twelfth birthday, his parents gave him picture books of ships and a pair of binoculars so he could better see the ships he was studying through the bay window in their dining room. From the last week of November 1917 through the first week of December, Ian would have more time to pursue his passion because his younger brother, Archie, had contracted whooping cough. In the days before vaccinations, when a child came down with whooping cough, the measles, mumps, or smallpox, they were kept at home, and a large red sign was placed on the door to warn visitors: "QUARANTINED." The fear of contagion was so great that the child's siblings typically stayed home, too, which is why all six Orr children had to remain in their new house for two weeks. To pass the time, Ian watched the ships with his binoculars and books and entertained his siblings with his descriptions.

Richmond was an ideal neighborhood in which to raise children, the kind of place where everyone knew everyone, kids played outside, and parents sat on their front porches and looked after all the neighborhood kids, not just their own. The only constraints on the children's freedom were school, chores, and church.

In 1917, most Richmond children attended St. Joseph's Catholic School, Bloomfield, and the biggest, Richmond School. The neighborhood was also home to a Protestant orphanage down by the docks, where one teacher taught all sixty-seven students, including the children of soldiers and sailors who'd died overseas or gotten someone pregnant before they left. (There was no effective birth control in 1917.) Because the boys' Catholic school on Young Street had burned down the previous year, they had to go to St. Joe's while their diocese finished building their new school. Until then, the girls attended St. Joe's in the morning, and the boys in the afternoon.

To accommodate the influx of children during the Great War, Richmond School built a new wing, but it was already overcrowded, so it added two more classrooms, which gave them seven classes for 421 students. In 1917 it wasn't uncommon to pack 60 students into a single room, but they still had to split the bubble group of 94 first-graders into two classes.

The principal of Richmond School, a stern-looking man named Mr. Huggins, also taught sixty students in grades seven, eight, and nine in one classroom. With only nine ninth-graders still in school, however, it wasn't as complicated as it sounds. Their subjects included algebra, physics, and Latin, plus current events about the war, a specialty of Mr. Huggins's. His students included Barbara Orr in the eighth grade; Ian Orr and James Pattison in the seventh grade; and Noble Driscoll who once dunked Barbara's pigtails in the inkwell—all close neighbors and friends.

Mr. Huggins and his family lived in Rockford, just up the tracks past Africville, but every morning he took the train into town with his daughter Merle, eleven, got off at North Street Station, and walked up the hill to Richmond School. They liked going to school together.

Richmond was also home to four churches: St. Joseph's Roman Catholic Church, which supported the school and a convent; St. Mark's Anglican on Russell Street, which had been expanded twice to accommodate the influx of military personnel and migrant workers in its pews; Kaye Street Methodist Church, with Reverend William J. W. Swetnam; and Grove Presbyterian, which had also built extensive additions to handle its growing congregation on the northerly slope of Fort Needham park, headed by the Reverend Charles J. Crowdis.

Most families in Richmond relied on their shared tempo of family, work, school, and church, which filled shifts, classrooms, and pews and connected neighborhood families. The Orrs went to Richmond School during the week and Grove Presbyterian on Sundays with Gordon, James, and Alan Pattison and Al and Noble Driscoll and their younger siblings.

Most Richmond kids shared a fascination with the Great War, especially the ships sliding past their neighborhood every day. If Barbara Orr's brother Ian was the most knowledgeable ship watcher in the group, his good friend Noble Driscoll wasn't far behind. The Driscolls' home, just across Mulgrave Park from the Orrs', offered a pretty view of the Narrows from its back windows. Their father was not a captain of industry, like the Orrs' father, but a railroad car inspector down at the Richmond Yards who had to support his wife, nine boys, and five girls, although two of their children had already married and left home. With fourteen kids, the milking cow in the backyard wasn't for show-and-tell.

Second only to watching the ships go by, Noble Driscoll loved going to the movies, a recent invention. The Progressive Era's sense of possibility spilled over into the arts, too, with Pablo Picasso creating Cubism, Charlie Chaplin developing the "Little Tramp," and the Original Dixieland "Jass" Band producing the world's first jazz record, "The One Step." Thanks to the dramatic growth of newspapers, movies, and records, farmers and factory workers could identify Al Jolson, Harry Houdini, and Mary Pickford and hum the tunes of Irving Berlin, George Gershwin, and Cole Porter. The arts were suddenly for everyone—even twelve-year-old boys from working-class homes.

With no theater in Richmond, Noble often hopped onto the street trolley for five cents to go to the Empire Theater downtown on Gottingen Street (pronounced locally like "cottage inn," with Gottingen's first "n" being silent). The Empire promised THEATRE COZY AND WARM. NEW HEATING INSTALLED. If Noble craved a candy bar, he'd skip the trolley and walk downtown to save the five cents for a treat at the theater, and still have five cents left to see a show featuring Mary Pickford, Douglas Fairbanks, or Charlie Chaplin, often accompanied by a live organ. The "talkies" were still a few years away.

The Great War had already spanned a good portion of the children's young lives, so it had been normalized, something they lived with every day. Nothing seemed strange about going to the movies each week while the war raged overseas.

The Pattisons' father held an important position as the mechanical superintendent at the Acadia Sugar Refinery, housed in the tallest building on the North End, at the edge of the harbor. The family lived just a few blocks away on the east side of Barrington in a house they rented from the sugar refinery.

The Pattisons had five children, including Gordon, fourteen; James, thirteen; and Alan, eight. In one photo, Gordon and James look like junior Wall Street moguls, with their hair neatly parted and slicked back, fancy ties, high-collared shirts, braces to hold up their pleated pants, and confident grins, each draping an arm over the other as though poised to take on the Halifax banking world.

Principal Huggins urged them to join the Junior Cadet Corps, where they were trained in drill, physical fitness, and rifle exercises. Noble Driscoll also tried to join the Cadet Corp, where his older brother Al was one of the team's best shooters, but he was too small for someone his age and couldn't handle the guns, so his cadet career ended before it started. In 1915, 625 teams of cadets from across the British Empire took part in the National Rifle Association competition, with Richmond's cadets winning two prizes.

Like their friends and neighbors Ian Orr and Noble

Driscoll, the Pattison boys were obsessed with warships. Because the Pattisons' house was so close to the dry docks, when James was walking to or from Richmond School, North Street Station, or his friends' houses, he liked to make a detour toward the docks to see what ship they were working on. James was in the happy habit of filling his homework book with sketches of the wide variety of vessels he saw every day.

Just a few blocks away, the handsome young Reverend William J. W. Swetnam, pastor of the Kaye Street Methodist Church, and his pretty wife, Lizzie Louise Swetnam, were tending to their six-year-old daughter, Dorothy. She was getting over the whooping cough, too, so neither she nor her brother, Carman, had been going to the Protestant Orphanage School that week, which they attended because it was closest to their home, and perhaps because their parents wanted them to meet children they wouldn't see in Richmond School.

Carman remained optimistic that he'd be allowed to sing in their "Mission Concert" that Thursday night. His mother, a skilled pianist, had kept his hopes up by rehearsing with him all week.

Just a few blocks away lived Vincent Coleman, a dashing man who looked younger than his forty-five years, with thick, dark hair parted on the side and swept up and back, and a carefully trimmed mustache. He was Hollywood handsome but humble, raising his five kids while working as a train dispatcher. Well-liked and respected in the neighborhood and a favorite with the kids, he had become a local hero the previous summer. In the *Evening Mail*'s account, Mr. Coleman "jumped on a runaway engine and stopped it in time to save a collision with a suburban train."

Richmond's recent success had spread to the neighborhood directly to the north, Africville. In 1848, William, John, and Thomas Brown bought some land immediately north of Richmond and welcomed other immigrants from the West Indies, and former slaves from the U.S., despite the name. As one older resident said, "None of the people came from Africa. You better believe it. It was part of Richmond, just the part where the colored folks lived."

In contrast to the brick and marble banks of downtown Halifax and the concrete and granite factories of Richmond, the commercial buildings of Africville were usually made of wood and produced basic goods like cotton, nails, and beef; there was also a bonemeal plant that manufactured fertilizer, and smelled like it. Most residents of Africville worked as laborers: stonemasons, garbagemen, and barrel makers, an Africville specialty. When business was humming, the men could get work as stevedores, loading coal from railcars to ships. The women often found work cleaning houses a few blocks away in Richmond, farther downtown, or in the mansions of Halifax's South End.

The Halifax city planners had laid down rows of train tracks from North Street Station around the shoreline of Bedford Basin and right through Africville, and turned much of the area into a dumping ground for the rest of the city, yet never gave its residents basic services like police protection, sewage, or schools. So, the people of Africville created their own. Despite these obstacles, Africville managed to produce a world-champion boxer, George Dixon; got Duke Ellington to visit when he was on tour; and organized its own hockey team, the Brown Bombers. But what bound Africville to the wealthier parts of Halifax was little more than proximity, and the mutual benefits of a thriving economy.

Directly across the Narrows from Richmond and Africville sat Turtle Grove, where the Mi'kmaq had lived for centuries. But after the Europeans arrived, they struggled to hold on to a portion of what they had—an all-too-familiar story. By 1914, they had been reduced to a few dozen residents on the shore, led by Germain Bartlett Alexis. His friends called him Jerry, but his fans knew him as Doctor Lone Cloud, the name he used when performing with Buffalo Bill Cody's Wild West show. The name stuck after he moved to New Brunswick, married Elizabeth Paul, a young Maliseet woman, and started his own family. Around 1892, the year Barss was born, Lone Cloud and his family settled in Nova Scotia. He continued to perform up and down the Atlantic Coast, then turned to politics when the band elected him the second sub-chief of Halifax County.

Lone Cloud didn't take his duties lightly, writing letters to the Canadian Department of Indian Affairs to ask why there was no government-sanctioned reservation at Turtle Grove. When the government replied that the tribe had no more right to the land than squatters, he asked if they could buy the land. When they told him they couldn't do that either, he urged them to let the Mi'kmaq relocate to another reservation, but that fell on deaf ears, too.

The Mi'kmaq people started migrating 300 years earlier during the first battle of global empires. It had still not been resolved by the mid-1910s, even as a far larger, more violent contest was unfolding all around it.

Chapter 11
Wounded Inside and Out

After Ernest Barss's parents received the initial postcard informing them that their son had been wounded, with no details, a few days later they received a short, censored note dated June 6, 1916, from "No. 4 Gen'l Hospital, Ward #2.a. Med.," one of the facilities on the huge British military base in Camiers, France, a tiny coastal town just 90 miles from Ypres, which also served as the French base of the Machine Gun Corps. On the same form, in a very small box under "Casualty," someone typed, "Cont' Back," above "S.Shock," indicating Barss had been diagnosed with a contusion of the back and shell shock.

Whatever Ernest knew, he was not going to tell his parents much. They received this message from "Corpl J. E. Barss."

"Dear Father and Mother:

"Just a few lines to let you know that I am in the [redacted] place due to the fact that I was blown up by a German shell of large caliber in our [redacted] the other day. I will try & tell you all about it later but don't feel up to it just yet."

He added that the "poor old" Princess Patricia had been virtually wiped out once more, an unhealthy tendency borne of their habit of fighting to the death. "I can't tell you how thankful I am that I was spared," Barss wrote, attributing his good fortune to chance, or faith. "I will never be able to understand how it was I was not killed a hundred times that day."

Although he had hurt his back and would have to lie "perfectly still for a while," he assured them "I am as good as new. Don't worry I shall be out by the time you get this." Normally a brutally honest correspondent, Barss's last two lines were almost completely false.

Barss filled in more of the mystery two months later on August 18, 1916, from Mission House Hospital in New Seaham, Durham, about a five-hour train trip northeast of London. He wrote that the shelling on Mont Sorrel was the worst he'd seen, and he felt deeply grateful to have gotten out alive. "I never will be able to understand how anyone lived through it all."

Despite his chipper tone, Barss had been seriously

wounded, and a full recovery seemed unlikely. His official records stated: "high explosive shell causing an injury to spine," specifically "Contusion of back. Lumbar," and "Regional paralysis of left leg." Barss's injuries would require him to wear a body cast for six months, and his doctors didn't believe he would ever walk normally again. Barss apparently didn't see the point in worrying his parents about that, nor the "shell shock" doctors had diagnosed, which could cover anything from simple sleeplessness to a complete nervous breakdown.

The good news was that Barss hadn't been killed, and he would never have to go back to the trenches. But he wasn't healthy, and he wasn't home either—far from it.

Receiving these mysterious missives caused his parents so much worry that they started battling the military bureaucracy to get a berth on a ship heading overseas, despite the difficulty of doing so for civilians during wartime and the obvious dangers for everyone on board. After several months of persistent appeals to the authorities, they were finally granted permission to ship from Montreal on the *Pretorian*, a 940-passenger liner, to Glasgow, Scotland, and arrived safely on September 29, 1916.

In a letter to her sister, Libby Barss described their first visit to the hospital grounds. "I saw a young man with a stick and a blue band on his arm coming along." She didn't recognize the man until they were much closer, when she looked up and realized it was her son. "You can imagine how glad we all were to see each other once more."

After emotional hugs, she sized him up. "He looks very well but his leg is pretty stiff and his back pains him all the time. He doesn't sleep very well but is doing better than when he was first wounded. He is having electric treatments on his leg now every morning. It had been paralyzed but is beginning to get better."

This left some things out, including Ernest's body cast and the depth of his shell shock symptoms, including insomnia and hand tremors, but that's probably because their son didn't tell them everything, lest they worry too much.

"Ernest says his appetite is better than it was," Libby said. "To look at him you wouldn't think there was anything the matter with him."

He'd been seriously hurt and had a long way to go, but he was very much alive, psychologically damaged but still in possession of his quick wit. For weeks on end, his parents provided company and encouragement, shared news from home, and helped him do just about everything, including walk. But the progress was slow, when visible at all.

After two months, Howard and Libby decided they had done all they could do for their only child for now, and it was time to go home. They booked passage on a converted luxury liner originally called SS *Vaderland* when it launched in 1900 but which was now a British troopship renamed *Southland* to avoid a German-sounding name. A year earlier, a U-boat had torpedoed *Southland*, costing the lives of forty Australian soldiers. But 1,360 men had survived in lifeboats and the ship was beached, so they repaired her and put her back into service a few months before the Barsses boarded her.

Their trip home was mercifully uneventful, but six months later another German submarine, the prolific UB-70, which is credited with sinking fifty-three ships, torpedoed *Southland* and finished the job. Barss's parents were also fortunate.

The military doctors determined that Ernest could return to Canada in January 1917, but before he could board he contracted either the mumps or the measles and had to be quarantined. The ship sailed without him—and was sunk by a German U-boat, killing all aboard.

After Barss had recovered from his malady, on Sunday, February 4, 1917, he boarded the SS *Missanabie*, a three-year-old British passenger liner, which made for a comfortable return. (A year later, *Missanabie* would also be sunk by a German U-boat.) After eight days on the ocean, *Missanabie* arrived in Saint John, New Brunswick. But Barss missed one of his trains, so they had to load him onto a sleigh for the last 18 miles to Wolfville, where he arrived at 10 p.m.—twelve hours late.

"He looks well," his father wrote, "but is pretty weak from the effects of his [appendix] operation."

He was finally safe at home, where he could slip between clean, starched white sheets and know that he was safe among people who loved him. But he was a mere shadow of the stout, self-assured young man who had left two years earlier for Europe. After two weeks at his parents' home, he returned to Halifax for three more months of rehabilitation at Pine Hill Military Convalescent Home, just over Citadel Hill.

The doctors' conclusions were not encouraging, reporting that Barss suffered complete paralysis "of left foot and up the leg to three inches above the ankle joint." Almost a year after Barss had been evacuated from the battle of Mont Sorrel, he still could not extend or flex his left foot or toes, and could walk only with "a marked foot drop," hardly the stuff of a hockey hero.

A question on the form asked the attending physician, "To what extent will injury prevent his earning a full livelihood in the general labor market?" The doctor answered, "30%."

On another form, under "Probable Duration of Incapacity," a doctor wrote, "Indefinite."

Almost a year after getting hit, Barss's shell shock hadn't abated either, including "insomnia, nervousness . . . some tremor of his hands." Today's doctors would likely call it post-traumatic stress disorder, or PTSD, the symptoms of which typically include a lack of "positive or loving feelings toward other people." As a result, victims tend to avoid relationships.

We can only speculate, but it might not be a coincidence that Eileen Clarke, the woman whom Barss had mentioned in so many letters while fighting overseas, seems to have disappeared after December 1, 1916. Barss quit sending her letters and his pay, and there is no more mention of her in his correspondence.

Some of the war's damages were as hard to calculate as they were to overcome.

Three years into the Great War, neither the Allied Forces nor the Central Powers could gain the upper hand, all the while sacrificing healthy young men by the thousands every day. The global conflict had been reduced to a giant game of tug-of-war, with neither side able to gain much ground before giving it back, while adding troops upon troops to both sides of the struggle. These additions didn't tip the balance but simply maintained it.

The war that was supposed to be settled when the leaves fell in the fall of 1914 was only getting bigger by the year, and worse for all involved. After Great Britain suffered tremendous losses on the Western Front, the Russians were about to pull out, so the need for more men increased just as the desire to join was dropping. Thus, Great Britain initiated the draft in 1916.

The wild card in this tired game was the United States. President Wilson had tried to remain neutral but felt compelled, as the German atrocities mounted, to side more frequently and more publicly with America's natural allies Great Britain and France. While most Americans remained vehemently opposed to entering the "European war" and were content to let the Old World settle its own scores, compelling reasons for the Americans to join the Allies became more obvious as the war ground on. A victory for the Central Powers would deeply damage American business, which depended on robust trade with Great Britain and France, and threaten the United States' national security. Anti-German sentiment—stirred up by the German practices of attacking soldiers with poison gas and civilian ships with U-boat torpedoes—was making it harder for President Wilson to keep his country out of the conflict.

A piece of paper soon tipped the scales. In January 1917, German foreign minister Arthur Zimmerman sent a coded telegram to Mexico, a page filled with ten columns of five-digit numbers, seventeen rows deep. Decoded, the telegram revealed that Zimmerman was offering Mexico a deal: if the Mexicans declared war on the United States, the Germans would help them win back the land they had lost in the 1848 Mexican-American War, including present-day Texas, New Mexico, and Arizona.

The British intercepted the telegram, decoded it, and informed the Americans. Although Mexico was unlikely to take Zimmerman up on his offer, the telegram provided President Wilson with the rationale he needed to persuade his nation to enter the war, which the United States officially did on April 6, 1917.

As of that date, no major world power remained neutral, making it a truly global war. The decision also made the United States and Canada official allies for the very first time in their history—if in name only.

Of course, the Americans would only make a difference if they bothered to show up. In the spring of

1917, the iconic poster depicting Uncle Sam declaring "I WANT YOU!" was created to lure America's young men into the war. But six weeks after declaring war the United States military had recruited only 73,000 volunteers. That forced President Wilson to propose a draft for able-bodied men from age twenty-one to thirty-one, which became law on May 18, 2017. But even that didn't have the intended effect. The United States was home to 23 million men between those ages, but 3 million who registered never reported, and 3.5 million never bothered to register at all. With only paper records sitting in D.C., the draft offices had few means of tracking down the violators.

Americans had always sought to stay out of Europe's wars, and felt no loyalty to the crown. Further, by 1917 it was easier to see the endless slaughter the war was producing. This forced President Wilson to sign another bill into law: "Work or fight," which made it mandatory for draft-eligible men to demonstrate that they were performing work vital to the war cause, or they would be drafted into the army. Baseball was not exempt. By mid-December 1917, no fewer than eleven Boston Red Sox players had been lost to the war—the most of any team in baseball—which encouraged their star left-handed pitcher, Babe Ruth, to give hitting a try.

By the summer of 1917, even Canada no longer had enough young volunteers to maintain its troop levels. This prompted the Canadian Parliament to pass the Military Service Act of August 29, 1917, which gave the prime minister the power to draft soldiers if he thought it necessary.

That triggered the next question: Who would be the prime minister to decide this? With this urgent question in the balance, the federal election to be held on December 17, 1917, became a referendum on the "Conscription Crisis." The current prime minister, Robert Borden, who had gained office when the 1911 Reciprocity proposal went down, was fiercely pro-war, like most of his fellow Haligonians. If he won reelection in 1917, he promised to approve conscription nationwide.

But the man Borden had unseated in 1911, French-Canadian Wilfrid Laurier, promised that if he won the 1917 election, he would drop the draft, which pleased most French-Canadians and growing numbers of those weary of the war. If Laurier returned to power, Canada's role in the Great War would likely wind down, with or without an Allied victory.

The lines were drawn. Expecting a close battle, Prime Minister Borden, a fierce political fighter, tried to tilt the election by allowing soldiers overseas to vote, but not conscientious objectors at home. The way the war was going, the election would depend partly on how much people at home really knew about what was happening there.

"One of the reasons that war has remained tolerable to civilian populations is they don't know most of what goes on," former PBS news anchor and native Haligonian Robert MacNeil wrote. "It was particularly true in the First World War, when the nature and quantities of casualties were so horrifying, and when censorship was not only very repressive but the press an . . . often willing cheerleader for the war effort."

MacNeil liked to shock American audiences with this fact: in World War I, Canada lost 60,000 young men, from a total population of 7 million. If the United States had lost a similar ratio in Vietnam, it wouldn't have lost 58,000 men but 1.7 million—or almost thirty times more.

"The First World War left indelible scars on the Canadian psyche," MacNeil wrote, "but it did not tear this country apart as Vietnam did America, with much smaller losses, because people at home knew very little of the reality and were fed, for the most part, jingoistic, uplifting accounts."

One German soldier named Manfred von Richtofen, better known as the Red Baron, found the public's habit of romanticizing warfare absurd. "I am in wretched spirits after every aerial combat," he wrote in his autobiography. "I believe that [the war] is not as the people at home imagine it, with a hurrah and a roar; it is very serious, very grim."

In the spring of 1917, Barss spent three months recuperating at the Pine Hill Military Convalescent Home in Halifax, where the Canadian doctors repeated what the English doctors had told Barss overseas: he was not likely to walk normally again—crushing news for a lifelong athlete. The same man whose ankles had been so strong before the war that he didn't need to lace up his skates was now being told he would never walk again without a cane, or severe pain.

Barss decided to ignore the doctors' prognosis. He forced himself to walk every day with his new cane, regardless of the weather or how he felt. His walks were slow, clumsy, and agonizing, but essential for his morale. He needed to believe that he was getting better, and that he would not be crippled the rest of his life.

Making his way down Citadel Hill to the waterfront, he could see how much Halifax had changed in just a few years. The harbor was crowded with ships, the streets were filled with sailors and soldiers, and civilians with strange accents were scurrying to keep up with the demands of Halifax's wartime economy, and automobiles were everywhere. The town was throbbing with a restless energy Barss had never felt in Halifax before.

Limping through the hospital and the town also allowed him to converse with the doctors, nurses, and orderlies at the facility, people who knew more about the war's realities than most, and with townspeople in the barbershops, restaurants, and city parks. The contrast between the macabre business of killing Germans and seeing his friends killed from bullets, shells, and gas and the romantic and naïve notions of the people on the home front, he found alarming and frustrating. Like most veterans who had seen combat, Barss quickly gave up trying to explain what was really happening "over there."

After three months at Pine Hill, Barss's doctors allowed him to go back to his parents' house in Wolfville. There, he kept up his daily walks, knowing that if he stopped, his half-healed leg would never recover. People in his small town eagerly welcomed him back as a war hero, but Barss found the ignorance of the war even greater in his small town.

And yet, Barss remained fiercely patriotic and fervently pro-war. He took a position as county secretary for Victory Loans—war bonds—which required him to walk all over Wolfville with his cane if he wanted to meet his sales goals. He also took a position as the military representative of the local exemption tribunals, where recruits made their cases for avoiding the trenches and Barss and his panel ruled on them.

The national election for prime minister and other posts was scheduled to come up in 1916, but the government postponed it due to the war. Rescheduled for December 17, 1917, it was already shaping up to be what historian Michael Bliss described as "the most bitter election in Canadian history," with Prime Minister Borden's conservative government pushing for conscription, and former prime minister Wilfrid Laurier's Liberal Party pushing against it. Thus, it was called the "Khaki election," since the principle issue at stake was Canada's role in the Great War.

Barss wrote to his American uncle Andrew Townson in Rochester, New York, that the election was, "keeping the country stirred up. We have never had a crisis such as this in the history of Canada where the mere representatives count for so little and the issue for so much."

Barss added that "If the Laurier party should get in, standing as it does for a policy by which Canada would do no more for the war . . . then I for one don't want to stay in Canada or say that I am a Canadian any more. That is how strongly we feel about it down here."

As determined as Ernest Barss was to support the war effort, he was more determined to walk again.

PART IV

A Dangerous Dance

Chapter 12
Two Ships

Fall 1917

In April 1917 alone, 15,000 troops, equivalent to a quarter of Halifax's population, boarded ships in Halifax Harbour heading for Europe.

But the more ships that left Halifax, the more chances the U-boats had to find them. That was the sole purpose of the U-boats' existence, after all, for which everything else was sacrificed, including speed, power, and comfort. During the Great War, possibly the only place on earth more miserable than a flooded trench near Ypres was inside a German U-boat, where twenty-five to fifty crewmen packed themselves inside a steel tube that typically measured about 230 feet long and 20 feet wide, and stayed in there, for three weeks to six months.

The vessels were equipped with one toilet and no shower. Bathing, washing, and shaving were banned to save precious fresh water. Each sailor was given only one extra pair of underwear and socks, with no change of uniform and no laundry.

The loaves of bread they ate grew white fungus so quickly in the humid confines that crews called them "rabbits." The scenery never changed, the odor of everything grew worse daily, claustrophobia had to be constantly suppressed, and almost half the 360 U-boats ended up on the ocean floor, taking 5,000 crewmen down with them. They called them "iron caskets" for a reason.

Life in a U-boat had only one justification: finding an Allied ship and blowing it up. And they were good at it, sinking so many that the U-boats alone threatened to turn the tide of war. The Red Baron and his eighty combat victories in the sky pale in comparison to legendary U-boat captain Lothar von Arnauld de la Perière and his 194 sunken ships.

By 1917, the U-boats had sunk an estimated 3,000 Allied ships, forcing the British to try the convoy system. When it actually worked, they quickly made the practice standard operating procedure. Typically, thirty or more ships would gather in Bedford Basin, sheltered and safe. When they got the order, they would head out single file through the Narrows and past McNab's Island to the head of the harbor, where they would meet an escort of powerful destroyers and quick gunboats—the perfect combination to transform the U-boats from the hunters to the hunted.

But to Noble Driscoll, the advent of the convoy system just meant more ships to watch. Whenever a group of ships started its journey out of Bedford Basin, Noble would shout, "A convoy is coming!" and urge everyone to come to their home's back windows, or out into the backyard if the convoy was big enough to warrant the extra attention. Usually his parents and siblings would indulge him for a few minutes, then return to what they were doing, leaving Noble by himself to memorize all the details he could to tell his friends at Richmond School.

While the Haligonians watched the big ships come and go, and Barss was back in Wolfville working "tooth and nail" to get the vote out for Prime Minister Borden's government and the conscription program it supported, *Mont-Blanc* was chugging up the coast, burrowing through the deep waves kicked up by a coastal storm and weighed down with 6 million pounds of high explosives to attack German soldiers. The waves crashed across the deck night and day, splashing the crew with salt water and making them fear for their lives every time their bow smacked into another wave.

The *Imo*, coming across the Atlantic from Rotterdam, Holland, was riding high and fast with nothing but ballast in her holds. Launched in 1889 when the White Star Line had christened a new steamer the SS *Runic*, she measured 430 feet long, a third longer than a football field, and 44 feet wide, a good-size all-purpose boat for transatlantic shipping. The ship was sold twice before the Norwegian Southern Pacific Whaling Company bought it in 1912 and renamed it *Imo*. In 1917, the Belgian Relief Commission chartered the ship to haul supplies from North America to Europe.

In theory, neutral ships could cross the ocean with impunity, but that theory was little consolation after a U-boat sent your ship to the bottom of the ocean. The company painted BELGIAN RELIEF in huge red letters on a white background on *Imo*'s side, so no one could claim they didn't know what the ship was hauling. Whether this actually helped ward off German U-boats or the *Imo* was simply running on luck was impossible to know, but it had crossed the Atlantic unescorted several times without incident, at a decent 12 knots, or 14 miles per hour.

Imo was operated by a crew of thirty-nine men from around the world, including Norwegians, Swedes, Danes, a Dutchman, and a French-Canadian. Their captain, Haakon From, was a native of Sandefjord, Norway, a town of 2,000 in 1870, when From was born there. He became a whaler at twenty-two and spent all his years at sea, the last twelve as a captain. He was fluent in English, had traveled twice to Antarctica, and had sailed in and out of Halifax twice the previous summer. While this hardly qualified him as an expert navigator of the Narrows, it certainly gave him more familiarity and confidence than the captain of the White Star Line's RMS *Atlantic* had in 1873, before her disoriented helmsmen crashed into the shore.

Now forty-seven, Captain From was generally considered an even-keeled, good-natured man, but an incident earlier that year suggested he was not always so sunny and calm. After Captain From had led *Imo* to Philadelphia to unload a shipment of grain, he hired a company to repair her boiler and engine room. When Schmaal Engineering Works completed the repairs for $9,000—a hefty $183,000 today—Captain From refused to pay them or even to explain why. When Schmaal's lawyer left the ship to file a lawsuit, "Captain From acted like a maniac," Gustav Schmaal recalled. "When I entered his cabin, he glared at me like a man out of his mind and snarled like a beast. Raising his big fists, he brought them down on my head, knocking me to the floor. Then, cursing horribly, he picked me up bodily and hurled me through the door of the cabin. As soon as I regained my feet, I ran for my life!"

Captain From pulled *Imo* out of port and hurried down the Delaware River to make his escape. Schmaal and his attorney chased the ship by train and tugboat, finally catching *Imo* in Wilmington, Delaware, where authorities made Captain From pay up, plus penalties, which more than doubled the expense. The best Captain From's attorney could do by way of explanation was this: "The *Imo*'s captain was intensely anti-German." Apparently, he was also prone to violent outbursts.

Mont-Blanc **had** already changed hands a few times when a Frenchman bought her in 1906 and used her as an ore carrier for almost a decade, giving her the "barest maintenance" to do her job. On December 28, 1915, the Compagnie Generale Transatlantique (CGT), also known as the French Line, purchased the ship, renamed it *Mont-Blanc*, and added guns fore and aft to make her suitable for use during the war. *Mont-Blanc* might have been on the smaller side, slow, and in subpar condition, but in the later years of the war, the French Line figured just about any piece of metal that could float would be in high demand. They guessed right: the French Admiralty hired her immediately, sending *Mont-Blanc* across the Atlantic several times without incident.

In October 1917, the French Line turned *Mont-Blanc* over to Captain Aimé Joseph Marie Le Médec, who was born on December 8, 1878, in the tiny seaside town of Penerf, Morbihan, in the northwest corner of France, almost directly across the Atlantic from Nova Scotia. Of his thirty-eight years, he'd spent fully twenty-two of them at sea, and half of those with the Compagnie Generale Transatlantique. He had earned a reputation as a competent if not spectacular skipper and a stickler for the rules.

Le Médec had achieved his rank of captain just two years earlier, as a wartime promotion, but he had never captained *Mont-Blanc* before. His two previous ships had been smaller, suitable for conventional commercial shipping, and he had never helmed a munitions ship either, let alone one weighed down with 6 million pounds of high explosives.

That might have been alarming before the war, but in the conflict's fourth year, the normal rules no longer applied. And so Le Médec finished his first trip on *Mont-Blanc* from Bordeaux, France, to New York Harbor on November 9, 1917. For security reasons, the British Admiralty did not inform *Mont-Blanc* what it would be loading, but *Mont-Blanc*'s crewmen took note when the authorities instructed them to bypass their usual slip, and dock in Gravesend Bay in Brooklyn instead, then gave the shipwrights detailed plans to cover every inch of metal in the holds with wood, cloth, tar, and rubber, and to secure it all with copper nails. If any crewman still harbored doubts about the volatility of the cargo to come, his questions were answered with the arrival of the rotating band of police officers that surrounded the ship for three weeks while stevedores loaded boxes and barrels into the hermetically sealed holds.

What made *Mont-Blanc*'s cargo so dangerous?

All explosives require two components: a fuel and an "oxidizer," usually oxygen. How destructive an explosive is depends largely on how quickly those two combine.

With "low explosives," like propane, gasoline, and gunpowder, it's necessary to add oxygen to ignite them and keep them burning. If a fire runs out of oxygen, it dies. Another factor is speed. The rate of the chemical reaction, or decomposition, of low explosives is less than the speed of sound, or 767 miles per hour.

In contrast, a "high explosive" combines the fuel

and the oxidant in a single molecule, making each one a self-contained bomb, with everything it needs to create the explosion. To ignite, a high explosive usually requires only extreme heat or a solid bump. Once started, the dominoes fall very quickly, ripping through the explosive material faster than the speed of sound.

When detonated, a high explosive produces a flash of light, a sonic boom, incredible heat from the rapid chemical decomposition, and immense pressure caused by the instantaneous production of gas and the expansion of hot air, creating the kind of airwave associated with nuclear weapons. A high explosive releases these forces in spectacular fashion, and that is what makes them so dangerous.

Low explosives like fireworks have been around for centuries, but the discovery of high explosives happened relatively recently. In 1863, a German scientist named Joseph Wilbrand discovered something called trinitrotoluene, which cleverly combined some pretty basic elements—carbon monoxide, hydrogen, nitrogen, and carbon—to create something truly destructive. It's better known as TNT.

In 1867, a Swedish inventor with 355 patents named Alfred Nobel found that nitroglycerin, an extremely unstable high explosive, could be handled safely if it were first absorbed in a porous material such as clay, sawdust, or cotton. Nobel called his invention "dynamite" and made a fortune off it.

When Nobel's brother Ludvig died in 1888, a French paper mistakenly thought Alfred had died, and titled his obituary "The Merchant of Death Is Dead." When Alfred read his own obituary, he was crushed to see how he would be remembered. To change his legacy, he rewrote his will to devote 94 percent of his fortune, or about $210 million in today's dollars, to fund five Nobel prizes to be awarded to those who had given "the greatest benefit [to] mankind" in the fields of physics, chemistry, literature, peace, and physiology and medicine, with a prize for economics added in 1968.

It is now debatable which of Nobel's two most famous creations has had the greatest impact on the world he left behind, but we know the production of high explosives did not end with dynamite. Four years later, in 1871, another German scientist, Hermann Sprengel, discovered a close cousin of TNT called trinitrophenol, sometimes called TNP or picric acid, which consists of carbon monoxide, carbon dioxide, hydrogen, nitrogen, and carbon. Again, it doesn't look too scary, but the damage picric acid can do is astonishing.

Alan Ruffman, editor and author of *Ground Zero*, explains that in both explosives, "the Nitro group

(NO2) acts as the oxidizer, and carbon and hydrogen provide the fuel. In the explosion process, the complex molecules decompose into a simple solid (carbon) and gases (carbon monoxide, carbon dioxide, hydrogen, and nitrogen). The energy released in the breaking of the chemical bonds that bind these molecules results in the high temperature of the explosion; the high pressures are produced by the rapid expansion of the gases as they are released from the dense solid bonding."

Because both TNT and picric acid are designed to be incredibly destructive, they were quickly adopted for military use, with the Boer War and the Great War serving as laboratories. By 1917, picric acid had emerged as the favorite because it was shown to be 10 percent more efficient than TNT. Both can become even more destructive if you heat the contents by igniting a low explosive nearby, which will multiply the power of the TNT or picric acid.

"She had a devil's brew aboard," Raddall states of the *Mont-Blanc*, a perfect combination of catalysts, fuel, and firepower. The ship's manifest included 62 tons of gun cotton, 250 tons of TNT, and 2,366 tons of picric acid, the least understood of the chemicals on board, but the most dangerous.

Picric acid is notoriously unstable, and even more so when dry, because it's especially sensitive to friction and shock—so sensitive, in fact, that when picric acid is stored in labs, merely turning the lid of a jar of the chemical, if dried particles are stuck between the bottle and the stopper, can blow up the entire lab.

Put it all together, and the power of *Mont-Blanc's* cargo works out to about 3 kilotons of TNT—or about a fifth of the 15 kilotons the "Little Boy" atomic bomb unleashed on Hiroshima.

After the shipwrights had so carefully built the magazines, hermetically sealing each compartment, and the stevedores had packed it all systematically, the French government agent operating out of Gravesend Bay received a last-minute order from his superiors in France to pack what little space remained on *Mont Blanc* with urgently needed benzol, an unusually volatile fuel, the latest "super gasoline." The stevedores followed orders, swinging 494 barrels containing 246 tons of the highly combustible accelerant into a few unused spaces belowdecks, on the foredeck, and at the stern, where they stacked the fuel three and four barrels high and lashed it with canvas straps, a somewhat slapdash approach compared to the thoroughness with which the shipwrights had built the magazines. When the crew walked past the drums on deck, they could smell the unmistakable reek of the benzol.

With the final addition of the benzol, *Mont Blanc*

now carried an impressive array of the most danger-ous chemicals known to man at that time. While ben-zol can't match the pure power of gun cotton, TNT, or picric acid—all high explosives—what the stevedores probably didn't know when they stacked the barrels of benzol on deck was that the airplane fuel needed only a spark to ignite, while picric acid doesn't explode until it reaches 572 degrees Fahrenheit, and TNT does not detonate until it reaches 1,000 degrees. But by mak-ing the last-minute decision to store most of the fuel on the deck and the TNT and picric acid below, the crew had unwittingly constructed the perfect bomb, with the easy-to-light fuse on top, and the most explosive materials trapped in the hold below.

Thanks to reforms instituted after *Titanic* sank without enough lifeboats for everyone on board, *Mont-Blanc* had two lifeboats with enough seats to carry all forty-one men to safety, including Captain Le Médec and Pilot Mackey, but it lacked a fire extinguisher. In-stead, the ship was equipped with a connection for a pressure hose on the forward deck, which would draw its water from the sea, and two anchors that could be dropped from the bow to secure her in an emergency. As a last resort, *Mont-Blanc* could be scuttled by open-ing the seacock to flood the holds, but thanks to the ship's history of poor maintenance, that would require a minimum of thirty minutes to coerce the rusted rivets and bolts to release the old-model valve, and another two hours for the holds to fill up with enough water to sink the ship.

But it's unlikely anyone gave all of this much thought, and perhaps even less likely that Captain Le Médec did, since he was still getting to know the vessel on his first round trip. Besides, a sudden shift or a single spark could render all those questions moot in a second.

As *Mont-Blanc* approached her December 1 departure date, Captain Le Médec returned to the British Admiralty with his interpreter for a second meeting with Commander Coates. When Coates asked him if the fully loaded *Mont-Blanc* could maintain 8 knots (about 10 mph) across the North Atlantic, Le Médec consulted the ship's incomplete logs and considered his only transatlantic trip on *Mont-Blanc*. He didn't have enough data to answer Coates's question confidently, but he admitted he did not think *Mont-Blanc* could keep up that pace.

Taking all this information in, Commander Coates said, "I will have to see about that," and left Le Médec at the table while he consulted with a superior officer. A few minutes later, Coates returned to tell Le Médec he would proceed unescorted to Halifax—the first time that port had been mentioned as a possibility—and once there, if *Mont-Blanc* couldn't keep up with a convoy to Europe, Le Médec was to open the envelope Coates handed to him to reveal their secret route to Bordeaux.

Once again, Commander Coates wasn't casting for Captain Le Médec's feelings on the matter, nor was he offering alternatives. Captain Le Médec was again disappointed by the plans, but he didn't waste time trying to think of a way out of this assignment but instead how they could get across the Atlantic without blowing up.

And so the sequence of events that brought a poorly maintained French freighter built in the nineteenth century, captained by a man unfamiliar with the ship and her cargo, into the service of the British Navy in Gravesend Bay during the most horrific war in human history was now complete: all these elements had combined in surprising fashion, with any number of safeguards eliminated, to produce a weapon of mass destruction floating up the East Coast in hopes of reaching Halifax safely. It was a fool's mission—but then, that was the Great War's specialty. An hour before midnight on December 1, 1917, *Mont-Blanc* eased out of Gravesend Bay as quietly as possible.

The *Halifax Herald* reported that in the last week of November 1917 alone, the British had lost one small ship, four fishing boats, and sixteen merchantmen of 1,600-plus tons each, for a total of twenty-one ships in seven days, or three a day. If the Germans caught sight of *Mont-Blanc* and added it to the list of hits, the resulting explosion would make international news. The U-boat crew would be received in Hamburg much as *Highflyer*'s crew was being celebrated in Halifax—provided, that is, they lived to tell the tale.

The *Mont-Blanc*'s crew scanned the surface for any signs of U-boats, watching the sky to judge the weather and feeling the roll of the ship more intimately than ever before. They could only hope the shipwrights' work would hold up. The sailors mindlessly reached for their cigarettes, only to remember that they had no matches, because lighting a match might be enough to ignite the bomb beneath them.

Captain Le Médec navigated up the East Coast as carefully as he could, trying to balance the competing demands of speed and caution. On the one hand, the longer he took to reach the safety of Halifax Harbour, the more time a U-boat had to find them. If *Mont-Blanc* bypassed a straight course to Halifax in order to hug the shoreline, where the sea was calmer but U-boats were more likely to lurk, especially near Boston, the odds went higher still.

But if Le Médec steered straight to Halifax, *Mont-*

Blanc's bow would pound into the bigger waves kicking up on the North Atlantic, with each impact threatening to disturb the cargo below. Even a sudden shift of the high explosives, separated only by plywood partitions, could send them to the sky. The French government marine services ordered Le Médec to stick to the coast and not worry about the time the route would add to his itinerary. Hugging the shoreline, he was able to push *Mont-Blanc* to 7 knots, or about 8 miles per hour, almost full speed.

The decision seemed prescient on *Mont-Blanc*'s second day at sea, when a northwest gale blew across Maine for two days. As the ship fought the wind and waves, it was clear the threat of *Mont-Blanc* blowing itself up was greater than that of a U-boat finding her to do the job. Le Médec rode up the Maine coast almost to the Canadian border, cut across the Bay of Fundy to the southern end of Nova Scotia, and then stayed within 10 miles of the coast the rest of the way. This route, past Boston and Portland, added some 150 miles, but time seemed no object when Le Médec's main concern was not being reduced to shrapnel.

On the morning of Monday, December 3, Commander Coates's New York office sent a standard coded telegram to officials at Halifax Harbour informing them of *Mont-Blanc*'s cargo and scheduled arrival early on Wednesday, December 5. F. Evan Wyatt, Halifax's CXO, received the telegram. Though he did not know that picric acid was a high explosive used to make shells, he did know, like almost everyone else connected to this story, that benzol was "very dangerous," and that TNT was a high explosive "by reputation." He also knew other officers received copies of the telegram, but he never confirmed if any had read it.

Le Médec and his crew knew the only real solution to their dilemma could be found inside Halifax Harbour. So it was with great relief that on Tuesday, December 4, a crewmen finally spotted Nova Scotia and yelled the good news across the deck. But what they had sighted was only the southern tip of the banana-shaped province, leaving some 250 miles to go to reach of Halifax Harbour, more than a full day's sailing at *Mont-Blanc's* top speed. As the *Mont-Blanc* crew finished dinner on board Tuesday night, they hoped it was their last one at sea before they sighted the Sambro Island Lighthouse on Chebucto Bay, which promised calm waters the rest of the way to Bedford Basin.

That night, Haligonians were relaxing at home with newspaper stories about the bravery of the Nova Scotia Highland regiment during the Third Battle of Ypres, also known as Passchendaele, where millions of shells filled with picric acid claimed 600,000 casualties to gain a few more yards of soggy turf. But they were heartened by the courage of their boys, and felt like the war might be slowly moving in the right direction, especially with the Americans finally on board.

The far more humble *Imo* left Rotterdam in mid-November 1917 carrying nothing except ballast, the crew, and Captain From's loyal dog. On Monday, December 3, *Imo* cruised into Halifax Harbour, where Captain From planned to refuel before heading on to New York to load relief supplies, then return to Europe.

Though a neutral ship, the *Imo* was still subject to wartime scrutiny to protect against spies, contraband, and attack, especially at a harbor as crucial to the Allied war effort as Halifax. *Imo* had to be cleared by authorities from both the Royal Canadian Navy and customs, and her crew was not allowed to communicate with anyone on shore. *Imo*'s neutral status also meant it ranked below the warships that moved troops, supplies, and munitions, which could create delays in getting everything from coal to permission to leave the harbor that could stretch to weeks.

After anchoring *Imo* on the Halifax side of Bedford Basin, Captain From ordered fifty tons of coal from Pickford and Black, based right in Bedford Basin. After waiting two days, Captain From expected Pickford and Black to deliver the coal on Wednesday, so he asked CXO Wyatt to send a harbor pilot that day to lead his ship out to sea that afternoon. Wyatt obliged by assigning William Hayes, one of the best.

When dawn broke on Wednesday, December 5, 1917, *Imo*'s mission seemed as simple as *Mont-Blanc*'s was nerve-racking.

Chapter 13
December 5, 1917

At about 2:30 on Wednesday, December 5, Halifax customs officer Arthur G. Lovett received the *Imo*'s clearance papers from Naval Control, reported that fact to the guard ship, HMCS *Acadian*, and then boarded *Imo* to give Captain From the good news that his ship was cleared to go.

But when Lovett reached From's cabin, he found the captain agitated. The coal tender from Pickford and Black was supposed to arrive two hours earlier, but was just pulling alongside *Imo* with its load when Lovett arrived. Captain From knew loading the coal would take at least a couple of hours, and they would not be able to get past the submarine gates before Wyatt ordered them shut for the night.

After Lovett disembarked from *Imo*, he failed to inform the guard ship that *Imo* would not be leaving that day but the following morning. Lovett explained later, "We never stopped at the guard ship on the way back. Our only purpose is to inform them what ships were going to clear," not which ones would be staying in the harbor to clear later.

When he learned *Imo* wouldn't leave until the next morning, Harbour Pilot William Hayes hopped onto a tugboat heading back to the wharf so he could enjoy a few precious hours to himself, and get a good night's sleep. But unlike Lovett, Hayes stopped by the pilotage office to inform fifteen-year-old Edward Beazley that *Imo* would remain at anchor in the basin for one more night, then go out first thing the next morning. Hayes then told shipping agent George R. Smith that he would get back on *Imo* at 7:30 a.m. to pilot the ship out of the harbor.

Beazley dutifully wrote down the information on the blackboard, but he did not pass it on to the CXO's office on *Niobe*. The following morning, Thursday, December 6, Beazley assumed that whoever needed to see the message he'd left had already seen it, so he erased it. CXO Evan Wyatt remained unaware of *Imo*'s status, as did the rest of the harbor officials.

While Captain From stewed about being trapped inside Bedford Basin, Captain Le Médec and his crew were just as anxious to get in.

In the early afternoon of Wednesday, December 5, 1917, *Mont-Blanc*'s fourth full day out of Brooklyn, Le Médec and his crew spotted the Sambro Island Lighthouse. They still had 18 miles to go to reach Bedford Basin, where they hoped to spend their first quiet night in four days, but just reaching the calmer waters past the lighthouse offered some peace. Their first fear, of a big wave jostling their cargo and setting off the explosives, was behind them. All they had to do now was steer their ship past the ten minesweepers keeping the entrance clear and head to Bedford Basin. Once anchored, their second fear—of getting hit by a U-boat torpedo or mine—could also be put to bed for a few days of rest and relaxation.

Around 4:00 p.m. that day, Le Médec stopped *Mont-Blanc* at the examination anchorage near McNab's Island so harbor pilot Francis Mackey could board. What time CXO Wyatt ordered the antisubmarine gates closed each night depended on what ships were scheduled to leave and when. But if no special arrangements had been made, he usually closed them by sundown.

When the gates slammed shut, they sent a visible vibration through the buoys holding them up.

On Wednesday, December 5, 1917, sundown would not officially occur until 5:06 p.m. Atlantic Time, but there were no ships scheduled to enter or exit, the sun had already slid behind the slope of Richmond, and darkness was descending fast. Wyatt ordered the gates closed at 4:30.

Since the war had started, all ships were inspected before entering the harbor to prevent a Trojan horse from sneaking in and wreaking havoc. At 4:36 p.m., six minutes after Wyatt had closed the gates, Terrance Freeman, one of Wyatt's examining officers, boarded *Mont-Blanc*, interviewed Le Médec in the captain's cabin, and inspected the cargo list, a routine part of Freeman's job.

But when he scanned *Mont-Blanc*'s manifest, he could see there was nothing ordinary about the cargo sitting beneath him. Halifax Harbour welcomed thousands of ships every year, but it was still rare during the Great War for ships carrying high explosives to enter port. In fact, Freeman thought *Mont-Blanc* might be the first one cleared to anchor in Bedford Basin. "I knew it could do some damage all right," he said.

But the examination office had no special procedure for handling particularly dangerous ships. Freeman's task was simply to ensure that the manifest accurately reflected the cargo aboard, which it did. When Freeman handed the manifest back to Le Médec, he said, "She can't go in until morning."

Any chance Le Médec might have had to appeal the decision and ask for special clearance ended when CXO Wyatt left the Examiners' Office on *Niobe* at 5:15 for a business meeting, after which he planned to attend a party with his wife to celebrate a friend's wedding. The *Mont-Blanc*'s crew anchored just outside the harbor.

Freeman understood Le Médec and Mackey were eager to get safely into Bedford Basin, however, so he instructed them: "Stay at the anchorage until morning and then proceed up the harbor at the usual time if you do not hear from me." To be sure *Mont-Blanc* could get into Halifax Harbour at the first opportunity, Freeman gave Le Médec and Mackey a code number to be used to expedite entry into the harbor the next morning.

Mackey ate his dinner with Le Médec in the captain's cabin, and when they finished, the two men sat and talked as best they could with the language barrier between them. Mackey offered a cigar to the captain, but Le Médec just shook his head. When Mackey lit a match, Le Médec said, "In here it is all right to smoke, but nowhere else. It is even prohibited to carry matches in your pocket when on deck. On this voyage, a fire or a big bump and the whole damned *Mont Blanc* is no more!"

The captain and crew settled in for their fourth night of fitful sleep. They would not need alarm clocks to roust them.

Noble Driscoll was watching the harbor that morning before school, and could tell something was a little off. From his house perched on the high ground of Richmond, Noble could clearly make out *Imo*, and noticed a lot of men walking on her deck, so he presumed the ship was getting ready to sail and would be gone before he returned home. That disappointed him, because he wanted to see the big ship sail past their house.

But when Driscoll came home from school that afternoon, he was pleasantly surprised to see *Imo* still anchored in Bedford Basin. When he saw a much smaller boat tie up alongside *Imo* and unload tons of coal, Noble told his brother, "That would be the problem. I bet it held them up. We'll see it leave after all. I expect they'll want to get away first thing in the morning."

Noble Driscoll went to bed that night with something to look forward to the next morning.

While harbor pilot Francis Mackey spent a nervous night on *Mont-Blanc*, Ernest Barss spent another eve-

ning at his childhood home in Wolfville. He had plenty
to think about, and thanks to his shell shock–induced
insomnia, lots of time to do so. His long list of worries included the outcome of the war, the December 17
election, and what he was going to do with the rest of
his life. Having decided against businessman, soldier,
pastor, and grocer, what did that leave? What was he
qualified to do? What did he *want* to do? And who
would hire an invalid with a severe limp and shaky
hands? That would bring him to his biggest question:
With his relationship with Eileen broken off, would he
ever again believe he was worthy of a good woman?

It was more than enough to keep him up at night—
and if it wasn't, he could count on his sleep being shattered by nightmares of trench warfare, with bagpipes
playing in the background.

The Orr family had another night to themselves in
their new home, because their younger son, Archie,
was still recovering from the whooping cough. While
Barbara and most of her siblings getting antsy from
cabin fever and were anxious to get back to school, Ian
looked forward to another day of ship watching with
his binoculars through the bay windows.

With less than three weeks to Christmas, the kids in
Halifax were already talking about what they hoped to
find under the tree. This was the era that commercial-

ized Christmas, after all, by purchasing teddy bears, Lincoln Logs, and Erector Sets, all available in stacks at a new institution called the department store—Eaton's in Canada, and Sears, Roebuck in the United States. If you couldn't get to one of their stores in person, you could use their great innovation, the catalogue, from which you could order almost everything—even a house. All their products also came with another innovation: fixed prices.

The Reverend William J. W. Swetnam, pastor of the Kaye Street Methodist Church just a few blocks away, and his wife, Lizzie Louise Swetnam, were putting their son, Carmen, and daughter Dorothy to bed. Carmen's wish had come true: he had been cleared to get out of quarantine the next night to participate in their church's Mission Concert. Carmen's mother promised to practice with him one more time the next morning before school.

While the parishioners of Grove Presbyterian were celebrating the retirement of the loan for building their church, children anxiously awaited the arrival of the Ringling Brothers Circus, and the soldiers and sailors a few blocks to the south pursued their own pleasures. The alehouses, the speakeasies, the bootleggers, and the brothels—and the complete darkness of Garrison Hill—all beckoned them for another night of revelry.

With hundreds marked for transport the next day, they always knew each night could be their last—and if nothing worked out, they could always start a fistfight on "Knock 'em Down Alley."

Others went on formal dates. With orders to ship out imminent, it might be their last chance to see their beaus or meet a new one for months, if not forever. Ethel Mitchell, the nineteen-year-old pianist hoping to go to the Halifax Conservatory of Music, knew she wanted to see the strapping young officer from HMS *Highflyer* again, and she sensed that he might feel the same—but she could ponder that tomorrow, after a good night's sleep with her cat at her feet.

It had been a long, glorious night.

Chapter 14
A Game of Chicken

Thursday, December 6, 1917

The next morning, Thursday, December 6, dawn came at 7:36 a.m., offering a clear winter day, the kind that makes everything look a little sharper. The snow would soon blanket the colors, but on this morning you could still see the green grass and dirt roads, and smell the horses and their hay wagons headed for market day—the kind of peaceful morning that made it easy to get started.

The warm air from the night before was blowing out to sea, but Haligonians knew the weather that time of year could be much worse. A light haze descended on the harbor, as it did most mornings, but the rising sun promised to burn it off, and visibility was already quite good. Of all forms of weather that could threaten a ship, sailors feared fog the most, because it forced them to steer blind. But that would not be a factor on this day. The winds were so slight that chimney smoke lingered lazily over houses.

Back at the Mitchells' home in Dartmouth, Ethel was still groggy from her late night spent on HMS *Highflyer*, but she got up when her alarm clock went off at 8:00 a.m. so she could put in her scheduled one hour of piano practice before breakfast. She knew that was the kind of dedication it would take if she was going to get into the Halifax Conservatory of Music. When her mother heard her practicing, she suggested Ethel could skip this one rehearsal and sleep in. Ethel quickly agreed and slipped back under her blankets.

Unlike Ethel Mitchell, the people aboard *Mont-Blanc* did not need an alarm clock to get them going that morning. A few minutes before 7:30 a.m., Captain Le Médec and Pilot Mackey climbed onto *Mont-Blanc's* bridge to ensure they were ready when the examination tugboat started the process of getting *Mont-Blanc* inside the harbor. The tugboat did not disappoint, sending *Mont-Blanc* her first light signal at 7:30 sharp.

Mackey read Le Médec the message: "*Mont Blanc.* Hoist identification. Proceed Bedford Basin to await further orders."

Pleased and relieved, Le Médec repeated the command to his crew and handed one of his officers a slip of paper with the code number Lieutenant Freeman had given him the night before to signal to the examination tugboat. The officer nodded, turned to go deliver the message, and then stopped to ask, "The red flag for explosives also, sir?"

The question surprised the captain. Raising the red flag outside the gates would have been as foolhardy as waving a red cape before an angry bull. Once inside the harbor, however, *Mont-Blanc* was more likely to be struck by another ship than a German torpedo, so raising the red flag to warn other captains to steer clear was not an unreasonable idea, though no longer required during the war years.

Captain Le Médec looked at his officer as though he was considering the idea, then shook his head.

"No," he finally decided. "It is not necessary."

At 7:50 a.m., *Mont-Blanc* lifted anchor and started slowly for the outer gate attached to the north end of McNab's Island. Captain Le Médec and Harbour Pilot Mackey had her cruising at a calm, conventional 4 knots, or about 5 miles per hour. At that rate, it would take her about ninety minutes to get to Bedford Basin and anchor for the day, but there was no reason to hurry, and 6 million reasons not to.

Mont-Blanc got in line to enter Halifax Harbour, the second of dozens of ships that were expected to come and go that day. When *Mont-Blanc* passed the harbor's threshold at the edge of McNab's Island, where the outer antisubmarine gate had just been pulled back, Captain Le Médec and crew were safer than they had been since boarding *Mont-Blanc* five days earlier in New York. After enduring their fearful, four-day journey up the East Coast, they had reached what would surely be the easiest leg of their journey.

Most of the crew went below to eat breakfast, leaving four crewmen on deck and Captain Le Médec and Francis Mackey at the helm. Le Médec still exercised great caution, cutting his speed in half when his ship approached the ferryboats making their morning shuttles between Dartmouth and Halifax and ordering the engines stopped altogether when a small boat crossed *Mont-Blanc*'s bow.

Captain Le Médec would not be rushed.

Mont-Blanc eased toward the inner gate, maintaining a generous gap between her and the SS *Clara*, an

American tramp steamer piloted by Edward Renner, who saw *Mont-Blanc* running behind him.

At the same time *Clara* and *Mont-Blanc* started coasting into Halifax Harbour, *Imo* was preparing to pull up anchor at the other end of the harbor, on the western side of Bedford Basin closest to Africville. Harbour Pilot William Hayes had gotten a good night's sleep at home and then hopped aboard *Imo* Thursday morning for an early start.

When the guard ship hoisted the signal flags that gave *Imo* permission to depart the basin, Captain From and Pilot Hayes pulled up the anchor to head out, the only ship to leave the basin that morning. But no one in the CXO's office seemed to know about *Imo*'s leaving, and *Imo* didn't know anything about *Mont Blanc*'s arrival.

With both ships now in motion, it's worth asking who knew what.

The list was quite small. The only people who definitely knew *Mont-Blanc* was loaded down with 6 million pounds of high explosives were the men on the ship, including Harbour Pilot Francis Mackey, and four harbor officials not on board: CXO Evan Wyatt; examiner Terrance Freeman; Rear Admiral Bertram Chambers, who organized the convoys; and his second assistant, Lieutenant Commander James Murray, a sea-transport officer who received the same telegram.

A few others that morning would catch wind of *Mont-Blanc*'s dangerous cargo, but not through official channels, and not until later. The telegram listing the cargo also went to three other officials, but there's no evidence they ever read the information or understood its import.

The few who did know of *Mont-Blanc*'s manifest did not communicate with each other, and certainly not with other ships in the harbor, least of all *Imo*'s Captain From. If they had—or if Captain Le Médec had put up the red munitions flag once safely in the harbor—the day likely would have unfolded without incident, just like the others before it.

With the war so far away, Haligonians probably thought the odds of anything going wrong at home were quite long. And yet, with several crucial safeguards having been removed one by one—from loading a single ship with 6 million pounds of high explosives to carelessly stacking the benzol at the last minute to relaxing the harbor's rules on munitions, to using old, slow ships led by captains with no experience with explosives to the breakdown of the chain of command in Halifax Harbour and the miscommunication and countless shortcuts that followed—the odds were getting shorter and shorter, because every day the people in charge put the war effort overseas ahead of safe practices at home.

To guard against lapses would require constant vigilance by individuals relying increasingly on their own judgment instead of the comforting protocols that had been established over the years and were still in place just three years ago. If it wasn't these people on this day, it could just as easily have been another group the next day. Throw the dice enough times and your number is bound to come up.

And this is where the unraveling accelerated.

All ships in the harbor operated under the international code of seamanship called the Collision Regulations. You could almost boil them all down to one simple rule: stay to the right of all oncoming boats, just as cars in North America stay to the right today.

When the channels were running normally, communication was easy. That was especially important in 1917, when ships communicated mainly through steam-powered whistles loud enough to be heard over the wind and the waves, ships' engines, and the area's trains and factories. When a ship wanted to let another ship know it was sticking to the right side, or starboard, it gave a single short blast on the whistle.

(Here's a simple mnemonic device: starboard, with two "r"s, means "right." Port, with one "r," means "left," and both have four letters.)

If a ship planned to make an exception and veer to the port, or left, side, it gave two short blasts on the whistle. Still, so long as the other ship understood the signal and could provide the space needed for a safe maneuver, it wasn't a problem.

If a ship decided it needed to go into reverse, or "astern," it gave three short blasts on the whistle. When it did so, the stern would typically swing to the port side, while the bow would swing out to starboard—so the decision to throw the engines into reverse, or "transverse thrust," could affect other ships nearby. Again, so long as the oncoming ship understood the signaler's plan and had time and space to maneuver safely, even a transverse thrust wouldn't create trouble.

These three signals—one short whistle for right, two for left, and three for reverse—were also used to "claim" a channel. When a captain asserted his plans first, using only his whistle, he was claiming that channel for his ship, with the expectation that other ships in the area would accede to his wishes—essentially calling dibs. For example, if a ship gave two blasts on her whistle, it meant, "I know I'm coming down the wrong side of the channel, but I have good reason for my course, and I'm now claiming the right to take it." If the second ship replied with two whistles, it meant the second captain understood the first captain's decision to cut across his bow, and had no problem accommodating him.

But all these scenarios assumed everyone was navigating as they should be. As Donald A. Kerr writes in *Ground Zero*, however, the rules are "made for mariners, not mathematicians, so there are exceptions." This was particularly true in Halifax Harbour during the Great War, where the pilots had taken the Admiralty's rules and bent them as they saw fit.

Because *Imo* was anchored on the western side of the basin, just to get to the mouth of the Narrows she had to zigzag around a handful of ships anchored in her way. This meant she could go only a couple of knots, and would end up veering farther to the left than she would have if the basin were clear. Instead of starting her journey through the Narrows on the far right side, hard by Richmond's factories, railyard, and piers, she was pointing toward the center of the Narrows.

After *Imo* had cleared all boats anchored in the basin, Captain From ordered the chief engineer to run the engines full speed ahead. She was running about 7 miles per hour, or about 50 percent faster than the other ships in the harbor, including *Mont-Blanc*, and climbing. By the time *Imo* approached the Narrows, Captain From had crossed the imaginary center line of the Narrows, with the *Imo* running closer to the Dartmouth side than the Halifax side, where she should have been—another breach of long-established protocol.

The tramp steamer SS *Clara* was running in front of *Mont-Blanc*. When *Clara* entered the Narrows, Captain Renner saw the *Imo* for the first time—and he was surprised to see her on his side of the channel, heading straight toward him. Despite the sun rising behind *Clara*, Captain From and Harbour Pilot Hayes saw the *Clara* clearly, and right behind the *Clara*, a tugboat.

To avoid any problems, Captain From pulled the cord to emit one short whistle blast to indicate his intention to keep to his right—the correct channel—which would have the *Imo* veering back toward the Halifax side, where it should be. Given *Imo*'s current line toward Dartmouth and *Clara*'s position, however, Captain Renner decided that it would be simpler and safer, under the circumstances, for him to keep *Clara* on her current course and pass the oncoming *Imo* on the left, not the right. Although it was not the ideal maneuver, according to the Collision Regulations, so long as both ships agreed and had room, it was entirely acceptable.

Captain Renner gave two blasts on the whistle to tell

the *Imo* he planned to keep to the left. Captain From could have insisted on the conventional course, but since his ship had plenty of time and space, he replied with two whistles, indicating he understood the request and agreed to it. The problem seemed solved.

"It was far easier to let him keep the side he was on," *Clara*'s Captain Renner said later. "We were both on the wrong side."

Captain Renner's decision would normally amount to nothing, but as the breaks with convention compounded, so did the odds of a disaster. At this early stage, however, no one seemed alarmed. When *Clara* passed *Imo*, Captain Renner used a megaphone to send salutations to her captain and crew and let Harbour Pilot William Hayes know that another ship was close behind. That ship was *Mont-Blanc*.

When Hayes replied, "What did you say?" Captain Renner immediately recognized the voice of his colleague. Renner repeated his message.

After *Imo* passed the SS *Clara* on the port side, Captain From decided not to return to starboard, back toward the Halifax shore, but to continue on the left side, through it was the wrong lane, past Turtle Grove, where Jerry Lone Cloud and the Mi'kmaq lived, and then Dartmouth. Captain From made this decision at the start of the Narrows, the neck of the wine bottle, which spans a mere 1,000 feet across, affording little room for ships passing through if the need should arise.

At 8:15 a.m., *Stella Maris,* a tugboat that had served as a British gunboat in the China Sea, pulled out of the dry dock on the Halifax shore at the south end of Richmond and picked up two scows loaded with ashes from the dockyard. The tugboat, the tow ropes, and the two scows together stretched out to about 320 feet, the length of a football field—an unwieldy caravan, perhaps, but not unusual for Halifax Harbour, and nothing too tricky to handle on her short trip to the basin.

Stella Maris was in the capable hands of Captain Horatio Brannen, an experienced seaman who looked the part. At a time when cameras were still a luxury, Captain Brannen had recently sat for an expensive studio photo of himself in full uniform, to be framed and presented to his wife as a Christmas gift almost three weeks later. His son, Walter, served as his first mate, which surely made the captain proud.

No sooner had Captain Brannen steered *Stella Maris* toward the Narrows on the right side, heading for the basin, than he spotted *Imo.* He told Second Mate William Nickerson that *Imo* "was going as fast as any ship he had ever saw in the harbor," Nickerson recalled, adding that Brennan thought *Imo* "looked to be making eight or ten miles an hour," or 6 to 8 knots. Nickerson saw *Imo* stirring up foam at her bow, a rare and unwelcome sight in the Narrows.

Still, if *Imo* righted her course back toward Halifax, as Captain Brannen assumed she would, then her previous moves would be a minor annoyance, something to grumble about to the harbor pilots. But when *Imo* blew two blasts on her whistle, indicating she intended to continue through the Narrows on her left, in the wrong water, Brannen cursed, "The bloody fool! He's taking her down against Dartmouth. We'll be cross bows. Go about!"

Given *Imo*'s speed, size, and position, Captain Brannen's choices were as limited as the time he had to make them. Although he had a well-earned reputation for following the rules, he quickly calculated that he could not haul the scows behind him to the right of *Imo* fast enough to avoid a collision with either his tugboat or, more likely, the cables or scows that trailed behind it. Brennan pulled his ship and scows to the left, back toward the Halifax shore they'd just come from, allowing *Imo* to continue on her path to the middle of the Narrows. While Brannen was also breaking convention, after *Imo*'s signals, he had little choice—another unwitting addition to this growing list of exceptions.

This, in turn, only reinforced *Imo*'s unconventional trajectory to the left. To avoid hitting *Stella Maris* and her scows, the *Imo* went closer to the Dartmouth side of the channel, moving still farther from her correct course.

With *Imo* now charging across the imaginary centerline at the upper end of the Narrows, sitting atop the water and churning bubbles at her bow, *Mont-Blanc* began her approach into the Narrows from the opposite end and in opposite fashion: with 6 million pounds of high explosives pushing her down in the water, she gently parted a path forward, creating no foam in front and barely a wake behind.

On *Mont-Blanc*, Harbour Pilot Francis Mackey stood next to Captain Le Médec on the bridge. Mackey provided directions to Le Médec while *Mont-Blanc* slid slowly past George's Island, where the second submarine netting was secured each night. That meant the *Mont-Blanc* was now unmistakably inside Halifax Harbour. The crew looked forward to a well-earned respite in Bedford Basin.

Le Médec and Mackey continued guiding *Mont-Blanc* alongside Dartmouth's modest houses and factories. When *Mont-Blanc* came upon the famous HMS *Highflyer*, anchored in the upper harbor, she had to veer a bit to the right to be safe, bringing her still closer to the shore. After Mackey told Le Médec of the *Highflyer*'s exploits, the captain ordered a crewman to salute the ship by briefly lowering *Mont-Blanc*'s huge French flag, and *Highflyer* responded in kind.

Highflyer's officer of the watch, Lieutenant Richard Woollams, appreciated the gesture, but he couldn't help raising an eyebrow at the fully loaded steamer with metal drums stacked on her decks, three and four barrels high, held in place by mere ropes. "Fuel oil, or perhaps petrol," he thought. "Whatever it is, she's damn sloppily loaded. . . . The convoy admiral won't be very happy about that one!"

Mont-Blanc's plan was simple: proceed slowly to the right along the Dartmouth coast to the basin, anchor to refuel and restock, and try to catch a convoy heading to Europe, one slow enough to accommodate *Mont-Blanc*'s top loaded speed of 7 knots. The crew assumed the final leg would be the most dangerous and nerve-racking, especially if they had to sail unprotected for three weeks. But that was not something they had to worry about that morning.

At 8:27 a.m., *Mont-Blanc* was about 400 feet from the Dartmouth shore. Then, just to be careful, she veered farther to the right until she was less than 100 feet from the shore, about as close as a ship could comfortably get without scraping the bottom—certainly one loaded with 6 million pounds of high explosives.

Better safe than sorry.

About this time, Captain Le Médec looked up to see *Imo*'s masts for the first time across the Narrows, about a mile away. Her four stacks were all Pilot Mackey needed to see to know it was *Imo*. He also knew the ship was being piloted by William Hayes—and not due to official communications but dumb luck: the previous afternoon, Mackey, Captain From, and Hayes had shared a tugboat while Captain From grumbled about the coal ship coming late. At that moment, Mackey put it together: the coal delay had kept them from escaping the harbor before the nets came across, causing them to leave this morning.

During *Imo*'s earlier visits to Halifax, Mackey had piloted her once or twice and found her easy to handle. When he saw *Imo* riding high that morning, he knew she was empty, which would make her faster, but it would also harder for her to gain "traction" on the water. Adding to Mackey's disquiet: he saw *Imo*'s bow plowing through the water fast enough to whip up the water in front of her. "Quite a ripple," he said. But his greatest concern was this simple fact: *Imo* was heading southeast, directly toward *Mont-Blanc*.

Because the morning sun was just starting to rise be-hind *Mont-Blanc* and the ship was riding so low, Cap-tain Le Médec worried the men on *Imo*'s bridge might not be able to see *Mont-Blanc*, which made Le Médec worry they were about to be run over by a temporarily blind captain.

Back on *Imo*, Captain Haakon From and Harbour Pilot William Hayes, having just avoided *Stella Maris* and her scows, saw *Mont-Blanc* for the first time. Despite the rising sun, they could see *Mont-Blanc* clearly. Cap-tain From had no idea what *Mont-Blanc* was carrying, like almost everyone else in the harbor. His thoughts were elsewhere: he had already been delayed one day, and was eager to get to New York as fast as possible.

Harbour Pilot Mackey, standing on the bridge of *Mont-Blanc* next to Captain Le Médec, was stunned to see *Imo* bearing down on them—and cutting through their channel, no less. He instinctively pulled the cord to give one short, sharp blast to let the oncoming ship know *Mont-Blanc* was on the correct side, she had the right to stay there, and she intended to. He figured the captain of the oncoming ship would see *Mont-Blanc* and slow down to change course back to the right side, and all would return to normal.

But Captain From responded to Mackey's message with two short whistles, nautical language for "No, we will pass on the left side." Unlike Captain Renner's request, which Renner had initiated and Captain From readily agreed to, Captain From was countering Mackey's announcement, which Mackey and Le Médec were not about to agree to. They didn't have to know what picric acid was to understand that they had a lot more at stake than any other ship in the harbor.

Hearing *Imo*'s two whistles, Mackey directed Captain Le Médec to steer *Mont-Blanc* even closer to the Dartmouth shore, to the edge of danger—both from the coastline and from the perilously shallow water—and pull her back to "dead slow." Fully loaded, *Mont-Blanc* sat so low in the water it risked running aground if it came too close to the Dartmouth shore, which ranged from 35 to 68 feet deep. If they managed to avoid *Imo* but run into the shore or aground, either could provide all the sparks or turbulence needed to set off their cargo.

At the same time, "so as to relieve myself of all possible doubt," Mackey said, "I blew another signal of one blast," which translated to: "We're on the correct [starboard] side. You are not. Move back to the other side, or stop."

To Mackey's amazement, *Imo* responded to his repeated request with two more short blasts, which meant: "I don't care. I am not changing my course."

Mackey was incredulous. "I did not understand," he said. "I had the right, and [Captain From] had no right to change my signal because I had given first one blast, meaning I am heading to the right, except . . . to avoid the collision."

Mackey had good reason to be outraged, but no time to indulge it. "Seeing [*Imo*] going at that rate of speed," he said, "I knew if I kept on going he would bang me ashore."

Now Captain Le Médec and Mackey faced one of the toughest decisions a helmsman has to make—and fast. The two ships were, in effect, playing a game of chicken, which helps us understand both captains' rapidly collapsing choices. You are in your car and see that an oncoming car is in your lane. What do you do? You go to the right shoulder—until you see he's going to your shoulder, too, while leaning on his horn. In desperation, at the last possible moment, you finally decide to cut to the left. You know it's normally the wrong move, but the situation you're in is not normal. It should work—unless the oncoming driver does the same thing.

With *Imo* now only about 150 feet away—half a boat

length—from *Mont-Blanc* and closing fast, Captain Le Médec froze. Mackey yelled at Le Médec to steer *Mont-Blanc* to the port side in the hopes that both ships would pass each other on the "wrong" side. Under the circumstances, being wrong paled in comparison to being dead.

Mackey's shouting snapped Le Médec out of his stupor. He quickly concluded that Mackey was correct, and ordered *Mont-Blanc* hard to the left, away from the usual safety of the Dartmouth shore. This pulled *Mont-Blanc*'s bow toward the middle of the Narrows, exactly where Le Médec did not want to be, but anything was preferable to smashing into *Imo*, the shore, or the bottom.

After *Mont-Blanc* had finally and reluctantly veered left, the two ships were briefly parallel to each other, and Mackey thought that everything might just work out. If both captains had maintained their last directions, that's just what would have happened.

It's called a game of chicken, of course, because one of the two drivers, or in this case captains, is expected to lose his nerve first, turn chicken, and avoid disaster for both vehicles. This works so long as the other captain doesn't also turn chicken and change his course. Judging by the behavior of *Imo*'s captain to that point—speeding down the wrong side of the harbor channel while repeatedly signaling that he had no intention of budging—Le Médec had to figure that the hard-charging captain would be the last man to lose his nerve.

Le Médec guessed wrong.

No sooner had Le Médec deferred to *Imo* and turned *Mont-Blanc* diagonally across the middle of the Narrows, generously giving *Mont-Blanc*'s channel to *Imo*, than Captain From also decided to end the game of chicken by issuing three blasts on his whistle, announcing his sudden decision to switch from full speed ahead to full speed astern. This precautionary maneuver had the predictable effect of pulling *Imo*'s stern to the left while swinging her bow to the right, toward the middle of the harbor—right into *Mont-Blanc*'s new pathway. For the first time all morning, *Imo*'s bow was heading in the right direction—but at exactly the wrong time.

The awkward dance would have been as comical as two people trying to walk past each other on the street who repeatedly move to the same side, unwittingly increasing the odds of bumping into each other—if the stakes weren't so incredibly high.

On the bridge of *Mont-Blanc*, Mackey was apoplectic, but he quickly dismissed the idea that *Imo*'s harbor pilot, William Hayes, whom Mackey had worked with for years, had made that final decision. "Knowing

Hayes as I do, I didn't think it was his order," Mackey said. "I didn't think Hayes would do that." Mackey was convinced the command came from Captain From, and Hayes had merely obeyed.

Mackey and Le Médec started shouting orders to the crew almost in unison. As *Imo*'s bow seemed to stretch toward *Mont-Blanc*'s nose in slow motion, both saw only one solution: simultaneously they grabbed the whistle cord, sent out two short blasts, indicating their intention to turn even harder to the left, and yelled below-deck to power *Mont-Blanc* across *Imo*'s bow.

Mackey yelled at Le Médec, "There is going to be a collision!"

Le Médec apparently agreed, bellowing to the crew below to make a last, desperate move: throw *Mont-Blanc*'s engines into reverse at full speed—a transverse thrust—in hopes of to back up as fast as possible to minimize the impact.

"Full speed astern!"

"I knew that in the No. 2 'tween decks was the TNT," Le Médec said, "and that was a dangerous explosive, I had heard in New York, which would explode under the least shock." Being no chemist, Le Médec did not know that the barrels of picric acid stored in the No. 1 hold were even more powerful and volatile than the TNT, but his intent was sound: mitigate the impact, and pray that the gigantic bomb packed beneath them was not disturbed.

On *Imo*, Pilot Hayes reached the same conclusion, yelling virtually the same words to Captain From: "There is going to be a collision!"

It looked like Captain Le Médec's attempt to avoid being struck at the point of the hold packed with TNT might work. Instead, *Imo*'s bow was now targeting the drums of benzol and barrels of picric acid.

Thanks to Archie Orr's whooping cough, the Orr children would not be joining their classmates at Richmond School that morning. They had plenty of time to play games, draw pictures, and watch the ships slide by. Just a few minutes after Barbara Orr waved good-bye to her father heading off to work, she stood at their dining room's big bay window, idly admiring the views their new home offered of the harbor below.

Then Barbara noticed something peculiar unfolding: one big ship coming out of the basin toward the Narrows, and a smaller one approaching the other way, from the harbor toward the basin. Even to her untrained eye, they seemed to be getting too close to each other, with the big one on the left going too fast. As she was drawn closer to the window, the two ships started acting strangely, blasting their whistles back and forth in a rare nautical argument.

Barbara was only fourteen years old, but years later she could recall that the two ships "looked like they were deliberately trying to run into each other . . . There was no need of a collision."

Barbara beckoned her oldest brother, the naval aficionado, "Ian, come and see what's going on!"

When Ian saw what his sister saw, he was transfixed. He had never seen the harbor traffic play out like this before.

"That's a neutral ship," Ian said, pointing to the *Imo*, with BELGIAN RELIEF on its side. "Otherwise it would have a convoy."

They continued coming closer.

Barbara cried, "They are trying to run into each other!"

Chapter 15

"Look to Your Boats!"

Both captains had thrown their ships into full reverse thrusts to pull their bows back, with their
engines loudly straining to overcome the momentum
of their last maneuvers. Their bows were still creeping forward, however slowly, with the tip of *Imo* lining
up on the right front flank of *Mont-Blanc* at an almost
perpendicular angle.

The roar of the engines drowned out the shouting
crewmen on both decks. Seeing that contact couldn't be
avoided, those on deck watched *Imo* advance the final
few feet. *Imo*'s bow crawled toward the side of *Mont-
Blanc*, until the awkward, dangerous dance ended in
the middle of Halifax Harbour at 8:46 a.m., Thursday,
December 6, 1917, when *Imo*'s bow struck *Mont-Blanc*.

The four crewmen working on *Mont-Blanc*'s deck

instinctively flinched, as if they were preparing to get punched in the face, but when *Imo* hit their ship, it did not blow up instantly, as they had expected. Because both ships had been backpedaling at full throttle, the impact was not particularly forceful. If the French freighter hadn't been hauling 6 million pounds of high explosives, the entire incident would have been a minor matter for the insurance adjusters and the wreck commissioner, and quickly forgotten.

But when the huge slab of steel that was *Imo* crashed into the other huge slab of steel that was *Mont-Blanc* at that angle, it was enough to carve a V-shaped hole in *Mont-Blanc*'s plating running from the waterline right up to her deck, where it spread five or six feet wide. Le Médec had succeeded in shielding the No. 2 hold, where the stevedores had stored the TNT, but in so doing he exposed the No. 1 hold, where they had packed some of the benzol and picric acid. And that's where *Imo* hit *Mont-Blanc*.

The jolt snapped the lashings that held the benzol in place and knocked over some of the carelessly stacked, thin-skinned barrels on top. When they tumbled to the deck, a few burst open, sending the unusually combustible fuel washing across the boards and down the gash into the cargo holds below.

When the steel plates of the two ships became entangled, Captain From continued to pull *Imo* back at full speed, which tore the entwined metal apart. One *Imo* crewman felt no shock and heard no noise on impact, but "could feel something like a little twist."

That little twist was enough to generate the very sparks everyone who had worked on *Mont-Blanc*, from the shipwrights to the stevedores to the crewmen who didn't even carry matches, had gone to such lengths to avoid. A fire started and spread across the foredeck with a *whoosh*. Within minutes, thick, black smoke poured out of the gash in the side and enveloped the deck. Whenever the flames penetrated a new drum of benzol, flames would shoot up through the smoke.

The Orr children's astonishment over the collision drew their mother and their six-year-old sister, Isabel, to the window. They were rapt when smoke started climbing out of a big hole in the smaller ship.

Ian ran to get his binoculars. When he returned, he pointed to the burning *Mont-Blanc* and told Barbara, "That's an ammunition boat."

"Which one?" Barbara asked.

"The smaller one that was hit."

"What do you mean, an 'ammunition boat'?" Barbara asked.

"That's the kind of boat that carries bullets and

gunpowder and things like that. I can see barrels on the deck, too. It's called the *Mont-Blanc*."

"Will it explode?" Barbara asked.

"No, not that I know," Ian replied.

The men on *Mont-Blanc* knew better. Having lived in constant fear of the slightest disruption or smallest spark sending their ship to the moon, the haggard and edgy crewmen were certain the ship would erupt at any second. Every moment spent not running for their lives was borrowed time.

They had been trained to stay calm under pressure no matter what the sea sent their way, but no one had ever prepared them for this. Seconds after the benzol fire swept across the foredeck, the men on deck rushed toward the bridge in retreat, and the men below rushed up the steep staircase, where they waited for Captain Le Médec's orders. His by-the-book approach had already paid off. They were disciplined and obedient—an extraordinary feat when they expected the 6-million-pound bomb heating up beneath their feet to obliterate them at any second. A few men strapped down some loose barrels of benzol at the stern, knowing that if a fire started in the back of the ship, where the two lifeboats were located, they would be trapped in the middle.

Captain Le Médec ran through his options on this unfamiliar ship as quickly as he could, knowing full well he might not finish the exercise. Could they put the fire out? They had no portable extinguishers on board, and the connection for the pressure hose came out of the forward deck—now covered by the benzol fire. Could they anchor the ship in the middle of the harbor and escape while other ships doused the fire, and at least minimize the damage if it exploded? No, he remembered: the anchors were also located in the bow, with none in the back.

Scuttling the ship was probably the most effective way to squelch the dangerous cargo, but it would take at least half an hour to loosen the rusted rivets and bolts to release the valve, and at least two hours to fill the hold with enough water to sink *Mont-Blanc*. If there was one thing Captain Le Médec knew they didn't have, as he watched the smoke grow so dark and thick that he could no longer see the gash in the side of the ship, it was a couple of hours to execute a plan.

Out of ideas, Le Médec rushed down from the bridge and spun around, giving orders to everyone on deck to find the rest of the crew and start lowering the lifeboats. While they sprang into action, Pilot Mackey later presented the captain another option: "Full speed ahead?"

Mackey's idea was simple and quick, with a decent chance of success: point the ship out to sea and mash it down. They would be traveling away from the most populated parts of Halifax and Dartmouth, and might even force enough seawater through the gash to douse the fire and swamp the explosives. That plan could also be cut short by the ship exploding at any second, but it could greatly reduce the potential loss of life.

If Le Médec heard Mackey's plan, he gave no indication. Instead, he shouted to his men, "Abandon ship!"

Le Médec started shouting at the crew in French, and Harbour Pilot Mackey in English: "Look to your boats!" The men didn't need any more encouragement to sprint to the sides of the ship, where they anxiously waited for the lifeboats on each side to be lowered. In their haste, someone cut the ropes holding up the lifeboats, which splashed into the water, empty. The sailors all but jumped from the ladders and ropes to save the boats, and did so in the nick of time. At 8:48, the men assigned to the starboard boat started rowing as fast as they could from the burning ship.

The men in the port-side lifeboat held on to a rope, waiting for the remaining men on deck. Mackey stopped one man rushing down from the bridge and told him to run back up to straighten the steering wheel and lock it in place. After he did so, he rushed past Mackey to the ladder, leaving Mackey to make a truly life-and-death decision: stay on *Mont-Blanc* to try to save hundreds or thousands of lives, or escape and save his own?

Le Médec went to retrieve his chief engineer, Anton Le Gat, and third engineer from their posts in the engine room three decks below, when a crewman grabbed his arm and said, "Captain, we must go. Le Gat is accounted for. When the others went up he remained to lift the safety valves on the boilers, but he is there now."

Le Médec replied, "You go, my friend; I am responsible and I must stay with the ship. It is correct, isn't it?"

"No, we will both go. Come, I don't think we have much time."

Herbert Whitehead, who captained a Canadian Navy drifter that delivered provisions to ships in his branch, heard "a lot of whistling." That was never a good sound in the harbor, so he maneuvered alongside *Mont-Blanc* to see what had happened. To be heard over the roaring fire, Whitehead poked his megaphone through the wheelhouse window to offer to take the men to Bedford Basin. Of course, Whitehead didn't know *Mont-Blanc* was carrying 6 million pounds of high explosives that were getting hotter every second he spoke.

"Jump into my boat!"

No one racing down the ropes was about to stop and chat with him, let alone take him up on his offer. But if they didn't seem to hear or understand him, he certainly heard them, yelling back and forth in French. One of his stokers, a French-Canadian sitting at the bow, "never heard any warning given in French, and I never heard any in English," despite the fact that Whitehead's boat now had the unenviable distinction of occupying the single most dangerous spot in North America.

If just one member of *Mont-Blanc*'s crew had taken a few seconds to do only that much, Whitehead could have gotten word to *Niobe*, which would have quickly spread the word and saved countless lives. Unaware of the cargo, Whitehead casually circled around the stern of the blazing ship while the crew loaded the lifeboats, until he witnessed three small explosions on deck. He concluded that *Mont-Blanc* was carrying oil, and it was probably best to head back to *Niobe*.

Ralph Smith, a marine engineer with Burns & Kelleher, was on a workboat headed for the basin when *Mont-Blanc* and *Imo* collided about 350 yards away from his boat. He went to help *Mont-Blanc* just as the men were scrambling into their lifeboats. "I never saw two boats filled as quick in my life," he said. "Slid down the tackles and over the side and in the boats in very quick time. Of course, I don't blame them for it either. They were rowing very hard, but the boats did not move very fast. They are heavy boats."

Smith recalled one of them stood on a bench in the boat, waved his arms, and started yelling something in French and pointing toward Halifax. Smith said the word was probably foreign, but sounded something like "explosion."

Like many onlookers, Smith didn't realize the harbor no longer required munitions ships to fly the red flag, so he didn't think *Mont-Blanc* could be carrying high explosives. More likely it was oil that threatened to ignite.

When Captain From's crew watched their counterparts on *Mont-Blanc* row past them, they didn't hear warnings from Mackey or anyone else, so they assumed the fire alone explained why they were escaping. That was hardly a crazy conclusion, as the flames on *Mont-Blanc*'s deck were later described as "ferocious." A few *Imo* crewmen speculated that gasoline or kerosene might be on board.

The other sailors in the harbor that day either didn't hear or understand *Mont-Blanc*'s crew, and the crew never slowed down to make sure their urgent message had been understood by anyone. But when Mackey saw a man on a tugboat called *Hilford*, he said he tried to warn him to stay away from the flaming vessel. The man Mackey saw happened to be Lt. Commander James Murray, who was one of the few in the Examiner's Office who knew *Mont-Blanc* was carrying immense amounts of high explosives. It's not clear if Mackey's message got through, or if Murray simply needed to see *Mont-Blanc* on fire to know urgent action had to be taken, but we do know Murray quickly ordered his ship to Pier 9, just below Richmond, so he could warn others.

The men in *Mont-Blanc*'s second lifeboat waited anxiously for Le Médec and Mackey to make the defining decision of their lives.

When Le Médec said he would stay on board, the first officer twice took him by the arm and told him to come down to the lifeboats. Le Médec finally relented, walked to the top of the ladder—and turned around. He did not have his coat or captain's hat, he explained, without which he could be confused for any crewman.

While the same crewman scurried up the ladder to chase the captain again, Harbour Pilot Mackey knew he had to make up his mind, and make it up now—if the ship didn't blow up while his mind was racing. He could stay on board *Mont-Blanc* to try to put the fire out, which he knew could spare his city and its people unimaginable harm. But putting out the fire was already looking like an impossible task for the entire crew to accomplish, let alone one man. Attempting to do so would almost certainly cost him his life, and his sacrifice might not make the slightest difference to anyone else.

Or he could stay on deck, waving his arms and yelling at nearby ships, sailors, and civilians about the ship's cargo and urging them to run away as fast and as far as possible. If he caught the attention of even a half dozen people who could spread the word, they might be able to evacuate the area. Perhaps a tugboat captain could even haul the boat back out to sea, past McNab's Island, where the potential damage would be much less. This plan carried the same danger, however: if the ship exploded in the next few seconds, as they all assumed it would, his life wouldn't save any others.

Or he could follow the crewmen into the lifeboats and save his own life. It would not make him a hero, but perhaps he could live with that—if he could get away before *Mont-Blanc* erupted.

Mackey looked at Captain Le Médec heading toward the rope ladder, then back at the benzol fire growing behind him, knowing what lay belowdecks. He then ran for the lifeboat and hopped in.

As Mackey later said, "There was nothing I could see that could be done to improve the situation."

While that is certainly debatable, Mackey's decision resulted in at least one unexpected outcome: he would live to answer for his actions.

While it's easy to judge Mackey in that situation, it's worth noting that even a soldier as gung-ho as Ernest Barss, a man who had eagerly volunteered for the army, had no qualms about killing Germans, and had chastised those able-bodied young men at home who were sitting the war out, eventually grew "heartily sick of the whole show" and hoped an officer's commission or even a bullet in the arm would pull him permanently from the trenches, alive. Barss's dilemma was simple: he wanted to be brave, but he wanted to live, and he knew his luck was bound to run out.

Those same thoughts were probably going through Mackey's head, but he was no gung-ho soldier, just a harbor pilot who had drawn the short straw the night before to guide a floating bomb into Bedford Basin. The same questions Barss had mulled over for a year Mackey had to process in a few seconds. For those of us who are certain we would perform the noble, selfless, and heroic act, perhaps we would—but our answers today don't count for much until we're standing where

Mackey was standing, with a few seconds to make such a monumental decision.

How many would sign up for a year in the trenches? How many would agree to pilot a floating bomb? These men did not seek out these choices, which were foisted upon them by a war started by much older men after the assassination of an Archduke 4,000 miles away.

When the *Mont-Blanc* crewman caught up to Le Médec, the captain once again insisted he would stay with the ship. The crewman argued there was nothing to be done, so the captain should lead his men to safety.

"I forced him, taking him by the arm to the ladder," the crewman said.

Le Médec surrendered again, to the relief of the frantic souls waiting in the lifeboat for him to make up his mind. When the captain joined them, he resumed his role, ordering the rowers to get away from the ship as fast as possible—and head toward Dartmouth, not Halifax.

Le Médec and Mackey had always assumed that if it ever came to it, they would go down with the ship. Perhaps they would have if the rowboats had not been available, if the ship hadn't already seemed doomed, and if they had more than a few seconds to think about the rest of their lives. But that was the predicament they were in. Their decision didn't make them heroes, of course, but perhaps it didn't quite make them villains either. Whatever the accounting, Mackey and Le Médec were the last to leave the ship.

Even though *Mont-Blanc* was drifting toward Richmond, which put the lifeboats' launching point an estimated 200 feet from the Halifax side and about 800 feet from the Dartmouth side of the Narrows, the men rowed furiously across to Dartmouth. Shortly into their urgent journey, one of the live shells on *Mont-Blanc's* forward deck blew up, inspiring them to row even faster.

En route, Mackey claimed, "I was shouting to the men in the vicinity. I called out to everybody in sight that the ship was in danger and likely to explode. . . . I think I was too far from Pier 8 [across the Narrows, in front of Richmond] for them to hear me. . . . I called out there and did everything I could possibly do to let everybody hear me."

Yet no one did.

The rowboats reached the Dartmouth shore near Turtle Grove, where Jerry Lone Cloud's Mi'kmaq family lived, in about ten minutes. The *Mont-Blanc* crewmen beached their boats without bothering to secure them, jumped into the shallow water, and ran for the woods at a full sprint. They couldn't fathom why their ship hadn't already blown up, but they didn't intend to stick around to find out.

Running for their lives, they passed a Mi'kmaq woman named Aggie March, who had wrapped her baby daughter in a blanket so she could go outside and see what the commotion was about. The men running past her were yelling that the boat was about to explode, but only in French, so she had no idea what these crazed sailors were trying to tell her. After a half dozen barrels of benzol launched into the sky, March had calmly turned back to her cabin when a *Mont-Blanc* sailor came up with a clever idea: he snatched March's baby from her arms and started running into the woods, following his crewmates. March screamed and chased after him, just as he knew she would. Once he was deep enough into the woods, he stopped, pushed her to the ground, then jumped on top of her with her baby girl between them, waiting for the explosion he knew was going to occur at any second.

Aggie March and her baby would be the only people the *Mont-Blanc*'s captain, crew, or harbor pilot would save that day.

Chapter 16
Box 83

While the crew of *Mont-Blanc* rushed past, *Imo* still lingered near the spot where she had collided with *Mont-Blanc*, halfway down the Narrows on the Dartmouth side. She had withstood only superficial scratches across her bow. Captain From and Harbour Pilot William Hayes decided to take *Imo* out of the Narrows and back to the open water of Bedford Basin to assess their situation. After trying for several frustrating minutes to turn the 430-foot-long ship around in the 1,000-foot-wide Narrows, with boats orbiting around the abandoned *Mont-Blanc* as it floated by, they decided to sail back out to sea and turn around, then return to the basin.

The crew of *Mont-Blanc*, meanwhile, lay on the ground of the Dartmouth woods, gazing in wonder at their burning boat drifting across the Narrows, dumbfounded that it hadn't exploded. Francis Mackey thought "it might blow off in an instant."

With no one on board to guide it and with the steering wheel locked, however, the ghost ship would follow Captain Le Médec's last rudder command and the current. She started drifting from the Dartmouth side of the Narrows, where the collision occurred, toward Richmond. To most onlookers, where she stopped was largely a matter of curiosity.

A ship named *Middleham Castle* had been tied up at the Halifax Graving Dock Company wharf, just outside the dry dock at the south end of Richmond. Her crew stared across the water at the smoking ghost ship, less alarmed than amused by the abandoned boat's hapless yawing across the Narrows toward their side, while their foreman grew irritated with them because they had stopped working.

Jack Tappen, nineteen, worked for marine engineers Burns & Kelleher, which had won the contract to do all the pipe work at the graving dock. Tappen was carrying a large cast-iron pipe to *Middleham*'s engine room when he heard someone on deck yell, "Two ships just collided off us!" Tappen set down the pipe and dashed up on deck, just in time to see *Imo* and *Mont-Blanc* pull apart. He then saw a fire rising from the waterline on

BOX 83 · 225

one of the ships as it floated toward them and the crew abandoning ship. By then *Mont-Blanc* was so close to the Richmond dockyard that Tappen could see *Mont-Blanc*'s cook, who had been serving breakfast when the ships collided, was still wearing his white apron.

One of the older Burns & Kelleher employees told Tappan, "I saw a coal ship burn like that once." When the same engineer saw the flames growing, he added, "If she has explosives aboard, this is no place for us." But no one took him seriously, because nothing like that had ever happened in Halifax. Some of the *Middleham Castle* crew put bumpers out in case *Mont-Blanc* rubbed up against their ship.

The foreman had more immediate concerns: getting Tappen and his coworkers to move the pipe they had left below deck. When the foreman snarled, they finished the job quickly so they could return to watch the ghost ship gently slip right alongside Pier 6—a perfect landing, as if guided by an invisible pilot. At 8:52 a.m., her nose grounded softly into the shore, directly downhill from the Richmond neighborhood and the Richmond Printing Company, between the Acadian Sugar Refinery and the Hillis & Sons Foundry.

The growing throng of observers gathering near Pier 6 viewed the raging *Mont-Blanc* not as a harbinger of imminent danger but as an oddity. In the face of deck fires, which were fairly routine during the chaotic days of the Great War and were usually started by scattered coal embers, the *Mont-Blanc* crew's hurried escape struck the locals as a strange display of cowardice, not as a caution that they, too, should head for the hills.

After they watched the *Mont-Blanc*'s crew dash to Dartmouth, they returned their attention to the far more interesting sight of the unmanned boat blazing in the harbor. The *Mont-Blanc*'s plume of thick, black smoke could now be seen for miles, luring more passersby going to work or school from Richmond, Africville, and downtown Halifax.

Crewmen from nearby ships, unaware of *Mont-Blanc*'s contents, rushed to secure her to Pier 6 so they could douse what they assumed was a conventional fire.

Captain Horatio Brannen's tugboat, *Stella Maris*, which had been towing the two scows filled with ash when it narrowly avoided the speeding *Imo*, was now cruising along the Dartmouth shore, just where it was supposed to be. When Captain Brennan realized the conflagration on *Mont-Blanc* was no common coal fire, however, he immediately gave orders to the first mate—his son Walter—and other crewmen to get the tugboat's hose ready while they anchored the scows so they could leave them behind to rescue *Mont-Blanc*.

BOX 83 · 227

Stella Maris made it over to *Mont-Blanc* at 8:53, just a minute after *Mont-Blanc* had settled into Pier 6. The *Stella Maris* crew trained their hose on the fire, but it had no effect on the flames, which were growing as quickly as the crowd around them.

Tom K. Triggs, the acting commander of the HMS *Highflyer*, picked six crewmen to join him in one of the *Highflyer*'s rowboats. At 8:55, they pulled alongside *Stella Maris* to see if they could help. Commander Triggs boarded *Stella Maris* to discuss the situation with Horatio Brannen, and they were soon joined by a *Niobe* officer and some of his sailors. After spending a few minutes deliberating the merits of this approach or that, the *Niobe* officer recommended that Captain Brannen attach a cable to *Mont-Blanc* and tow her away from Pier 6.

By 8:58, the fire on *Mont-Blanc* had gotten out of control, spreading to the wharf and threatening the other ships and buildings around it. If they couldn't extract *Mont-Blanc* from the dockyards soon, the entire town, built mainly of brick and wood, with mature trees lining every block, could burn down.

Brannen agreed with Commander Triggs and ordered a *Stella Maris* crewman to fetch a five-inch-thick hawser—a cable used for towing ships—but Triggs recommended something stronger. Brannen then sent

Second Mate William Nickerson and a deckhand below to fetch a ten-inch cable, with Brannen's son, First Mate Walter Brannen, holding open the entrance to the hold.

From the woods across the Narrows, Mont-Blanc's crew watched the expanding conflagration, astonished. Perhaps the shipwrights in Brooklyn had built the custom-made holds so well that the high explosives really were hermetically sealed, the benzol was not leaking into the other compartments, and the explosives wouldn't detonate. The ship was still burning at 9:00 a.m., after all, fourteen minutes after the collision had started the fire on deck. Anything seemed possible.

About this time the barrels of benzol started putting on a show for the folks walking up to Pier 6. From Halifax's first battle with Louisbourg in 1758 through the American Revolutionary War, the War of 1812, the American Civil War, and into the first three years of the Great War, Halifax had never been attacked, and nothing had ever gone seriously wrong in the protective arms of the harbor. They had little reason to suspect anything would be different this time, especially with the professionals working around the ship to put out the fire appearing so calm. Hundreds of people watched from the harbor's brand-new pedestrian bridge, made of concrete and steel, which spanned the railyard to allow people to walk over the rows of tracks safely.

BOX 83 · 229

On the *Curaca*, an American ship docked nearby at Pier 8 to load wheat and horses to ship overseas, a Scottish crewman named Edward McCrossen joined the entire crew of his ship standing at the stern to watch the fire. He counted at least seven small explosions, each followed by a missile firing into the air and bursting. After one of the explosions, the *Curaca*'s chief engineer said, "That's gone a couple thousand feet at least."

The spectacle seemed sufficiently routine for McCrossan to decide he could spare a few minutes to go belowdecks and roll a cigarette.

After the fireworks show had been running for a few minutes, word of the ghost ship spread beyond the docks. By nine o'clock, workers at just about every factory and office within sight of the plume of smoke had stopped what they were doing to go to the windows and gaze at the blooming black cloud and wonder aloud what was happening down by the docks.

The Burfords had emigrated from England to Halifax, where the senior Burford now operated the engine room at Hillis & Sons. His son, fifteen-year-old Frank, was the firm's youngest and newest employee; he had taken a temporary position at his father's company until he could enroll in a plumbing apprenticeship. When the workers clustered around the window, Frank squeezed past some of the older, bigger men to sneak a peek. But while he watched *Mont-Blanc* burn not far from the home the Burfords rented on the Flynn block, just up the hill from North Street Station, he heard the company telephone ring and his boss answer.

"Frank's not here to run errands," his boss barked. "He's not going . . . Oh, well, in that case. Just this once, then."

His boss summoned Frank from his post at the window and told him he needed to deliver a package to the dry dock a few blocks away. "You won't need your coat," he told Frank. "It's not cold, and you'll run faster without it. When you come back, we'll find a good place [at the window] for you again."

In the harbor, sailors climbed on decks to watch *Mont-Blanc* burn. In Africville and Turtle Grove, the black and native Haligonians, respectively, paused to watch the smoke climb skyward. At Camp Hill Hospital, some 200 Canadian casualties used their crutches and wheelchairs to move closer to the big windows. In the Protestant Orphanage the children went to the windows to watch, but the orphanage was so close to Pier 6 that the windows grew too hot to touch.

In the blue-blood blocks of Gottingen Street, where the more elegant homes featured horsehair couches, waxed floors, and varnish on almost every wooden

BOX 83 · 231

surface—all of which burn voraciously—anyone who had not already gone to work climbed the exterior staircases to their upper floors to watch the spectacle. Their homes had electricity, but many still used oil lamps, and plenty were heated with gas.

The collision and the fire that followed were perfectly timed to draw Haligonian fathers on their way to offices, factories, railyards, and dockyards; to lure children on their way to school down to the docks; and to attract the attention of their mothers, who'd just finished cleaning up after breakfast, with their kitchen stoves still burning, to watch from their bay windows. The longer the boat burned, the more people dropped their work to watch, or left their homes and workplaces to see it for themselves.

The onlookers were not disappointed, as rockets of flame climbed through clouds of smoke whenever a drum of benzol caught fire or grew hot enough to erupt on its own. One woman compared the pyrotechnics to the fireworks held at the Exhibition Grounds nearby, while an artist riding the Dartmouth Ferry counted four distinct sheets of flame—a beautiful effect.

When someone pulled the fire alarm labeled Box 83, located just south of Pier 6 near the dry docks, it made a familiar sound back at the West Street Fire Station, the outpost closest to the alarm. The ten-man crew answered the call every time a ship's boilers dumped coals on the wooden docks and started a small fire. Whenever they heard the alarm they would run to their brand-new fire engine—which they had christened the Patricia—the city's first completely motorized, chemical fire engine, the pride of the Halifax Fire Department and one of the first of its kind in the Maritimes.

Billy Wells, a clean-shaven, round-faced, and cheerful-looking thirty-six-year-old, would jump into the driver's seat and take the wheel. He liked to race to the sites against the other station's horse-drawn trucks and his brother Claude Wells, who would take off from the Brunswick Street Fire Station, near the Citadel, in Fire Chief Edward Condon's Buick Roadster. Racing through the city streets made of brick, cobblestone, wood, and dirt to get to a small fire and put it out was all good fun. Billy Wells couldn't imagine a better way to pay for his pints.

On this day, however, Constant Upham, who owned a general store on the North End, could see that the growing blaze on *Mont-Blanc* was no longer a routine fire, and he wanted to make sure the firemen knew it. Fortunately, Upham's store featured a new invention: a telephone. Upham placed calls, which still required operators to complete them, to four fire stations in the

BOX 83 · 233

area to tell them the situation on Pier 6 should not be taken lightly.

Billy Wells and his crewmates at the West Street Fire Station had already heard the alarm from Box 83 when Constant Upham called to say that it was serious. They hopped into the Patricia while someone banged on the bathroom door to get one of their crewmen, who had come to the station in spite of a bad flu, or possibly a hangover. Unwilling to wait any longer, Billy Wells pulled out of the station, started the sirens, and left their crewmate behind.

Wells looked forward to racing his brother to the docks, until he remembered Claude had the day off. He then recalled that he needed to pick up part-time firefighter Albert Brunt on the way. When Brunt heard Box 83, followed by the Patricia's sirens, he pushed his paint cart out of the way and rushed to the corner of Gottingen Street, where he knew the Patricia would be passing. As the Patricia slowed to turn onto Gottingen, Brunt reached to grab the rail on the back of the truck, but his hand slipped and he fell back onto the street, scraping his hands and knees. His friends on the truck hooted and hollered at Brunt, picking himself off the street while Wells kept speeding toward Pier 6.

Down the road, fifteen-year-old Frank Burford had just picked up the parcel at the dry dock, as his boss had ordered, then run as fast as he could to *Middleham Castle* to watch *Mont-Blanc* burn. He passed Constant Upham's store on the way, while a shiny new motorized fire engine flew by at top speed: 30 miles per hour.

By the time the Patricia stopped near Pier 6, the fire on *Mont-Blanc*'s deck had already become so big and hot that the firefighters could not look straight at it, averting their eyes and shielding their faces. Chief Condon could see that Constant Upham was right: this was no ordinary dock fire. He pulled Box 83 again to roust all the help they could get.

A retired fireman named John Spruin heard the call, pulled on his fire suit, got into his old horse-drawn pumper, and headed down Brunswick Street to Box 83.

Chapter 17

"Oh, Something Awful
Is Going to Happen"

Because so many families in Richmond had a passel of kids, with three on the low side and a dozen not uncommon, each weekday morning the neighborhood homes buzzed with everyone hustling to get off to school and work on time.

In the Pattisons' home that morning, their daughter Catherine, ten, had a bad cold, and would be staying in bed. Gordon, fourteen, and James, thirteen, had packed their leather school bags with their books and their homework for Principal Huggins. Their little brother, Alan, eight, would tag along on their way to Richmond School.

A few days earlier, the Pattisons' parents had taken the two older boys to a jewelers' shop to pick out timepieces, in recognition of their status as growing young men. Gordon had selected a handsome silver wristwatch with a face designed like the spokes of a wheel, while James had opted for a classic pocket watch. He quickly developed the habit of pulling it out of his pocket and flipping it open to check the time, even when no one asked.

But on this morning, when James dug into his pocket for the watch, he remembered he had lent it to his father, the mechanical superintendent at the Acadia Sugar Refinery just a block from their home, because his father's watch was in for repairs. It was Gordon, therefore, who had the pleasure of checking his wristwatch and telling his brothers it was time to go. School started a half hour later that week, at 9:30, due to "winter schedule," which schools implemented to save money on heating and lighting during the winter, and make it safe to walk to school in daylight.

James and Gordon Pattison might have been on the cusp of manhood, but their mother still insisted they wear their thick sweaters and button up their jackets. The sun was out, but she knew the winter cold was coming. A few minutes before 9:00 a.m., they kissed their mother good-bye, grabbed Alan, and walked out the door. As soon as they stepped outside they heard the fire alarm from Box 83, then saw the Patricia race by, siren blaring, with the firemen hanging on to the side while Billy Wells careened through the streets.

The Pattison boys looked at each other, wide-eyed, and quickly forgot about school to chase after the Patricia. They could hear the roaring fire and see the black smoke billow, but they couldn't see either ship until they stepped into the gap between the graving dock and the Acadia Sugar Refinery. Out in the middle of the Narrows they spotted a big ship with BELGIAN RELIEF on her side. When they walked past the Protestant Orphanage, all sound suddenly stopped.

At the other end of Richmond, Noble Driscoll played with his little brother, Gordon, in their backyard where the family kept their milking cow. They had not yet adjusted to Richmond School's "winter schedule," so they were ready to go to school by 8:30, giving them half an hour to kill.

More than three years into the Great War, Noble and his brother had watched hundreds of ships from the family's backyard, which faced the harbor. When they heard whistles being sent between two ships that morning, they ran to the corner of the yard just in time to see the bigger boat cut into the smaller one.

"I'm going to get Pop," Noble told Gordon, who was less impressed.

Noble found his father sitting next to a window, eating his breakfast before walking down to the Richmond railyards, where he worked as a car inspector. He had heard his son race into the house to deliver big news from the harbor many times, so he listened patiently to Noble's latest story. When Noble finished, his father said, "I'll just finish my breakfast first, and then get my things together for work. I'll come and see what's up as soon as I've done that."

When Noble returned to the backyard, Gordon was gone. Noble assumed he must have seen one of his friends and headed off to school, so Noble figured it must be time for him to go, too. But instead of walking to Albert Street and then going four blocks south to Richmond School, he decided to take a detour along Campbell Road to get a better look.

When he got closer, he saw *Mont-Blanc* burning ferociously and "two small boats, crammed with men, heading quickly away from the ship." When he heard the West Street Station's Patricia racing through the streets with Billy Wells at the wheel, he couldn't contain his excitement any longer and ditched school to follow the Patricia.

Along the way, Noble walked up to Mr. Creighton's store, where his older brother, Al, delivered groceries with a horse and wagon. The people there knew Noble well, so when the owner's son, Cam, saw Noble, he warned him, "Don't go any closer, Nob. There's bullets exploding, and you might get one in your leg."

The fire was so close and so loud by then that Noble could barely hear Cam's warning, but he did as instructed.

"Just at that moment," he recalled, "an unnatural silence fell."

Mr. Huggins, the principal at Richmond School, arrived on the train from Rockingham, just a couple of miles around the bend, with his daughter, Merle, just as they did every school day. They ignored the commotion by the docks on their way up the hill a couple of blocks to the school, because Mr. Huggins liked to get there a solid half hour before his students. But when he ran into the father of one of his Junior Cadets, he stopped to chat, telling his daughter, "You run along, Merle. I'll catch up."

She was only too happy to, because that meant she could play with her friends on the playground before school. While her father wasn't terribly worried about the burning ship, he figured the school would be safe.

"That's quite a fire down there," Mr. Huggins said to his friend. "I hope those students of mine are not getting too close and making nuisances of themselves."

The owner of Richmond's general store, Constant Upham, had a brother, Charles, who worked the night shift as the yardmaster of the Richmond railway. Shortly after dawn broke, Charles finished his shift and walked two blocks up the hill to his home. Tired as he was, he always looked forward to digging into the big, hot breakfast his wife would have waiting for him. Then he'd stoke their furnace and stove with coal from the cellar before trudging upstairs to his bed for some much-needed rest.

His oldest children, Ellen, Archie, and Millicent, were not going to their classes at Richmond School that day because they would be attending their grand-father's funeral that afternoon at their cousin's house up the hill, where their grandfather's body lay in state in their parlor. When Charles Upham lumbered to the top of the stairs, he was not surprised to see Archie, a feisty, happy-looking kid, and Millicent, her hair in curls, playing in one of the bedrooms.

"Don't make too much noise," he said. "I'm going to sleep."

Charles went into his bedroom, shut the door, swapped his work clothes for his nightshirt, and climbed into bed, pulling the blankets over his head to keep the daylight from stirring him.

In the room next door, Archie grabbed a book from the shelf, hopped onto the bed, and started to read. Millicent played near him with her dolls' tiny tea set, a favorite of hers. On top of her bureau she kept a piggybank in which she saved her pennies for Christmas, just two and a half weeks away. Unlike Archie, who couldn't keep a penny in his pocket, Millicent was a good saver.

They were quiet as could be, but they soon heard the tumult coming from the docks.

"Daddy will be angry about all that noise," Millicent told Archie.

"He'll never hear it," Archie laughed. "He always pulls the blankets right up over his head. You can't even see his nose. I don't know how he breathes."

The two sat on the bed, reading and playing, Archie with his back to the window, Millicent facing it.

The Orr children remained engrossed by the drama unfolding out their window. When they asked their mother if the burning ship might explode, she saw the dockworkers and sailors nonchalantly watching the action, some laughing, and reasoned that they would know if there was any real danger, and no one seemed too worried. She replied calmly, "Oh, I don't think so."

When the fire grew, the Orrs noticed their classmates

and friends dashing down the hill past their new home to get a closer look. So strong was the Haligonians' sense of security that when Barbara and Ian asked their mother if they could join them to see the burning ship for themselves, their mother gave permission, provided they wore their coats and boots and didn't get too close.

Barbara wanted to see if a neighbor friend would join her. Before Ian and Isabel went their own way, Barbara told them, "You go on if you like. We'll join you in a minute or two."

Ian took little Isabel with him, and together they ran straight down Kenny Street toward the waterfront and the crowd around Pier 6. Barbara walked down to Mulgrave Park, which sat just across Campbell Road from Pier 6. She then started walking toward her friend's house, her high-laced boots crunching the frosty grass, but she did not run. She was too absorbed by the fire rising higher and higher to go very fast.

The fire roared so loudly, Barbara couldn't hear anything else. Then, suddenly, the noise stopped. Barbara stood in the middle of the park lawn, mesmerized, and stared at the ship.

"It was so still, so calm," Barbara recalled. "This awful column of smoke went up. And then these balls of fire would roll up through it, and then they'd burst. But there was no sound. It was the strangest thing.

"I stood spellbound in the middle of this field.

"I thought, 'Oh, something awful is going to happen.' "

The onlookers, longshoremen, firefighters, and sailors didn't know that the benzol on *Mont-Blanc*'s deck was seeping into the hold below. They didn't know that, a week earlier in Gravesend Bay, stevedores had stored tons upon tons of TNT and picric acid down there. And they certainly didn't know the fire they were watching on deck was heating up the volatile contents below, minute by minute. Most of the people who did know—Francis Mackey, Captain Le Médec, and his crew—were watching from behind a hill across the Narrows in Dartmouth.

Lt. Commander James Murray was one of only four people in the Examiner's Office who knew what *Mont-Blanc* was carrying, and the only one out on the water that morning. So when he saw that *Mont-Blanc* had caught fire, he immediately turned his boat, *Hilford*, back to Pier 9 near his office, hoping to send out a general warning by telephone—if he could get there before *Mont-Blanc* blew up.

After docking *Hilford* at Pier 9, Murray started running up the jetty to his office, but he also sent one of his sailors to the railway dispatch office to warn them of trouble ahead. The sailor did as he was told. As chief clerk of Richmond railway yards William Lovett and train dispatcher Vincent Coleman were sitting at their desks talking about the ship in flames just 200 yards outside their window, their door burst open, giving them a jolt.

"Everybody out!" the young sailor shouted. "Run like hell! Commander says that bloody ship is loaded with tons of explosives and she'll blow up for certain."

William Lovett (not to be confused with Arthur Lovett, the customs officer who gave *Imo* clearance) immediately called Henry Dustan, the terminal agent of the Canadian Government Railways, in their new building a couple of miles away in South Halifax and said, "This is Lovett talking. There is a steamer coming into the wharf on fire, loaded with explosives. There is likely to be an explosion."

Coleman, who'd already been a hero that summer when he hopped onto a runaway engine and stopped it before it collided with a suburban train, commanded his staff to run for safety. Coleman led the way, until he remembered the overnight express train No. 10 from Saint John, New Brunswick, was scheduled to arrive at the North Street Station in Richmond, right by Pier 6, in just a few minutes, with 300 passengers.

If Ernest Barss faced the horror of the Great War over several months, and the crew of *Mont-Blanc* wrestled with the Great War's power for four days, Francis Mackey and Vincent Coleman both had to face life-and-death decisions in a matter of seconds. Mackey ultimately ran for the rowboat, but Coleman ran in the opposite direction. He stopped, turned back toward his office, and rattled off an urgent telegraph to the train station just 4 miles around the bend in Rockford, the last stop before Richmond's North Street Station, hoping to stop the No. 10 train before it left.

Coleman's telegram, sent at 8:49, marked the first word to anyone outside Halifax of potential trouble ahead. But he didn't know whether his message had been received, if it was passed on to the appropriate people, or if it would do anyone any good. But he was pretty sure it would be his last.

"Hold up the train," he wrote. "Ammunition ship afire in harbour making for Pier 6 and will explode. Guess this will be my last message. Good-bye, boys."

PART V

9:04:35 a.m.

Chapter 18
One-Fifteenth of a Second

At 9:04:35 a.m., while firefighters and crews from other ships battled the blaze, the fire on *Mont-Blanc* either penetrated the magazines storing the TNT and picric acid or finally nudged the temperature in the cargo hold just past the 572-degree-Fahrenheit threshold needed to detonate picric acid. Regardless, the result was the same.

The instant *Mont-Blanc*'s cargo ignited, it started a chemical chain reaction an immense string of dominoes knocking the next one over in rapid succession, with each domino self-contained microscopic bomb that is the molecule of a high explosive.

To try to grasp the magnitude of this unprecedented explosion, Robert MacNeil offers this simple comparison: when a rifle is fired, one ounce of explosive powder in the shell burns rapidly, fomenting hot gases. These gases expand, forcing the bullet out of the shell—and in a hurry. *Mont-Blanc* held the equivalent of 83 million ounces of gun powder, which did collectively what one rifle shell does, with 83 million times more force, shooting out in all directions at once.

The detonation itself took one-fifteenth of a second, five times faster than the blink of an eye. The epicenter of the explosion instantaneously shot up to 9,000 degrees Fahrenheit, about six times hotter than molten lava.

The explosion started in the gigantic steel casement of the cargo hold, which had been packed tight and was far too small to contain such an exponential expansion. The blast shot outward in all directions at 3,400 miles per hour, or four times the speed of sound. It tore through the ship's steel hull like wet tissue paper, converting the vessel into a monstrous hand grenade. The heat vaporized the water surrounding the ship and the people trying to tie her up and put out the fire. The remains of these victims were never found because there were no remains to find.

Small chunks of metal from the ship crashed through roofs, punctured other ships, and killed and maimed people both nearby and hundreds of yards away. Retired fireman John Spruin, the man who had heard the fire alarm, put on his old uniform, and driven his horse-drawn pumper to the site, was ripped apart by shrapnel and killed instantly.

Mont-Blanc disintegrated, leaving only two recognizable parts: the anchor shank, which weighed half a ton and was found 4 miles away in the woods of the Northwest Arm; and an iron deck cannon, intended to protect the ship from U-boats, which landed 3 miles away in Little Albro Lake behind Dartmouth, with its barrel drooping like a warm candle.

The explosion also produced something we recognize all too readily today: a mushroom cloud. The extremely high temperatures involved created a gas fireball filled with vaporized particles of the ship, the cargo, oil, coal, and humans, skyrocketing directly upward to form the stalk of the cloud, which rose 2 miles into the air. When the blistering-hot debris reached its zenith, they cooled, slowed down, and spread out, making it look something like a mushroom cloud, though it lacked the perfect symmetry nuclear bombs produce.

The cloud was so big and thick that it made it seem as though dusk had arrived at 9:05 a.m. When the cloud could no longer hold the particles, it started shedding the oil and debris, which changed the color of the cloud from black to white.

This attracted the attention of observers miles away, who were often unaware of the cloud's significance. Rear Admiral B. M. Chambers, who was saying good-bye to his wife outside their home near the Royal Artillery Park on the south side of the Citadel, heard the explosion and looked toward the Richmond docks. He noticed, "there, right in front of the house . . . was rising into the air a most wonderful cauliflower-like plume of white smoke, twisting and twirling and changing color in the brilliant sunlight of a perfect Canadian early winter morning."

Another wrote to an American friend, "The smoke cloud following the explosion was a wonderful spectacle and for a few minutes we never realized the seriousness of it."

The seriousness was clear enough to those beneath it. When the cloud released its contents—including the carbon by-products of the explosion, the fragments of bunker coal, and the steel pieces and particles of *Mont-Blanc* itself, plus tons of oil and airplane fuel—it created what witnesses described as "dark rain." But anyone caught underneath the fallout could tell you it wasn't water coming down but a thick, black precipitation of hot oil and soot, like liquid tar, mixed with heavy, scalding shrapnel that cut, burned, and blackened everything in its path.

The eruption also sent ground waves through the bedrock at about 13,000 miles per hour, which caused bystanders to feel a "thump" and houses to shake. These were picked up by the stylus on the new seismograph at Dalhousie University, a mile and a half away. People in Sydney, Cape Breton, about 250 miles northeast, felt the mysterious shock. One hundred ten miles away in Charlottetown, Prince Edward Island, plates and glasses shook for a few seconds, as if from an earthquake far away.

The explosion itself and the ground waves were quickly followed by the third force, air waves, concentric circles of gas bubbles racing outward from ground zero like those seen in 1950s instructional films about atomic bombs. This invisible force initially traveled at supersonic speeds before dropping to a sonic velocity of 756 miles per hour, similar to what atomic bombs generate.

Ian Forsyth, a student at the Halifax County Academy, not far from the Citadel, felt two blasts as the school principal was reading Psalm 103.

As a father has compassion on his children,
so the LORD has compassion on those who
fear him;

for he knows how we are formed,
he remembers that we are dust.
The life of mortals is like grass,
they flourish like a flower of the field;

When they heard a "dull boom" coming from the north produced by the ground wave, "the principal looked up and we focused our eyes on him." After a moment's hesitation, he returned to Psalm 103.

the wind blows over it and it is gone,
and its place remembers it no more.

A second later the air wave hit, throwing windows inward and bringing plaster down on the students.

Although the air wave was invisible, its effects were not. As it moved out from the epicenter, the walls of air simply blew buildings apart, without leaving a trace. Also called shock waves, and concussions, they smashed the Halifax City Hall clock tower in the center of downtown, 2 miles from Pier 6, stopping its arms at 9:06. "The city hall itself is something of a wreck," wrote Stanley K. Smith, the editor of the *Saint John* (New Brunswick) *Daily Telegraph*. "The face of the clock, though this building is over 2 miles from the scene of the explosion, is blown in and the hands register the hour and minute at which the horror fell upon the city."

Although the vibrations traveled more quickly through the earth than the air, the air blast created far more damage. "The enormous volume of gaseous products of the explosion," the authors of *Ground Zero* write, "rushed outward from the doomed ship, pushing the air and water ahead of them."

Whatever the initial explosion had left intact, the shock wave seemed determined to finish off. *Mont-Blanc*'s concussion rushed outward from the epicenter at 2,100 miles per hour, seven times faster than the most powerful tornado. It shattered virtually every window in Halifax and blew out some as far as Truro, Nova Scotia, 50 miles away.

Because of the speed and power of the shock wave blasting the homes, however, "shattered" isn't quite the right word. Many witnesses said the windows— tens of thousands of them—simultaneously "popped" like plastic packing bubbles, sending daggers of glass inward toward the onlookers who had been watching the ship from their factories, schools, and bay windows. The last thing hundreds of people saw was the burning *Mont-Blanc*, followed by an incredible burst of white light, eclipsing everything else. The next second, their faces, eyes, and bodies were riddled with glass shards, leaving them bleeding, blind, or dead.

When the powerful concussion collided with the slope of Richmond, it hit the ironstone and granite bedrock that lay just two feet below the topsoil and deflected upward toward Fort Needham park.

On its way to Fort Needham, the blast wave picked up debris from crushed buildings—and often the people in or near them—and sent them up the hill. This "push broom" effect, in which the invisible air wave knocked down everything in its path including hundreds of homes, drove those pieces in a solid front to the next obstacle, plowing over the people in its way and then continuing toward its next target.

For people still at home, their walls and windows came crashing in on them before they could comprehend what was happening. The blast struck when most homeowners in Halifax had just stoked their furnaces and finished making breakfast and coffee on their stoves, which provided more deadly raw materials for the shock wave to pick up and send hurtling into the next home. Fire never had a better friend than the air wave radiating outward from the explosion's epicenter and igniting dry wooden homes filled with horsehair couches and varnished floors.

The explosion, the ground waves, and the devastating air waves were quickly followed by a tsunami. The explosion created a bowl-shaped hole in the water, then sent gigantic waves in all directions.

Some observers said the explosion literally parted the sea, momentarily exposing the harbor floor. This sudden displacement created a thirty-five-foot wave that crashed against Richmond thirty feet up the hill, flooding the foundations of all the buildings that had been torn open by the initial blast and the shock wave that followed. The tsunami then ran up the bedrock surface of the slope, rolling up the hill thirty feet more, flooding still more buildings and homes, and leaving people in its path thousands of feet from where they had been standing a few seconds earlier, trying to figure out what the hell had just happened—provided they had survived all that. While they were trying to put it all together, some were pulled back down the hill by the undertow, and drowned in the harbor.

The shock waves and tsunami also went in the other direction across the Narrows, crashing against the Dartmouth shore a quarter-mile away. Phillip Mitchell, the grandfather of Ethel, who had danced on *Highflyer* the night before, lived in Dartmouth. When *Mont-Blanc* started burning, Phillip, who was lame, stood on the Dartmouth shore near an electric wire pole with a loose board at the foot of it. When the ship exploded, Phillip grabbed the board and held it over his head, which shielded him from the "black rain" that soon came down from the sky. Seconds later, the tsunami headed his way, still about twenty feet high when it hit Dartmouth. Mitchell dropped the board and wrapped his arms around the pole. The wave went way over his head, but as it receded he looked behind him to see that it had soaked the boxcar on the track twenty feet above him. The second and third waves followed, each smaller but still more than powerful enough to toss a man to the ground and pull him out to sea. Phillip kept clinging to the pole until the last wave passed, and he was still standing.

The blast crushed about half of Dartmouth, including all of Turtle Grove, where the Mi'kmaq lived and which took the brunt of the tsunami. George Dixon worked at a small shipbuilding plant near the Mi'kmaq, where the tsunami rumbled toward him like boiling liquid filled with pieces of metal. Single-story homes were swamped from the roof to the basement.

The Mi'kmaq homes were destroyed, killing at least nine people, including Jerry Lone Cloud's two daughters. The village, which he had been begging the government for months to move to a reservation, had effectively been wiped out. Starting with Halifax's first battle against Louisbourg in 1758, every conflict between Europeans in North America had squeezed the Mi'kmaq onto smaller and smaller parcels of land, but the explosion and tsunami finally finished off their little village.

When the black cloud fell to earth, the sun returned, exposing the truth of what the explosion had done. Pier 6 was gone, leaving only a bank of mud behind, while the materials that comprised Piers 7, 8, and 9 and the buildings near them had all been scooped up the hill. Trees and telegraph poles that ran along the railroad tracks around Richmond and Africville had been snapped like twigs and added to the pile.

All told, the explosion turned two square miles of this calm, orderly, postcard-pretty town into a nightmare of chaos, destruction, and death in a split second.

The explosion's force threw railroad tracks into knots, crushed concrete factories, reduced wooden houses to kindling, and ripped open cement schools, brick churches, and stone houses. It destroyed 6,000 buildings, rendering 25,000 people—almost half the population of Halifax—homeless in one ear-splitting *whoosh*.

The cataclysm killed 1,600 instantly. Some were destroyed on the spot, while others were thrown half a mile, often shot out of their shoes, which were left where they had been standing a moment before. At least 300 died when their homes, factories, or schools were demolished by the blast or the bubble. Corpses were scattered throughout the rubble as though a mannequin warehouse had been bombed, leaving bodies contorted in strange positions, often with their clothes torn off, and many missing arms, legs, or even heads.

The blast also wounded 9,000 people, leaving them stumbling about their leveled city like drunks, bleeding and bewildered, their expressions frozen in blank surprise.

Chapter 19
Parting the Sea

When the black cloud cleared, the survivors could not find *Mont-Blanc*. The ship, all 320 feet of it, had vanished, reduced in a flash to atoms.

Pier 6 had been built to withstand hurricanes, but there was virtually no sign of it, the area having returned to the rough, muddy, natural landscape the Mi'kmaq had walked for centuries.

Seconds after the blast, the tsunami sent several ships near the epicenter down to the sea bottom, then sent them up with the thirty-five-foot waves, snapping thick steel anchor lines like licorice sticks.

Farther from Pier 6, the USS *Old Colony* was thrown about like toy boats in a bathtub, but suffered no casualties. HMS *Highflyer*, anchored in the basin, had been built for battle and survived the explosion, but suffered a damaged hull, with fifteen crewmen wounded and three killed.

The rowboat of the HMS *Highflyer*, led by Acting Commander Tom K. Triggs, coming to the rescue of *Mont-Blanc*, had been blown to pieces. Commander Triggs and all but one member of the crew had been killed.

Stella Maris, the tugboat captained by Horatio Brennan, had been rent asunder and then launched skyward, landing where Pier 6 had been. Of Brennan's twenty-five-man crew, twenty were killed, including William Nickerson, who had been sent to fetch the ten-inch hawser. Horatio's son, Walter Brannen, who had been standing at the entrance to the hold, escaped with cuts, bruises, and a punctured eardrum—about the best he could hope for, given the circumstances. His father, Horatio, had been killed instantly. The photo he had sat for to surprise his wife for Christmas would remain at the studio, unclaimed.

Curaca, the American ship loading wheat and horses for Europe, had been docked at Pier 8, so there was nothing between her and *Mont-Blanc*. The blast had snapped off her masts and knocked her stern in like a dented tin can. Of *Curaca*'s thirty-five-man crew, thirty-two were killed.

In an irony that would not have been lost on the men crouching in trenches overseas, where the fickleness of fate was an all-too-familiar presence, Edward McCrossan, who had been so desperate for a cigarette that he had gone belowdecks to roll one while *Mont-Blanc*'s fireworks display entertained his crewmates, was one of the few crewmen not on deck when it exploded. Cigarettes don't normally save lives, but that one saved his.

McCrossan was not out of danger, however, as the heavily damaged *Curaca*, with nothing securing her to the dock and no crew to steer her, was now in the throes of waves emanating from the epicenter and soon headed toward the Bedford Basin. Quickly sizing up the situation, McCrossan jumped onto *Calonne*, which had been docked at Pier 9 right behind *Curaca*, and was now also drifting toward the basin. Though shielded, *Calonne* had still lost seven of her crew. After McCrossan hopped aboard, he looked back at Richmond, where he saw that the hillside was now covered with collapsed homes and women and children "covered with blood."

Smaller vessels, so much easier to flip over or break apart, often had worse luck. The tugboat *Hilford*, for example, which had been tied up on the far side of *Calonne*, had been partly blown apart by the explosion before the tidal wave tossed her atop the wharf, where she was left lying some thirty feet above the water. Another tugboat had been launched clear over Pier 6.

Just a few hundred feet farther south along the Halifax Harbour coast, the Halifax Graving Dock Company's wharf offered some protection, with the dry dock's high walls providing a buffer against the harbor's waves. But that wasn't enough to spare the men on *Middleham Castle*, docked just off the wharf, including the workers from the marine engineering firm of Burns & Kelleher. They had been watching *Mont-Blanc*'s barrels of benzol rocket into the air when the foreman sent nineteen-year-old Jack Tappen down below to move a cast-iron pipe to the engine room. After Tappen dropped off the pipe, he stopped to chat with another worker standing against the bulkhead, who put his hand on Jack's shoulder. While they talked, *Mont-Blanc* exploded.

The force of the blast shot Tappen backward through an open doorway behind him, and straight down a narrow hallway at full speed. When Tappen regained his wits, he was relieved to discover that he had landed on a pile of something soft. Because it was pitch black, he couldn't see his hand directly in front of his eyes, let alone whatever it was he had landed on. It didn't take him long to figure out that the softness, the cloth, and the occasional hard struts and spheres constituted a pile of human corpses—the very colleagues he had been talking to just a few minutes earlier. The bodies had not begun to stiffen yet, but they "bled profusely, and the smell was profound."

While Tappen tried to get his bearings, the ship soared upward and plunged down with each wave of the tsunami, tossing him back and forth on the pile of bodies. When the boat settled and his eyes adjusted to the darkness, he could see that he'd not been hurt, but every button on his vest had popped off.

Tappen soon realized he was not alone. Two other apprentices, who'd been thrown into the same room, had also survived. They looked around and found the man who'd been talking with Jack in front of the bulkhead a few seconds earlier. The force had slammed him into the bulkhead and crushed his skull.

When the trio of survivors climbed back on deck, they saw huge round boulders weighing several tons each, possibly from the bottom of the sea, sitting on the deck. *Middleham Castle*'s hull had been ripped open, and the ship was starting to sink. The three men weren't eager to jump into the water, which was now swirling with unpredictable currents and undertows, tons of oil and coal, and shrapnel, dead bodies, and drowning men. While *Middleham Castle* bobbed, rolled, and began sinking, they waited for their chance to jump to the *J.C. McKee* then slide down its ropes to the wharf.

From there they could see people floundering in the water, yelling for help, with dead bodies floating among them. The three young men pulled out as many of the flailing swimmers as they could before they realized they had to leave the disconnected wharf before it drifted out to the Narrows. They hopscotched their way across floating debris to get to shore, where they discovered the shed where they'd hung their coats each day had been flattened and was on fire.

The Dartmouth Ferry started its scheduled trip right at 9:00 a.m.—fourteen minutes after the collision, and four minutes before the explosion. Dorothy Chisholm, a Dartmouth resident who worked at the Royal Bank in Halifax, boarded the 9:00 a.m. ferry, just like she did every morning.

By the time the ferry departed Dartmouth, *Mont-Blanc* had been secured to Pier 6. The ferry passengers lined up along the rail to watch the freighter burn. The ferry had made it only halfway across the channel when *Mont-Blanc* blew up.

Due to the distance between *Mont-Blanc* and the ferry, the passengers had a few seconds to dive for cover; Chisholm, however, was slow to react. The blast sent passengers flying across the ferry, with Chisholm landing on top of the pile of bodies. It might have seemed like a break, until the explosion sent debris flying overhead and the black cloud eventually dropped its heavy, hot, and oily debris on her. As the tsunami tossed the ferry up and down, Chisholm thought the Germans had attacked them, and she wished she had been under the pile of passengers to avoid getting shot.

Confusion gripped almost everyone near the harbor. And why not? This was not peacetime. Fear of the Germans had permeated their lives since the Great War had started three years earlier, so blaming the Germans was their first reaction.

The stunned passengers gradually sorted themselves out, stood up, and started to assess the damage. Again, contrary to expectations, those sitting belowdecks in the saloon had suffered greater harm, much of it from flying glass.

Despite the blast, the determined ferryboat captain finished his trip to the terminal in Halifax, got his wounded passengers to safety, and continued his regular routes throughout this horrific day. Although he and his crew were surely as anxious as everyone else to find out what had happened to their homes and their families, they remained at their posts, knowing that thousands depended on them—a quiet bit of heroism.

Shortly after the detonation, the displaced water tossed the 5,000-ton, 430-foot-long *Imo* several hundred feet across the Narrows, where she beached in the shallows of Dartmouth, listing toward the shore and riddled with holes from the shrapnel. Five *Imo* crewmen, Harbour Pilot William Hayes, and Captain Haakon From were killed instantly. When the authorities arrived to talk to From later that day, they found his loyal dog guarding his body, barking at anyone who tried to come close. To retrieve the captain's body, they felt they had little choice but to shoot his dog.

A full half mile from the explosion *Mont-Blanc*'s crewmen were knocked down, some unconscious. Captain Le Médec and Pilot Mackey were pinned under a spruce tree. When they regained consciousness, they had to free themselves of the heavy branches on top of them. Neither had been seriously wounded, but Le Médec was so dazed, and everything surrounding him seemed so strange, that he did not initially recognize Mackey, who had lost his cap and the bottom half of his raincoat, which had been torn off.

Le Médec assessed his crew, finding four wounded, one with a broken arm and severe bleeding. The crew walked toward Windmill Road, where Le Médec flagged down a car. They would get help, but the bleeding crewman would later die of his wounds.

Mackey walked by himself to the Dartmouth Ferry

landing. There he saw Captain Peter Johnston, Nova Scotia's superintendent of lights and buoys, who had been on the ferry with 300 other passengers when the explosion hit. When Johnston saw Mackey waiting for the ferry by himself, wearing a ripped raincoat and no hat, he knew something must be seriously amiss.

He asked Mackey, "What caused the explosion?"

"The ship I was on exploded."

Mackey explained what had happened. When their ferry reached Halifax, Mackey walked to the Pilotage Authority to tell his story.

If it was nearly impossible to predict who would survive, it was just as difficult to anticipate what any one individual would do in the face of such danger. The split-second, spontaneous choice was often irreversible.

And this is what makes Vincent Coleman's actions that day all the more remarkable. After he had ordered his men to run and began following them, he turned around, against the tide of people running for their lives, to save others.

Chapter 20
Blown Away

Minutes after the lethal black cloud had deposited its contents back on earth and the sun returned, people looked to the Halifax shore and saw a barren landscape that could have passed for a picture of Ypres. Almost all of Richmond—the factories, businesses, schools, churches, and homes, most of them made of wood—were "smashed to flinders," Raddall recalled.

The North Street Station, the city's main depot, had been crushed, with the stylish glass and steel roof crashing down on the trains, the tracks, the platforms, and the people below. The Richmond railyards ran eight tracks across at their widest along a plateau just above the docks. In an instant, the rails had been tangled up in knots, bending this way and that—or they were just gone, replaced by a muddy slope.

Downtown Halifax didn't take the full force, but its stores appeared as if they'd been shaken hard by a vengeful giant, with their goods tumbled in all directions and piles of plate glass covering the floors and streets.

After the fire on *Mont-Blanc* started, Frank Burford, the fifteen-year-old plumber's apprentice working for Hillis & Sons Foundry on Barrington, had been sent by his boss to fetch a parcel at the dry dock when the ship blew up. A moment later, everything was dark, he was choking on plaster dust, and his legs were pinned under a heavy timber. He started struggling to free himself, but a sudden, shooting pain forced him to stop.

Knowing that the wrong move could upset the pile of beams and trap him forever or crush him, he slowly twisted and turned, careful not to shift the timbers or aggravate his leg wound. Thin and nimble, he worked his way through the scattered beams toward a small opening, a little ray of light. When he finally slithered through, he looked around to see a hellscape of destruction, with not a single intact building anywhere in sight and fires burning everywhere. Having lived in this vibrant town his entire life, he could not recognize this as his home.

Since it had all happened in a flash, he had to think

hard to remember how he'd gotten there. He'd seen a freighter in the Narrows on fire, with men racing over the sides to board rowboats. That must have been it, he thought. Their ship must have blown up.

While Burford was sorting out what had happened, two sailors broke his reverie.

"Mister, have you seen our boat?" they asked.

Frank just shook his head. He was as confused as they were.

When he got down off the pile that had been his factory a minute earlier, he saw a smashed wagon next to a dead horse, and then the Patricia, driver Billy Wells's pride and joy, torn apart. It was hard to imagine how anyone anywhere near that fire engine could have survived; Fire Chief Condon, his deputy, and five of the six crewmen had all been killed.

The Hillis & Sons Foundry didn't fare much better. Forty-one employees, including general manager Frank D. Hillis, assistant manager James B. Hillis, and his father, had all lost their lives. Burford would soon learn he was one of only three who survived.

The scale of the disaster is almost impossible to grasp, except in its details.

Amelia Mary Griswold lived on Needham Street with her three daughters, one of whom, Edna, had two daughters of her own. After the shock wave raced up the hill and crushed their house, the remains soon caught fire. Although Amelia had received a serious cut on her face, she managed to pull Edna out of the house and lay her on the ground. But she couldn't find Edna's two-year-old daughter, Sadie.

Edna's other daughter, Vera, survived, but the trauma left her speechless for years afterward, and "extremely nervous." In the tumult, Edna's body, which Amelia had just left on the ground outside the house, somehow disappeared, and its resting place remains a mystery.

Amelia's oldest daughter survived unscathed, but her youngest, Rita, fifteen, was burned and blinded. Amelia's two sons, Alfred and Frederick Griswold, both worked at Hillis & Sons Foundry and were among the employees killed that day. Frederick left behind his wife and four children, aged eleven years to seven months.

Alfred Griswold's home, just a few blocks away, was destroyed. Inside, his wife and five-year-old son were both killed. When St. Joseph's School was destroyed, their six-year-old daughter was also killed. Her sister, Mary, eight, also attended St. Joe's, but somehow survived—only to discover her entire family had been wiped out.

If you had survived the explosion, the shock wave, and the tidal wave, you were not yet out of danger. Because this was the era of wooden stoves and clapboard houses, and the explosion had occurred just after breakfast, fires started everywhere at once, while survivors were still trapped under bricks and boards.

Jack Tappen, the nineteen-year-old apprentice who had survived the explosion by landing atop a pile of dead men, made it back to shore with the two other surviving apprentices, all of whom were told to help anyone they could. They walked until they reached the Richmond Printing Company, owned by the Orr family. The once proud, strong structure, built to last of granite, now looked like a pile of blocks a baby had knocked over during a temper tantrum.

The trio walked toward the rubble, now burning rapidly. The building's collapse had killed thirty employees, most of them women, in an instant. The fire that followed threatened to burn to death those still trapped by the stones and beams.

Barbara Orr's grandfather, Samuel Orr Sr., was one of the lucky few. Although more than seventy years old, when he saw his bookkeeper trapped under a granite block, he summoned the strength to heave the block off the man, and save him. But when the senior Orr heard his youngest son, David, thirty—Barbara's uncle—yelling for help, pinned under another huge granite block, the elder Orr could not reach him before the fire did. Samuel Sr. would never forget his son's desperate screaming.

Barbara's other uncle, William MacTaggart Orr, could not be found inside the building either. He had last been seen standing near the Lorne Rowing Club, probably watching the fire.

Samuel Jr., Barbara's father, had been late to leave their new home that morning, and did not seem to have made it to work. Samuel Sr. assumed his son had stopped to see the commotion near Pier 6, but no one could be certain.

When Jack Tappen and his fellow apprentices stumbled onto this tragedy in progress, they hurried to rescue a few women before the fire took over. They did not realize until later that the women they were carrying out were already dead. Such adrenaline-fueled decisions were commonplace that morning.

In the midst of Tappen's recovery efforts, it suddenly occurred to him that he should check on his mother and grandmother a few blocks away. When he got there, he found that every window and most of the doors had been blown in, but the building was still standing. He searched for his mother and grandmother on the first and second floors, but didn't find them until he looked in the basement laundry room. Before the explosion, they had gone downstairs to watch their cat having kittens. After the explosion they stayed there, fearing that the Germans had attacked and more was coming.

At twenty-one, Joe Glube already owned a successful tobacco and stationery store, not far from his home on Gottingen. Thanks to Christmas sales, he did brisk business that Wednesday, and worked late.

He returned home beat, and fell into a deep sleep. But when his mother and sister came through his bedroom door, both covered in blood and screaming, he jumped to attention. Their roof had caved in, and outside he saw the black cloud to the north. Like others, he assumed the ammunitions magazine by Bedford Basin, on the Dartmouth side, might have blown up. Then he watched a coal driver stop next door, leave the coal in his truck, enter the house, and return with a dead body to put on his truck. Glube realized they had been fortunate to survive.

The two biggest general stores in Richmond, Isaac Creighton's and Constant Upham's, were both blown away. Constant's brother, Charles, the yardmaster who had finished his night shift, had eaten a big breakfast, then stoked the furnace and stove before burrowing himself under the covers, figured he had only a few hours to sleep before his father-in-law's funeral that afternoon. Two of his two older children—Millicent, nine, and Archie, almost seven—were in the bedroom next door. Millicent was sick, but since Archie was almost ready for school, he visited her for a few minutes. When the explosion hit, he had his back to her window, while she was facing it.

They heard a "huge rushing wind" tear through their house. A second later, a piece of glass shot into the back of Archie's head but did not penetrate his skull. As alarming as that must have been, he was more shocked when he saw his sister's face sliced by flying glass, and her left eye wrenched out of its socket.

Their father, Charles, asleep in the room next door, didn't remember the explosion jolting him awake, but he did hear his children screaming "in pain and fright." The blankets had protected Charles from harm, but when he ran from the room barefoot in his nightshirt to find his children, the broken glass strewn about the floor shredded his feet. With his adrenaline eclipsing the pain, he rushed to find his two children in the next room cut and bleeding, and his daughter missing her left eye. Charles identified the more pressing issue: they were on the second floor of a house about to collapse.

When Charles led them out of Millicent's room,

he discovered that the entire east side of the house which faced the harbor was gone. The stairs had been knocked out—save for the oilcloth that had covered them. It remained attached to the top stair. Mr. Upham used the oilcloth as an escape rope, sliding down to the first floor. He then pulled the oilcloth as taut as he could and persuaded both children to slide down. As he spoke, the beams and walls were caving in, giving them a clear view of the harbor.

The children, both covered in soot and blood, did as he urged and slid down the oilcloth. No sooner had they escaped than the house went up in flames. From there, Charles picked up his daughter and carried her piggyback, and led Archie by the hand to safety.

All over town, the strongest, most important parts of buildings—beams, joists, and bricks—often became the most dangerous, while the least important, like the oilcloth, frequently became lifesavers.

Mr. Upham set his two children on a door lying flat on the ground, telling them to stay put while he ran back into the house to save his wife and three younger children. He tried one entry point, then another, and then a third, but the collapsing house and raging fire wouldn't let him get close. He would later take some slight comfort in the fact that he'd heard no cries from inside their burning home.

When Charles saw his boots and trousers had fallen from his bedroom to the first floor and hadn't caught fire yet, in a moment of practicality he retrieved them and put them on, squeezing his boots over his bleeding feet. There was nothing else to do but hold his son's hand, carry his daughter on his back, and start walking up the hill to their cousins' house on Longard Road, where they had scheduled the funeral of Mrs. Upham's father for that afternoon in the Rasleys' parlor. But when a heavy piece of a ship smashed through the Rasleys' roof and destroyed a chair next to the coffin, Annie Rasley, nine, suffered a cut to her eye, another child was also cut, and her little brother, Reg, ran out of the house screaming. They had no idea where he went, and could only hope he would return safely.

The morning after Grove Presbyterian had celebrated paying off their building loan, the Reverend Charles Crowdis climbed to a higher point on Fort Needham to get a better look at *Mont-Blanc* burning in the harbor. He would later recall that "Jets of flame and spiral puffs of smoke shot heavenwards."

At 9:04, the blast knocked him off his feet. He ran back to Grove Presbyterian and found the church and the manse had both been crushed, but were not yet on fire. His five-year old daughter and four-year old son were standing outside the house and appeared safe but his wife, Jane, and her two sisters, Marjorie and Marie, were still in the wreckage. Frantically digging through the rubble, Reverend Crowdis found Marjorie, who had badly injured legs and feet but was alive. His other sister-in-law had broken her collarbone, and would also survive.

Reverend Crowdis finally discovered his wife, Jane, under the organ on the first floor. A moment earlier, she had been upstairs. Her face was "almost unrecognizable, her eyes in a frightful state." Reverend Crowdis fetched his wheelbarrow from the shed, loaded his wife and son in it, and, with his daughter running behind, headed to the nearest hospital. Although it was set up to treat infectious diseases, the doctors there managed to remove Mrs. Crowdis's damaged eye, and she survived.

When Reverend Crowdis returned to their former address, both his sisters-in-law were gone, with no explanation. He soon found Marie but not Marjorie, whose name would soon appear on a long list of fatalities. She was later found alive, and lived to be ninety-five.

The disaster played no favorites, conspiring to destroy all four Richmond churches, and a large swath of their parishioners. Grove Presbyterian, which the Orrs,

Driscolls, Pattisons, and Uphams all attended, lost 148, while St. Mark's lost 200 and St. Joseph's an astonishing 404. The Kaye Street Methodist Church, where Reverend Swetnam presided, lost 91 members.

That morning, Reverend Swetnam's wife, Lizzie Louise Swetnam, sat at the grand piano to accompany their son, Carman, who was rehearsing the song he would sing that night at the concert. Their daughter, Dorothy, sat in a rocking chair across the room, while the Reverend leaned against the doorway, taking in the pleasant scene.

Their next-door neighbors, the Bonds, lived with two daughters in their early twenties: Ethel (not to be confused with Ethel Mitchell, of Dartmouth), and Bertha, who was engaged to a soldier named Sandy Wournell, serving on the front lines in France. In a letter to him, Bertha explained that she and Ethel were just waking up from a late night, when Ethel invited her sister to stay in bed while she went downstairs to make them breakfast, Bertha slept until about nine o'clock, when she stirred, saw the time, and hustled out of bed and into her "underclothes and corsets, stockings and an old pair of boots, which I didn't button."

She wrapped a heavy bathrobe around her and went to the bathroom—and that's when *Mont-Blanc* exploded.

"The first shock didn't stun me," she said, probably referring to the ground wave that followed the explosion. But then the church next door collapsed, "and I saw it go. Maybe a shell struck it or maybe it was simply the concussion," the latter being far more likely. A split-second later the concussion knocked Bertha into the hallway, facedown, and rained plaster on her back.

"I was sure that was the end of me and all I was thinking of was you," she wrote, expressing a sentiment familiar to thousands of soldiers. "I remember saying, or rather thinking, your name over and over but when I hit the floor first and for a few seconds I was stunned and if I had never lived I'd never have known what happened to me or felt any pain but as it was I began to move and wiggle out from under the stuff.

"My face and head was bleeding considerably. I could tell by the look of the floor and also by the way the blood was dripping off my chin but for all that my knees didn't shake a particle."

Bertha then called down for Ethel at the same time Ethel started calling for her while running up their damaged stairs. When Ethel saw that Bertha's face was bleeding and her two front teeth had been chipped, she never expected to see Bertha's face "whole again." But after Bertha cleaned up her wounds, she saw that she wouldn't need stitches.

"I had a most miraculous escape and for that we are so thankful," she wrote. The Great War had turned on itself, transforming the home front into a war zone, with soldiers overseas anxiously awaiting word that their loved ones back home were safe.

When they saw that the manse next door had been destroyed, Bertha wrote, "I didn't expect to find a soul there."

Next door, when Lizzie Louise Swetnam had begun playing the song on their grand piano, Carman started to sing but was quickly interrupted by a gigantic boom. A beat later, their house imploded, and the floor beneath them gave way.

The explosion knocked Reverend Swetnam out cold. When he regained consciousness, he saw that all but his underwear had been torn from his body, but he seemed to be okay. Then he saw that the grand piano had landed on top of his wife and son, crushing them both. He stood there in disbelief until he heard Dorothy's voice from underneath the ceiling beams, now strewn about the floor.

"Where are you, Daddy?"

Reverend Swetnam followed the voice and found his daughter so severely trapped that she could not get through the tiny gap between the beams and wall slabs piled on her. Swetnam searched frantically for his saw to cut the timbers, but when he started ripping through one of the beams it shifted, and Dorothy screamed. He stopped, unsure of what to do.

At that moment, Bertha and Ethel appeared. They could see Dorothy was "completely hemmed in" by pieces of a broken wall that had fallen on her. Reverend Swetnam was immobilized, afraid that if they tried to pull the wall off her, Dorothy could be crushed.

By this time the fires were "blazing in pretty good shape," Bertha said. "I'll never forget Mr. Swetnam's look when he saw us."

He seemed catatonic, and might have been in shock. With the back of the house on fire, the sisters recognized the impending danger faster than he did. They pleaded with him to keep sawing until they pierced his paralysis. He told Dorothy she would have to be tough and brave while Daddy rescued her. He clenched his jaw and sawed through the beam with a strength his neighbors never suspected he had.

Swetnam's saw stirred up a swirl of smoke and plaster dust that gave Dorothy a violent bout of coughing, but this time he didn't stop until he had cut out a small opening. With the fire now consuming what used to be their home, Swetnam dropped the saw and waved Ethel and Bertha to join him so all three could leverage a board sticking out of the pile. With all the force they could muster, they lifted the load just enough for Reverend Swetnam to pull her out.

"Then it was time to run," Bertha wrote, "so we ran to our place and grabbed what clothes we could. We got upstairs and I thought of my ring. It had been in my jewel box on the bureau. I found it among the plaster but the tray had gone. In a minute I located it, but no ring. I just had to get it," and after more hurried searching, she did.

The sisters gave the Swetnams some clothes to cover themselves and were about to leave when Bertha remembered their safe. She dropped her load, ran into the ruins of their home, and raced around looking for the safe, while the fires came for her. She found it and, on the first try, opened it. She tore up two cushions to create "rude bags" and stuffed them with the safe's most valuable contents: her letters from her fiancé at the Western Front. She grabbed them, then ran from the ruins before the fires caught her.

The sisters started looking for their "dear dad," who had walked down to the mill to get some sugar from a barrel inside the door. "There we found his body," she wrote. "I can't describe the sensation I had . . . Our greatest comfort is that his death was instant and that he was ready to go. You know, Sandy, that neither Ethel or I are of a collapsing nature, so, as hard as it was, we had to cover the body and leave it."

The schools fared no better than the churches. The explosion blew in the windows of St. Joseph's Catholic School and caved in the ceilings. Four girls were killed, and four later died in the hospital.

Missing school didn't improve the chances of surviving either: fifteen girls who had been absent that day were killed in or near their homes. Boys who would have attended St. Joseph's school that afternoon due to the split schedule they had adopted while the boys' school was under construction might have been safer at school. Fifty-five lost their lives.

Precautions were often pointless. Behind the Acadia Sugar Refinery's tall brick tower, which had snapped off "like a carrot" and tumbled onto a nearby dock, the Protestant Orphanage stood right in the path of the blast. The school's matron knew they were in peril well before *Mont-Blanc* blew up, so she ordered their twenty-seven children into the basement to be safe. When the shock wave thrust their building down upon them, they were flattened, killing all twenty-seven orphans and the matron herself.

When the Richmond School building collapsed, school had not started yet, and the building was largely empty—but not completely. When the ship exploded, Mr. Huggins was knocked to the ground and injured, but his first thought was "At least Merle would be safe."

When Principal Huggins rushed to the school, he discovered that the concussion had crushed the building, with his daughter inside. No one could find her.

There was simply no predictably safe place to be in Richmond that morning. Eighty-six students died on their way to school or in their homes, where they had stayed to get well and to keep their classmates from getting sick.

In the first two hours after the explosion, the normal order was breaking down quickly, with people, even children, left to rely on their instincts. In the schools that survived largely intact, usually those far from Pier 6, most teachers dismissed their students, leaving them to walk home unescorted despite the obvious risks. Many children returned to their neighborhoods to discover their parents and homes had vanished, although it often took them some time to confirm they were looking on the correct street.

Chapter 21
They're All Gone

Where there had been a vibrant shipping town abuzz with some 60,000-plus people all starting their busy day, just a few seconds later there were no piers, no train station, no factories, no schools, no homes, no people, and no sound—a desolate, silent moonscape. The explosion and its aftereffects had left only a few standing walls, some trees ripped clean of leaves and most of their branches, and fires burning everywhere.

A few moments later, survivors put to use every siren that still worked, racing around Halifax and Dartmouth to find their loved ones and help strangers, who filled the air with their agonizing wails.

One witness predicted, "The real nightmare is just beginning."

After one victim's building had been flattened, he recalled, he "crawled out through the windows and everything was black. Can't begin to tell ya of the awful sights. Dead bodies laid out in rows, arms and legs sticking out of the debris, burned to the bone. And the whole North End, nothing but charred embers. The whole thing just turns your heart sick."

On Russell Street, survivors saw a naked man walking down the street, his skin falling off his body "like wood shavings." Bewildered victims walked, crawled, and dragged themselves out of their destroyed homes like zombies, with horrendous injuries: arms and legs blown off; faces burned, lacerated, or smashed beyond recognition; and some whose bodies had been cut in half but who kept breathing for a few minutes with shocked, helpless expressions, too stunned to speak.

The survivors who could walk stumbled about aimlessly, hoping to find anyone who could lend a hand. On their directionless searches, they kept encountering symbols of their naïveté: the shattered bay windows they had rushed to so they could *watch* the ship burn; the fire alarms strategically positioned around a city now ablaze; and the small-bore hoses and buckets at each station that everyone had assumed would be enough to keep them safe.

To get a better view of *Mont-Blanc* burning at Pier 6, hundreds of people had climbed the stairs of the harbor's substantial new concrete-and-steel pedestrian bridge, which spanned the eight tracks of Richmond railyard. An instant later, the only evidence that the bridge had ever been built was the concrete moorings and deformed steel beams that had been thrown about Halifax and Dartmouth. The people who had been standing on the bridge had disappeared.

The Patricia, the gem of the Halifax Fire Department's fleet, had been transformed into a twisted hunk of metal. The blast ejected the driver, Billy Wells, from the Patricia's driver's seat and shot him up the hill. He was still clutching the steering wheel, which he had apparently ripped from the vehicle. The explosion, the shock wave, or a combination of the two also snatched Wells's clothes off his body, tore the muscles from his right arm—probably the result of his clenching the wheel—and injured his right eye. But he was alive—for now.

Just a few seconds later, the thirty-five-foot wave picked up hundreds of people, including Billy Wells, and washed them up to Fort Needham. When the water reached its zenith, it came rushing back down, bringing with it everything it had just carried up the hill.

On Wells's return trip, he became tangled in telephone wires, which fortunately were no longer live. Still, Wells knew he had to free himself or he would die there. Using only his left arm, he got loose, then saw that most of the people he had been trying to save seconds earlier with his fire engine were in worse shape.

"The sight was awful," he recalled, "with people hanging out of windows dead. Some with their heads missing, and some thrown onto the overhead telegraph wires."

One sailor felt he was being squeezed on all sides by the whirlwind, then picked up and pulled through the air until the wind's energy was exhausted. Fortunately for him, that occurred when he was atop a hill, shortening his fall to earth after it released him. Another sailor recalled watching *Mont-Blanc* burn at close range, then lying on top of Fort Needham a quarter mile away, in shock but not critically injured. He, too, would probably have died if the slope had not softened his landing.

Fourteen-year-old Barbara Orr had been standing on the hillside of Mulgrave Park. When it exploded, Orr felt herself moving strangely, as if in a dream, riding a great wind while twisting and turning along the way.

"I was thinking that I was going down in deep holes all the time," she said. "Almost like an unconsciousness."

Just as soon as the wind started, it stopped, leaving Orr on a nice field of grass. But it wasn't Mulgrave Park. It was Fort Needham, a third of a mile up the hill.

She laid on the ground, half conscious, trying to make sense of what had just happened. A sharp pain in her foot and ankle snapped her out of it. She slid her fingers down her leg to check, and bolted upright when she felt that her knee-high, lace-up leather boot was gone. The blast must have pulled it off.

She then noticed that she was soaking wet and covered in oil and soot. Although she couldn't remember it, after being blown off her feet by the shock wave, Orr almost certainly was swept up by the wave going up the hill, the same one that had sent firefighter Billy Wells up the bank.

When Barbara got up to walk home, her ankle could not bear her weight, and she collapsed on the ground. She looked down to see that she'd been burned, and her foot and ankle were banged up. After sitting there for a few minutes, wondering what to do, she decided that perhaps she could gather her strength in a few minutes and make it home.

She saw people who had been launched up the hill like her, by the air wave or the tsunami or both. Most were more injured than she, but all were coated in the same black, oily grime that now covered her.

"People were all crying," she recalled, "and saying, 'The Germans are here! The Germans are here!'"

She knew better, because she'd seen the munitions ship burning before it blew up. She tried to tell them, "It isn't the Germans! A boat exploded!" but her voice failed her, turning as silent as a dog whistle. "Nobody would have paid any attention, anyway," she said. "But everybody thought it was the Germans."

When Barbara Orr looked down the hill toward her home, all she could see was a thick, dark wall of smoke and fire. She forced herself to start moving, walking as far as she could before she had to crawl for a bit, then go back to walking. But when she was close enough to her street to realize the fire was devouring everything made of wood, she stopped, knowing there was no point in walking closer. Her family's new home was gone.

Her aunt Edna and uncle William Orr lived on Gottingen Street, not too far away, but far enough from the growing fire that Barbara thought they might be safe. But with each few feet she became more aware of her injuries, including sharp cuts on her face and arms, which stung when the salt water and oily grime seeped into them. She wiped her brow repeatedly to keep the acidic goop from getting in her eyes.

She was surrounded by other disoriented survivors, but she did not seek help. She needed all her focus to get down the hill and find her aunt and uncle's home. She relied more on instinct than evidence, since every house she passed had collapsed or disappeared, leaving only a foundation in flames.

When she got to Gottingen Street, she was relieved to see that her aunt's house was still standing. The windows had been knocked in and some of the ceilings had collapsed, but the walls were still standing, qualifying it as one of the best houses left in Richmond.

As Barbara approached, she saw her aunt and her aunt's two children, Gladys and Bill—Barbara's cousins—standing outside, looking around. They all appeared to be unharmed but muddled, worried about their husband and father, a partner at the Richmond Printing Company with Barbara's father. They expected to see him walking the few blocks back to check on them.

When Barbara's aunt saw her, she did not recognize the strange figure. "Who are you?"

"It's me, Barbara!" she cried, surprised that her aunt did not run to her immediately.

"But you can't be Barbara," Aunt Edna said, looking at Barbara's now tangled black locks. "Barbara has red hair."

When Barbara finally convinced her she was her niece, Aunt Edna asked her, "Where are your mother and the other children?"

Barbara had not been back to her home, nor to the Richmond Printing Works, and she hadn't yet talked to anyone other than her aunt. But she still replied, with complete conviction, "They're all gone. There isn't anybody left."

"Oh, that's not true," her aunt said, with no more information than Barbara had.

Aunt Edna wanted to help Barbara, but she couldn't offer much. Yes, their home was still standing, but it was filled with broken glass, some fallen beams, and piles of plaster. She needed to find her husband and children, and was reluctant to leave their home before they returned. She could do only so much for her niece, unable to find so much as a decent coat in the house for Barbara to stave off the coming cold, or a decent hand towel to clean her cuts. But looking at Barbara, she decided they had to go to Mrs. Moir's house for help.

"Come along," Aunt Edna said. "It may not be so bad there."

Aunt Edna helped Barbara make the painstakingly slow trek to see Mrs. Moir, whom they found standing in her doorway, gazing at all the destroyed homes.

"Come in," she said. "Isn't this dreadful?"

Mrs. Moir listened to their story but could not come up with anything to say to comfort Barbara. She tried to clean up Barbara's skin and cuts, but the greasy filth seemed to be embedded in Barbara's skin, and scrubbing harder risked aggravating the cuts. Mrs. Moir's gentle approach didn't finish the job.

Mrs. Moir then gave Barbara a cup of hot tea and sent her upstairs to lie down. But Barbara could not sleep, endlessly rolling over the day's traumatic events in her mind, feeling helpless and alone.

On Noble Driscoll's walk to school, he'd taken a detour toward Pier 6. When he passed Creighton's Store, the owner's son, Cam, warned him not to go any closer. The two were chatting, and then Noble was flying through the air.

The force sent him backward about a quarter of a mile. Like his friend Barbara Orr, whose pigtails he'd once dunked in ink, he thought he'd been dreaming. When he landed, he looked up to see smoke and flames and a thick haze everywhere, blurring what he thought was a full moon—but it was actually the sun, behind the black cloud of oil, gas, and debris.

He looked down to see that he was sitting on a pile of roof shingles and rubble, which had probably been someone's house, or maybe several houses. His cap was long gone, and so was his coat, which the blast had picked off clean, but Noble's body seemed to be in good shape.

When he surveyed the bleak terrain, with no people in sight and no sound, he wondered if he was the last person on earth. How would he live? What would he eat? For a thirteen-year-old boy who loved to eat, that was more than a question of survival.

Driscoll started walking. As his bearings returned, he realized that he must have been carried all the way to Duffus Street, right behind Richmond School, which had been converted into the biggest pile of rubble on the block.

When he recognized a workman from the crew that had been putting the addition on the school to accommodate the growing population, Driscoll knew he was not alone.

The man asked, "Was it the Germans?"

"I don't know," Noble said, and that was the end of the conversation—one of many oddly brief exchanges that occurred that morning. Noble set off for his home, hoping to find his family safe and sound. But when he got to where he thought their home had been, he saw that only one wall was standing, so Noble kept walking.

He soon saw his classmate Bill Swindells, in tattered clothes, covered in soot, with blood oozing down his neck. Still, Noble was glad to see that someone his age was still alive. There could be others.

"I saw your brother Lou," Swindells told Driscoll. "Look, here he comes now."

When Noble turned to look, he thought Swindells must have been mistaken. Noble thought it was some-one from Africville. But when the kid smiled, revealing his big buckteeth like white pearls on a black canvas, Noble knew it was his brother Lou.

The Driscoll brothers walked back to their address in silence. Noble held on to the slim hope that he had gone to the wrong address the first time, but they soon came upon the same scene: one wall standing, the rest gone. They were about to leave when they heard some faint sounds. They followed the murmurs behind the only remaining wall, where they found their mother, their father, and some of their siblings all huddled around the kitchen stove, trying to stay warm.

Incredibly, only Noble's little brother Gordon was

still missing. They hoped he had found refuge at a friend's house and would return home soon.

A little after 9:00 a.m., Gordon, James, and Alan Pattison had been running across Barrington Street, taking a considerable deviation from their normal route to Richmond School. When they finally got a glimpse of the burning ship, the vessel exploded.

The blast hurled them all. Like Barbara Orr and Noble Driscoll, James could not comprehend how he got from where he was—standing near the Acadia Sugar Refinery with his brothers—to where he ended up: lying on Barrington Street, trapped under heavy trolley cables, which were no longer live. James struggled to free himself but lost consciousness again. When he woke up the second time, Barrington Street was awash in water, and he was soaked, thanks to the tsunami, and covered in a thick, black soup.

After rising to his knees, James collapsed again, smashing his face on the pavement. He fought to get his feet underneath him once more, but they were still wobbly. He noticed he had a bloody nose and a shingle nail stuck in one of his hands. When he pulled it out, blood spurted, but that was easily stanched, the least of his worries.

It was stranger than any nightmare he'd ever had. Was it real? To find out, James climbed a high pile of stones nearby to get a better look at his surroundings. When he reached the peak, he saw the playing field of the Protestant Orphanage, but no orphanage. It had been flattened. But in that field, he saw a boy on the ground covered in black goo, as dark as a chimney sweep. When the boy started stirring, James noticed something flash on his wrist: a silver watch.

James and Gordon Pattison were too stunned to give each other more than a brief acknowledgment. Both boys had lost their jackets, blown away without a trace. The blast yanked off one of Gordon's laced leather boots, too, damaging his foot in the process. They were banged up and bloody, but they could both still walk without too much pain. They started searching the rubble for their little brother Alan, but they couldn't find any clues.

After the cloud dissipated, the artificial fog lifted, and the sun returned, they looked around and saw a world unlike any they had seen before. The Acadia Sugar Refinery, the tallest building in Richmond, was now a heap of concrete blocks covered in thick steel rods that looked like cheap netting. Their father worked there, so they had to wonder how he could have gotten out alive.

They decided to see if Alan had gone home, but it

was impossible to tell where their neighborhood streets had been. Along the way they came across something that looked like a huge beaver dam, which they soon realized had been someone's house. On top was a man with a horrible gash on his face, tearing at his home's broken wooden beams with his hands. Underneath, somebody was screaming. A house nearby had just caught fire, and the man knew time was running out.

When they went to help him, a soldier told them, "Get away from here. The magazine in Wellington Barracks might go up next. Go up to open ground, up that way," he said, pointing to Fort Needham on the hill. "You'll be safer."

James knew the magazine at nearby Wellington Barracks was filled with explosives. If it caught fire, the scene they had just survived could be repeated, though it was hard to imagine what additional damage was left to be done.

With Gordon limping on his bare foot, they made their way up the hill. All around them, people were walking silently over the bleak terrain, seeing but not understanding. They were too stunned to speak and vaguely nervous about a second explosion, be it from the magazine at Wellington Barracks or the Germans.

This was the moment when the instinct of human decency, which appeared to have survived the explosion, slowly broke through the fog of the survivors' uncomprehending shock. Strangers started helping strangers. On the Pattison boys' slow walk to Fort Needham Park, someone gave James a coat and a hat, and Gordon found a boot on the ground. When he stuck his foot inside, it fit well enough, but he wondered what had happened to its original owner.

Thousands of children in Halifax and Dartmouth returned to similar scenes.

Eileen Ryan, eleven, had been trapped under the wreckage at St. Joseph's School but managed to climb through the boards and plaster and walk to her home on Macara Street. She was relieved to see it still standing, but as she walked closer she could see that the windows, sashes, and frames had all been smashed to bits. Inside, her mother and younger brother huddled, laboring under the illusion that only their home had been attacked. When Eileen's three brothers returned, Mrs. Ryan looked at them tearfully and said, "Boys, our home is gone."

But the boys and Eileen had already seen far worse on their way home.

"Mother," the oldest answered, "you're lucky to have your life."

Eileen's friend and classmate Helena Duggan, also

eleven, left school and went straight to her home on Russell and Barrington. Her mother had been recovering from delivering another baby girl, while still struggling to absorb the death of her two-year-old daughter, Alma, months before. When Helena saw her mother, she had a large sliver of a mirror stuck in the side of her head. A soldier tried to remove it but couldn't, which was fortunate, because doing so might have caused Mrs. Duggan to bleed to death.

The soldiers urged the Duggans to leave their home before it burned, and led them down Russell Street. But Mrs. Duggan, still muddled, forgot that she had left her newborn daughter in the house. While walking down the street, she was having an imaginary conversation with the daughter she'd lost only months earlier. It was not until they stopped to rest on a curb that they realized they had left the newborn in the house. Someone ran back to retrieve her, only to find the house in flames. It was too late. Mrs. Duggan had lost her second daughter that year.

Across the harbor in Dartmouth, Ethel Mitchell accepted her mother's invitation to skip her usual 8:00 a.m. piano practice to sleep in after her big night with a few of the *Highflyer*'s officers.

After Mrs. Mitchell wished her daughter more sweet

dreams, she walked downstairs, but got only halfway when the floor beneath them collapsed, dropping Mrs. Mitchell about twenty feet into the basement. The roar of destruction woke Ethel. All the windows in her room had been smashed in, but her lazy start to the day had likely saved her life. Tucked snugly into her bed under a thick winter blanket, she was largely protected from the flying glass shards. Her pink dress, hanging just a few feet away, was shredded, and her cat Buttons, sleeping at the foot of her bed, had been killed.

When she got out of bed to look around, glass shards stuck into her bare feet. She ignored the pain to hurry to the staircase, but it was gone, and so was the floor beneath it. Recounting her journey later, Ethel could not remember how she had gotten down from the second floor to the ground, one of many unsolved mysteries that day. For Ethel that included the identity of her rescuer, which she never learned.

About an hour later, someone found her with a man's coat over her shoulders and large boots on her bleeding feet, sitting on a biscuit box outside a neighborhood store, and took her to her grandmother's house nearby. There she found her mother, alive and looking for help.

Jack Tappen, who had been shot through the narrow hallway of the *Middleham Castle* onto a pile of dead bodies, made it back to shore with his two fellow apprentices.

On Barrington Street, the Tappen trio came across a house that had one side blown in and was beginning to burn. Then they heard cries for help from a man and a woman at a second-floor window. When they looked closer, they saw that the woman was holding a baby, and then they heard some young men standing underneath the window, urging the couple to toss their child to them first and then jump themselves. Tappen's trio joined them.

The mother refused to let go of her child until it became clear that she had no choice. When her husband tossed the child gingerly to the young men, one of the boys caught it safely.

The woman then urged her husband to jump next. Tappen was puzzled by this reversal of chivalry, until he saw why: she was visibly pregnant, and by jumping she risked losing this child, too.

The encroaching fire provided the motivation she needed. She jumped.

The boys softened her landing. Her husband, her baby, and her unborn child were safe.

Chapter 22
The Panic

At 10:00 a.m., a young lieutenant named C. A. McLennan noticed red-hot coals scattered near Wellington Barracks, which sat on the southern edge of Richmond near the docks. The Barracks had been badly damaged by the blast and suffered plenty of casualties, but that hardly made it unique—destruction was the rule in Richmond that morning. The problem was that Wellington Barracks contained a large, well-stocked magazine, which sat perilously close to a furnace room.

McLennan grabbed a fire extinguisher and doused the embers, potentially saving thousands of lives. But the quenched coals sent great clouds of steam and smoke spiraling upward, visible for miles, prompting onlookers to assume the worst and run and for the hills, yelling at people they passed to do the same.

Lieutenant McLennan had acted wisely to avert a potential disaster, but in the process he inadvertently set off a panic among already panicked people. Soon, firemen, policemen, and soldiers were patrolling the surrounding area with megaphones to warn everyone that Wellington Barracks was going to blow up at any moment and ordering them to get to the nearest open ground, posthaste.

An hour after *Mont-Blanc* exploded, people were as obedient as they had been nonchalant an hour earlier. This time their curiosity didn't compel them to wander down to take a closer look. They immediately dropped everything—their homes, their possessions, rare photos, family heirlooms, and sometimes family members trapped under beams, bricks, and boulders—to head to the safe, open spaces of Citadel Hill and the North Commons just behind it, and as far away as Point Pleasant Park at the southern tip of Halifax.

The underwater cable between Halifax and Dartmouth had been badly damaged, probably when *Imo* landed on it. The explosion knocked down telephone lines, snapped poles like toothpicks, and destroyed the main cable lead and the 800 individual lines running from it. Communication with Halifax's North End was effectively cut off. This prevented officials from asking other cities for help, and greatly limited their ability to assess the extent of the damage, to communicate what needed to be done next, and to squash rumors when they arose—particularly the widespread belief that the Germans had attacked and were about to do so again.

What did calm people down—perhaps the only thing—was the sincere work of strangers helping strangers. Rescuers, whether professionals or amateurs, appeared by the thousands all over town, an instant army of mercy reporting for duty—unofficial and unorganized but utterly committed to providing aid to anyone who needed it. It was these spontaneous acts of generosity, courage, and selflessness that did more to reassure victims than any formal communication could have achieved. On December 6, 1917, there were no substitutes for uncommon courage and basic human decency.

Unfortunately, this vital work all over town was interrupted when officials told everyone to head for higher ground. Some grabbed what they could salvage from their collapsed, burning homes and walked away, knowing everything they owned would be gone when they returned.

Thousands of people formed a stream of speechless, roughed-up refugees trudging from the harbor to the top of the hill. Those who could walk carried those who couldn't: the sick, the injured, the very small. Many had lost all their clothes, but were often given something to wrap around themselves from strangers along the way.

Richmond's Chebucto Road, Kempt Road, and Quinpool Road "became rivers of bloody and smudged humanity hurrying westward to the safety of open fields," Raddall remembered, "and through the long afternoon hours they stood in the snow watching the smoke pall over the burning North End, waiting for a blast that never came."

The people who had been fortunate to survive with open wounds and glass embedded in their skin were all corralled up the hill. Those left behind included people pinned down in the wreckage. Many could not yell for help, including babies. But with thousands heading to higher ground, the odds of survival for all the trapped survivors went down precipitously as the fires came for them.

In this, like so many other circumstances that week, the plight of the people in Halifax closely mirrored those of their sons, brothers, husbands, and fathers overseas, where cries for help came from the wounded in no-man's-land every day, while their comrades, desperate to do something, had to wait in the trenches until the enemy snipers abandoned their posts, lest they create more victims. In both France and Halifax, survivors most vividly recalled the shattering screams of the wounded they could not reach in time to help.

The survivors climbing the hill were following orders—sensible ones, given the information available. While Lieutenant C. A. McLennan's quick action might have saved thousands of lives by preventing a second explosion, the panic that followed not only stopped what progress had just been made in the rescue effort but added to the suffering of thousands. In the fog of war, such well-intended decisions were made with grave consequences every day.

When a soldier ordered Joe Glube, the tobacco and stationery store owner, to find higher ground, the twenty-one-year-old took his bleeding mother and sister up to North Commons. When his mother realized she had left behind her new fur coat, Joe dutifully went back through the quiet, empty streets to retrieve it. But when he returned to the North Commons, so many victims had packed the park that he couldn't find his family.

While he searched for his mother and sister, the scene he'd just walked through caused him to worry about his store on Barrington Street, not far from City Hall.

He wondered if it was still standing, on fire, or being looted. At a time when competing priorities seemed to pop randomly into peoples' heads, this thought grabbed Glube's attention and compelled him to hurry back to his store.

On the way he saw other store owners gripped by the same fears, hurriedly boarding up shattered windows and doors. Glube's block happened to be far enough away from Pier 6 to have suffered minimal damage and no fires, and no one had reported seeing a looter yet.

Glube followed the lead of his business neighbors, breaking up crates and nailing the boards to the window frames. As he was completing that task, Deputy Mayor Henry Colwell appeared on the Grand Parade—a military parade square created at Halifax's founding—with a megaphone to admonish the store owners.

"What are you people doing? Do you realize there have been thousands of people killed or hurt? They're starving in the North End. We need help!"

That's all Glube needed to hear. He dropped his hammer and shouted, "Where do we report?"

"The Armories!" Colwell shouted back. "Bring transport if you have it."

Glube rushed back home, put the tires back on his secondhand Ford, took it off its blocks, and drove to the Armories. As Glube drove north, he was amazed to see that entire rows of homes had been completely wiped out. As he drove through Richmond, the stripped homes, trees, and electrical lines made it almost impossible to discern where the narrow Halifax roads had been, and he became disoriented. He passed dozens of bodies strewn across yards and roads in every imaginable position.

When he got to the Armories, volunteers who had been on the job for no more than an hour or two loaded his Ford with food, blankets, and other supplies to give to whomever needed them. On his return trips to the Armories to retrieve more supplies, Glube started picking up seriously injured victims and dropping them off at the nearest hospital or makeshift aid station, which were already popping up around town. All were quickly deluged with more patients than they could handle, with thousands more on the way.

That newfangled invention, the automobile, was suddenly in great demand. As of that morning, the snow and ice hadn't come to Halifax yet, so those who owned "a motor," as they called it, got busy taking their cars off their blocks; adding air, oil, and gas; and getting them back on the road.

Some car owners used them to speed out of town. T. J. Wallace, an optometrist, and his wife and their seven kids lived on Chebucto Road near the West Arm, which seemed a safe distance from Pier 6. But when a big chunk of metal, possibly from *Mont-Blanc,* landed in their garden, narrowly missing a few of them, Dr. Wallace decided they were leaving. When one of their sons tried to sacrifice his seat so their Newfoundland dog could have it, Dr. Wallace refused. They headed out to Tantallon, about 20 miles away, but Herring Cove Road was clogged with people who had had the same idea and were driving and walking out of town, some of them limping.

Others got their cars out of their barns, carriage houses, and garages to help survivors, many of whom would owe their lives to these amateur ambulance drivers. The entire city was now in a race against time, which could be measured in pints of blood.

When Eileen Ryan's older brother rushed home to get his shiny new 1917 Chevrolet going, his mother had to tell him he had already missed their next-door neighbor, who had come over to their house distraught because his young daughter's jugular vein had been cut and she was bleeding to death. The neighbor begged Mrs. Ryan to get the Chevrolet out to take his girl to the hospital, but no one knew how to get the car ready, let alone drive it. His daughter died in their home.

The Ryans were preparing to leave for high ground,

as they'd been instructed, when some sailors showed up at their door. If you owned a functional vehicle, word traveled quickly. When the sailors inquired if it could be driven, he assured them it was in fine shape. They asked if he could drive the wounded to the various hospitals, a request that some car owners refused because they feared the blood of the victims would ruin their upholstery. But the young Mr. Ryan, probably still thinking of the girl next door, eagerly volunteered his car and his help. His brand-new Chevrolet would never be the same. But then, nothing else would be either.

While he headed out to help, Mrs. Ryan and her four younger children grabbed a few things, including their pet parrot, which could mimic bugle calls from nearby Wellington Barracks, and started walking to the city's outskirts. After a few blocks, Mrs. Ryan's handbag felt too heavy, so she left it on a fence post. After seeing the girl next door lose her life, her handbag no longer seemed so important.

Apparently the other survivors who passed that way felt the same. When Mrs. Ryan came back a few hours later, her handbag was still hanging on the fence post, untouched.

After Charles Upham had coaxed his wounded children, Millicent and Archie, to slide down the oilcloth staircase cover, he had to execute one of the thousand acts of triage being performed throughout Halifax that day: leave his burning house behind, with his wife and three of his children in it, all presumably dead, and get his two surviving children help as fast as he could.

But when the panic struck, they had to change direction, joining a crowd walking to a field behind Dean's Nursery off Longard Road. There they watched the fires raging in their neighborhood below, and another one at the cotton factory behind them, which had quickly become an inferno.

Volunteers from St. John's Ambulance Brigade, the Salvation Army, and the Red Cross roamed the parks and open fields where survivors had gone to avoid the second explosion they'd been told was coming. The volunteers handed out food, clothing, and blankets; provided basic first aid; and tried to identify and deliver the most seriously wounded to hospitals. But, being badly outnumbered, the volunteers couldn't get to all the victims quickly enough, and some died waiting.

On this day, it only made sense that a prison built to keep criminals in became one of the safest places for innocent victims to keep danger out. A savior emerged in the form of George Grant, the governor of Rockhead Prison on Gottingen Street near Bedford Basin, where the day before the prisoners had been breaking rocks to make gravel and stone chips for roads. After the explosion, the inmates took advantage of the confusion and escaped.

Instead of trying to chase down the escapees, Grant realized that their departure presented an opportunity. With the weather turning colder by the hour, and so many people with serious injuries in need of proper clothing, shelter, and first aid, Grant opened his prison to some seventy survivors, many of them fellow parishioners at Grove Presbyterian Church.

Charles Upham knew Grant, who agreed to take Archie into the prison so Charles could take Millicent to the Cogswell Street Military Hospital, where the wounded soldiers gave up their beds to the explosion victims almost as eagerly as the prisoners gave up their cells. Charles Upham's children were hurt and scared but safe enough in their new temporary homes for him to board a sleigh to search for his relatives.

Rockhead Prison's newest little inmate, Archie Upham, was comforted to find one of his aunts, Mrs. Rasley, whose family had expected to host his grandfather's funeral that day. Although her son Reg, Archie's playmate, was still missing, and two of her daughters had already gone to the hospital, one with a cut eye, Mrs. Rasley devoted herself to Archie's immediate needs. When she saw that his head wounds had produced so much blood they had glued his shirt to his back, she found clean water, soaked his shirt, and peeled it carefully off his body. In the process she discovered the source of all that blood: a serious cut on the back of his head from the glass that had shot toward him and Millicent while they played. No one had noticed how much blood Archie had lost because he had dark hair, and his head was already so black from the grunge that it was hard to see.

Aunt Rasley did her best to clean the wound, and then George Grant gave Archie some of his older son's clothes. They were much too large, but fashion was even less important at Rockhead Prison on December 6 than it had been on December 5. If you had something to cover your torso, you qualified as one of the best-dressed people in Richmond that day.

At 9:04 that morning, Mrs. Rasley's son Reg had been in the storeroom off the kitchen where Mrs. Rasley kept the jars of preserves she bottled so her family could eat fruit each winter. While Reg examined the tempting goods on each shelf, a piece of hot, heavy metal came crashing through the roof and smashed a chair a few feet away from him. He assumed it was a German shell, and that German soldiers would be busting through the

Rasleys' front door at any minute, guns blazing, looking for captives. Reg's unproven theory was confirmed in his mind when a few heavy jars of preserves shattered on the stone floor behind him. He didn't need to wait any longer for the Germans to come barging in to get him. He ran out of the house and kept running.

When he eventually slowed down, he met one of Governor Grant's sons, who told him, "Come home with me." When they ran into more of the Grant boys, they decided they should check on their aunt at her bakery on Tower Road, a few miles away. When they finally got there, Reg's considerable energy had fizzled, and he was exhausted.

Mrs. Grant asked Reg a lot of questions about his family, but, like so many dazed kids that day, he didn't have many answers. The Grants' aunt surmised enough, however, to send one of her nephews to find Reg's mother to tell her that her son was being looked after at her home. When Mrs. Grant put him to bed, Reg dropped right into a deep sleep.

Years later, he recalled that being with strangers who cared had a profound effect on him, "I wasn't afraid anymore."

Gordon Pattison, fourteen, and his brother James, thirteen, found themselves on their own—a common predicament for Halifax children that day. With nowhere to go, they joined the other "instant refugees" walking to North Commons to avoid a second explosion. On the way, a stranger gave both of them coats and James a stocking hat, which he appreciated until he discovered it was crawling with head lice. He was amazed the lice could get through all the oil and tar on his head to his scalp, but that was the least of his problems. They could only hope their younger brother, Alan, whom they had not seen since they had all been watching the ship together, had survived.

The crowds of refugees filling the parks and open fields endured almost two hours of cold, pain, and gnawing uncertainty. Shortly before noon, the Seventy-Second Battalion of Ottawa flooded the magazine at Wellington Barracks, then carried most of the ammunition to the harbor, where they dumped it. (Protecting the environment was not a priority in 1917.)

With that, officials decided the threat of a second explosion was over, and told everyone they could return to their homes—if they still had them. The survivors left the parks and fields of Halifax as slowly and silently as they had arrived, but many weren't sure where to go.

Gordon and James Pattison tried to make their way back to their home on Barrington Street, but the fires had grown so big that officials there turned them away. With few options, they headed for their grandparents' house across the Narrows on the Dartmouth side. They planned to board the *Ragus*, which shuttled Acadia employees back and forth between the refineries on both sides of the channel (*Ragus* is sugar spelled backward), but the boat never showed up.

When the captain of a government boat patrolling the harbor saw them, he told them to hop on, and dropped them off at the agency's wharf in Dartmouth. The captain might have been breaking the rules, but by then just about every societal norm had already been suspended, leaving the survivors to rely on their common sense, innate decency, and each other.

The superintendent at the dock in Dartmouth "gruffly ordered them to clear out," they recalled, which might have been because the captain had broken the rules, or because the boys were covered in black grease. The boys had to walk another mile and half along the railroad track and through the fields of the Mount Hope Lunatic Asylum to get to their grandparents' home.

It was already getting dark when their grandmother opened the door. "She could hardly believe her eyes," James recalled. She was so relieved to see them that she didn't care that they were covered in dark muck, scooping them into her arms for a big hug.

The boys had hoped to see the rest of their family at her home, but no one else was there. Their grandfather and uncles had gone to Halifax to find them, their siblings, and their parents. While their grandmother tried to clean them up, she asked them what had happened, but the still shaken boys could not tell her much, and could offer no clues as to where their parents and siblings might be.

The windows of their grandparents' house had all been smashed, but fortunately their grandfather had not yet installed the storm windows. His procrastination was rewarded when the boys found the storm windows safe in the basement and installed them, making theirs one of the few warm, dry homes in the area that night.

Their grandmother made them a hot dinner and then sent them to bed. Tired as they were, they could not fall asleep, too worried about their mother, father, brother, and sister. Hours later, their grandfather and uncles returned. Their grandfather hurried upstairs to see his grandsons, probably as much for his sake as for theirs. The boys sat up when their grandfather came in, hoping for good news, but he didn't have any to share.

They had not learned anything on their search, except that the Acadia Sugar Refinery, where their father worked as the mechanical superintendent, had been reduced to rubble.

Their grandfather explained that the sugar refinery shuttle boat, *Ragus*, had not picked them up because it had been close to *Mont-Blanc* and was ruined, her crew of five killed. It was a sobering report for the boys, who had started the day happily saying good-bye to their parents and sister at their home before walking to school with their little brother. It would end with the brothers not knowing if any of them were still alive.

Barbara Orr was grateful for Mrs. Moir's help and hospitality, but lying in her guest bed on the second floor brought Barbara no peace. Her mind raced with the day's incomprehensible events.

Outside Mrs. Moir's home, the horse-drawn Boutlier's Fish Truck came through—not to deliver Atlantic salmon on its normal route but to pick up people to take to the nearest hospital. Some of the wounded on the truck were still and quiet, while others moaned softly.

Mrs. Moir asked them to wait, then walked upstairs. When she got to the guest room door, she was afraid to wake Barbara. But when she opened the door slowly and quietly, she found Barbara wide awake, and happy to have her thoughts interrupted.

"They are taking people to hospital, dear," Mrs. Moir said. "And we think that you should be seen by a doctor as soon as possible."

Orr, still weak and confused, was relieved to have someone else make the decisions. The men from Boutlier's carried Orr to their truck, where she recognized the name on the side because the store delivered fish to the Orrs, too. It provided a little comfort to see something familiar, a slim bit of evidence that perhaps not everything had been destroyed.

When Mrs. Moir watched Barbara be loaded onto the truck, still redolent from its fish deliveries, she was close to tears. The truck made its way gingerly through the streets of Richmond, trying not to jostle its passengers while avoiding the destroyed homes and factories, the dead bodies and body parts, and the people trying to make their way through the mess, usually in shredded clothes.

Boutlier's Fish Truck dropped Barbara Orr off at Camp Hill Hospital, whose entrance was now clogged with wagons, trucks, and cars trying to deliver many times more victims than the 240 veterans the hospital had been designed to help. Because Orr was in much better shape than those around her, many of whom were near death, she waited for some time before two soldiers put her on a stretcher, carried her just inside the entrance, and set her down in a corridor surrounded by other victims, where she fell unconscious. When she awoke, the patients around her seemed unnaturally still.

"Then I realized there was something funny about the people," she said. "Most of them were dead."

Because she had been left among the lost causes, no soldiers, nurses, or doctors had bothered to come through her corridor looking for patients. When she finally saw a young orderly walking by, she called out for help. The orderly jumped, startled to hear a voice among the dead and dying.

"I'll be back in a minute," he promised her.

He returned with a helper to carry her stretcher up to a long ward filled with beds, a scarce commodity. After they helped her into one of the few still available, someone washed and treated her burned leg. But her injury was clearly not life-threatening, so the rest of her head and body, covered in greasy filth, would have to wait. She was ignored for days.

"I was shy, scared, and wouldn't like to ask," Orr recalled. "I don't think I had anything to eat. Nobody paid any attention. You just laid there and hoped that somebody would come that knew you. That's just the way you went."

When Barbara Orr awoke on Thursday morning, December 6, 1917, she had been surrounded by nine family members from three generations in a beautiful new home. The Orrs's dreams were coming true, and the future was bright.

But as the sun set on that surreal day, she had to face the possibility that her grandparents, her father, her mother, and her four sisters and brothers, including twelve-year-old Ian, who had ventured down to the docks for a closer look with Isabel, were all dead. She feared that she might have been right, after all, and she would have to make her way in the world without them. Barbara lay quietly in her narrow bed, feeling deeply alone, wondering what would happen next. Who would come for her?

At Camp Hill Hospital, Barbara Orr's heartbreaking story did not qualify as exceptional.

As great as the losses were throughout Halifax and Dartmouth, they would have been much worse had it not been for the selfless souls who stayed at their posts during the panic and beyond to help others, despite the obvious danger. It would be just as foolish to judge those who followed orders to find higher ground as it would be to forget those who ignored that command so they could help others in immediate need, such as the volunteer firemen who stayed behind to battle the flames. Hospital staff overwhelmed with incoming patients didn't budge, and the linemen working on the torn network of cables kept at it, restoring limited service by 1:00 p.m. that day, and clearing 200 lines by that night.

One of the more stirring examples came from the Children's Hospital. After receiving orders to evacuate, the superintendent, whose face had been seriously cut by flying glass, told her staff: "No one shall leave this building. It would mean the death of many of the children if they had to be moved to the Commons, and it is the duty of everyone to stand by our post, and if it should be that we are to die, we will die at our post."

After the panic, some of the Driscolls returned to their home: Noble, Al, and older brother Cliff; their five-year-old brother Art; and their mother and father, whose eye was filled with glass shards and covered with a bandage. They all huddled around the family's kitchen stove, which sat against their home's one remaining wall, trying to stay warm.

Since Noble and his younger brother Gordon had been playing in the backyard before leaving at different times for school that morning, the family held out hope that Gordon was alive. Cliff decided to go looking for him. He returned with no news of their little brother, good news about an option to get help faster, and sad news about a neighborhood friend.

He told his family the story he had heard about Vincent Coleman, who had decided to return to his post to try to stop the No. 10 coming in from Saint John. They were saddened to hear that their friend almost certainly died in the explosion, but were heartened by his bravery on such a horrible day. There were still good people out there—lots of them, it would turn out. While the stories of loss and horror traveled fastest, the competing tales of decency and bravery were beginning to catch up.

Cliff had also heard of a means for them to get help. Not long after the explosion, he'd been told, the conductor of the No. 10 train rolled slowly into Rockingham, a Halifax suburb just north of Africville. Given the rubble and the severe damage to the rails ahead, the conductor decided to stop there. He concluded that the most effective way for him to contribute was to let his passengers off there, then fill his train with the injured and homeless in Halifax and take them to other towns back up the line, around the province.

"Come on," Cliff urged. "There's room for you, too."

The family agreed. Mrs. Driscoll carried five-year-old Art while the others walked. They left their one-walled home and walked up the tracks to Rockingham, while discussing how to find Gordon.

When the Driscolls approached the train, they encountered the passengers from Saint John, New Brunswick, who'd just gotten off. They were aghast by the tattered survivors walking past them, like new recruits watching grizzled veterans emerge from the trenches and pass them without a word. If the signs of destruction in Rockingham impressed the newcomers, they were hardly noticed by survivors like the Driscolls, who knew far worse lay behind them.

The family settled into a compartment, with Art lying limp on his mother's lap, barely conscious. While Cliff helped the other passengers board the train, the two younger Driscoll children, Noble and Al, complained of hunger. Mrs. Driscoll and a neighbor on board recalled that they had Christmas cakes in sealed tins back home, and asked Cliff to fetch them before the train departed. He returned triumphant, bearing two large containers. Noble, Al, and Lou greedily gulped down the sweet cake.

At 1:30, the conductor pulled out of Rockingham for a slow, two-hour trip to Truro. He messaged the station in Truro, about 60 miles away, to tell them to expect the first train of Halifax refugees.

Major de Witt, a Wolfville doctor, had been on a train heading to Halifax for a conference when it stopped in Rockingham. Fortunately, he had his medical bag with him. When he saw the victims boarding the train in Rockingham, he decided to stay aboard and treat the most urgent cases first, including two eye removals performed on the rocking train with only his basic instruments.

At Windsor Junction, 10 miles from Halifax, another doctor and a nurse boarded: Major de Witt's father and sister. While they were getting on, Cliff Driscoll got off to look for their little brother back in Halifax.

With every Halifax facility overwhelmed with patients, the trains continued to send injured and homeless victims to Truro for medical attention and safe, secure homes to spend a few nights, while towns in Nova Scotia, New Brunswick, and beyond were sending relief trains into Halifax filled with doctors, nurses, and medical supplies.

At 3:30 p.m. that day, the Driscolls' train slowly eased into Truro. Although the medical professionals and hundreds of volunteers in Truro were ready to receive the train, nothing could prepare them for what they saw. A young Truro teacher named Josephine Bishop described the scene in a letter to her mother in Digby, Nova Scotia.

"I hardly know what or how to write my heart is so full," Bishop wrote. "Yesterday morning we were pursuing the even tenor of our ways when an awful calamity happened in our midst. School had just assembled and I was reading the Bible when two awful explosions shook the building with great force," even though it was some 60 miles from Pier 6. She is probably describing the sensation of the ground wave, followed by the air wave. "Thought at first that the Germans must have opened fire on Halifax. It proved to be as bad or even worse."

She was most affected by the children, "black as coal and horribly disfigured," including an infant who had lost both parents and both eyes. "So many little children injured, and their parents gone."

The seriously injured, including Mr. and Mrs. Driscoll and Art, were taken to the courthouse, Truro's fire hall, the civic building, and the old William Street school, which had all been prepared by the locals to serve as medical shelters while the train was coming from Halifax. The healthier survivors were invited by Truro residents to stay in their homes, including Noble and Al Driscoll, who jumped at the chance to spend a few nights at an experimental farm. Before they hopped onto the horse-driven cart to take them there, however, Noble realized that the Christmas cake he'd eaten so eagerly did not mix well with the soot and oil on his hands, face, and mouth, which the cake had probably delivered to his stomach. He had to find a bathroom to get rid of his lunch.

When they boarded the cart, the boys could not see anything in the complete darkness of their long, bumpy ride. But when they reached the house, they received a hot meal and a hot bath to get the grime off their skin and hair. The boys were pleasantly surprised to find that the house had hot water gushing from the taps—a luxury in 1917, as was the double bed with clean, white sheets that they shared.

They were too tired to talk much before falling fast asleep.

PART VI

Help

Chapter 23
No Time to Explain

The explosion instantly established Halifax as one of North America's worst disasters, putting it on a short list with the Great Chicago Fire of 1871, the Johnstown Flood of 1889, the Galveston hurricane of 1900, and the Great San Francisco Earthquake of 1906.

The Great Chicago Fire consumed 2,000 acres, destroyed some 17,500 buildings, and left a third of the city's 300,000 residents homeless, killing 300. But thanks to strong leadership and visionary planners, Chicago came back stronger than before, confirmed by the 1893 World's Fair, which attracted 21 million visitors.

In 1889 in Johnstown, Pennsylvania, several days of heavy rain brought tragedy when the dam at Lake Conemaugh finally broke, sending a gigantic wave of water and smashed houses hurtling toward the blue-collar town below, killing more than 2,000 people. When some victims sued the country club where the Carnegies, Mellons, and other local millionaires vacationed, which owned the faulty dam, the courts ruled it was "an act of God."

By the turn of the twentieth century, Galveston, Texas, had been the state's biggest city in three of its first five decades. But after a 1900 hurricane killed a third of the 38,000 residents, the deadliest natural disaster in U.S. history, Galveston never recovered, ceding its throne to the upstart Port of Houston.

Six years later, in 1906, the people of San Francisco were awakened at 5:12 a.m. when a massive earthquake ripped the earth open from Oregon to L.A., swallowing thousands of San Francisco's buildings, rupturing water pipes and gas lines, and lighting fires across the city. The quake left 200,000 homeless and 3,000 dead. In the immediate aftermath, Oakland's population doubled, but San Francisco's rebuilding program caused an economic boom and lured its residents back, and then some.

Four very different events—a fire, a flood, a hurricane, and an earthquake—created four very different disasters, with a lot in common: poor preparation usually coupled with a natural disaster, resulting in massive destruction of property, infrastructure, and human life.

How the cities emerged afterward depended almost entirely on the quality of their leadership, community spirit, and a little luck.

On that basis, Chicago and San Francisco engineered the most robust recoveries. Even Johnstown's population tripled after the flood, and didn't start its long descent until heavy industry faded and the town suffered its third major flood in 1977. But Galveston never recovered, dropping from leader to footnote. Still, it responded better than Vanport, Oregon, a city constructed to house workers for the World War II effort. It was briefly Oregon's second-largest city, with 50,000 people, until a broken dam wiped out all of its homes in 1948. The citizens never bothered to rebuild it, which is why you've probably never heard of Vanport, Oregon.

Halifax's losses of land, property, and lives put it squarely in the middle of this pack. Its disaster was entirely man-made, but its fate would depend on the same factors that determined the future for its peers: leadership, community spirit, and a little bit of luck.

Survivors often suffered from shock. They had just seen their city turned inside out, their homes crushed, and their loved ones dismembered, decapitated, and blown apart. Many were convinced that the Germans had attacked them and worse was coming. But even in a city consumed by chaos and paranoia, thousands of Haligonians put aside their fears and got to work helping those who could not help themselves.

Firemen, policemen, and soldiers seemed to appear all over town to do whatever they could, from putting out fires to extracting survivors to getting them help as fast as they could. Individuals like Joe Glube and businesses like Boutlier's Fish Truck put their cars and horse-drawn carts to use picking up victims to take them to hospitals. Packed as they were, they usually represented the victims' best chance.

With the phones and cables down, hospitals could not contact their doctors and nurses. But the medical professionals didn't need to be called to know they were urgently needed. They packed their medical bags with all the supplies they had, walked down to the nearest hospital, and offered their help unconditionally—then started the toughest, longest, and most important shifts of their lives.

Within hours of the explosion, amid burning buildings, broken water mains, and gas pipes, and the nauseating smell of smoldering human flesh, the all-female Halifax Red Cross fanned out to tend to the wounded, whom they found strewn about every city block.

In a town suddenly facing severely limited resources,

View of Halifax and its harbor as it would have looked on the morning of December 6, 1917. (*Library of Congress*)

The North Halifax neighborhood of Richmond before the blast. "Here dwelt the artisan, the railroad man, the independent man of moderate means, the home maker, the man of enterprise building the city's newer part." (*Nova Scotia Archives*)

After launching a promising career with Imperial Oil in Montreal, Joseph Barss (*center*) quit to join the legendary Princess Patricia Canadian Light Infantry and fight in the Great War—against his parents' wishes. (*Barss family*)

The Battle of Mont Sorrel, June 1916, where Barss was wounded while manning a machine gun. On June 2, during some of the war's worst fighting, a German shell exploded near Barss, injuring his spine, paralyzing his foot, and giving him shell shock. (*Archives Canada*)

Barss recovering from his wounds at a military hospital, where he spent six months in a body cast. His doctors said he would never walk without a cane again, but he was determined to prove them wrong. (*Barss family*)

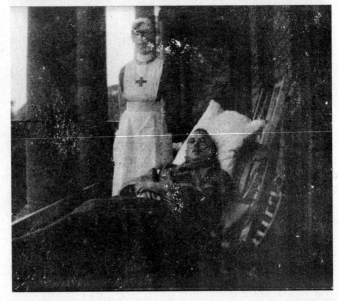

Barbara Orr's family had just moved into a new home. When she saw *Mont-Blanc* burning, she knew, "Something awful is going to happen." (*Barbara Orr and Janet Kitz*)

ABOVE: On their walk to school, James and Gordon Pattison took a detour to Pier 6 to watch *Mont-Blanc* burn. After the blast, they couldn't find their younger brother. (*James Pattison and Barbara Orr*)

After the collision between *Mont-Blanc* and *Imo*, train dispatcher Vincent Coleman returned to his post to send an urgent telegraph: "Hold up the train. Ammunition ship afire in harbour . . . will explode. Guess this will be my last message. Good-bye, boys." (*PANS*)

The only thing Noble Driscoll liked more than going to the movies was watching the endless parade of warships go past their home in Richmond. The explosion threw him back about a quarter-mile. Driscoll is front row, center, in this class photo. (*Maritime Museum of the Atlantic*)

Undated photos of the French freighter *Mont-Blanc,* which was old, poorly maintained, and slow by the time it was pressed into service during the war. In November 1917, in Gravesend Bay, New York, it loaded six million pounds of high explosives to deliver to the trenches across the Atlantic. (*Alain Croce; MMA*)

BELOW: Crewmen of *Mont-Blanc* in detention after the blast. (*MMA*)

ABOVE LEFT: As the Chief Examining Officer of Halifax Harbour, F. Evan Wyatt warned, "It is not possible to regulate the traffic in the harbor, and it is submitted that I cannot in this regard accept the responsibility for any accident occurring." (*Original photograph provided by Janet Maybee and the Mackey family*)

Francis Mackey, forty-five, could earn $1,000 a month as one of Halifax's fourteen harbor pilots. He had a spotless twenty-four-year record until he boarded *Mont-Blanc.* (*Courtesy of Joel Zemel*)

The Great Halifax Explosion, as captured by Royal Navy Lt. Victor Magnus.
(*Ann Foreman*)

At 9:04:35 a.m., the explosives on *Mont-Blanc* finally erupted. The center shot up to 9,000 degrees Fahrenheit, and shot outward at 3,400 mph, creating a mushroom cloud that could be seen for miles. (*NSA*)

Contemporary map of the explosion's epicenter. (*Royal Society of Canada*)

The harbor minutes after the blast, while smoke still hung in the air. (*NSA*)

SS *Imo*, the Belgian relief vessel that collided with *Mont-Blanc*, setting in motion the explosion. The blast created a ground wave, an air wave, and a 35-foot tsunami that sent the 5,000-ton *Imo* across the Narrows, where it beached in the shallows of Dartmouth. (*MMA*)

The explosion wiped out 325 acres in one-fifteenth of a second, obliterating the Richmond neighborhood and leaving 25,000 people—almost half the city—homeless. (*City of Toronto Archives*)

Panoramic view of the destruction. (*NSA*)

While *Mont-Blanc* burned, Richmond School Principal Huggins let his eleven-year-old daughter Merle go ahead to the school. A few minutes later, the building was demolished. (*MMA*)

"I saw some terrible scenes of desolation and ruin at the [Western] Front," Barss said, "but never, even in that old hard-hammered City of Ypres, did I ever see anything so absolutely complete." (*City of Toronto Archives*)

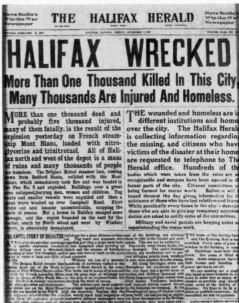

Headlines of December 7, 1917.

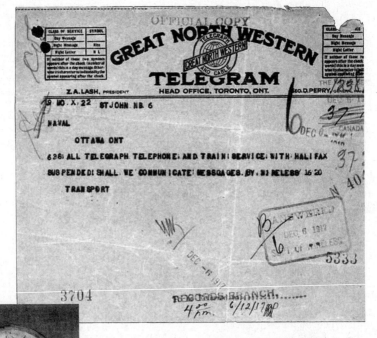

ABOVE: December 6 telegram noting loss of communication with Halifax. (*Library and Archives Canada*)

A local clock that forever stopped at the moment of the blast. (*MMA*)

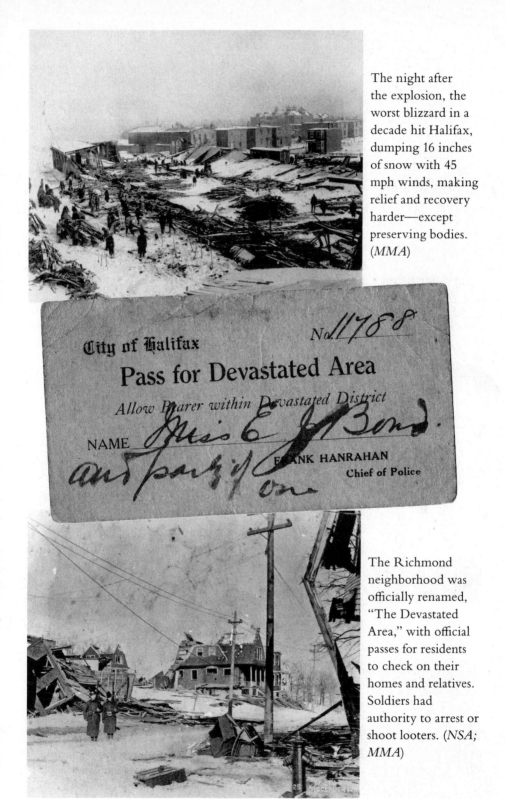

The night after the explosion, the worst blizzard in a decade hit Halifax, dumping 16 inches of snow with 45 mph winds, making relief and recovery harder—except preserving bodies. (*MMA*)

City of Halifax
No. 11788

Pass for Devastated Area

Allow Bearer within Devastated District

NAME *Miss E. J. Bond.*
and party of one

FRANK HANRAHAN
Chief of Police

The Richmond neighborhood was officially renamed, "The Devastated Area," with official passes for residents to check on their homes and relatives. Soldiers had authority to arrest or shoot looters. (*NSA; MMA*)

Officials decided to bury ninety-five unidentified bodies at a mass funeral for December 17, 1917—the first of many. (*NSA*)

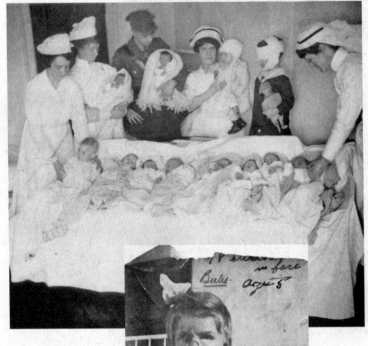

The explosion created thousands of orphans, many wounded themselves. Families from around the world offered new homes. (*MMA*)

A young survivor of the blast.

Medical relief workers, likely including some from the Harvard medical team, upon their arrival into Halifax. (*International Film Service/NSA*)

About an hour after the blast, word spread that another explosion was coming (either from the explosives in Wellington Barracks, or the Germans), sending thousands of victims to North Commons. The threat was false, but the panic was real, and cost more lives. (*Canadian Red Cross*)

After the support from Massachusetts, the city of Halifax passed a formal resolution to thank the state.

Boston doctors stand in front of Bellevue, which they converted to a hospital within hours. Canadian Premier Robert Borden exclaimed, "The hospital is a triumph of organization ability!" (*NSA*)

Within two hours, Massachusetts Governor Samuel W. McCall (in bowler hat) telegrammed Halifax: "Massachusetts ready to go the limit." They gave doctors, nurses, money, even housing— and named it for him. (*NSA*)

A 1919 poster proclaimed, "As though over night . . . A new city has risen out of the ashes of the old. We rub our eyes and look again—but the vision does not fade." (*NSA*)

After witnessing so much tragedy, Barss decided to become a doctor. While in medical school, he married Helen Kolb and started the University of Michigan's hockey program. (*Lora Durkee/T. J. Garske*)

LEFT: The Halifax Memorial Explosion Bell Tower. RIGHT: Barbara Orr had her parents' and siblings' names engraved on a bell. When they dedicated the church, Barbara was asked to play the bells, but was afraid to make a mistake. She played anyway—and it was beautiful. (*Dennis Jarvis; MMA*)

A view of Halifax and its harbor today. (*Tony Webster*)

including doctors, nurses, hospital beds, and drugs like anesthesia, the entire city, from the soldiers to the surgeons, was now practicing triage. They had to make thousands of snap decisions about who needed help the most, who could wait, and who was in such bad shape that saving them would cost the lives of five others who required less extraordinary measures. The wartime rules of triage applied here: comfort for the helpless, care for those who might pull through. If a patient was between these two states, managing to just hang on, they were probably on their own. If they endured long enough, they might get the help they needed to survive. If they didn't, their death only confirmed that the medical staff had made the correct, if difficult, decision to tend to others. Under normal circumstances the severely hurt victim would be saved, but "normal" had left Halifax at 9:04 that morning.

The caregivers naturally emphasized urgency over organization. With thousands in desperate need of immediate help just to make it through the day, doctors, nurses, and others frequently failed to record where their patients were when they had been injured, what wounds they had suffered, where they lived, or even their names. When a soldier found a woman bleeding to death in her blown-out home, it made no sense to wait for her husband to return from the factory to tell him where his wife had gone. Even if her husband was still alive, where, exactly, would the soldier leave the note? Just about everyone wanting to help had to figure out what to do for themselves.

Likewise, when a solider rushed a grandfather to a local hospital, or a police officer picked up a mother with glass in her head, or a fireman rescued a baby from a burning house, tracking the patients' journeys seemed like a truly trivial pursuit. But this essential expedience would help explain why hundreds of victims went unidentified, making it much more difficult for family members to find their loved ones in the days that followed.

None of this kept common citizens from performing heroic deeds all over Halifax and Dartmouth, deeds that seemed to multiply as the hours grew. The habit of extraordinary effort from ordinary people took root and proved contagious. Watching a neighbor rip through a wall to rescue another neighbor or a stranger find the strength to pull a timber off a factory worker he heard screaming as he walked by seemed to inspire others to test their own limits. What the resilient Haligonians did best was simple but hard: they kept going.

Before the Americans had declared war the previous spring, Boston had started preparing for it. On February 10, 1917, two months before the country officially joined the conflict, Massachusetts formed the nation's first Committee on Public Safety, designed to react to disasters and even anticipate them. Led by Governor Samuel W. McCall, the committee included leaders from a cross-section of Boston society: government officials, bankers, and the nation's biggest shoe manufacturer, Henry B. Endicott, whom McCall had tapped to chair the committee, which sought to ensure that the people of Massachusetts would retain their way of life despite the inevitable drain of the Great War, even if they were struck with a catastrophe at home. This meant setting aside resources and preparing skilled professionals in transportation, medicine, agriculture, housing, and accounting to respond to whatever came their way. Remarkably, Governor McCall managed to do all this without raising taxes through private donations of money, goods, and services, particularly free labor.

Boston was way ahead of its peers, while Halifax was like most cities: unprepared to perform the city's basic duties during an emergency. Because Halifax's leaders had never made any emergency plans, they would have to make them up—just as soon as they figured out where everyone was. That Thursday morning, Deputy Mayor Henry Colwell, president of a local men's clothing company, was walking to his day job when the shock wave knocked him off his feet. When he got up, unhurt, he remembered that Mayor Peter Martin was out of town, so Colwell was now the man in charge.

Where Boston had a governor preparing it for the worst in advance of the war with the full cooperation of the city's leaders, Halifax had a glorified clothes salesman who didn't realize he was in charge until the explosion bounced him onto his backside. At that moment, you might have predicted Halifax was less likely to rise from the ashes like San Francisco than fall hopelessly behind like Galveston.

Colwell walked straight to City Hall, where he saw the wind running through broken windows and sending legislative papers flying everywhere, and barely a soul inside because they had gone home to check on their families. When Colwell found Chief of Police Frank Hanrahan, the police chief told him Fire Chief Condon and his crew had been all died at the scene of the explosion, the *Patricia* had been destroyed, and Richmond had been reduced to ruins, with fires burning everywhere.

Colwell had to make some big decisions with little information or experience to draw on, and he had to make them fast.

Shortly after the explosion, word started spreading

that a winter storm was coming up the coast from North Carolina to Halifax. Colwell and Hanrahan headed out to visit the military headquarters a few blocks away to meet with Colonel W. E. Thompson about two urgent concerns: heating and housing. Thompson offered to have his men set up a "tent village" on North Commons with mattresses, blankets, and soldiers to help the victims and protect the area. Satisfied, Colwell and Hanrahan headed back to City Hall.

As they approached the steps with a thousand thoughts racing through their minds, a stranger approached them to ask if he could be of assistance and handed Colwell his business card: W. A. DUFF, ASSISTANT CHIEF ENGINEER, CANADIAN GOVERNMENT RAILWAYS.

Yes, Colwell thought, he could. Colwell asked Duff to follow them upstairs, while Duff shared what he had already seen that morning. After the explosion, he had left his room at the Queen Hotel, borrowed a car, and drove to North Street Station to inspect the Canadian Government Railways (CGR) property. The station was the gem in Richmond's crown, a gorgeous building with a glass dome. But the explosion had ripped the roof open like a can of sardines. The farther north Duff traveled, the worse the city looked.

Desperate to do something, Duff picked up as many

wounded as he could, drove them to area hospitals, and then went back for more, until he realized he could never help more than a dozen or two victims at the most—facing the day's common dilemma between the most urgent and the most important. Duff concluded he could help thousands if he could get word to the outside world about what had happened.

Because all lines were down in Halifax, Duff drove to Rockingham, where he cabled his general manager in Moncton, New Brunswick, to tell him the extent of the damage and of the urgent need for medical assistance and relief supplies.

Hearing Duff's descriptions of the damage, Colwell exclaimed, "For God's sake! Send out additional messages to the different towns of Nova Scotia and New Brunswick asking for further relief. And sign them, 'The Mayor of Halifax.' "

The part-time politician had quickly assumed full power. Someone had to.

Unbeknownst to them, word of the disaster was already getting out, thanks to a few folks taking the initiative. George Graham, the general manager of Dominion Atlantic Railway (DAR), also happened to be in town the night before. While he and his daughter were eating breakfast in his private railcar at the North Street Station, their car suddenly rocked. They went outside to see 400 ruined railroad cars—crushed, tipped over, on fire. When Graham's attempt to send a telegram from the Halifax office failed, he walked to Rockingham, counting twenty-five dead employees en route.

In Rockingham, Graham sent a telegram to Kentville, Nova Scotia, asking for a relief train of doctors, nurses, medical supplies, and forty-five DAR trackmen and bridge builders to repair the railway lines. Graham wrote, "Organize a relief train and send word to Wolfville and Windsor to round up all doctors, nurses, and Red Cross supplies possible to obtain. No time to explain details but list of casualties is enormous."

These messages confirmed the buzz that had started when Vincent Coleman got his urgent telegram out from the railyard dispatch office at 8:49, just four minutes after the collision and fifteen minutes before the explosion. It turned out that his telegram to Rockingham arrived after the No. 10 express train from Saint John had already left the station, but the train had not yet reached Richmond's North Street Station when the *Mont-Blanc* blew up. Nothing lost. But crucially, Coleman's telegram got through, and was the only one to get out prior to Halifax's lines going down at 9:04 a.m. His message sparked a series of telegrams that had spread throughout Nova Scotia and New Brunswick by 9:26 a.m., then reached Montreal (9:50), Boston (10:13), New York (10:27), and Ottawa (10:37).

It's worth noting that the first round of missives did not include the American government in Washington, D.C. The Americans might have been allies on paper for the last few months of their 141-year history, but that didn't make the American government something the Haligonians would think to call in their hour of need.

The information passed down to the cities was typically incomplete and inaccurate, stating that the explosion had occurred anywhere from 8:00 a.m. to 9:30 a.m. and might be the result of a bomb, with the damage grossly underestimated. "It is believed a number of people near the scene were either killed or injured," one message said, "including several telegraph employees."

But all these cities knew that something horrible had happened in Halifax and the town would need help. This early start was crucial, because Halifax could not get its lines restored to get another telegram off until 12:26 p.m., more than three and a half hours after Coleman's missive, and they had to send it to Havana, Cuba, which forwarded the message to the American Red Cross in Washington, which sent it on to its office in Boston—which already knew about it.

While Colwell was urging Duff to send out more telegrams, a soldier burst in to tell them Wellington Barracks was about to explode. They had no reason not to believe him, and headed toward Point Pleasant Park on the southern tip of Halifax.

With each city block Colwell could see just how bad the situation was, with so many victims bleeding from their faces and hands, and others being hauled in wheelbarrows by parents and children. When Colwell had seen enough, he stopped short, grabbed Hanrahan, and convinced him they were duty-bound to return to City Hall and get to work, even if there might be a second explosion. Hanrahan readily agreed. Along the way they gathered other city officials and civic leaders and brought them all back to City Hall.

There, at 11:30 a.m., they called the first meeting of the Halifax Relief Committee to order. They didn't waste any time standing on ceremony. The impromptu body included the chief of police, the city clerk, and about twenty city leaders of various sorts, some of whom had instinctively gone to City Hall to see what they could do without being asked. Colwell and his leadership team quickly formed subcommittees to address every critical need, from transportation, emergency shelter, food, and finance to mortuary. Then they appointed well-known, capable leaders and assistants to run each committee and outlined their immediate tasks.

The Food Committee, for example, opened grocery warehouses in Halifax and Dartmouth. Rotary Club members and volunteers packed boxes with bread, butter, tea, baked beans, sugar, condensed milk (which wouldn't spoil), and precooked meat and fish, because they correctly assumed many victims would not have a working stove. They delivered these boxes to any places housing refugees and any homes with people in them.

The leaders leveraged their strengths—a newfound civic spirit and a generally hardworking, selfless, and honorable citizenry—to cover their weaknesses, particularly a lack of organization and preparation, to create in minutes a skeletal version of what Boston had taken months to build. As one relief worker said, "Quick decision at the risk of occasional error was preferable, in the first hours, to extended deliberation and discussion."

After agreeing to meet again at 3:00 p.m., they adjourned the meeting at 12:15—just forty-five minutes after convening it— fanned out across the city, and got to work. For a government that hadn't bothered to develop any plans for disaster relief in the three and a half years since the war had started, it was catching up fast. It was a business case study in how to put egos, titles, and territoral battles aside to work for the greater good. Never had so much work been done in City Hall so quickly.

Most of these committees capitalized on the one advantage Halifax had over most North American cities: it had been mobilized for war, and was the temporary home to five thousand sailors and soldiers. Hundreds of them were supposed to ship out that day, but those orders were now delayed so they could stay and help.

Colwell's team granted military and naval forces complete emergency powers, allowing them to act as police, rescue workers, guards, and transport controllers. That afternoon, the soldiers secured the Richmond neighborhood, which they officially renamed "the Devastated Area." Residents who needed to check on their homes and retrieve what they could were issued official passes to the Devastated Area, which had to be shown or they would be arrested for trespassing. Those guarding the Devastated Area were given the authority to arrest looters, or even shoot them.

Assistance soon started coming in from other sources, too. In Dartmouth, Colonel Ralph B. Simmonds, a partner in Jas Simmonds Ltd., a large hardware firm, went to military headquarters at Spring Garden Road in the center of Halifax and offered his services. They asked him for supplies. By 11:00 a.m., Simmonds had equipped a hundred men with shovels, axes, saws, and ladders from his store, and sent them by boat with orders to clear a passage through the rubble on Barrington Street, a major artery.

Supervising this work, Colonel Simmonds recognized another need that wouldn't have occurred to him if he hadn't been on the scene. He sent a messenger back to his company to get all the three-by-five index cards they had to record where each article or corpse had been found and tie the label to the object or the body itself. They tagged the corpses and piled them on the side of the road three high until they could figure out where to move them.

But due to Halifax's lack of preparation, civic institutions were immediately overwhelmed by the tasks in front of them. In 1917, the Halifax Police Department consisted of a chief, a detective, eight sergeants, and twenty-nine officers, plus eight temporary men who had been hired to help with the wartime surge in population, soldiers, and criminal activity. This staff hadn't stamped out crime in the city—witness the profits bootleggers and brothels were enjoying—and it wasn't expected to. Cracking down on the evils along "Knock

NO TIME TO EXPLAIN · 351

'em Down Alley" would require diverting resources the city and nation needed to spend on getting soldiers and supplies from North America to Europe. But while the police department hadn't made Halifax heaven on earth, it was doing a decent job keeping the city safe for the many constituencies that called it home.

Likewise, the Halifax Fire Department had been hiring only part-timers since 1894, but the city had suffered few major fires during the intervening twenty-three years, even with the extra pressure of the Great War. The explosion, however, inflicted such heavy losses that the department's presence was barely felt in the aftermath.

Colonel Thompson and his staff were trying to figure out how to come up with enough guards to secure the city when he received a knock on his door. Two American naval officers, Captain Stanford E. Moses of the USS *Von Steuben*, which had taken minor damage when the steamship *Northwind* drifted into it, and Captain Howard Symington of the USS *Tacoma*, which had felt the concussion 52 miles off Halifax and returned to port, asked, "Is there anything we can do?"

It was no time for prideful stoicism. On behalf of Halifax, Colonel Thompson had to speak up. "Can you give me any men to patrol the streets?"

"Any number?"

"Can you give me two hundred fifty?"

"Yes," they said, without hesitation. Almost as fast, the "efficient Americans" produced the required number of bluejackets and Marines to monitor Halifax's streets and shore, allowing the Canadian troops to get some sleep.

"This thoughtful consideration on the part of the American officers is characteristic of the people they represented," Halifax historian Blair Beed writes, "and was manifested in a thousand ways by the measures of relief which they put in operation later."

No matter how well-prepared a city was, having one-sixth of the population wounded in an instant would strain any health system.

Between Halifax and Dartmouth there were four public hospitals: the Victoria General, with 175 beds, was already at capacity before the explosion; the Nova Scotia Hospital for Infectious Diseases had 200 beds, but was set up for a very specific mission; the Children's Hospital; and another small facility for infectious diseases on Gottingen Street. The city was also home to a few military hospitals—Camp Hill Hospital, with 240 beds; another on Cogswell Street with 150 beds; and Pine Hill Military Convalescent Home near Pier 2, where Barss had recovered in one of the 125 beds near the South End—plus seven small, privately run facilities, the largest of which was the Halifax Infirmary with a mere 30 beds.

In all, the two cities had about a tenth of what was needed to handle the 9,000 people who'd been seriously wounded by the explosion. The situation was actually worse than that, because most of those beds were already in use, mostly by wounded veterans. To make the best of this horrible situation, Haligonians would have to be resourceful, generous, brave—and a little lucky.

That week, Ernest Barss had been recuperating at his parents' home in Wolfville, a slow and painful process consisting mainly of willpower and grit—and precious little progress, if any, with his left leg and his shell shock–induced nervousness, insomnia, and hand tremors. He was pushing himself to get better, but he had every reason to doubt that he ever would. He had continued to work for the war effort while wondering what he could do with his life. And then he received a call.

George Graham's long walk to Rockingham, where he sent a telegram out to the rest of the province asking for urgent medical help, got quick results. Less than two hours after the explosion, a Wolfville physician named Dr. Elliott asked Barss, whom he knew had learned basic first aid overseas, to join him on the train to Halifax. All Elliott knew was what Graham's cable had told him, "Simply that there had been an explosion and part of the city had been wrecked and was in flames," Barss recalled. "Of course we thought it greatly exaggerated, but when about half an hour later an urgent call came for doctors and nurses we began to think there must be something in it."

Barss was being recruited to return to a war zone—not to fight this time, but to help. Despite his infirmity and shell-shock symptoms, all of which could be aggravated by this demanding mission, once again Barss didn't hesitate to answer the call to duty.

"A special train was made up and left about noon," Barss said. "I just had ten minutes [to pack a bag], but I made it."

If Barss's outlook had changed dramatically during his first trip to the trenches, slowly turning his optimistic bravado into fatalistic defeatism, this second call would transform his life once again.

Chapter 24
Ready to Go the Limit

At 10:13 a.m., Boston received a telegram about the tragedy in Halifax.

Of all the cities that received telegrams about Halifax's plight, Boston was probably the most unpredictable. Halifax is about equidistant from Montreal and Boston by train, but twice as close to Boston by sea. So it wasn't a question of whether the closest major city could help Halifax, but whether Boston would.

On the one hand, Halifax had fought for or supported the opposite side of every battle Bostonians had ever waged, starting with the American Revolutionary War—the very conflict that sent 30,000 United Empire Loyalists fleeing New York and New England to Halifax in the first place, forming a big part of the foundation of Halifax's current population. One of

Nova Scotia's favorite sons, Joseph Barss Jr., gained his status by capturing, sinking, or burning dozens New England ships in the War of 1812, while Dr. William Johnston Almon and Jock Fleming risked life and limb sneaking a Confederate ship past Union forces under cover of darkness.

For the Bostonians' part, when U.S. congressmen were openly advocating annexing Canada just six years earlier, Massachusetts's representatives didn't make a peep of protest. They had even supported the idea themselves more than once over the years. And there was the simple matter of identity: this was Halifax, Nova Scotia, not Providence, Rhode Island; Canadians, still British subjects, not fellow Americans.

But the bonds between these two shipping towns went even deeper. They had more in common with each other than either had with the cities to the west. Boston was home to thousands of Halifax cousins, who still visited, and transplants like James Earnest McLaughlin, the architect of Fenway Park. It certainly didn't hurt that, as of April 1917, the United States and Canada were officially allies in war for the first time in their long histories. That by itself probably didn't compel Boston to action—Russia was also an ally in the Great War, after all—but it removed one more obstacle. Plus, Boston had something no one else had: a

Committee on Public Safety. Boston had prepared for something like this, and now had an opportunity to show it.

The telegram from Halifax was quickly forwarded to Henry B. Endicott, the shoe magnate who chaired the Massachusetts Relief Commission. He promptly paid a visit to Governor McCall at the State House at about 11:00 a.m. Given the telegram's scant information, neither man could be sure what had happened or what was needed, but they wasted no time firing off a telegram to the mayor of Halifax: "Understand your city in danger from explosion and conflagration. Reports only fragmentary. Massachusetts ready to go the limit in rendering every assistance you may be in need of. Wire me immediately."

While waiting for a response, Governor McCall called a meeting of his recently formed Committee on Public Safety for 2:30 that afternoon, then made the short trip down from Boston's golden-domed State House past the expansive Boston Commons to convene a "town hall" meeting. There, a hundred leaders from across the state formed the Massachusetts-Halifax Relief Committee.

After confirming that Halifax had not replied to the governor's first telegram, and that no one in Washington had any information either, the committee decided to take action anyway, organizing a relief train to leave that evening. Governor McCall sent the following message by wireless: "Since sending my telegram this morning offering unlimited assistance, an important meeting of citizens has been held and Massachusetts stands ready to offer aid in any way you can avail yourself of it. We are prepared to send forward immediately a special train with surgeons, nurses and other medical assistance, but await advices from you."

When Governor McCall received no response to that message either, he sent another: "Realizing time is of the utmost importance we have not waited for your answer but have dispatched the train. —Samuel W. McCall, Governor of the Commonwealth of Massachusetts."

To lead Boston's relief effort in Halifax, McCall tapped Abraham C. Ratshesky, officially listed as A. C. in print, but called "Cap" in conversation. Born in Boston to Jewish immigrants in 1866, he founded the United States Trust Company thirty years later to serve the immigrants other banks often turned away. His bank succeeded, allowing Cap to give the Boston chapter of the American Red Cross its first headquarters, mount a campaign to save "Old Ironsides"—the USS *Constitution*—devote his time to the war effort after the United States entered that spring, and serve as the vice president of the Massachusetts Public Safety Committee.

On Thursday, December 6, at Governor McCall's direction, Cap Ratshesky assembled a relief train consisting of two Pullmans, a baggage car, and a buffet car. They were filled with boxes upon boxes of medical supplies; eleven surgeons and doctors, an ophthalmologist and an anesthetist; ten nurses; six American Red Cross representatives, each with a different specialty; four leaders of different railroads; and five reporters from the Associated Press and four Boston papers: the *Globe*, the *American*, the *Herald*, and the *Post*.

The reporters were usually the least-noted members of the contingent, but in some ways they were the most important. In addition to getting complete access to a major international story, these reporters had a couple of crucial advantages. Unlike covering wartime stories in the United States, which were closely watched by military censors, in Canada they could write freely to a public hungry for authentic war stories. At the same time, because it was Halifax, a city close to Boston in almost every way, the reporters knew their subject, and knew their audience would care about it, too. In the process, they had the chance to provide a vital service: reporting on the true severity of the situation in Halifax and publishing it across North America.

The relief train pulled out of Boston a little after 10:00 that night, some thirteen hours after *Mont-Blanc* exploded—an impressive turnaround time for a committee that had not yet communicated with the people it was trying to help. The train had received special permission to pass all other train traffic en route to Halifax. The sooner it reached Halifax, the sooner those aboard could start helping.

The reporters wrote stories from the train, long before they arrived.

Boston Post, December 7, 1917:

BOSTON RUSHES RELIEF SPECIAL

Trainload of Physicians, Nurses, Red
Cross Workers and State Guard Officers
on Way to Halifax

By Roy Atkinson, ON BOARD RELIEF TRAIN EN
ROUTE TO HALIFAX, Dec. 6—

John F. Moors, chairman of Boston Red Cross civilian relief committee, together with colleagues, spent the first part of the journey planning to supplement organizations of relief in Halifax, especially [for the] Homeless, sick, injured, children, and rehab of victims, especially handicapped.

They still were just guessing, working with only a patchy telegram from Halifax as their guide. When the train pulled out of Boston, the people on the Massachusetts-Halifax Relief Committee thought they might be overdoing it with four train cars packed with medical professionals and supplies. But when the Boston party arrived in Saint John, New Brunswick, on Friday, December 7, and dozens of relief workers boarded with more stories about crushed buildings and broken windows, the Boston contingent surmised they might have underestimated the city's needs.

"The most we obtained were rumors," Cap Ratshesky said, but "the more we obtained the worse they sounded." At the next station, Ratshesky wired Boston for a trainload of building materials, particularly glass and putty.

The people already in Halifax couldn't afford to wait. Once the Haligonians had organized their committees, they put them to work.

The Transportation Committee was authorized to secure automobiles to take the newly homeless to shelters, the injured to hospitals, and the relief workers to the damaged areas most in need. But when only twenty-five car owners volunteered to lend their autos or driving services to the committee, the leaders authorized their committee members to commandeer any car whenever they saw one or heard of one in storage.

The Emergency Shelter Committee opened an office at City Hall where people who needed shelter, or who had shelter to offer, could register so supply could be matched up with demand. Committee members toured the North End to find survivors in destroyed homes and help them find shelter elsewhere, and set up first-aid dressing stations at drugstores, shelters, and the YMCA downtown.

The Finance Committee opened a line of credit at the Bank of Nova Scotia, which was eager to help, while the Food Committee arranged for suppliers to deliver boxes of food staples to emergency shelters, hospitals, and dressing stations, and to set up a food depot at City Hall.

The Mortuary Committee would be burdened with many unenviable tasks, but the first was straightforward: instead of storing the corpses at a half dozen locations around town, which made it more difficult for soldiers to transport the bodies and record-keepers and families to find them, they needed to select a single building to house an official, temporary morgue. They quickly settled on the Chebucto Road School, which, despite its broken windows, had a lot to recommend it: it was large, it could be quickly cleared out and converted to its new purpose, and it was close to Pier 6, minimizing the transport of corpses and travel for their relatives. The committee also needed a place that could keep bodies for as long as possible, giving them the best chance of being identified.

They designated the upper floors for offices and the wide-open, cooler basement for the bodies, which they planned to lay in rows and cover with sheets. The Royal Engineers quickly fixed up the damaged school, covered its windows, and cleaned the space. As soon as people learned of the location, bodies began to pile up outside the building, stacked two and three high until morgue workers could retrieve them.

The Relief Committee also dispatched crews of volunteers to put out fires and turn off water mains, faucets, and spigots, and to pick up the dead—tagging their names, when they knew them, to the victims' wrists, or simply attaching a number when they didn't—loading them onto rudimentary flat wagons dozens at a time.

They soon learned to conduct this dispiriting job late at night so as not to offend the friends and relatives of the deceased. But because everyone could hear the horses' hooves each night, the rolling midnight morgue was a poorly kept secret, one that woke many Haligonians whose homes still lacked windows.

Chapter 25
A Steady Stream of Victims

I f the sight of the survivors on the No. 10 train pulling into Truro stunned the locals helping them off,
it was nothing compared to the shock of those who took
the train the other direction into Halifax.

Dr. Percy McGrath had graduated from Dalhousie
Medical School in May, and like so many of his classmates, he immediately signed on to serve the Crown in
the Great War. He was stationed at Camp Aldershot,
about 65 miles from Halifax and just 9 miles from Ernest Barss's hometown of Wolfville. When McGrath
heard about the explosion, he and his wife, a nurse,
gathered their equipment and all the medical supplies
they could find and boarded a relief train in Kentville
heading to Halifax. The seats were already filling with
medical personnel and track and bridge repairmen.

Word of the calamity had spread quickly throughout the province, although no one had much accurate information about it. When the train pulled into each town along the way, the people boarding the train knew progressively more about the disaster, and consequentially more fully grasped Halifax's desperation.

That included Dr. Elliott and Ernest Barss, who likely boarded the same train at the next stop in Wolfville. The conductor made the journey to Halifax—or as close as he could get to it—in record time. The relief workers got off the train in Rockingham and walked the remaining distance. It wasn't easy trekking either, especially for Barss and his cane, requiring them to navigate the wreckage until they reached the northern tip of Barrington Street, which the military had cleared with great efficiency that morning.

On Dr. McGrath's walk, he saw survivors being pulled from basements even as their houses were collapsing on them. People bumped past them carrying victims in bundles or sometimes a basket, on their way to the hospital or the morgue. A doctor walking with McGrath "muttered something about Dante's Inferno."

It's no surprise that a doctor like Percy McGrath, who had never seen trench warfare, would be astonished by the scenes in Halifax that day. But it says something that Ernest Barss, who had experienced just about everything a soldier could, was just as shocked. This carnage wasn't coming from trenches stretching for miles but from the home front, a picturesque town Barss had grown up loving, which now produced casualties at a rate that would rival Ypres, the very place Barss had been willing to take a bullet in the arm to escape.

"Of course you have read of the terrible disaster down there," Barss wrote to his uncle Andrew Townson in Rochester, New York, in a typed letter that ran to five single-spaced pages. "No reports could exaggerate the terrible damage and loss of life. We couldn't get within three miles of the city for the whole space in between was a blazing mass of ruins."

The relief workers were guided by an army officer and his men. When they passed Richmond, Barss was aghast.

"I saw some terrible scenes of desolation and ruin at the front, but never, even in that old hard-hammered City of Ypres, did I ever see anything so absolutely complete. In that entire area of over three square miles in the immediate vicinity of the explosion there was not one stick or stone standing on another. Every house and building had just crumpled up and the whole was a raging mass of flames."

Because the heat from the fires was so intense, their

army guides kept Barss, Dr. Elliott, and company moving along at a brisk pace. That wasn't easy either, thanks to the "mud about up to our knees caused by the tidal wave, which swept over everything." He didn't mention the toll such hard walking took on his damaged left foot, but he kept up without complaint.

The entire city had been placed under martial law just a few hours after the event, Barss noticed, and parties of soldiers were working everywhere among the ruins, "pulling out the dead and the almost dead, and trying to get them identified. We had to walk between long rows of hundreds and hundreds of dead. Men, women, and the most pitiful part of it all, little children. They were lying in every conceivable position, their bodies in many cases crushed or burnt out of all recognition, and all so blackened and charred that one would hardly know them for anything but heaps of charred rags. The blood was everywhere, and even when we got up to the less ruined part of the city the sidewalks and streets were strewed with it everywhere."

After Dr. Elliott and Barss got past Richmond, they were able to commandeer "a motor" to take them to City Hall, which must have been welcomed. The drive into town also gave them a better sense of the damage done.

"Practically the whole water front was wrecked,"

Barss said. "All the large new steel and concrete piers just completed recently were wrecked beyond repair. People were killed everywhere, all over the city, and there was hardly a whole ceiling or pane of glass in the city or within a radius of five miles."

A few hours later, an eye doctor named G. H. Cox boarded the first relief train from New Glasgow in northwest Nova Scotia. He described the Devastated Area as "going from one corner of hell to another."

Captain Frederick T. Tooke, an ocular surgeon from Montreal, wrote, "The sense of depression was almost unbearable. Not a sound could be heard, railway stations were not running, ours had only been the second to arrive in Halifax, electric cars had been suspended, one could not even hear a motor horn. The streets seemed empty. The silence was intolerable and Halifax at first impression seemed in fact a city of the dead."

When the various groups of relief workers reached what used to be the North Street Station and King Edward Hotel in Richmond, the guards arranged transport to City Hall, where committee members assigned doctors, nurses, and other volunteers to various hospitals, centers, and makeshift facilities of all sorts, a task that was more complicated than the committee members had expected.

When a committee leader instructed one of the volunteers to take a group of wounded to St. Mary's Hospital in Richmond, he was informed that wasn't possible. Not because of the blocked roads, the fires, or the downed wires, but because the hospital—the rooms, the beds, the doctors, and the patients—was gone, blasted away by the explosion. Another volunteer had been sent to the Canadian Infantry's North Barracks to solicit more help, only to discover that it, too, had been obliterated.

The military, civilian, and private hospitals were all swamped with patients. Wounded mothers had to bring their children with them, which added to the crowding and confusion, as did hundreds of desperate family members searching the halls for their relatives. Because the records of those admitted were either woefully incomplete or nonexistent, the only way people could find relatives was by walking slowly past each bed, trying to recognize faces that had been covered in black gunk, lacerated, severely bruised, or broken.

Most facilities were severely damaged. The explosion had cost Rockhead Hospital, which housed eighty convalescent soldiers, all its windows and many of its steam pipes. Nonetheless, by the first afternoon, the soldiers recovering there had sacrificed their beds for about ninety newly injured explosion victims.

If the facilities were pushed to their limits, so were the doctors and nurses. "I wish I could describe the scene at the hospital adequately," Halifax's Dr. Murphy wrote of Victoria General, one of the city's biggest and busiest hospitals. "The ground in front was jammed with autos, wagons and every conveyance capable of carrying a sufferer. The hallways, offices and every bit of floor space was littered with human beings suffering with all degrees and manners of wounds and injuries."

Dr. Murphy, two other doctors, and two local eye specialists operated nonstop for three days and nights, treating 375 wounded on the first day alone. Before they finished, they had received 575 victims at a hospital that had enough space and staff to handle only 200 beds.

"The predominance of facial injuries," Victoria General superintendent W. W. Kenny wrote, "rendered the scene all the more ghastly because of the freely flowing blood."

A doctor at another hospital praised the small staff of nurses, who "controlled the frenzied patients, some of whom attempted to escape and to take their lives, amidst the initial confusion following the explosion."

Able-bodied survivors set up the wounded on every flat surface they could find in the hospitals, the city buildings, and even the doctors' homes. On December 6, hundreds of emergency surgeries were performed on store counters, front porches, and dining room tables, often without anesthesia.

The YMCA was converted from the unofficial home of bootleggers into a makeshift emergency hospital within a few hours. When Dalhousie's medical students responded to the call for volunteers, some were sent to the YMCA, including fourth-year medical student Florence J. Murray, the minister's daughter from rural Nova Scotia. When the blast broke the windows at Dalhousie University 2 miles away, the medical students knew their time had come to help.

When Murray reported for duty at the YMCA, the commanding officer asked her, "Has your class had instruction in anesthesia?"

"Yes, sir," Murray replied, although years later she admitted, "There was no opportunity to say that all in the class except myself had had this training. In the army one doesn't explain. One answers questions."

Murray's answer was good enough for the C.O. "Go

to the operating room and give anesthetics," he ordered, and she did as instructed. Her first patient was six years old, which gave her pause. "Did a child require the same amount of anesthetic as an older person, or should she have a smaller dose?" she wondered. "I didn't know. I knew I should watch the eye reflexes to help judge the depth of anesthesia, but this unfortunate child had lost both eyes."

Murray simply had to wing it. "In fear and trembling," she recalled, she gave the child a smaller dosage, then watched very closely for a reaction of any sort during the operation. Fortunately, she had guessed correctly, and the patient came through nicely. She kept going with the patients that followed.

"The next morning," she said, "the commanding officer appointed me official anesthetist for the hospital."

Throwing everyone from first-aid practitioners like Ernest Barss to medical students like Florence Murray right into the mix wasn't an issue with the patients, who weren't inclined to spend much time investigating their caregivers' medical credentials.

When a volunteer at the Armories asked Joe Glube, the young tobacco shop owner who had been delivering victims to hospitals, if he could chauffeur a doctor, Phillip Gough, on house calls, he readily agreed.

When patients required more care than Dr. Gough could deliver from his medical bag, they drove them through the accumulating snow to the nearest hospital, then went back to visit the next house.

It turned out that Dr. Gough was not a medical doctor but a veterinarian, yet on that day no one complained about his work.

Murray's classmate and close friend Hector J. Pothier had also been thrust into administering anesthesia at the Victoria General Hospital. "For the following week," he recalled, "it was work around the clock, with precious little time to eat, sleep, or change clothes." But, he added, "When you face a problem yourself and you solve it yourself, it always stays more embedded in your mind. . . . The practical experience acquired due to the explosion, although so dearly paid for by the people of Halifax, was a tremendous value for studies during the remainder of the semester."

"Never did doctors, students and nurses work harder than through-out that Thursday and into the small hours of Friday morning," said Dr. George A. Murphy of Victoria General.

Camp Hill Hospital, located on the Halifax Commons where thousands had sought refuge during the panic thanks to its location near the Citadel, was the closest major facility for Richmond's victims, and the busiest.

A committee official at City Hall sent the McGraths, Elliott, and Ernest Barss to Camp Hill to help with the throng of patients, including Barbara Orr.

Finished the year before to serve convalescing soldiers, Camp Hill's entrance became choked within an hour after the explosion with every manner of vehicle, from ambulances to wheelbarrows, bringing a flood of casualties. The hospital's convalescing soldiers were quickly converted to orderlies and tasked with hauling stretchers throughout the building. In the first twenty-four hours alone, Camp Hill provided shelter, food, and medical care for more than 1,400 victims—more than five times its capacity. And yet, due to its new clientele, Dalhousie University professor Archibald MacMechan wrote, "Camp Hill will almost always be a synonym for horror."

Another doctor remarked, "You couldn't tell the living from the dead." The Camp Hill patients were like nothing the doctors had seen before, "bathed in blood and the flying dust and debris of 'the black rain' soaked their clothes and dyed the skin underneath a dark, dirty gray."

Dr. W. B. Moore of Kentville, Nova Scotia, confessed, "Many of us had seen terrible sights of human tragedies and suffering but nothing like this in the immensity of the number, and the frightful and various character of the injuries. Men, women, and children of all sorts and classes were literally packed in the ward like sardines in a box, the cots all occupied, and the floors covered so that it was difficult to step between them."

Like every other building within a few miles of Pier 6, Camp Hill's windows had been smashed. The staff draped blankets across the empty frames, which left the rooms both cold and dark.

The McGraths didn't bother waiting for someone in charge to give them orders. The day called not for obedience but initiative. Their directives came from the desperate and dying lying wherever they turned, from those quietly asking for help to others crying "Here! Come over here!" The McGraths jumped in, stanching bleeding wounds, setting broken bones, bandaging burnt skin, and stitching wounds of all kinds, which was made trickier due to the bits of wood, glass, and plaster often embedded in them, not to mention the oily soot that covered almost everyone. No amount of careful scrubbing seemed to get it off.

Stores of anesthetics throughout Halifax quickly ran low. But if the doctors, nurses, and volunteers were heroes that day, so were the patients. Almost everyone aiding the victims was struck by their remarkable fortitude, allowing the doctors to operate

without anesthesia—"unthinkable under normal circumstances"— the kind of desperate measure even
the medics at the Western Front tried to avoid. True,
many victims were still in shock, but this quiet tough-
ness continued throughout the weekend, after the initial
symptoms had usually worn off.

Dr. Murphy recalled, "There were pale faces enough,
but their eyes were dry; there were no tears. . . . The
suddenness and horror of the disaster was too great to
find expression in that way."

The depleted cache of medicine forced doctors
to decide who would get a tetanus shot. Because the
serum was also in short supply, the medics disciplined
themselves to use it only on the deepest wounds. They
guessed right: out of 9,000 patients, only two cases of
tetanus were reported.

Like most people aiding the injured that day, the
McGraths "lost all track of time and all sense of fatigue
and hunger." At about six that evening, relief trains
carrying more doctors, nurses, and volunteers arrived
from New Glasgow, about 100 miles north. Every
helping hand was a godsend—and never enough. The
McGraths stayed on.

Dr. G. H. Cox started operating in Camp Hill's
kitchen at half past six by the light of a single bulb,
with the few surgical tools he'd brought with him. He

operated until half past seven Friday morning. Thirteen hours of nonstop surgery, working as fast as he could to get to as many bleeding patients as possible. By the time Dr. Cox was relieved by Captain Frederick T. Tooke, his surgical instruments had become so dull from cutting and ripping through so much skin, muscle, tendon, and bone that "they could no longer cut."

In Halifax, Cox mended "faces torn to tatters, as if clawed by a tiger. The wounds were stuffed with plaster and dirt. Some eyes were literally bags of glass."

If seasoned surgeons were often overwhelmed by what they saw, the children at Camp Hill, whether visiting, helping, or staying, often got more than they bargained for. Helena Duggan, an eleven-year-old girl who had survived the destruction of St. Joe's in Richmond, had accompanied her father to Camp Hill so he could be treated. To pass the time she walked around the hospital, where there was plenty to see. But when she looked into a bucket on the floor and saw that it was filled with human eyes, she was done looking around.

C Company was a group of local teenage girls who volunteered to knit hats and provide other sundries for the soldiers. On December 6, they offered to help out at the hospitals until more nurses arrived. They followed surgeons around holding bowls of water containing dissolved blue tablets to disinfect surgical implements. This necessarily put them in position to watch surgeons treat glass wounds, disjointed limbs, and oozing burns. Several members of C Company became nauseated and had to leave, but one sixteen-year-old girl not only stayed but came back the next day.

Although Barss had no medical training beyond the basic first aid all soldiers received, the city was grateful for anyone who could still walk, see, and lend a hand, so he was permitted to perform tasks normally reserved for medical professionals. He threw himself into the frightful work for three days, working on only a few hours of sleep.

He told his uncle Andrew that as soon as he and Elliott arrived at Camp Hill, they "got to work—and believe me there was plenty of it to do. Poor, wounded people everywhere. On the beds, between the beds on the floor, in the corridors, on mattresses and blankets, everywhere they could find a place to put them, and still they were coming in.

"And the wounds were terrible. There was every kind I ever saw at the front, but a great majority have head wounds. Hundreds of people lost their eyes. In one of the operating rooms where they took only eye cases, the surgeon took out one hundred eyes the first day, and then handed them over to the next man to operate.

"The stench of blood was almost overpowering. Several of the trained nurses keeled over at the sights. As for me, I had seen so much of that kind of thing that it didn't bother me at all. I was assigned a trained nurse and a V.A.D. [Voluntary Aid Department nurse] to help me, and my how we worked; I dressed every kind of wound, set several fractures, and did a number of [surgeries] as well."

When Barss was relieved at four the next morning, Friday, December 7, he had completed a nonstop fourteen-hour shift. He got a few hours of sleep somewhere, then came back at 8:30 Friday morning for more. If he ever wondered whether medicine might be his calling, it would be hard to construct a more intense introductory course to find out.

For all the inhuman demands on everyone in that hospital, they all benefited from patients who insisted on waiting for others with more serious injuries to go first, and a volunteer medical staff that refused to complain about functioning at the highest levels for the longest hours without proper operating tables. Quite the opposite: there was a chorus of comments on the remarkable esprit de corps and sense of mission that defined their crews, not to mention a surprisingly high degree of calm and order throughout the facilities, amid the most chaotic days Halifax had ever seen.

Having inherited a horrible situation, the medical professionals from Halifax and beyond were making the very best of it, and very quickly.

Chapter 26
Blizzard

Friday, December 7, 1917

The sunny, balmy conditions of Wednesday night, December 5, had already given way by Thursday afternoon to more typical overcast skies, colder temperatures, and light snow. Deputy Mayor Colwell anticipated the need for more housing and heat that evening, but few expected any unusual weather that night.

The *Halifax Herald*'s "Maritime forecast" for Friday, December 7, was quite routine for the season: "Moderate westerly winds. Fair and colder." The *Amherst Daily News* predicted "North and north-west winds. Mostly cloudy and cold. Local snowfalls near the Nova Scotia coast."

Once again, Haligonians had little idea what they were in for. Severe, sustained snowstorms are rare in Nova Scotia before New Year's Day, due largely to the ocean's moderating effect. But the world once again made an exception for Halifax. Throughout Thursday, a storm that had started brewing off the Carolinas was making its way up the East Coast through a thick cloud cover, timed to land in Nova Scotia at the end of the most tragic day in the city's history.

But Colwell was surely right about the housing crisis. The explosion destroyed 1,630 buildings and damaged 12,000 more, leaving some 25,000, almost half the population of Halifax-Dartmouth, without adequate housing and dangerously exposed to the elements.

After Deputy Mayor Colwell asked Colonel W. E. Thompson for help with temporary shelter, the Engineer and Ordnance Corps outdid itself, putting up tents on the North Commons for 250 people, equipping them with canvas floors, cots, blankets, and oil stoves, and adding temporary hospital accommodations, more than enough to keep people warm through the cold night ahead, in a clean, safe environment—a rare commodity that first night.

But while the soldiers and volunteers waited for a crowd to arrive, a funny thing happened: no one showed up. Patients refused to be transferred, even from the most crowded corridors, and thousands of uninjured Haligonians opted to ride out the night in homes missing windows and walls, heating, and often plumbing, rather than spend the night in a canvas tent. After seeing granite buildings toppled like toys, Haligonians weren't too interested in swapping their heavily damaged homes for tents, no matter how much sense it made.

Thousands of survivors decided to make the best of their homes. To make just one room suitable for human habitation usually required shoveling out piles of broken glass and debris, boarding up open windows and doors—when they could get their hands on some boards—or just tacking up tarpaper, blankets, or cardboard. Stores soon ran out of those supplies, too. After doing all that, the best many residents could hope for was a cold, dark, and drafty home, but they didn't complain, frequently pointing out that others had it worse—and they knew that was true, because as soon as they were done patching up their homes, they helped neighbors who were less fortunate.

For thousands of others whose homes could not be made livable anytime soon, the best bet was to think of a relative or friend who lived far enough away to have escaped most of the explosion's wrath, but close enough to walk to, then hope they opened the door and let you in. There was no way to ask beforehand, and if it didn't work out, you had to think of someone else, and start walking.

Volunteers working for the Transportation Committee relocated 5,000 people to the homes of friends and family and to hospitals, relief centers, and temporary hostels set up in a handful of downtown buildings. This relocation effort created a new breed of hero: the emergency drivers, who worked as hard and long as the doctors and nurses. At City Hall volunteers fed them in a lunchroom that they staffed day and night.

When Thursday, December 6, 1917, came to a close, few homes contained the same people they had that morning. Many families had been split up in the confusion, and didn't know where their relatives were— or if they were still alive. People felt unanchored, and hallucinations were common. In the Devastated Area, which had been stripped of power, plumbing, and infrastructure of any kind, heat and light were provided by fires and torches.

But most of the 25,000 Haligonians who lost their homes found somewhere safe to sleep. It was a good night to rely on the kindness of strangers, who seemed particularly ready to help, and thousands did.

To the horrors of the biggest man-made disaster in the history of the world were added the caprices of Mother

Nature. That night the temperature fell more than twenty degrees, from a high of almost 40° Fahrenheit down to 16°—bone chilling on a good day, but particularly painful on this one.

Far worse was the wind and snow that came with the temperature drop, howling through open windows, burying the dead, and forcing the living to spend the night bent over their stoves, trying to stay warm enough to make it to the morning.

During that long, cold night, many of the seriously wounded, some still trapped in their homes and factories, could not endure the additional trauma and died. Premature births and stillbirths were brought on by falls, injuries, and shock. Yet in the windowless shelters and overcrowded hospitals, babies came into the world. Against all odds, the forces of life were stubbornly reasserting themselves.

When morning broke on Friday, December 7, the world had flip-flopped yet again. Thursday's hellscape, with half the city crushed and fires burning everywhere, had been covered in a sixteen-inch-thick blanket of pure white snow, freezing everything beneath it. The storm that had sneaked in the night before revealed itself to be a roaring blizzard the next day, the worst in a decade, with gale-force winds attacking the town at

40 to 45 miles per hour, snapping twigs off trees, tearing tar paper off broken windows, and knocking down what had remained tenuously standing up.

By Friday afternoon, December 7, the rescue workers who had spent the previous day navigating through boards, bricks, broken glass, and dead bodies now had to contend with heavy, damp snow that soaked their clothes, clouded their vision, and covered the roads and everything left on them in thick drifts.

When a sailor named D. G. O. Baillie saw Halifax for the first time that morning as his ship entered the harbor, he noticed that "a pall of smoke hung over the ravaged city, and infernal gloom half-hid the remaining buildings so that at first we thought the whole town had been destroyed."

They were eager to help, but their goodwill was tested when their commanding officer ordered them ashore to dig out "the innumerable bodies known to be buried in the ruins." They had no training in the very particular craft of rescue, so "at first we stumbled about aimlessly over piles of masonry and shattered timbers. The bodies were frozen stiff as wood or stone so that often the blow of an axe or shovel would slice off an arm or leg. It was a gruesome experience and more than once I saw a shipmate turn aside to be violently sick."

Their nonstop hard work was not enough to keep away the cold, which nearly cost Baillie a toe to frostbite.

The train tracks that had just been painstakingly cleared of rubble from the explosion were now smothered once again in deep drifts. The snow covered the ruined factories, the schools, and the homes, some with survivors still trapped inside. Soldiers were directed to stop removing debris and start removing snow.

In the harbor, the high winds wreaked almost as much havoc as the tsunami had, tossing ships about until their anchor lines snapped and sending them wherever the wind and waves wanted them to go. Naval crews had to leave needy victims to secure drifting vessels and remove heavy flotsam before they created yet more damage.

The weather affected the recovery mission in other ways, too, discouraging some victims from leaving their broken homes to seek medical attention, increasing the chances of them freezing in their homes and preventing rescue workers from getting to them, or even getting to their own homes for a few hours of much-needed rest.

The Transportation Committee reported that practically all the automobiles they had commandeered the day before had broken down in the storm. But the "motors" had done their job, helping to move nearly a thousand people, many of whom likely would have died if they had not been rescued in time.

The age of the horseless carriage was coming, but it hadn't arrived yet. While the horse-drawn sleighs had their own troubles getting through, they fared much better delivering warm clothing and blankets for the homeless than the cars, which could be seen abandoned on roadsides all over town.

One day after workers had restored 200 telephone lines, the blizzard knocked them out again, forcing the workers to start all over—and this time in the worst weather. Underwater cables had been broken by anchors dragging behind distressed ships. Given the bare-bones service available, the phone company asked its customers to place only urgent calls until the emergency passed, though a case could be made that all calls going out of Halifax were urgent.

An underwater cable between Halifax and Dartmouth had served as Dartmouth's lifeline to the outside world, but when workers tried to lay a new cable, the storm forced them to abandon the effort. Just a few years into the telephone age, what used to be a luxury was quickly becoming a necessity—and, in a crisis, a lifesaver.

But if the Haligonians could face the explosion and keep going, the biggest blizzard in a decade wasn't going to stop them either.

St. John's Ambulance Brigade began canvassing the hardest-hit areas district by district. The Red Cross supplied 150 Voluntary Aid Department (V.A.D.) nurses to military hospitals. The Halifax School Board mobilized teachers to help. The Halifax Relief Commission, quick to address unanticipated needs as they arose, created four more committees: Clothing, Medical Relief, Fuel, and Dartmouth Relief.

The Clothing Committee set up a system to distribute clothes and footwear out of the Green Lantern Restaurant downtown after it had been reasonably cleaned up and repaired. The volunteers there soon saw heavy two-way traffic, with as many people dropping off clothing and shoes as picking them up. The Fuel Committee delivered coal to hospitals, shelters, and homes, trying to unburden the victims from another layer of discomfort.

The Dartmouth Relief Committee received a generous gift from Imperial Oil, Ernest Barss's former employer in Montreal, which provided three bunkhouses big enough for 200 people to move into, plus trained caretakers, and $10,000. Relief workers soon set up twenty-one shelters, plus some private homes, which fed about 6,000 people in the week following the disaster.

The Food Committee added new depots across the city. By Friday afternoon, with the blizzard now delivering snow from the ocean at the rate of an inch an hour with very little visibility, volunteers drove to the North End to persuade the remaining residents there to leave their homes for shelters—not always successfully.

More than 300 servicemen searched homes for survivors, but the odds of finding anyone alive went down with each passing hour. Their role gradually shifted from rescue to recovery, the dispiriting, nightmare-inducing task of pulling dead bodies and body parts out of broken buildings.

From its inception, Halifax had been a staging area for war, backing battles on at least three continents. It sent its sons to war and saw some of them return as casualties. But the city itself had never been touched directly by it, until it was hit in the most unexpected way. While Haligonians guarded the front door, the devil snuck in the back—a shock to the system that Raddall, a Halifax teenager when the explosion hit, captured perfectly:

"Since Indian days no foe had dared attack the

town. The strength of the fleet and the fortress for six generations had made the place too formidable. Yet here was all the slaughter and destruction of a modern bombardment concentrated in a single blast; and now in the most populous part of the city the survivors lay besieged by the winter weather, not merely for this night but for many days and nights to come."

The frigid temperatures did have one unexpected benefit: the dead could be stored on pallets in the basements of destroyed buildings without embalming fluid, which was in short supply, and preserved for weeks until the deceased could be identified or buried.

Chapter 27
Lost and Found

For the many families who were missing someone, there were few alternatives to slogging through the snow from hospital to hospital—half of which hadn't existed the day before—and crowding around newspaper offices searching the long lists of the patients at each facility, the missing, and the dead.

If their relatives' names didn't turn up on any of those lists, they placed ads themselves, taking care to include any details that might help find their loved ones, and left their contact information—as incomplete as that often was, with phone numbers and even addresses effectively useless. As the days mounted, they started reading other ads, some of which were placed by good Samaritans who had found someone, usually a child, and didn't know how to help them find their home.

In this era of already limited communication, made much more onerous by the destroyed homes, the blizzard, and the downed telephone lines, journalists proved to be a tremendous asset. Reporters trudged to the hospitals and all thirty-six official shelters, plus many of the private homes that had taken in survivors, to perform the dicey and tedious work of compiling lists of survivors.

Jim Gowan, seventeen, watched his father do this work for the *Halifax Herald* and saw how difficult it was. Many survivors had been sent to surrounding towns like Truro, Amherst, and New Glasgow, which all promised to send the refugees' names as soon as possible, but that could take days. But when a reporter discovered that someone assumed missing or dead was alive, it brought great relief and joy to the family, and a bit of light to the journalist's often dark duties.

Tragedy comes quick and loud, while the small acts of decency that follow come slowly and quietly.

Gordon and James Pattison woke up on Friday, December 7, at their grandparents' home in Dartmouth, where they had trekked by foot and ferry after the explosion.

The boys finished breakfast while watching the snow come down and kept their grandmother company through the long, anxious day while their grandfather and uncle took the ferry back to Halifax to renew their search for the boys' father, mother, ten-year-old sister, Catherine, and eight-year-old brother, Alan. They bought every newspaper in Halifax that morning to look for any information on their missing relatives, and were rewarded with a notice indicating that the boys' mother was being treated at the YMCA. They immediately headed off to see her.

The listing proved accurate, which was not always the case. When they found her, they saw that one of her hands had been cut and crushed, but she was otherwise fine, and very much alive. They were disappointed to learn that she had no news about her husband; her daughter, Catherine, who'd been quarantined at home; or Alan, who'd walked toward the piers with Gordon and James.

Their grandfather placed an ad in the papers: "Pattison Allan [sic] 8 years old, missing. Pattison Catherine, 10 years old, missing. Pattison, V. J. missing, adv. R. F. Grant, Victoria Road, Dartmouth."

When Mr. Grant came home that night and told the boys their mother was alive and would be getting out soon, it gave the boys relief, and reason to believe the others might be found, too.

That same morning, Friday, December 7, the Pattisons' friends and classmates Noble and Al Driscoll woke up 60 miles away on an experimental farm in Truro. They felt lonely being separated from their parents and siblings, most of whom were being taken care of at the Truro courthouse-turned-care-facility. The boys had no way of getting information about their missing brother Gordon, whom Noble believed had left for school before him that day.

Still, it was good to be in the country on the outskirts of Truro, with a fresh blanket of snow outside their window. When Noble got up to look, Al saw that the sheets where Noble had slept had become a black, grimy mess.

"Nob!" Al shouted. "I thought I told you to get properly clean last night!"

"I did!" Noble protested. But when he looked back at his pillowcase, he was shocked to see the dark stains.

When Al sat up, Noble pointed. "Just look at your own side!"

Al looked behind him to discover his pillowcase was just as soiled as Noble's. They would have to try again.

Bertha and Ethel Bond, who had helped Reverend Swetnam rescue his daughter, were staying with distant relatives in the South End. Bertha's letter to her fiancé fighting overseas summed up the feelings of many:

"We can hardly realize what it means. So many of our friends and relatives are gone," she wrote, and North Halifax was "burnt to the level, but," she added, almost quoting Ernest Barss's letters to his parents verbatim, "we are looking at our trouble with never a waver because there are so many worse off than we are."

Dorothy Swetnam and her father, the Reverend William Swetnam, had found safe haven at a friend's home in Dartmouth. The morning after the explosion, the Reverend took the ferry back to Halifax, where he saw that Richmond's four churches had all been destroyed. Because so many of their parishioners had lost their homes, health, or lives, all four clergy spent their energies aiding their flocks, despite their own losses.

In the wake of tragedy, people are often tempted to tell the mourners "Everything happens for reason," "It will all work out for the best," or "This is all part of God's plan." Reverend Swetnam, a devoted man of the cloth, was having none of it.

"If this was the work of God," he said, "I'll tear off this clerical collar."

Swetnam found time to sift through the manse, now crushed, to salvage whatever he could bring back to Dorothy for safekeeping. While almost everything had been destroyed, somehow the Reverend found among the ruins one of Dorothy's fragile teacups, completely intact, adorned with old English letters: "Remember Me."

While family members longed to find missing loved ones, those who were injured often pined for someone to find them.

Barbara Orr lay in her bed at Camp Hill Hospital, her eyes fixed on the doorway to her ward, scanning every face that appeared there. She watched visitors come in from the cold, stomp their feet, and brush the snow from their coats, looking eager, anxious, and cautious at the same time. She examined them carefully, hoping to recognize an aunt or an uncle or any familiar face. Even after she didn't recognize them, she would continue to study them as they walked slowly between the beds and stretchers, scrutinizing every patient for a match. Usually they passed through quietly and deliberately, disappointment growing with each step. But once in a while, Orr would hear the happy outburst when someone found someone they loved, still alive.

She did not hold out much hope of seeing her parents, but one of her aunts had helped her just a couple of hours after the explosion. She had to know Barbara was alive. Of course, that aunt was now consumed with finding her missing husband, brother-in-law, and father-in-law—Barbara's father and grandfather—but perhaps her relatives would send a neighbor or friend for her.

But there she was, lying in her hospital bed with her burns, too shy and scared to ask for so much as a glass of water. As it grew dark that first Friday, with the snow showing no sign of letting up, the number of visitors dwindled, and Barbara began to wonder if anyone was looking for her. She concluded that perhaps she had been right from the start: her family was all gone, and she was not a high priority for her remaining relatives.

Barbara Orr was a mature, quietly self-confident young woman, but she was nearing her breaking point. As the second day dwindled to a close, she was on the verge of crying, of letting it all out, but she "gulped them back," and closed her eyes, hoping to get some sleep.

Barbara was unaware of it, but someone had put her name on a list: "ORR, Barbara, Kenny and Alberts Sts., Camp Hill."

In the midst of the worst tragedy in Halifax history, Haligonians were uplifted by more than a few heart-warming stories. Rescuers found hundreds of people trapped and badly injured but alive, pleading for someone to find them.

The rescuers discovered one baby who had been sleeping in his crib when the blast blew the closet door over it. The door shielded him when the ceiling collapsed moments later. When the rescuers cleared the ceiling plaster and beams off the closet door and lifted it, they found the baby as healthy as could be.

Company Sergeant Major Davies led several soldiers on a rescue mission through the Flynn block, just 200 yards from Pier 6. At about 11:00 a.m. on Friday, December 7, twenty-six hours after the explosion, Private Benjamin Henneberry thought he heard a sound coming from a house cellar.

Henneberry had more incentive to find survivors than most. He had returned from overseas before the explosion, which blew up the apartment his family rented on the Flynn block. His wife had been pinned under the collapsed structure for five hours before someone heard her cries and came to her rescue. She was now recovering in the hospital with two of their children, but five were still missing.

The devastation in Richmond was so complete that residents often couldn't be certain where their homes had been. It was not uncommon for survivors to sift through the ruins, only to discover they were going through a neighbor's wreckage, not their own. Likewise, victims could end up far from their original homes.

Thus, when Henneberry heard a baby's cry, he jumped, shouting to the others to come quickly. They rushed to help him find the source, tearing through the still-smoldering ruins until they unearthed a wood-stove, still warm, and found a twenty-three-month-old girl under the stove's ash pan. She had some burns but was very much alive. Though the combination of soot and tears made her difficult to identify, when Henneberry scooped her up in his arms, he was convinced she was his.

The little girl became an instant celebrity and a favorite at the Pine Hill Military Convalescent Home, where her sweet disposition cheered the staff.

A few days later, a woman searching for family members heard the baby girl instinctively cry out, causing the woman to turn around, stare at the girl, and then run over to her to give her a hug. The woman looked down at the tag on the cot, which said "Henneberry," and told someone at the hospital: "That is not a Henneberry child. That is a Liggins!" As the girl's aunt, she would know.

The Liggins family had rented an apartment near the Henneberrys when Mr. Liggins was called to fight overseas. On the morning of December 6, the girl's mother and four-year-old brother had gone to the window to watch *Mont-Blanc* burn. When the blast leveled their home, they were killed. But the concussion sent little Annie Liggins shooting across the kitchen and under the stove, next to the ash pan, which protected her when the house collapsed, and kept her from freezing during the blizzard.

Before Liggins's father returned to claim his daughter, the legend of "Ashpan Annie" had already spread.

Private Henneberry was not Annie Liggins's father, but he might have saved her life. Ashpan Annie's story inspired thousands to keep searching for survivors, which might have saved more lives. That the story of Ashpan Annie spread so quickly showed how thirsty all of Halifax was for some good news, and a little hope, to keep everyone going during this dark time.

The blizzard also seemed to be working against the doctors, nurses, and other volunteers who packed the four train cars from Boston, and the dozens they picked up along the way in Maine and New Brunswick.

After covering almost 500 of the trip's roughly 650 miles in less than twenty-four hours, the engine broke down in Moncton, New Brunswick, the last stop before the tracks turned to the southeast into Nova Scotia and toward Halifax. The relief workers ate their Friday-night dinner while the mechanics hustled to get the train moving again.

As soon as the mechanics fixed the engine, the tracks were covered in snow. The blizzard had moved inland, slowing the train down with each passing mile. The train had to grind through as much of the snow as possible, then pull back and slam forward again until it broke through the drift blocking its path, and repeat the process over and over. Instead of setting a record for the fastest train trip to Halifax, the Boston & Maine was now in danger of setting a record for the slowest.

Outside the appropriately named Folly Mountain, the drifts were finally too deep for the train to go any farther. The conductors found Ratshesky to give him the news. Ratshesky was no hothead, but he was not about to let this mission be aborted on the tracks of Folly Mountain. He reasoned aloud that if the blizzard was this bad for them, sitting on a heated train with all the food and supplies they could want, what was the storm like for the victims in Halifax? After his short sermon, Ratshesky recalled, "I pleaded with them to do everything in their power known to railroad men to clear the track."

Ratshesky stepped off the train to address a band of men with shovels, telling them everything he had heard about the Halifax tragedy: the crushed buildings, the thousands of wounded, the children, and how the blizzard was making everyone that much more miserable. "The men, realizing this," Ratshesky said, "and knowing that every moment was precious worked like Trojans."

Each time the diggers cleared some track, the engineer would send the 135 tons of train smashing into the next layer of snow and release the steam to help melt it, and the diggers would start again, sweating so hard that they took their coats off. About an hour after they started, with the passengers urging the shovelers on, the train finally broke through the drift.

The passengers cheered, and the train crawled ahead, with the diggers running to grab a rail and hop back on.

Chapter 28
The Last Stop

To help with the massive task of collecting, identifying, and storing the bodies, Halifax benefited from having an embalming professor and an undertaking expert come in from Toronto.

But the man put in charge of the grim work was Halifax's own provincial civil servant Arthur S. Barnstead, the son of Dr. John Henry Barnstead, the local doctor who had created the first system for handling mass casualties when *Titanic* victims had arrived by the hundreds just five and a half years earlier. Inspired by his father's work, Arthur became one of the world's first licensed coroners, while assuming the position of Nova Scotia's secretary of industries and immigration. His father offered to work under his son as he took on this immense task, and he accepted.

Under the junior Barnstead's directions, sailors and soldiers combed the area looking for corpses. Some of them carried big wicker baskets to pick up body parts—arms and legs, hands and feet, ears and fingers—on the chance that these might help someone construct a final answer about a relative. They put the bodies and their parts into the body bags the senior Barnstead had introduced during the *Titanic* recovery.

They were instructed to put all the victims' effects in carefully labeled cloth bags, of which they had plenty left from the batch used for the *Titanic* victims. They were big enough to hold a pair of shoes and a few other identifying items, with one number assigned for each victim's effects. They used the extra manila tags to record where the body was found, its approximate age, and any other details that might help someone make an identification. Then they attached the tag to the items, the bag, or one of the victim's big toes.

This entry was typical: "Three lots from . . . Veith Street, possible Mrs. . . . and two children." Another: "Lady at NW corner of basement, Flynn Block. Lying with children."

The harder cases required workers to determine how many bodies were present after they'd been burned. "Charred remains" was a common answer to that riddle, attached to a bag of undetermined bodies. One tag read, "Remains of three or possibly six bodies brought in a clothes basket." Another: "Two or possibly three children."

Once the remains arrived at the Chebucto Road School, the junior Barnstead directed his new assistants to strip the bodies and wash them as best they could with water retrieved from nearby homes. (Although the Chebucto Road School had been hastily repaired, it still lacked running water.) They kept the victims' clothing if possible, though most of it had to be thrown away to avoid disease.

They tried to assign everything associated with a single victim the same number to help identify them later, but many bodies did not have any clothing or effects, or were impossible to identify, and sometimes the tag identifying it became illegible or fell apart in the blizzard.

One destroyed home demonstrates just how difficult this work could be. A two-story house near Pier 6 had been partitioned into apartments and rented out by six families. When it had collapsed and burned, it left a pile of charred planks, plaster, and ashes. A team of soldiers dug through the basement and discovered a dead boy lying next to a stack of letters, bills, and receipts, which had rather miraculously escaped damage. They sent the boy and the papers to the Chebucto Road School, where someone from the family's Catholic church identified the boy and the rest of his family. All were buried at Mount Olivet Cemetery. As there were no close family members left alive, the contents of the mortuary bag were never claimed, and the papers stayed in the child's cloth bag in the morgue and were buried with him.

They later determined that the letters had belonged to a woman from Ireland who lived in the same building. Her body and that of her only child, a girl, had probably been near the boy's body. Her husband had been fighting in France. Four months after the explosion, he was discharged. After two years of risking his life for his country, he returned to find that his home, his wife, and his daughter were all gone. All that remained were his letters to his wife, but those had been buried with the boy.

Nothing could bring his family back, of course, but his affectionate letters home, clearly valued by his wife, would have given some comfort. She had cut out a poem from a newspaper to keep with his letters, with each verse ending, "The song he sang in the trench that night, / Was the song of a girl back home."

He would never see his letters, nor his wife's favorite poem.

Barnstead and his temporary staff organized the morgue with admirable alacrity. By the second day, Barnstead and company decided they were ready to receive the record keepers, reporters, and relatives. To handle the throng, they kept their makeshift morgue open for thirteen hours a day, from 9:00 a.m. to 10:00 p.m., long after dark.

Each day they provided the newspapers a list of victims they had identified and descriptions of others, which brought in more visitors. The *Halifax Herald* described the morgue as "a place of soft-going feet and lowered voices."

Barnstead's staff handled the visitors with great care. To keep out the gawkers, a volunteer in the lobby interviewed each visitor to determine whom they were looking for, asking enough questions to gauge the sincerity of their search. For female visitors, the interviewer would summon a "sympathetic woman" to accompany her on her short tour of the basement.

Downstairs, the staff draped sheets over all the bodies and arranged them so a visitor would first see the least-damaged unclaimed bodies, progressing to the most damaged, followed by the bags of effects and file-card descriptions. If a visitor was able to make a positive identification, they still needed a burial permit to release the body. "I think it might be my brother-in-law" would not suffice, lest a distraught, possibly confused mourner bury the relative of another visitor who might come by hours later.

If you were missing a loved one, you most likely would have visited their home first, then the temporary shelters, then the hospitals, and finally the Chebucto Road School—your last stop. Here, you faced two possibilities, both heartbreaking: you would find your loved one's remains, and your worst fears would be confirmed: they were gone. As tough as that was, the second option was worse—not finding them. True, their absence from the morgue gave hope that they could be alive, but that meant your search was not over, and was more likely to end in eternal uncertainty. The gift of hope was eventually eclipsed by the pain of not knowing.

It was with these conflicting emotions that thousands of fearful survivors walked up to the front door of the Chebucto Road School, often escorted there by a soldier or a volunteer. This anguish was captured in thousands of notices posted in the local papers.

Mr. Huggins, the principal of the Richmond School who let his daughter walk up to the school herself that morning while he talked to a parent, posted the following: "Merle Huggins, aged 11 years, who was at Richmond School at the time of the catastrophe, is missing. The little girl is the daughter of Principal Huggins, who will be deeply grateful for any information regarding her."

After the morgue had closed on Friday night, November 7, a young woman was so desperate to search for her brother that she would not take no for an answer from the soldier who told her she would have to come back the next day. She dashed around the school building, banging on each door she passed, pleading for the guard inside, Donald Morrison, to let her in.

"Help. Help. Please help me."

Her voice sounded young and very sincere. Morrison repeated the soldier's instructions, but the woman continued to plead with him to let her look for her brother, whom she said was only eleven years old. Morrison used his lantern to guide himself. The instant his key unlocked the door, the girl "tumbled into the room," he recalled.

She introduced herself as Elizabeth Fraser. "Is my brother here? Please help me. I have looked everywhere and I cannot find him."

Morrison lifted his lantern to see her face. "She was sixteen or seventeen," he recalled. "Her face was dirty and tear-stained and she was wet and cold. She told me she had been looking for her brother for two days."

He could not refuse her. He escorted her down the

first row. When they reached the first body, he lifted the sheet, shined his lantern on the corpse, and then looked to see if she recognized the deceased.

"Body after body we checked," he said. "From time to time I stole a look at my companion but she seemed unaware of anything, working with a fervor that I had to admire. Cold, hunger—everything was forgotten."

When they finished the row of teenagers, Morrison's lamp happened upon a canvas leaning upright against a column. Elizabeth thought she recognized the grungy canvas, so they went to take a look. Once Morrison turned the canvas back, Elizabeth emitted a brief scream, then dropped to her knees to clasp her brother, repeating, "I found you. I found you."

"She cried as I have never seen anyone cry before or since," Morrison said. Once she finished, she straightened her brother out, carefully pulled the canvas back over him, and stood up, gathering herself.

She thanked Morrison, saying she would return as soon as possible. A few minutes later she did so with two men carrying a stretcher, and they removed her brother from the morgue.

"Under ordinary circumstances," Morrison explained, "I would have been court-martialed but my C.O. only reprimanded me. I guess he realized I was only human."

Chapter 29
The Yanks Are Coming

Saturday, December 8

Despite an almost complete lack of preparation for such an emergency, after suffering the worst man-made explosion in history, Haligonians got organized, helped each other in every way imaginable, and treated an estimated 90 percent of the wounded within twenty-four hours, in a herculean effort. The majority of victims received attention through the twelve emergency dressing stations, doctors' offices, and home visits, while 2,500 people packed local hospitals and still others were treated in towns as far out as Truro.

It was undeniably impressive, but even that high

achievement would not have been enough by itself to restore the city. Fortunately for Halifax, native son Sir Robert Borden had won the pivotal election of 1911 and was still in office when the explosion occurred. He cut short his trip to Prince Edward Island to help his hometown, and lent the full power of the entire Dominion of Canada to Halifax's recovery effort. Haligonians appreciated that, of course, but probably expected it. What they didn't anticipate was the river of aid that came from the United States.

"Doctors and nurses arrived from outlying provincial towns and substantial help was on the way from Montreal and Toronto," wrote explosion survivor Thomas Raddall, "but the first and most valuable assistance came from the ancient foe beyond the Bay of Fundy."

That ancient foe, Boston, had taken up arms against the United Empire Loyalists in two wars and almost did so in a third, the American Civil War. Boston, the rebellious soul of a nation that had, just six years earlier, spoken openly on the floor of Congress about annexing its longtime neighbor, was now coming to its rescue, unbidden, in full measure.

After the grueling train trip through the blizzard, A. C. "Cap" Ratshesky and the Massachusetts contingent rolled into Halifax's new South End Station at about 6:00 a.m. on Saturday morning. Ratshesky headed straight for the CGR's temporary headquarters, and got an education along the way.

On the train to Halifax, Cap Ratshesky had repeatedly ratcheted up his orders for supplies and people to be sent from Boston, but once he traveled through the city he could see that even the most dire reports grossly underestimated the devastation—a misimpression the American journalists who came with him corrected, telling the outside world of the scale of the disaster and the specter of Halifax's heroes meeting the challenge with grit, teamwork, and integrity. Those dispatches soon inspired city, state, and national governments, businesses, and individuals around the world to give generously to the Halifax relief effort.

The Boston party's immediate mission was to find the survivors and help them medically, then materially. When Ratshesky reached Canadian Government Railways headquarters, he met A. Hayes, CGR's General Manager, and handed him Governor McCall's letter, in which McCall assured him, "I need hardly say to you that we have the strongest affection for the people of your city, and that we are anxious to do everything possible for their assistance at this time."

When Hayes finished reading, Ratshesky recalled, "He was so affected that tears streamed down his cheeks." Hayes rose to greet Ratshesky, saying simply, "Just like the people of good old Massachusetts."

After Hayes collected himself, he offered the Boston group the use of the temporary wires they had just connected to City Hall, which had restored communications with the outside world. He also informed Ratshesky that the private railcar of Sir Robert L. Borden, Premier of Canada, was close to theirs. Hayes then messaged the PM to let him know the Massachusetts relief party had arrived and would be glad to "call upon him in his car as soon as possible."

Borden's "answer came most informally," Ratshesky wrote. "He joined us in person in a very few minutes, expressing to us in appropriate words his profound appreciation of the quick action on the part of the Commonwealth of Massachusetts. . . ."

Because Prime Minister Borden owed his rise to power in 1911 to a tidal wave of anti-American sentiment and fear of annexation—fear he had stoked—his deep expression of gratitude marked a considerable turnabout, and was utterly sincere: he had lost many friends in the explosion himself. The prime minister asked the Bostonians to join him on his way to City Hall so they could present Governor McCall's letter "and learn what disposition we should make of our party and supplies."

At City Hall, Ratshesky's party met Lieutenant-Colonel McKelvey Bell, the chairman of Halifax's newly created Medical Relief Committee and head of military hospitals in Halifax, who helped the Bostonians pick a suitable building to convert to a temporary hospital. They settled on the Bellevue Building in the center of the city.

"The building was turned over to us in very bad condition," Ratshesky said, "not a door or window remaining whole, and water and ice on the floor of every room" due to exposed pipes bursting from the cold. It says something that this was deemed the best building available. "Apparently, under ordinary circumstances, it would have been impossible to have put into shape for a long time."

But these were not ordinary circumstances. About fifty crewmen from a U.S. training ship, a company of Canadian soldiers, and the British Military Stores Depot got Bellevue ready to receive patients by 12:30 that afternoon, a mere five hours after the Boston party had pulled into Halifax. Bellevue had been transformed into one of eight emergency hospitals that opened that weekend, which added a much-needed one thousand beds to the city's capacity.

At about the same time Bellevue started receiving patients, the snowstorm stopped for a few minutes, and the sun broke through the clouds. The clouds soon returned with yet more snow, but the sunshine was delicious while it lasted.

More good news from Boston: the previous day at historic Faneuil Hall, Governor McCall and the Massachusetts Relief Committee had held a follow-up meeting and decided to send Halifax $100,000, or about $2 million today, plus more medical and trades personnel, and two supply ships: *Calvin Austin* that Saturday night, and *Northland* on Sunday. When newspapers told their readers where *Calvin Austin* had docked so they could bring their donations, the docks soon overflowed with Samaritans eager to contribute to the cause, including a "society lady" who was so inspired by the outpouring that she doffed her fur coat and added it to the cargo heading north.

When *Calvin Austin* pushed off from the pier under a large Red Cross flag flowing from her masthead to ward off German U-boats, according to one reporter, "a lusty cheer went up from the crowd of workers and spectators who lined the docks."

Shortly after Bellevue was up and running, some fifty leaders, including Cap Ratshesky and Prime Minister Sir Robert Borden, met to streamline the relief work, form the Reconstruction Committee, and meet with the city engineer's office to make plans to hire 500 employees to start working on the future. The level of organization they brought to the task was impressive, one of the great underestimated qualities of any serious undertaking, lightyears away from where the recovery effort had started two days before.

If Halifax was shattered in one instant, it had begun to recover in the next.

By Saturday night, thanks to the unexpected infusion of doctors, nurses, volunteers, and medical supplies from Boston and elsewhere, many of the medical personnel who first took up the herculean task of treating 9,000 victims finally got a respite, and some were able to go home for some long-overdue rest.

After Percy McGrath was relieved following his third day at Camp Aldershot, he spent a few days making home visits around Halifax by sleigh before returning to camp.

Ernest Barss and his mentor, Dr. Elliott, had finished their third full day with almost no sleep when they finally turned things over to the next wave of volunteers and headed to the train station on Saturday afternoon. Just getting through the blizzard required commandeering a sled and a pair of horses, then waiting in a signal box for a couple of hours. The ride was painfully slow, with the snow-covered tracks adding several hours to their journey before they got home at 10:30 that night.

But the long ride gave Barss time to reflect on all that he had just seen and done. In addition to the horrific scenes of destruction and disfigurement, Barss recalled the quiet heroism of so many victims and responders. He also had a changed view of Canada's neighbors. He had been highly critical of the Americans before the explosion, as you'd expect from Joseph Barss Jr.'s great-grandson, but he now felt compelled to say something in his letter to his uncle about the Boston contingent.

"I tell you we'll never be able to say enough about the wonderful help the States have sent," he wrote. "The response was so spontaneous and everything done even before it was asked for. It brought tears to all our eyes when they came and told us a little of what had been done by the U.S.

"You know we have always been a trifle contemptuous of the U.S. on account of their prolonged delay in entering the war. But never again! They can have anything I've got. And I don't think I feel any differently from anyone down here either."

1911 felt like a century ago.

Chapter 30
A Working Sabbath

Sunday, December 9

Three days after the explosion, the weather made another surprising turn, switching from winter to spring.

This was initially a very welcome change, providing some relief from the bitter cold and snow flying through broken windows and busted doors. But on the whole it created more problems than it solved for the beleaguered town. The warm spell that began on Sunday, December 9, melted twenty inches of snow into slush, creating new rivers running down already muddy roads and into open basements and soaking the boots of everyone trying to rescue or recover the victims and their belongings. In the days before weatherproof outerwear, their coats, hats, pants, and boots became as waterlogged as the streets their owners were trying to clear.

Beyond discomfort, the brief warm spell made the snow heavier, causing already damaged roofs to leak and occasionally collapse. To the long list of chores local homeowners were tackling, they could now add roof repair.

The worse the roads became, the better the horses looked. The few autos that had survived heavy use during the blizzard were rendered all but useless in the slush and mud. The Transportation Committee wisely secured more horses to get through the streets, lest they create one of the world's first cases of gridlock.

Halifax normally honored the Sabbath, closing stores and canceling most activities except church and Sunday dinner. But with far too much work to be done the city decreed that Sunday, December 9, would be a working day.

That included the crews repairing telephone and telegraph wires, which had been snapped and severed all over town. Adding to the area's communication woes, radio operators on the Atlantic coast transmitted only under strict wartime regulations, and wireless communication wasn't yet good enough to cover the gap, so even the normal channels of communication available in this era were greatly hampered. As a result, several out-of-town newspapers received their first telegrams about the explosion from Havana, Cuba. From certain parts of Canada, cable communication had to take strange detours, with the most effective route to Halifax running through London.

But once again, ordinary people rose to perform acts of generosity, and creativity. One clever man gathered messages from survivors to their relatives letting them know they had survived and boarded a train to Truro to send them out from Truro's telegraph machine. Then he picked up telegrams that had come in to Truro for people in Halifax, hopped onto the next train going back, and delivered the highly coveted notes. Problem solved.

The linemen worked without rest to establish partial service, which Western Union and Canadian Pacific restricted to official messages only. Knowing people were desperate to reach their families, the linemen continued to work through the wind, the snow, the muck, and the slush to restore some 300 telephone lines. They also hooked up temporary emergency lines to relief centers, where the need to get word to fretful relatives that people were okay, and to give them the sad news of who wasn't, was at its greatest.

The Western Union station on Hollis Street brought in twelve extra operators to handle the load, but they were still overwhelmed by the volume of 5,000 cables a day for a month. Operator Leo Campbell recalled, "We worked day and night."

Delivering the cables was harder. Boy Scout volunteers could not get past the soldiers guarding the Devastated Area, who were not letting anyone in without a pass, and certainly not a bunch of teenage boys. When Western Union sent their own employees to do the job, they had a hard time finding the street addresses—provided they could find the street, or a house still standing. If they got past all that, they still needed someone to be home. If they couldn't, operator Leo Campbell recalled, they talked to any neighbors who might still be there or someone searching the area who knew the residents and gave them the message. The Relief Committee set up an Information Committee that day to create a log listing where survivors had relocated.

"We would deliver to shelters and wherever people were," Campbell said. "If that did not work, we would put notices in the papers, with the names of the people. The telegrams came for years," many of them from people who had not heard from a relative, friend, or associate since 1917, who concluded that perhaps their relatives and friends in Halifax hadn't responded to them because they had been in the explosion. This was often wishful thinking, but if you were trying to ignore someone far away, the explosion was as good an excuse as any.

Bertha Bond, who had helped Reverend Swetnam save his daughter Dorothy, sent a cable to her fiancé, Sandy Wournell, fighting overseas. She said only SAFE WELL BERTHA BOND, a message that reached him in Boulogne, France. Her descriptive letters would arrive later, but for now, that was all he needed to hear.

Thanks to the restoration of those wires and the journalists from Boston, news of the disaster spread fast. Although the explosion happened at the height of the largest war the world had ever seen, and initial information was sketchy at best, in the major papers of Europe, Asia, and the Americas, the story of the Halifax explosion jumped ahead of the Great War for a week.

When Jerusalem surrendered to Britain the same week and the U.S. declared war on Austria-Hungary on Friday, December 8, those stories took a backseat to Halifax. This was probably due to a number of factors: the explosion was bigger than any bomb dropped in the Great War; casualty lists from the battles overseas that week were much shorter than those from the explosion;

it occurred at a well-known port far from the trenches of Europe, the first time the horrors the soldiers were experiencing visited North America; and unrestricted American reporters were there to write the stories. If the daily butchery of trench warfare barely qualified as news by 1917, the leveling of a peaceful port town was not.

Since Cap Ratshesky and company had walked all over Halifax for twenty-four hours, they could give the people back in Boston a better idea of what was needed most. The day after *Calvin Austin* set sail for Halifax, the three-day-old Massachusetts-Halifax Relief Commission loaded *Northland* with more supplies for Halifax.

Henry B. Endicott asked H. J. McAlman, the president of the Massachusetts Automobile Dealers Association, to buy $25,000 worth of trucks to load onto *Northland*—more than half a million dollars' worth today. It was a sizable request, with nothing in it for McAlman, but a few hours later McAlman returned to Endicott's office with this news: "We bought the trucks, we hired ten first-class chauffeurs to go with them," and, if Endicott was willing to bypass a few regulations, McAlman promised to throw in enough gasoline to "run 'em for a while."

Massachusetts sent ten trucks whose names even car buffs would not recognize today: five Republics, three Whites, and two Stewarts, adorned with signs that said MASSACHUSETTS TO HALIFAX, plus ten drums of gasoline.

Back in Halifax, Prime Minister Sir Robert Borden went to see how the visitors from Boston were making out, then issued the following statement: "This afternoon I visited the hospital established at Bellevue by the Massachusetts hospital unit. They took possession yesterday . . . and within a few hours had every arrangement made for receiving patients, of whom nearly 75 are being accommodated." He concluded, "The hospital is a triumph of organization ability!" If Barss's views of Americans had changed, it seemed Borden's had, too.

On Saturday, the *New York Times* ran a story headlined "OUR BLUEJACKETS HELPING IN HALIFAX. Warship Furnishes Aid to Police and Establishes a Hospital. PRESIDENT SENDS MESSAGE."

To "His Excellency, the Governor General of Canada," President Wilson wrote an unwieldy but unequivocal message of support, in which he underscored the admiration the people of the United States had for "their noble brethren of the Dominion" and expressed "their heartfelt sympathy and grief." He then reinforced "the ties of kinship and community of speech and of national interest" the countries shared, in addition to "the strong bonds of union in the common cause of devotion to the supreme duties of national existence."

It wasn't poetry, but it wasn't a threat to annex Canada, either. Far from it—President Wilson might have delivered the clearest statement of unalloyed respect any American president had yet given to Canada.

That next day, Sunday, December 9, the *New York Times* released the response Canada's governor general, the Duke of Devonshire Victor Cavendish, sent to President Woodrow Wilson:

CANADA'S GOVERNOR GENERAL THANKS THE PRESIDENT, HAILING HIS MESSAGE OF SYMPATHY AS SIGN OF UNITY.

OTTAWA, Dec. 8—The Governor General [Duke of Devonshire] has sent this reply to the message of sympathy and offer of assistance from President Wilson to the City of Halifax:

I desire to thank your Excellency for your message, which the Canadian Government and I have received with profound appreciation and gratitude.

We recognize in it and in the generous offers of

assistance to the stricken City of Halifax, which have been received from many quarters of the United States, a further proof of that community of feeling which unites the two peoples in a bond of mutual sympathy and interest, so particularly appropriate at the present time, when both are engaged in a common purpose to vindicate the principles of liberty and justice upon which the foundations of both Governments rest.

The contrast of these unqualified messages of respect, gratitude, and peace to the animosity and suspicion that separated these governments in 1776, 1812, and 1911 is striking. It came from the top, and echoed throughout both nations.

Wilson's administration then offered $1 million in relief aid, but Halifax did not need it after so many individual Americans had given so much to Halifax. The people beat him to it.

If the disaster brought out the "better angels" of the Canadian and American character, it didn't transform Halifax into a haven of forgiveness that week. Haligonians' immense, unnecessary suffering fueled the very human emotions of fear and anger, and the desire for justice. The impulse to blame someone was great, and the object of that impulse was obvious: the Germans.

Taken broadly, this conclusion was entirely right and fair. It was the Germans, after all, who had started the war that was killing Canada's sons, often by ignoring international conventions of warfare. Without the Germans, Halifax would not have reprised its role as the conduit for soldiers and supplies heading to Europe—and that would include ships loaded down with 6 million pounds of high explosives.

But we know the Germans had no direct role in the collision on December 6, nor in the explosion that followed—all unintended accidents between Scandinavians and Frenchmen. But that answer was not particularly satisfying.

On Sunday, December 9, sixteen people of German birth, who had been reporting to the local police once a month since the war started, were arrested. Following a military inquiry, some were released immediately, and others in a few days, but anti-German sentiment still ran high. Locals smashed the windows of a few houses whose owners had German-sounding names, but for the most part, Haligonians were too busy putting their city back together to pursue revenge, especially uninformed revenge.

While some officials were trying to find the culprits, soldiers sorting out the rubble of the dispatcher's former office discovered Vincent Coleman's body, and near it, his tele-key.

They cleaned up the device that had probably saved hundreds of lives, and presented it to his wife.

Chapter 31
"It's Me, Barbara!"

Monday, December 10, 1917

On Monday, December 10, Halifax was hit with yet another violent snowstorm, continuing a ridiculous run of bad weather.

Now four days after the explosion, Barbara Orr remained in her bed at Camp Hill Hospital, largely ignored by doctors, nurses, and the steady flow of visitors. Barbara's hope waned by the hour, but her mother's other sister, who lived in Dartmouth, had seen Barbara's name in the newspaper and came down to find her.

When Barbara saw her aunt at the doorway, her

heart raced. But when Barbara called out, her aunt turned around and stared at her for a long moment, puzzled. It was not the reunion Barbara had imagined.

"It's me! Barbara! Barbara ORR!"

Barbara's bright red hair was still black from the "black rain." She had suffered so many cuts, scrapes, and bruises that her face was discolored and swollen— all of which rendered her unrecognizable to her aunt.

"I'm Barbara Orr!" she repeated.

But her aunt still didn't believe her. "Oh, no, no," she said. "You're not Barbara, because she has red hair."

But Barbara persisted, telling her aunt things only a family member would know until her aunt came to her bedside for a closer look. When she realized it really was Barbara, she was elated, and gave Barbara a gentle but heartfelt hug. She arranged to take Barbara back to their home in Dartmouth, which was still in decent shape. Barbara could not walk very well by herself, but that night, she was back in a familiar home, surrounded by caring relatives.

Having spent four days in a hospital with no visitors, however, Barbara was even more convinced that she had lost her entire family. Picturing the scene from her block over and over, she concluded that no one could have survived that explosion, or the fires that burned what was left to the ground.

Using the same logic, she couldn't imagine how her father, two uncles, and grandfather could have lived after the printing factory fell in on itself. Without any word from anyone, she decided she had been right from the start: they were all gone, and she was her family's sole survivor.

Her aunt had to tell her that there had been no listings from shelters or medical centers for her father, her mother, her three brothers, and her two sisters. One of her uncles, the owner of the nearby home she had first visited after the explosion, had also died in the printing works. And yet, somehow, the imploding building had spared her grandfather, and her uncle William had happened to be outside the building watching the ship burn when it blew up. He had been injured, but survived. The day after her aunt had found Barbara, she read his name on a list in the paper, and they went back to find him.

Barbara Orr's premonition, however, had been largely correct. Her once robust family had been reduced to an uncle, a grandfather, two aunts, and a few cousins. Of the eight people in their happy home Thursday morning, she was the only one who was still alive.

Millicent Upham was moved to a hospital that had been set up in St. Mary's College by some of the American doctors and nurses. They removed her left eye, and her cousin Annie Rasley's, too. They were in the same ward and talked often, sharing visitors.

While Millicent's father and brother Archie were visiting her, her father asked the doctor to look at Archie's head, which had bled so much the first day that his shirt had stuck to his back. The doctors discovered his wounds were more severe than they first appeared. They operated on him for eight and a half hours, removing twenty-two pieces of glass from his head, and inserted a silver plate to reinforce the back of his skull.

Frank Burford, the fifteen-year-old plumbers' apprentice at Hillis & Sons Foundry whose boss had sent him to fetch a parcel when the ship blew up, incurred only a deep cut on his leg from a falling timber, while almost everyone back at the foundry was killed.

The Burfords had the misfortune of living on Richmond's Flynn block, which had been all but wiped out by the blast, killing an estimated sixty people. The Burfords listed three family members as missing: Frank's father, who worked at the foundry, and his younger brother and sister. His mother had survived and was being treated by the Bostonians at Bellevue.

Eventually the two children were identified in the morgue, and on that Monday, December 10, Mr. Burford's body was recovered from the Hills & Sons Foundry.

A few days after the explosion, the local papers' thick obituary sections started listing funerals, including one for "Coleman, Vincent, funeral Sunday Dec. 9, 2:30 from home of H. E. O'Toole, brother-in-law, 126 Edward Street."

The Monday, December 10, edition of the *Evening Mail* included the following obituary:

VINCE COLEMAN, 31 RUSSELL STREET.
"A hero in death as in Life"

After describing Coleman's heroic deed that summer, when he had leapt onto a runaway engine to stop it before it collided with a suburban train, the article explained Coleman's selfless actions minutes before the explosion, followed by a letter to the editor: "I would appreciate highly if the relief Committee will ascertain whether or not any of his family are left alive and if so to give them special attention. Supervisor CGR [Canadian Government Railways] Truro."

The editors answered: "Mr. Coleman's wife was badly injured; their five children only slightly injured."

That week, it might have been tempting to call that lucky.

Chapter 32
Small Gifts

Tuesday, December 11

The Great War didn't take a minute off, with the Canadian troops overseas in as much danger the day after the explosion as they had been the day before. Troops, munitions, and weapons from across North America and beyond would soon be massing in Halifax again, then shipping across the Atlantic, just slightly delayed.

None of these things had changed, but their purpose had become much clearer to the Haligonians. Instead of viewing the Great War as an abstraction, something happening far away that Haligonians knew very little about, the actual point of the exercise—tearing apart more of the enemy's people than they could of yours until one side quit—was now at their doorstep, the full costs of the conflict everywhere apparent.

The bootleggers who had been doing brisk business out of the YMCA were pushed out when the Y was converted into one of a dozen temporary hospitals. But even when they relocated, bootleggers and brothels found demand for their services dramatically reduced. It wasn't due to the lack of a client base—volunteers and soldiers were coming to town on every train—or the fact that just about every building had smashed windows, but a cultural shift: the hedonism the speakeasies and brothels offered now seemed trivial or even offensive while thousands of people were sacrificing their comfort to help others. The prostitutes who had come from all over Canada soon left because business bottomed out.

While many landlords generously allowed their unoccupied properties to be used free of charge, with some even advertising this fact, a few others, recognizing a sellers' market if ever there was one, started demanding exorbitant rents. Likewise, many merchants gave away their goods freely for the cause, while some cranked up their prices.

These less-noble impulses infected the recently formed unions, too, which had been established to give the common man a better chance at a good life. Yet after the explosion, some bricklayers refused to allow plasterers to help repair chimneys, as that was brick-layers' work by union rules. Other tradesmen stub-bornly insisted on overtime rates for extra work. If the thousands of volunteers, from the local girls knitting balaclava helmets to the Boston doctors, had taken a similar stance, the cost to Halifax would have been many millions.

Six days after the explosion, Deputy Mayor Henry Colwell issued a proclamation warning that profiteering would be rigorously punished. People were encouraged to report transgressors, but the only reported convic-tion was a soldier accused of selling relief supplies.

If gouging was distasteful, looting was criminal— though amazingly rare. Newspapers warned that sol-diers had been instructed to shoot anyone attempting to steal from unattended houses, shops, or corpses. While some looting had been reported in the morgue, with visitors and even volunteers said to have pocketed rings and watches from the dead, most stories of loot-ing boiled down to false rumors, including a tale about a looter being hanged from a lamppost, and another about one being shot. In fact, the shooting story started with a joke from Colonel Ralph Simmonds, who was pleased to see it circulate as fact; it "Kept people away like the plague." Chief of Police Frank Hanrahan said he'd heard of only one case of a possible attempted burglary. Potential looters might have been dissuaded by the mounted, armed guards around the Devastated Area or the threats of shooting or hanging, but historically those threats have not stopped others after disasters. Looting was virtually non-existent in Halifax.

The calamity and chaos presented a once-in-a-lifetime chance for another class of people burdened with legal troubles, crushing debt, dysfunctional families, or unhappy marriages. If they wanted to make their current selves vanish and resurface far away as people new to the world, this was their moment. While we know the inmates at Rockhead Prison escaped after the explosion, it seems possible that a few dozen folks with other problems realized that this was their chance to start a new life.

In the days before computers, moving south to Boston or west to Calgary with a completely new identity was almost as simple as getting on the next train out of town. By its very nature, it would be difficult to prove anyone actually did this—unless they were caught or confessed—but that fact only confirms to the believers that the escapees pulled it off.

Oftentimes children who had suffered only minor injuries went to live temporarily with other families because their parents had been seriously injured. "There were good people who came around just till we got organized better," recalled Helena Duggan. She was eleven when she moved in with a kind woman named Mrs. Eaton, who hosted Helena "for quite a time. She was lovely."

Some families had to be more resourceful. Jean Hunter was a ten-year-old student at Richmond School when the blast ruined her home. So Jean and her remaining family, consisting of her grandmother, aunt, cousin, mother, and brother, moved into a boxcar at Willow Park railway terminal and lived there for twelve days. They managed to outfit their new metal home with beds, a stove, and chipped dishes, and dedicated one corner of the car for a bathroom consisting of a bucket and a curtain. They visited St. Mary's Hall to pick up some clothes, including a "lovely, warm coat," for Jean's aunt, and a "pretty corduroy-velvet" one for Jean—plus much-appreciated baths for the entire family.

Because the boxcar was too high off the ground to get into or out of very easily, the resourceful family spent almost all their time in the boxcar, in relative comfort. It was not the kind of arrangement a family of six would seek out under normal circumstances, but given the situation, perhaps it's not surprising that Jean

Hunter looked back on those twelve days with a certain fondness, and pride in their perseverance.

The severe weather hindered the work of the Emergency Shelter Committee, but more than forty cities offered to take in homeless Haligonians. Montreal volunteered three five-room flats, rent-free until May, but that paled in comparison to the offers of Berwick, in Nova Scotia's Annapolis Valley, to take thirty orphans, and Lunenberg, on Nova Scotia's south shore, which pledged food and shelter for 500.

Most of those who found themselves suddenly homeless preferred to remain in or near Halifax, with 800 people staying in shelters hastily fitted with sanitation and cooking capabilities, while 8,000 remained in damaged homes or moved in with neighbors. For this reason, the city leaders decided that the need to fix existing homes should take priority over building new ones. But home repair wasn't easy that December, since workers had to contend with frozen mortar, high winds, snowdrifts, and sudden thaws, not to mention a scarcity of almost every item needed.

To keep people warm in the meantime, the chairman reported that the committee had distributed 16,700 blankets and 1,800 quilts in the first two weeks alone. With a little help from their friends, the Haligonians toughed it out.

The Society for the Prevention of Cruelty to Animals (SPCA) found shelter for countless dogs, cats, horses, cows, pigs, and hens, and even repaired a few barns. But it didn't take long before the SPCA accommodations were overflowing, so they asked local citizens to take in animals, and many did. That still left so many animals that had been injured beyond help or that were simply homeless that the SPCA had to work overtime destroying them. Boston helped the SPCA, too, with its own SPCA chapter sending two inspectors and $1,000.

Cliff Driscoll found the family cow in the care of the SPCA, but when he claimed her, they asked him to pay for her board and lodging during their absence. Cliff countered by asking what they did with the cow's milk, which was enough for the SPCA to release the Driscoll family cow without further questions.

Rank, station, prestige—the explosion erased all those lines for a time, too. After the calamity ended so many lives and forever altered others, standing on ceremony was no longer a popular position. When the veneer of class was peeled back, it revealed a basic human decency. And this, not the rules of etiquette, is what drove the vast majority of Haligonians to make great sacrifices for their fellow man.

Women from South Halifax and Richmond who had always relied on maids rolled up their sleeves to start doing the work themselves, often for people they'd never met. They canceled their dinner and bridge parties that month and scotched their Christmas social plans in favor of long hours helping in homes and hospitals, doing clerical work for relief committees, setting up canteens for volunteers, and taking in victims and relief workers.

"The leaders of society took charge but it was only successful because everyone pulled together," Blair Beed wrote. "Businessmen took up shovels to look for their workers' families. The poor made sacrifices to assist those who had been well-to-do. Society women stood shoulder to shoulder with their ladies' maids cleaning the wounded and caring for the orphaned. After years of sending loved ones away to war, the war had come home to their doorsteps and the people of Halifax and Dartmouth were ready to respond."

The city's theaters closed out of respect, while local restaurants made free meals for many of the 25,000 homeless.

"December 6 was a day of unspeakable human agony," Dalhousie professor Archibald MacMechan wrote in January 1918. "Men and women saw their own burned to death and were unable to help them. But it was a day of heroism, of golden deeds. As a matter of course, men, women and children risked their lives for the sake of others. The spirit of helpfulness was everywhere, in all ranks and classes. There was no sacrifice which the more fortunate would not make for the homeless and the injured."

MacMechan was right, but it's worth remembering that these acts weren't performed by superheroes but by ordinary men, women, and children who met extraordinary circumstances with basic goodness. During these trying days, that was heroic enough.

It didn't get the attention the other committees received, but the Clothing Committee had to be among the most appreciated, especially in a town where half the residents had lost their entire wardrobes. The Committee set up five centers in Halifax and Dartmouth, with the Green Lantern restaurant serving as their headquarters. Every day trains and ships pulled into Halifax with so much donated clothing and footwear that the committee opened a special department at the Royal Mail Steamship Company to display and distribute it all.

Immediately after the explosion, the Clothing Committee, like the others, enforced few rules and kept no records of what they had given to whom. With people in dire need, the goal was speed. When they discovered some people who had not been victims were making off with new coats and clothes, they started keeping better records, but that in turn prevented them from helping the truly needy as fast as they could.

They ultimately decided to err on the side of speed and generosity. It was better to give a new coat to someone who didn't need one than to make someone who'd lost everything wait two days for their request to be processed.

One survivor recalled getting a new overcoat at a Dartmouth school. "Boy, did I look sharp! It was grey herringbone tweed, a lot better than the new one I had lost. There was one mass of clothing in the room, and all volunteer help, of course. I just took one look at that coat, and that was that."

Helena Duggan went to the Green Lantern to get a stocking hat and a black imitation sealskin coat. "I was so happy with it."

Amid all the losses, a new coat, freely given, would always be treasured.

If Halifax being turned upside down tempted a few to take advantage of the opportunity, far more frequently it inspired those with better intentions to perform selfless acts that were remembered by their recipients for the rest of their lives.

Al and Noble Driscoll had woken up their first morning in Truro with black oil from their hair and faces on their pillowcases, so they scrubbed every day to try to get the grime off. They still hadn't gotten all of it out when their mother gave them a dollar to go into Truro for a haircut.

When the barber started working on Noble's hair, the young boy winced, prompting the barber to look more closely at Noble's scalp. "Ah, you must be from Halifax," he said quietly. He spoke briefly to the other barber, who was about to start cutting Al's hair. They decided to give the boys a comprehensive treatment: one deep-cleansing shampoo, followed by another, both done with great care, with occasional pauses to remove small splinters of glass and wood before returning to the first task, cutting their hair. They took their time, telling other customers they'd have to wait or come back later.

It felt wonderful for Noble and Al to have their scalps so thoroughly cleaned, and it was a relief to have the painful fragments removed. But as the barbers were finishing up, both boys grew anxious. Their mother had given them a dollar for two haircuts, which didn't seem nearly enough for the special treatment they'd just received.

When the barbers were done, the boys stepped down from the chairs looking sharp, clean, and healthy, but feeling guilty. Al sheepishly held out the single dollar he had for both of them. The barber chuckled and shook his head.

"You come with me," he said, and led them across the street to a clothing store, where he bought both of them complete new outfits. When the boys tried to thank him, he just smiled, patted their shoulders, and waved them on their way.

The horrors the survivors endured surely dwarfed whatever small kindnesses they received afterward. But years later, they seemed to remember those tender mercies as clearly as the horrific scenes they had survived, as if they were somehow imbued with equal power.

After such traumatic suffering, it was striking just how far a little generosity and goodwill could go, perhaps because they provided tangible proof that human kindness had not been erased, even by the greatest man-made explosion the world had ever seen.

Under the most trying circumstances, the local papers kept putting out daily editions that provided the crucial service of getting the word out about the help being offered by the various committees, information about survivors in other towns, and the lists of the missing and dead. The journalists from Boston, particularly the Associated Press reporters, dispatched accurate reports of the disaster, including its unimaginable scale, to the rest of the world, which attracted millions of dollars in gifts for Halifax from governments, companies, and individuals. It came in big checks and small gestures, and, just as important, it came in quickly, when Halifax needed it most.

The Canadians came through, of course. The Province of Ontario sent $100,000, while Canada's own Dominion government, led by Prime Minister Sir Robert Borden, initially gave about $6 million, and would ultimately provide $18 million. The Strand Theater in Truro, where hundreds of survivors were staying with local families, donated a day's ticket sales. The Ford Motor Company of Canada donated three touring cars—but that actually represented a mere drop in the bucket for the Transportation Committee, which, at its height, received 3,000 calls a day for cars and 2,500 for teams of horses and trucks.

When Sir John Eaton, president of the Eaton Co., one of Canada's biggest department-store chains, heard about the disaster, he packed several train cars with food, experienced staffers, a medical unit, and enough goods to open a clothing and supply depot that carried building materials and other necessities, and headed for Halifax. If you had a requisition from your pastor or a committee chairman, anything you wanted was free. Although no one calculated just how much Eaton gave away, conservative estimates put the total in the six figures—millions today. He gave it all away on one condition: that there be no publicity.

Every corner of the vast British Empire gave generously. Local newspapers reported financial gifts from Newfoundland—still a separate British colony—the West Indies, South America, China, and New Zealand, as well as other parts of North America and the U.K. The Australian government gave $250,000, and the British government voted to send £1 million, then worth $4,815,000, and now almost $100 million—confirmation of the close connection between the Crown and her most loyal Canadian city.

The Lord Mayor of London set up a fund for the public to contribute to, which the Canadians and Brits called a "subscription list," with the *Times* of London printing the daily results. The fund eventually reached $600,000, or about $12 million today—remarkable during a war that was costing Britain billions. The British Red Cross donated £125,000, while King George V, the grandfather of Queen Elizabeth, recalled enjoying "so many happy times" in Halifax decades earlier when he was a prince that he felt compelled to send a telegram of sympathy and a personal check for £5,000, almost $100,000 in today's dollars.

Perhaps inspired by Boston's example and the uncensored newspaper accounts they read, the city of Chicago, which had survived its famous fire forty-six years earlier, sent $250,000. Mayor Thomson said, "Halifax had been among the first to assist after the 1871 fire so Chicago should return her kindness."

On December 10, the New York pharmaceutical supplier McKesson & Robbins wired the mayor of Halifax:

We offer five hundred dollars [about $10,000 today] in drugs and medicines, wire us your needs.

McKesson & Robbins,
Wholesale Druggists

They received a reply from Lieutenant-Colonel McKelvey Bell, the chairman of the Medical Relief Commission, who did not need to ponder his answer. "Many thanks for kind offer. Please send ether, chloroform, tincture of iodine and antistreptococcic serum."

Sometimes the gifts were quite specific, and usually quite helpful, saving Halifax the need to procure vital materials itself. New York sent prefab homes for temporary winter quarters, while Portland, Maine, sent five carloads of telegraph material, groceries, and dry goods. The governor of Maine sent 2,000 blankets and 1,000 cots from the state military stores in Augusta, and 8,000 other blankets from Bangor, plus staff medical officers, crews of carpenters, and other volunteers. "All ready for any emergency," he wrote. "Notify me of other needs."

Schenectady, New York, whose population shot up from 32,000 in 1900 to 73,000 in a decade, chipped in $4,000—or about $130,000 today. That might not sound like much, but in 1917, the average American worker made about $800 a year.

Sometimes the kindness arrived in person. As soon as he heard about the catastrophe, Dr. C. C. Hubly, a native Haligonian who worked for the Battle Creek Sanatorium in Michigan, run by the same Kellogg brothers who invented cornflakes, boarded a train with his secretary, Mr. Smith. Three days later the two were making unsolicited house calls in the poorest parts of the city, working every waking hour for a week.

Once again, Boston led with gifts of all kinds—money, supplies, personnel, even a benefit concert and a memorial service. At a benefit luncheon, Harry Lauder, the Scottish singer and comedian, pledged

$1,000 of his own money—about $25,000 today— which prompted others to donate an additional $1,203.

A benefit concert was arranged at Boston's Symphony Hall for Sunday, December 16, drawing some of the biggest names in entertainment, headlined by the world-famous Australian soprano Dame Nellie Melba, who inspired both "melba toast" and "peach melba." She was accompanied by Austrian violinist and composer Fritz Kreisler, conductor Dr. Karl Muck, and the Boston Symphony Orchestra. More than a hundred musicians played for free.

The broadside promised "A concert given for the Relief of Sufferers from the Recent Disaster in Halifax," the Farm-Aid of its time, featuring the overture "In Memoriam" by Sir Arthur Sullivan.

The sentiments, gestures, and money were accompanied by a seemingly endless stream of supplies and personnel. For more than a week, trains and ships left Boston almost daily, loaded with everything from doctors and nurses to X-ray machines and horse-drawn ambulances.

The city's generosity would not be forgotten.

Chapter 33
A Toast to Allies

Wednesday, December 12

The *Calvin Austin* left Boston late on Saturday, December 8, with $200,000 in medical personnel and supplies, engineers, glaziers, glass, and the society lady's fur coat, amid ringing cheers. After three full days of rough seas, on Wednesday, December 12, she was cheered once more—this time by the people lining the harbor in Halifax—receiving the kind of reception usually reserved for combatants like the Highland regiment and the HMS *Highflyer*.

As Halifax's homegrown historian Thomas Raddall remembered it, "With splendid heart and quick efficiency the State of Massachusetts sent by sea a complete relief expedition—food, clothing, bedding, medical supplies, doctors, nurses, trained welfare workers, together with a fleet of motor trucks complete with drivers and gasoline and loaded with carefully selected supplies—all ready to move off as soon as the ship came alongside. It was a perfect example of American generosity and quick-wittedness, and the city greeted it with a gasp of relief. And this was only the beginning. Financed entirely by American funds, the Massachusetts Relief Commission continued its clinics and its housing and welfare work in Halifax long after the disaster, a memory cherished by Haligonians to this day."

The *Boston Evening Globe* had a reporter on board who told of the "huge crowds who cheered the ship, the captain, the crew and her precious cargo."

The day after *Calvin Austin* left Boston Harbor, *Northland* followed her up the coast with more medical and reconstruction professionals, plus $100,000 worth of supplies and $25,000 worth of trucks, plus the gas and chauffeurs needed to operate them.

The rest of New England followed Boston's lead. Tiny Calais, Maine, sent its Red Cross unit, consisting of two doctors and nine nurses. The State of Maine hospital shipped thirty-six medical professionals to work in a temporary hospital, and the Rhode Island Chapter of the American Red Cross sponsored more than 100 who made house calls in the Devastated Area until a temporary hospital opened up.

With all these doctors and nurses coming into Halifax, the Halifax Relief Committee felt comfortable letting the first exhausted group head back to their towns across the Maritimes, Canada, and New England.

On Wednesday night, Nova Scotia's lieutenant governor and his wife held a reception at Government House to provide official recognition of Boston's contributions. The Boston doctors pulled up in the flatbed trucks that had arrived that day from Boston on *Northland.* According to the report of Boston's Major Giddings, all present enjoyed "a delightful and informal dinner," followed by a toast by His Honor the Governor to "the President and the King," which might have been a first, and the singing of both national anthems.

"Thus," Giddings wrote, "the event assumed a certain international significance. In fact, Governor Grant during the course of his remarks expressed what we all felt, namely, that, lamentable as the disaster was, it had undoubtedly furthered the cordial relations between Canada and the United States."

Subsequent reports and correspondence confirmed this transformation between the often-uneasy neighbors. As Halifax's Dr. Harris reported, "A terrible catastrophe had been the occasion for that expression of practical sympathy which the quick-witted American is always ready to display. . . . One of the chief features of the medical aspect of the Halifax disaster is the extreme promptness with which the great Republic to the south sent, all unsolicited, the resources of its own preparedness to the help of our stricken people."

The help didn't stop with the healing. Governor McCall's relief committee would send a complete warehouse of household goods—everything from new stoves, bathtubs, and beds—so hundreds could replace what they'd lost and feel like they were shopping while doing it. The help received felt less like a national handout than a gift from a neighbor. This respect for the victims' dignity was not lost on the locals.

To explain Boston's "splendid outburst of help and sympathy for this city," the *Halifax Herald* outlined the history of "ancient ties of blood and kinship," emphasizing all the two nations had in common, instead of their differences.

On December 13, 1917, before the Boston contingent returned to Massachusetts, R. T. MacIlreith, chairman of the Halifax Relief Committee, sent a copy of a formal resolution to Boston's Major Giddings, which expressed the Committee's

deep appreciation of the prompt and humane action of the authorities in Boston in dispatching your
corps to Halifax, and of the professional efficiency
and noble spirit which you and all members of your
unit have exhibited since coming to our stricken
city. We shall always bear you in grateful remem-
brance, and wish you a safe journey home.

Yours Truly, R.T. MacIlreith, Chairman, Relief
Committee.

Massachusetts's contributions to Halifax totaled more
than $750,000—$15 million today—and that was probably conservative. So surprising was the overwhelming
help from Boston that what most survivors mentioned
first when being interviewed years later was the "instant
and unstinting aid from the State of Massachusetts."

After Major Giddings returned to Boston, he sent the
following telegram to Lieutenant-Colonel McKelvey
Bell: "At Hospital you will find packages of cigarettes,
chocolates, etc., from Colonel Brooks who wishes you
to accept it with his compliments for personal or any
other use you see fit. We arrived home safely and all
so glad of opportunity to contribute our bit. —H. G.
Giddings."

Just six years earlier, Canadian Conservatives were
portraying Americans as "a corrupt, bragging, boodle-

hunting and negro lynching crowd from which Canadian workingmen and the Canadian land of milk and honey must be saved."

Six years later, the American response to the Halifax tragedy inspired Clark Hall to write a poem titled "Record of Halifax Explosion," which includes this stanza:

"God bless our neighbours to the South,
God bless them one and all
Who responded so magnificently
To humanity's urgent call. . . .

It sounded like the start of a great relationship.

PART VII

Rebuilding

Chapter 34

The Missing and the Dead

Thursday, December 13

A week after the explosion, the searchers digging through the Richmond ruins continued to find survivors, badly damaged but alive. Most of their work entailed shoveling charred remains into baskets, buckets, and washtubs, then passing them on to the corps of undertakers who had arrived from across Canada, to sift the remains for rings, dentures, and other clues that might help a relative identify them.

And yet for weeks afterward, families, friends, and colleagues continued to fill the Halifax newspapers' newly created "Missing" sections. These entries didn't require many words to affect the reader, including this one about Noble Driscoll's family:

"Walter Driscoll, 1549 Barrington Street, his wife and several children are in hospital in Truro. Wife and children practically uninjured. Driscoll's injury is severe. Enquiring for Gordon Driscoll, 11 years old, reported to have been seen by several people. If any information is received I will be pleased to have it communicated to me. H. O. McClatchy, Truro."

In just fifty-four words, Mr. McClatchy touched on the family's blessings, their injuries, and their painful uncertainty, without mentioning Art Driscoll's mute state, brought on by trauma.

"Missing: Donald Cameron. Answers to Donnie, 4-1/2 years, fair hair, dark grey eyes. Wore red sweater or nightgown. Was moved on first ambulance from Roome Street on Thursday morning. Father anxious."

"Would the soldier who rescued baby from unconscious woman's arms on Longard Road the morning of the explosion return baby to its parents, 9 Longard Road."

Stories like this no doubt gave hope to the thousands of people missing loved ones, but it would almost always prove a false hope.

The page included a less-common "found" notice: "The owner of the girl baby about 2 months old which was handed to a young lady on Gottingen Street, being previously picked up on Almon Street by a soldier, in a pasteboard box covered with an older child's check coat, can get same by applying at 1461 Shirley Street."

Except for the increasingly rare cases of people being found in another home in Halifax, Dartmouth, or an hour away in Truro, Amherst, New Glasgow, or another outpost, a week after the explosion getting news of missing loved ones was almost always bad news. But even finding out they had died provided some closure.

On December 12, Gordon and James Pattison learned that their missing eight-year-old brother, Alan, who had walked with them to the dockyard en route to Richmond School, had been identified by Mrs. Pattison's brother at the morgue. A day later, the same uncle identified the body of their ten-year-old sister, Catherine, which had been exhumed from the wreckage of their home. That left only Mr. Pattison still unaccounted for, but since he had been working at the Acadia Sugar Refinery, whose ten-story tower had been "snapped like a carrot," Mrs. Pattison had to face the fact that she had probably lost her husband along with two children, and sank deeper into despair.

But with her parents, her brother, and her sons Gordon and James all surviving, Mrs. Pattison had more motivation than many. After ten days "in hospital" at the YMCA, she joined her sons at her parents' home in Dartmouth.

On December 16, Bertha Bond wrote another letter to her fiancé, Sandy, in which she described one family that now had to live in the kitchen, their only sound room. She mentioned one friend was "grieving dreadfully" because her son, who had been working at the Richmond Printing Company, had not yet been found. Another friend had just received the great relief that her daughter was alive and well in Truro.

Her note then turned to her fiancé. "Those little things you sent me for safe keeping, and all you had given me but my ring are gone, and I did prize them so much."

But when her fiancé replied with a Christmas card from the Western Front, she replied that it now ranked as one of her most cherished possessions.

In 1917, fingerprints and dental records were not commonly used to identify corpses, and DNA hadn't been discovered. Furthermore, the military knew within days that it had lost hundreds of servicemen, but it didn't know how to account for them, and the Royal Canadian Navy decided not to publish a list of its deceased.

Some sailors could be recognized by the documents they carried, including military paybooks and leave passes, indicating they had been in Halifax to enjoy a few days of rest and relaxation before heading back to the trenches. A crewman from the British *Calonne*, who had just received his honorable discharge from the service and was now free to do whatever he liked with the rest of his life, was labeled victim No. 209. His name, John Hurley, was on the certificate in his pocket.

Some could be distinguished by their tattoos, like the sailor from the British *Picton* who had one of Buffalo Bill's head on the back of his right hand, and another of a serpent and a butterfly on the top of his right arm. These helped to determine that he was twenty-five-year-old Charles Dunn from Scotland.

But even such direct means often fell short. Another sailor had a flag of Norway tattooed over his heart, alongside a female figure. On his right arm, he had a horseshoe and the words "Sailor's Grave" and "Good Luck." Despite such telling marks, he was never identified, perhaps because anyone who might have seen those marks had also been killed.

Even with the new vulcanized asbestos dog tags British soldiers had been issued in 1916 and 1917, identification could still be difficult, and identifying civilians was much harder. A boy of about seven had carried a

Canadian soldier's coat button, another marked "N.S. Forces," and a shoulder insignia, CANADA, the kind of souvenirs Halifax boys loved to collect during the Great War. The young boy was never identified, which had to be agonizing for his parents—unless the reason was a wider tragedy: there weren't any relatives left to search for him.

After holding these corpses for eleven days, pushing the limits of safety, officials decided they needed to bury ninety-five of the unidentified, badly charred bodies. They scheduled a mass funeral for Monday afternoon, December 17, 1917, at the Chebucto Road schoolyard. The weather that day was similar to that of Thursday, December 6: cold, clear, and calm, with the addition of snow-covered streets and a haze that settled over Halifax before the service.

Three thousand mourners gathered, standing a block deep on each side of the school. Those who still had missing loved ones had to wonder if they were in one of those caskets. The thought might have even brought some peace.

They needed a funeral to gather as a community and acknowledge all those losses and pay their respects to the dead. This was the first of many, but perhaps the most important. The service they witnessed echoed the kind a platoon of soldiers received overseas after a costly battle.

Soldiers carried the wreath-covered caskets from the mortuary and laid them in rows on the snow-covered ground, placing the children's small white caskets closest to the crowd, while the Princess Louise Fusiliers band played the funeral march.

Each coffin included a plaque recording where the body had been found; the victim's likely age, sex, hair color, build, distinguishing marks or tattoos, and clothing; the contents of their pockets; and any jewelry they might have been wearing. There was an optimistic decency in this final extra effort. Everyone involved, from the soldiers recovering the bodies and effects to the people recording all they could before burying the remains, had to know that the odds of the corpses being identified were slim, and yet they went to these lengths, outside in cold, miserable conditions, instead of simply bagging the body and moving on, for a simple reason: someone, somewhere was missing this person, and one more scrap of information could make all the difference in identifying a loved one. Those present could take some comfort in knowing everyone had done all they could for the dead and for their families.

Still, no one could mitigate the sadness of the event. One deceased mother had been found clasping a baby so closely that they could not be separated, so they were placed together in one coffin.

Even in death, the mourners maintained the divide between Protestants and Catholics as best they could. The Protestant service was conducted first. After the band played "O God, Our Help in Ages Past" with the crowd singing, the Anglican archbishop of Nova Scotia delivered his sermon.

"It is not by the hand of the Almighty these unfortunate human beings have suffered, but by the mistakes of others," he said, echoing the sentiment of Reverend Swetnam. The Bishop urged his audience to take care of the children still with them, then ended the service with "Abide with Me."

> When other helpers fail and comforts flee
> Help of the helpless, oh, abide with me

The soldiers lifted the caskets onto large trucks, with the Protestant victims sent to the Fairview Cemetery off Windsor, where most of the *Titanic* victims had been buried, and the Catholic remains heading to Mount Olivet on Mumford Street. Both caravans were preceded by a band playing "The Dead March in Saul."

The dead march in Saul
Blood must be shed
Now time for eternal rest
The reign of terror is coming to an end now

They loaded the caskets on trucks and flat wagons. When they realized they had too many caskets and too few motors, a policeman commandeered horse-drawn sleighs, whose drivers were hard-pressed to decline. With caskets stacked two and three high on trucks and sleighs, the dignitaries and citizens walked solemnly behind to the cemeteries.

The *Morning Chronicle* reported, "No such procession had ever trod the streets of this city, and the prayer of all people here, of all creeds and no creed, must be, 'God grant so sad a sight may never be witnessed here again.'"

Wherever the unidentified were interred, their stories were buried with them.

The ninety-five unidentified victims were only a fraction of those the Mortuary Committee had to address. For two solid weeks fifty soldiers were assigned the task of burying the dead, right up to Christmas Eve. On the chance that the unidentified victims might be identified later, they used the same numbers to hold the victims' effects to mark slabs at the head of the graves and inside the coffins, with a chart recording all the information they had.

Thus, by Christmas, hundreds of lives had been reduced to numbers.

Chapter 35
The Inquiry

December 13, 1917–February 4, 1918

Haligonians still wanted to know what happened in the harbor that day, and to to hold people to account.

The Canadian and British legal systems pursued this question over the next two and a half years during four judicial tribunals: the Wreck Commissioner's Inquiry, which convened on December 13, 1917; a trial in Halifax, starting in April 1918; an appeal to the Supreme Court of Canada in Ottawa in March 1919; and finally an appeal to the Privy Council in London in January 1920.

The first of these, the Wreck Commissioner's Inquiry, was automatically opened whenever a serious accident occurred in the harbor. Its mission was to determine what caused the collision and to provide recommendations to ensure it didn't happen again. But because *Mont-Blanc*'s attorney and the judge assigned to the case perceived it as a dress rehearsal for the trial that was bound to follow, they approached the Inquiry as a practice trial, less interested in discovering what went wrong and how to fix it than in assigning blame.

The objective pursuit of truth was impeded by the fact that *Imo*'s captain, Haakon From, and Harbour Pilot William Hayes had both been killed when the tsunami tossed *Imo* toward Tufts' Cove, and that the captain and crew of *Mont-Blanc* were French. The tension between British-Canadians and French-Canadians goes back to the first European settlers and came to a fever pitch in the 1910s, with the French Liberals campaigning for Reciprocity and against conscription, and the English Conservatives opposing them on both issues, which threatened to tear the country apart. Add to this the persistent rumors that Captain Le Médec's last-second decision to cut across *Imo*'s bow was actually intentional, designed to create the collision, fire, and explosion that followed, and the men of *Mont-Blanc* clearly had their work cut out for them when it came to public opinion.

An editorial in the *Truro Daily News* expressed a common opinion when it said those responsible for " 'such a needless collision' in clear weather 'should be hung in good old-fashioned style' from the yardarm."

Yellow journalism was still in vogue, and was practiced widely. But even if it hadn't been, people recovering from the greatest man-made disaster in North American history should expect some answers. If the investigation proved some were guilty of criminal negligence or worse, the death penalty would not seem unreasonable at a time when sons overseas were being executed for desertion.

It was in this twitchy atmosphere that the Wreck Commissioner's Court convened on December 13, 1917, exactly one week after the explosion, while families were still digging out their homes and trying to find loved ones.

The lawyers on both sides were considered the best of the Nova Scotia bar. The *Mont-Blanc*'s company, captain, and crew were represented by Joseph Nolan, an established New York attorney retained by the French government, and by Humphrey Mellish, who would prove to be every bit as mushy as his name. On the other side, defending the *Imo*'s company and crew, was Charles J. Burchell, forty-two, in the early stages of a sterling six-decade run in the Nova Scotia courts. He was widely regarded as a first-rate attorney but a bit of a brawler.

With the Inquiry convening just a week after the explosion, legal experts felt reassured to see an experienced and respected Halifax jurist, the Honourable Arthur Drysdale, sixty, on the bench. He served on the province's Supreme Court and had a federal appointment as a district judge in the Admiralty for Nova Scotia. Thus, the feeling was that Drysdale would know both the law and the sea, and how they intersected.

The old courthouse on Spring Garden Road featured a large room with twenty-five-foot ceilings, befitting a Hollywood movie set. Its boarded-up windows and two oil lamps substituting for electric lights made the room even darker than usual, which radiated venerable English authority, designed not to comfort but to intimidate. From an elevated pulpit, Justice Drysdale, a lean man with a thick, dark mustache, would look down on witnesses, the counsel, and the gallery, which was packed each day.

Although there were forty-eight witnesses to cross-examine, the pattern quickly became clear: *Mont-Blanc* attorney Mellish was surprisingly timid, *Imo*'s Burchell was predictably aggressive, and Judge Drysdale sided with the latter. According to legal analyst

John Kerr, writing in *Ground Zero*, Burchell repeatedly "browbeat and misled witnesses, disregarded all the rules of courtroom etiquette and, on a number of occasions, violated the standards of legal ethics."

The problem was, it worked. Burchell was as skilled at pandering to the press as the press was unable to resist. Whenever Burchell intimated some misdeeds by a witness, the papers would publish them as established fact, regardless of how the witness responded.

Burchell understood something his adversary Mellish didn't: this first case was being adjudicated less by the Wreck Commission than by the court of public opinion, and public opinion was on his side. Burchell shamelessly fed the public's and press's anti-French prejudice, too, with similar success.

Burchell warned witnesses whose testimony favored *Mont-Blanc* not to lie, yet he lied to at least two witnesses. When Burchell presented chief examining officer F. Evan Wyatt as a prime example of English snobbery, he probably thought Wyatt would lie down, but he was in for a surprise.

Wyatt brought the confidence and courage of a seasoned seaman, and he wasn't about to roll over for a grandstanding attorney. When Burchell told Wyatt he had two witnesses ready to testify that Wyatt had ordered the dockyard evacuated, Wyatt called his bluff, demanding to know who those witnesses were. Burchell had no such witnesses, and started to back-pedal. Wyatt went on the attack, accusing Burchell of impropriety and embarrassing him badly—but not for long. Burchell quickly recovered and returned to his assertive approach. With Judge Drysdale, the press, and the public on Burchell's side, he paid little price for his ploy.

On February 4, one week after the final witness had appeared, Judge Drysdale published his opinion, laced with vituperatives toward Wyatt, Mackey, Le Médec, and *Mont-Blanc*'s crew. He managed to summarize the largest man-made explosion, with millions in damage and thousands of lives changed forever, in a single page, finding that Pilot Mackey and Captain Le Médec were "wholly and solely responsible for the collision." Further, Drysdale recommended that French authorities cancel Le Médec's master's ticket, that Mackey's license be canceled, and that he be prosecuted in criminal court. Finally, he found Wyatt guilty of neglect and recommended that he be disciplined—while making no mention whatsoever of *Imo*'s captain and pilot.

Mackey, Le Médec, and Wyatt were soon arrested and charged with manslaughter in the death of *Imo*'s harbor pilot, William Hayes.

Some observers were outraged by the conduct of

Mr. Burchell and the ruling of Judge Drysdale, but the majority of the press and the public cheered the decision. The people needed someone to blame, and to know that the universe was not as randomly cruel as it seemed. Burchell and Drysdale offered both, and the public accepted it.

Chapter 36
Christmas 1917

M ost Haligonians found the idea of shopping for Christmas gifts, singing carols, or celebrating too frivolous, even disrespectful. But on Monday, December 17, 1917—the day of the mass burial, eleven days after the explosion, and eight days before Christmas—a piece appeared on the front page of Halifax's *Daily Echo* suggesting that the surviving children should be given some joy this Christmas.

The children's section of the paper, called the "Sunshine Club," started a fund for children in hospitals and institutions to give them "the best Christmas they ever had." Cousin Peggy, editor of the Sunshine Club, wrote of one "wee maiden" who had taken the ice cream and presents from her birthday party to the Children's Hospital. In the same spirit, Cousin Peggy invited her young readers to donate their toys or money so the less fortunate could enjoy a bit of the Christmas spirit.

Newspapers in 1917 commonly sponsored "children's clubs" to provide a better Christmas for poor children. But the explosion greatly expanded the list of needy, directly affecting about 10,000 children, according to the paper, who had lost their homes or family members, or both. Adding insult to injury, the gifts their parents had purchased that year had often been destroyed.

One little girl, Marjorie Drysdale, lived in the middle of Richmond. She had asked her parents for a popular, expensive doll, but they didn't have much money, so she didn't think she would get it. One day before the blast, curiosity got the best of her, so she peeked under the tree, peeled back a corner of the wrapping paper, and saw that her parents had, in fact, bought her the special doll. A day later, their house was flattened by the explosion and burned to cinders, killing both parents. But Marjorie was always grateful for her indiscretion, knowing how far her parents had been willing to go to make her happy.

On December 19, the *Echo* reported that its appeal had worked: toys, books, and money for young survivors were pouring in. The next day, local stores felt it was acceptable to advertise again. A big store called Went-zells ran this ad: "Mister, do you think Santa Claus will be around this Christmas? Many and many a little kiddy has asked that question in the last few days. Is he going to come around to your home? Don't darken the kiddies' Christmas any more than you can help. Don't let them 'know' more than you can help. Life's trials and sorrows enter only too soon into their lives. When you are ready to buy your Christmas supplies, we are ready."

Because Halifax merchants had missed most of their holiday sales after the explosion while simultaneously giving generously to the recovery effort, the *Halifax Herald* urged Nova Scotians to eschew mail orders to central Canada or the U.S. and spend those dollars shopping at local stores. On December 20, Halifax merchants held a meeting to set up "Santa Claus Limited," a public appeal for money, workers, gifts, and automobiles to deliver Christmas to needy children. They figured they needed to raise $5,000 to provide 10,000 packages, one for each needy child.

On December 21, the *Mail* carried the appeal, with photographs of six wounded and homeless children: "Although the people of Halifax have performed veritable miracles," the merchants wrote, "greater efforts must be made. Tangible Christmas cheer must enter every home over which hangs a shadow cast by the great disaster."

They hoped to deliver a package of fruit, candy, and cake on Christmas morning to every child who had lost their home. They asked for "250 ladies" to volunteer for the task, and fifty cars loaned to distribute them. "You can't refuse THEIR call."

On December 22, the *Echo* reported a crowd of volunteers had shown up, with $183 already donated. It was just the start.

Little by little, everyday life returned to Halifax, including crass commercialism. The H. H. Marshall store advertised *The Halifax Catastrophe*, a book of forty photos, for fifty cents by mail. The curious could also buy *Views of the Halifax Disaster* by Royal Print & Litho, which sold 10,000 copies by December 25. Or you could buy *Devastated Halifax, 50 views*, published by Gerald E. Weir. "This book is interesting and instructive," he wrote, "and you will be glad to have it in later years—a book that your friends will be delighted to receive—especially the boys at the front. Mailed to any address in Canada, United States, or overseas."

For the survivors and their loved ones fighting overseas, "delighted" might not have been the most accurate description of their reaction to a picture book of the disaster.

Collections for Santa Claus Limited were conducted in rural schools, at concerts, and almost anywhere people gathered. More than a few kids donated their pocket money. Contributors' names were printed in the paper, including the children's. On Christmas Eve, the *Echo* reported that the Sunshine Club, whose goal was to raise $5,000 to provide 10,000 presents, had raised more than $13,000, plus gifts of every kind.

They now needed cars and drivers, which they thought would be difficult to find after so many cars had gone out of commission during the blizzard. But fifty drivers and their automobiles assembled at the Halifax Academy to distribute the parcels.

When the YMCA, which still housed victims, put up a Christmas tree, other facilities followed. At the Waegwoltic Club, a temporary hospital, the Christmas tree was enjoyed "as much by an eighty-five-year-old grandmother as it was by an eleven-month-old girl who had lost one eye." Only one facility, Camp Hill Hospital, had no tree, because it was still too crowded with explosion victims to spare the space for one.

In spite of the tremendous effort, for many families Christmas merely provided a poignant reminder of their losses.

Frank Burford, the fifteen-year-old who had unwittingly saved himself when he went to fetch a parcel, had lost his father in the blast. He was staying with relatives outside the city and received no presents. Instead, he got a letter from his older sister confirming his father's death, and that his mother was still in the hospital. As he recalled, "We had nothing to rejoice about."

James and Gordon Pattison remembered Christmas 1917 as a "blank day." They had lost two siblings, and assumed their father was dead. As hard as it was, James said, "It made you sensitive to other people's anguish, too."

Christmas for the Driscolls had always been a highlight of the year when they exchanged small presents, none costing much. In 1917, however, they had just left Truro for a big house in South Uniacke, about 30 miles northwest of Halifax. Their father had lost one eye, five-year-old Art was still in the hospital and had not spoken, and Gordon had not been found. They gathered for Christmas as before, but without Christmas cake or much cheer.

The week before Christmas, the morgue made several more identifications, including a young mother and her four children, and the Mortuary Committee conducted another large burial.

The atmosphere didn't stop people from trying, and with some success. The Overseas Club, a social organization, invited twenty-four destitute children aboard the *Lord Kelvin*, docked in the harbor, where they were served turkey with all the trimmings, followed by ice cream. Then, from behind a tree, the hosts brought out a "mystery box" for each child, to their delight.

Mrs. Michael Dwyer donated a part of her large house for a temporary home for children leaving the hospital, and helped finance it, too. Christmas there was a great success with the boys and girls, who received nice toys including granddaughter Eileen's fancy dollhouse, which she insisted on contributing.

With the young patients worried that Santa Claus would not be able to visit them because their hospitals lacked chimneys, the staff worked yet more overtime to assuage this fear. Doctors and nurses decorated the facilities and began their morning rounds by singing Christmas carols. Santa visited every hospital, and young patients woke to find a well-stuffed stocking on their bed.

Evelyn Johnson, an eleven-year-old student at St. Joseph's who had almost had her arm amputated before her mother intervened, was recovering at the YMCA, where an unusually jolly Father Christmas was making the rounds. She realized he was actually her favorite doctor, an American who had a knack for making the children laugh.

At St. Paul's Hall, Samuel Prince, a distinguished professor who would produce a seminal report on the catastrophe for Columbia University, traded in his black robe for a red gown to play Santa Claus "with gusto."

The children's fears that Santa wouldn't find them were quickly dispelled.

Those who spent Christmas day working in the crowded hospitals often remarked on the patients' depth of appreciation, giving the workers their most meaningful Christmas. One woman, tired and foot weary after hours of volunteer work, said "I think that today brought me to a greater understanding of the true meaning of Christmas."

After returning to Wolfville near midnight on Saturday, December 8, Ernest Barss collapsed at his parents' home. After three days working nonstop with only a few hours of sleep, even his shell-shock symptoms could not keep him from sleeping that night, or the next. In fact, he said, he had to rest up for a few days before he could muster the energy to write a proper letter to his uncle Andrew about what he'd seen and done in Halifax.

Ernest Barss closed his letter to his uncle, dated December 14, 1917, with an apology. "Well, this isn't much of a Christmas letter, is it? We don't feel particularly hilarious at the present time, I tell you. There is only one good result that I can see in the awful accident. It may make people realize that there is a war on. It had been awfully hard to bring it home to a great many even yet."

But the explosion did something else, too: it changed Barss's outlook. Instead of obsessing about all that he'd lost—his career in Montreal, Eileen, his health, and his prospects—he started looking forward to what he wanted to do next. When he had boarded the train to Halifax with Elliott, Barss knew he didn't want to run the family grocery store in Wolfville or work for a corporation in Montreal, and he certainly didn't want to stay in the military. But he didn't know what he wanted to do—or what he *could* do. Three days spent helping people whose lives had been upended more dramatically than his quenched a thirst inside him that nothing else could reach. On the long train ride home it came to him: he wanted to become a doctor to heal others.

Now, back in his parents' home, he had to figure out how—without the academic prerequisites, any money to speak of, steady hands or two good feet—he could make that dream a reality.

Chapter 37
Orphans

The blast left thousands of children orphaned. Others had lost one parent, while the other parent was still in the hospital or in recovery, leaving the children effectively orphaned for at least a few weeks or more.

The problems specific to children started with the registration process, with babies who couldn't speak, children with no documents, and many faces hard to recognize due to stubborn soot or disfiguring wounds. They were also susceptible to being mis-identified by desperate parents or even uncles, aunts, or cousins convinced that this was their child, and if they didn't claim them immediately, they might never see them again.

In the first days after the explosion, unauthorized adoptions prompted the authorities to institute a more rigorous identification process on both sides, while making appeals for the return of children mistakenly taken from the centers. It appears most cases were probably resolved, but since poor records were kept initially, no one can be certain how many there were, and if they were rectified. For the many parents who couldn't find their babies, these widely publicized errors added untold grief, but also a tempting hope that their toddlers might be alive and well somewhere.

In recognition of these unique issues, on Tuesday, December 11, the Relief Committee formed a special Children's Committee. By the end of December 1917, the committee had made contact with 500 families and 1,500 children: 200 needed hospital treatment, 48 suffered eye injuries, and 8 had been completely blinded. According to their records, the explosion created 180 fatherless children, 120 motherless children, and 70 orphans who had lost both, often in an instant—and these numbers are probably low estimates.

Cases read like this: "Four children, mother dead, father blind."

"Three children, father dead, mother badly injured."

In one family, both the mother and father had been killed, so their eighteen-year-old daughter took over responsibility for raising her three younger siblings.

In 111 other families, the mothers had been seriously injured or killed, and the fathers were fighting overseas. Even when the surviving parent lived in Halifax, they usually had to work long hours, so they often boarded the remaining children with others until their load lightened, visiting when they could in the meantime.

In 1917, before the explosion, Halifax was home to a half dozen orphanages, usually supported by private donations and churches. Two served Protestants, and four served Catholics. All six would have been overwhelmed by the influx of orphans after the disaster, but the situation was exacerbated because the Protestant Orphanage was destroyed. Given the pressing need, the Protestant Orphanage soon reopened as a temporary accommodation and was eventually rebuilt.

That still left a great demand for adoptive parents, both temporary and permanent. If the mother had been debilitated or killed while the father was off at war, family or friends often took their children, with a catch: they had to be of the same religion. This stipulation precluded Protestants and Catholics from adopting children of the other faith, with some heart-wrenching results.

The registration form of one soldier's family read as follows: "Daniel, soldier, killed. Mary, his wife, missing. Anna, 9-1/2, O.K. Kathleen, 11, missing, Helen, 7, missing. Ethel, 5, killed. Gerald, 3, killed. Michael,

1, killed. Everything destroyed." This left nine-and-a-half-year-old Anna by herself. When relatives from another town offered to take Anna in, the committee performed a basic background check, and determined it would be a good fit. Anna moved in with them, and all seemed well until the local church objected that Anna was not the same religion as her relatives. The committee brought her back to live in the orphanage in Halifax, adding another disruption to an already interrupted childhood.

A month after the explosion, the committee published a list of eighty names in local papers of children who were still missing, with few or no signs of their fate. Headed INFORMATION WANTED REGARDING MISSING CHILDREN, it assured readers that all communication would be confidential. A few of those children were actually found, but most appeared later on a list of the dead in the 1918 Halifax City Directory.

If the mother had been badly injured or killed while the father was fighting overseas, the military would not grant compassionate leave quickly, if at all. When no parents were left to care for their children, the committee took over, assuming the role of in loco parentis while working to find suitable homes for as many orphans as possible. The committee was blunt in its assessment of its new wards: "Coloured or feeble minded orphans," the committee believed, constituted a "special problem." Likewise, the committee stated that "disobedient or incorrigible" boys or girls would need to be considered in a different light.

But the committee members also seemed sympathetic to what the children had just endured. "It is of great importance to fully realize now, before it is too late, the tremendous change which this disaster has wrought in the lives of so many Halifax children, and to provide, in so far as human wisdom can, every safeguard, every advantage and opportunity for the children."

The committee didn't have to look very hard for takers, with more than a thousand offers coming in from across North America, though some were more suitable than others. Some writers had no qualms about expressing a preference for blue-eyed, fair-haired children. One man went so far as to say he would like to take in two healthy children, a boy and a girl, aged ten to twelve, who had good family backgrounds, dispositions, and manners, while hinting that children with red hair, upturned noses, or "weak chins" would not be welcome. The man received a response, but no orphans.

But his was not the crassest request they received.

An official from a state in the Deep South wrote, "Send fifty colored girls at once." His wish was not fulfilled.

Committee members replied to each and every letter or telegram—no matter how offensive, apparently—including those asking for strong boys, because the writers were probably looking for cheap farmhands. The worst sides surfaced, but once again, simple humanity ultimately won. The vast majority of correspondents were sincere in their desire to help.

From Charlottetown, Prince Edward Island, a telegram said: HAVE SIXTY PRIVATE HOMES FOR CHILDREN MOSTLY PROTESTANT / SOME FOR PERMANENT ADOPTION / REST WILLING TO HOME INDEFINITE TIME. Charlottetown authorities offered to send a committee to handle the transition.

Some were touching, including this letter from a Dutch immigrant near Edmonton, Alberta, who wrote, "I hope you excuse mine writing but I am only four year in Canada . . . and I cannot explain myself the way I wanted, but I do feel sorry for all the poor little ones. Please let me know, I was an orphan child myself and know what it is, to be without a home." Due to the distance, he was not given a child, but thanked sincerely for his heartfelt offer.

One of the nine nurses sent by the Calais, Maine, Red Cross gave a speech when she returned, telling her neighbors what she'd seen and how Halifax was recovering. When she finished, a dozen families approached her, offering to take in some of the Halifax orphans. The nurse promised to help them navigate immigration.

Despite the flood of offers from afar, the committee decided it would be best to place the orphans in Nova Scotia homes whenever possible, because it would be less disruptive for the children, easier to keep an eye on them, and Nova Scotia would not lose more of the next generation—an important consideration for a province that had already lost so much of its younger population to Quebec, Ontario, the Great War, and the explosion itself. For all the heartbreaking situations the children faced, most of them were taken in by caring families, usually relatives, and often had the chance to choose among several good options.

But even a good match couldn't guarantee a successful transition. The newly orphaned children had been deeply affected by what they had seen and lost, but there was no grief counseling in 1917. Some children were placed with relatives they barely knew who lived far away or already had more children than they could care for. If behavioral problems surfaced, children were often moved from home to home or separated from their siblings—the only people who might truly understand what they were going through. If these matches failed, they ended up back in the orphanages.

As a result, some children's lives were filled with a flash of tragedy followed by a lifetime of sadness, where they couldn't settle in anywhere, hold down a steady job, or maintain a healthy relationship. In these cases, perhaps, they might have been better off bypassing the closer options for one of the warm invitations from farther away.

Barbara Orr was one of the "explosion orphans." Her story seemed to unfold like so many war-child tales that tell of the long, hard struggle to piece a normal life back together. She often worried that her two youngest siblings, to whom she loved to read, had been found somewhere but could not give their names. Because their house had burned down, she knew it was unlikely, but the thought still troubled her.

Barbara moved in with the aunt who found her and her husband. Later her uncle had to tell her most of her family had not yet been found and that it was assumed they were dead. When their bodies were later discovered, Barbara had to identify them at the Chebucto Road School morgue.

Barbara received offers from three related families to move in, and she was old enough to choose for herself—two silver linings. After careful consideration, she decided the quiet of the Dartmouth home, which had no other children, was too much for her to take. She missed the constant noise of five siblings in one house, and liked the idea of living with her aunt Edna and uncle William MacTaggart Orr, who had children about her age, including lifelong friends Gladys and Bill.

This left Barbara with the difficult task of telling her Dartmouth aunt and uncle that she wanted to move back across the harbor to Richmond. Though it's clear Barbara made the right decision, it's hard not to feel something for her Dartmouth relatives.

For someone who had lost almost everything, however, it's even harder to judge Barbara for this simple preference.

Chapter 38
"Don't Stare"

Of the many doctors who traveled to Halifax to help, 102 were Canadian out-of-towners, usually from Nova Scotia and New Brunswick, and 120 came from the United States, most of them New Englanders who set up shop at Bellevue, Halifax Ladies' College, and the USS *Old Colony*. The number of out-of-town nurses, both Canadian and American, who worked incredible hours for days was even more impressive: 459.

Lieutenant-Colonel McKelvey Bell later reported that the suddenly robust medical staff in Halifax had performed 250 eye removals and 25 amputations over about two weeks. But even these figures are low, as they do not include house calls or patients treated in doctors' offices, homes, and any number of impromptu operating rooms, some of which converted back to dinner tables a week later.

The doctors and nurses gave generously of their time, expertise, and effort. Some paid a price for it long after they returned home, unable to shake the sights they had seen. The *Halifax Herald* told the story of one doctor from Sydney, Nova Scotia, at the northern tip of the province, who could not reconcile all that he had witnessed, and probably experienced something similar to the shell shock Barss and others experienced. Back in Sydney, he talked incessantly of the horrific scenes he had encountered. When he concluded he could not shake them, he committed suicide.

The gratitude shown to the Boston doctors from the Canadian prime minister and the patients was sincere and well earned. But eventually it threatened to obscure the vast and vital work of the "first responders," those doctors who lived in Halifax, Dartmouth, and nearby, and came running without being called to administer to thousands of victims—presumably the worst of the worst, since they were in the most urgent need of help—a full day or two before most outsiders arrived.

This habit of heaping praise on the foreigners eventually made many Halifax doctors bristle, some of whom reached a breaking point when an article appeared on February 2, 1918, in the Halifax *Evening Mail* crediting local doctors with merely "materially helping with the wounded." This outraged the local doctors, who felt compelled to write letters to the editors of the *Halifax Herald* on February 16 and the *Morning Chronicle* on February 18.

"Some of the medical men of this city have resented this manner of describing the part played in the surgery arising out of the explosion," they wrote, correctly pointing out that local doctors and nurses "bore the whole burden" of medical work for the first forty-eight hours, when the majority of victims were first treated and before the Americans showed up on Saturday morning.

"The splendid work done by the American surgeons is hereby not in the least minimized," the Halifax doctors continued, "but the local practitioners naturally resent being described merely as helpers during a period in which, unquestionably, they and their provincial brethren were the chief performers."

This tendency to discount the contributions of local doctors continued for decades, but it's worth clarifying that they had no quarrel with the American doctors themselves, just the journalists and historians who too often diminished their efforts. Quite the opposite—the Canadian and American doctors performed one of the great acts of international cooperation, putting aside recent national politics and petty egos in the service of a greater good. They departed exhausted but exhilarated, with a profound sense of shared purpose and respect.

"The best traditions of the medical profession gained greater glory during the calamity at Halifax," Dr. Thomas A. Foster of Portland, Maine, said. "The heroic devotion of the Canadian physicians" was a "stimulant to their willing and eager American counterparts."

Perhaps the final word is this: of the hundreds of doctors and nurses from near and far who helped the 9,000 explosion victims, all of them were necessary. Years later, when the doctors and nurses who helped out began passing away, their heroic work in Halifax decades before was often highlighted in their obituaries.

With the advantage of a century of hindsight, we can add this: the moment people had the luxury of weighing who contributed how much, the crisis had passed, and the business of returning life to normal was well under way. The truth was simple: all the doctors and nurses did everything they could, and they did it remarkably well.

The soldiers continued exhuming human remains from the ruins until January 11, 1918—a full thirty-four days after the explosion. As doggedly as they had worked, they finished with hundreds of people still unaccounted for.

Coroner Arthur Barnstead could not solve all the mysteries the explosion had created. While Barnstead is credited with identifying about 60 percent of the estimated 1,951 victims, 242 could not be identified because they were too disfigured, or no family members were left to claim them. Another 410 were listed as missing, but their bodies were never found—entire lives erased in less time than it takes to blink.

On February 4, 1918, the Mortuary Committee reported that it had interred some 1,400 identified victims, and 150 more who had not been identified. But even this figure is low, because hundreds of bodies never reached the Chebucto Road School morgue. Some of the victims, like Captain Brennan, were so close to *Mont-Blanc* that they literally vanished, like the ship itself. Other bodies weren't discovered until the spring, when construction workers clearing sites for new buildings found more bodies in the rubble, mud, and dirt. Clearing away the wreckage of Hills & Sons Foundry, the Acadia Sugar Refinery, the

Richmond Printing Works, the cotton factory, Exhibition Hall, and the other Richmond buildings took months of steady work, which produced the remains of hundreds more victims.

The recovery crew removed the bricks, blocks, and broken glass that had been the sugar refinery well into the hot summer months, finding corpses throughout. When they finished, they moved on to Exhibition Hall, which they had thought was empty when the explosion hit. But, in the summer of 1919, a year and a half after the disaster, while clearing out one of the cattle sheds they found the shattered bones of a presumed vagrant, the last victim of the Halifax explosion to be found.

All told, officials determined that 1,953 people were killed in the explosion and its aftermath, about 400 more than *Titanic* had claimed, more even than the entire province of Nova Scotia had lost during four years of fighting the Great War. But this almost certainly underestimates the total, as it fails to count those whose bodies couldn't be found, those who died weeks and months later from injuries and illnesses caused by the explosion, and those officials simply failed to count.

If this is hard for us to imagine today, when authorities can definitively identify victims with just a few strands of hair, it's worth noting that fifteen years after the attack on the World Trade Center, the remains of 1,113 victims—some 40 percent of the 2,753 who died—have still not been identified. After such a cataclysm, even modern science can do only so much.

This brings us to a final accounting. No list was ever compiled of all the victims known to have died, let alone the unknown and those who died weeks and months after the explosion. Although the figure most commonly used is 1,953, almost every researcher I've encountered believes the actual figure to be much higher—perhaps as high as 3,000, which would represent about 5 percent of the population of Halifax. While there are no hard numbers to back that figure up, given all the considerations above, it cannot be discounted as absurd.

While none of the respectable Halifax scholars claims to have the final number, a consensus has developed that some 1,600 people were killed instantly, and probably 400 to 800 died afterward, in addition to 9,000 wounded and 25,000 homeless. These numbers will likely stand as the best estimates we have.

With most of the 9,000 wounded still living in the city—fully 15 percent of the population—the sight of cripples, amputees, and victims of facial disfigurements passing on the street would be a familiar scene for decades. Many victims never sought treatment for their wounds, with shards of glass emerging from their skin years later.

Haligonians born after the explosion learned to recognize the trademark scars, tinged in black and blue from the soot and TNT, and avert their glance without comment.

"Don't stare," their parents taught them. "It's the Explosion."

Unlike hundreds of other victims, there was never any doubt about Vincent Coleman's fate. But in the personals of January 7, 1918, this notice appeared: "The many friends of Mrs. Vincent Coleman now with her mother Eleanor O'Toole 126 Edward Street will be gratified to learn that she and her children are rapidly recovering from the injuries received in the explosion. Mrs. Coleman speaks in terms of deep gratitude of the many kindnesses of friends."

A few years later, Mrs. Coleman married a Mr. Jackson, who had also survived the explosion, which had permanently injured his arm. In 1923, working in the railyard with his weakened arm, he fell between moving cars and was killed.

Surviving the tragic death of two husbands, Mrs. Coleman Jackson lived past ninety.

Gordon Driscoll was never found or identified, and

the family could only conclude that he had been killed. His younger brother, Art, five, who had been unconscious on the train to Truro, recovered, but took months to regain his ability to speak. The family stayed together, which proved a great help to all of them. In 1919, Mrs. Driscoll gave birth to a baby girl.

In April 1918, workers clearing out the rubble of the Acadia Sugar Refinery found the remains of James Pattison's father, Vincent, among his many coworkers buried there, and returned his effects to his wife. These included the pocket watch the Pattisons had given to James the week before the explosion, which he had set five minutes fast. He had lent it to his father that day because his father's watch had stopped and was being repaired. When they found it, the face had been smashed and the hands torn off, but they had left a clear imprint on the face, the shadow of two hands stopped forever at 9:10. James saved it as one of the few keepsakes he had of his previous life.

Millicent Upham stayed in the hospital past Christmas, but never took off the little gold ring her mother had given her the previous Christmas. When a doctor thought the ring was getting a bit tight and wanted to take it off, Millicent refused. Her finger's swelling went down, and the ring stayed on.

While Millicent Upham recovered in the hospital

from losing an eye, Archie and their father, Charles, moved in with an uncle and aunt. A couple of months after Millicent rejoined them, spring had arrived, so Charles Upham decided it was time to search the foundation of his house, knowing that his wife, two of his daughters, and a son had been buried there. He did not want soldiers to find his family and possibly damage remains or heirlooms they might come across. So he steeled himself to perform the hard but necessary task, a final expression of the awful labors of love.

He enlisted the help of his brother and surviving son, Archie, and together they dug through ashes, cinders, and pieces of wood, brick, glass, and metal.

"All we found of my mother, two sisters, and brother we put in a shoe box," Archie recalled, "just a few bones. They were buried in Fairview in that shoe box, but by then it was nearly summer."

The Uphams lost thirty-three close relatives.

Millicent had clung to the ring her mother had given her, her last tangible connection, but when her father was digging through the burnt remains of the family home, he found a few more: the tiny dishes from Millicent's tea set, which she had been playing with that morning when the ship exploded. Rather amazingly, in a site filled with shattered chairs, beds, and couches, the tiny tea set had survived intact. Charles recognized it immediately, and carefully removed the little cups from the rubbish one by one. Not far away, he found the contents of Millicent's piggybank. The pennies had fused together from the heat.

Two years after the accident, when doctors were taking out the metal plate in Archie's head, they found yet another piece of glass.

The loss of possessions seemed of minor importance at first, but their value rose over the years, especially those keepsakes that could not be replaced.

Because cameras were rare in 1917, families usually had professionally taken photographs of special events such as weddings, but little else. Not one photograph of the Orr family survived, leaving Barbara with nothing but memories of her entire family.

Horatio Brennan, the captain of the *Stella Maris* who was working valiantly to pull *Mont-Blanc* out to sea when it blew up, a week earlier had taken an expensive studio photo of himself in full uniform, proud and dignified, to be framed and presented as a gift to his wife at Christmas. When no one came to the studio to claim the photograph, the studio found Brennan's wife and presented her with an unexpected memory of her noble husband.

Chapter 39
The Trials

1918–20

The Wreck Commissioner's Inquiry started December 13 and ended in a ruling from Judge Drysdale on February 4. But it marked the beginning of legal proceedings, not the end. *Mont-Blanc*'s owners sued *Imo*'s owners for $2 million in damages (about US $40 million today), and *Imo*'s owners returned the favor for the exact same amount.

The trial started on April 6, 1918, exactly four months after the explosion, while crews were still digging through ruins now covered in mud. *Mont-Blanc*'s owners replaced the highly ineffective Humphrey Mellish with Hector McInnes. *Imo*'s owners retained

Charles J. Burchell, which seemed a smart move when it was announced that the judge picked to handle the case would be Justice Arthur Drysdale, who had presided over the Inquiry. Five minutes into the trial, Drysdale made a rather incredible comment for a jurist: "So far as I'm concerned, I have been over [my notes] and have my mind made up." Perhaps realizing his faux pas, he added, "Although other witnesses may vary it."

Because Humphrey Mellish had inexplicably stipulated at the Inquiry that the original forty-eight witnesses' testimony could carry over to the trial, there would be only one new witness this time: John L. Makiny, master of the naval tug *Nerid*, which had been in the Narrows the morning of the collision. Makiny had seen the entire accident unfold, he was a respected man in uniform, and he had no connection to either ship—an ideal witness. He testified that *Imo* had been on the wrong side of the channel until the last few seconds, and that *Mont-Blanc* had been on the correct side until its last, desperate turn to port, which was made in the "agony of collision" in an attempt to avoid contact.

But Judge Drysdale had already decided at the Inquiry that the two ships had collided on the Halifax side of the imaginary centerline, when many reliable witnesses saw them hit on the Dartmouth side, resulting in the following exchange:

Burchell: "Where do you think the collision occurred?"

Makiny: "I don't think at all. I am positive," he said, stating that it had happened two-thirds of the way across the Narrows on the Dartmouth side.

Judge: "You are all wrong. I am satisfied about that."

When Burchell later asked Makiny why his testimony didn't agree with anyone else's, a statement Burchell himself knew to be false, since a number of witnesses had already described the point of collision as being on the Dartmouth side, Makiny responded, "If you let me explain what I know, I can give it, but I must confess I don't understand [the way you put the question]. I want to tell the truth."

Judge Drysdale interjected: "Quit talking and listen to the questions."

The trial was over in an hour. Drysdale had the last word, stating that Makiny was "all wrong about the place of the collision. It was caused by the improper starboarding of the helm of the *Mont-Blanc*. I will file a memorandum."

Three weeks later, on April 27, Judge Drysdale entered his decision, which again ran only one page long. In it, he said of Makiny, "His manner was bad and his matter worse. In short, I did not believe him." Drysdale went on to suggest Makiny had been coached by

Mont-Blanc's new attorney, Hector McInnes, to provide false testimony, "*the result of instruction*, and that on behalf of the French ship. I do not believe him."

Drysdale therefore felt justified in disregarding testimony from all previous witnesses who had stated *Imo* had been on the wrong side, *Mont-Blanc* on the correct side, and they had collided on the Dartmouth side of the Narrows. For Drysdale, these claims were not worthy of review.

Hector McInnes knew his clients, *Mont Blanc*'s owners, captain, and crew, didn't have much of a chance with Judge Drysdale, but he hoped for a fairer shake from the Supreme Court of Canada in Ottawa. His appeal was heard a year later, in March of 1919, by the five Supreme Court justices. Not insignificantly, three of them were English, two French.

MacInnes and his now all too familiar foe, Charles J. Burchell, spent three full days arguing the case for their clients. While the five Supreme Court justices conducted themselves during the trial far more professionally than Judge Drysdale had, and McInnes was more assertive than Mellish had been, those were low standards indeed, especially with Charles J. Burchell up to his usual antics. But when the decision came down two months later in May of 1919, it was still a surprise.

The Chief Justice, Sir Louis Davies, one of the English-Canadians, acknowledged that *Imo* had been on the wrong side of the Narrows at one point, but agreed with Drysdale's conclusion that it had returned to its proper side of the Narrows "in good time," so "the fault lay entirely in the fatal port manoeuvre of the *Mont Blanc.*" The second English-Canadian Justice agreed, and joined Justice Davies in moving to dismiss the appeal.

If the third English-Canadian justice, Francis Alexander Anglin, went with his two peers and decided for *Imo*, it wouldn't matter how the French-Canadian justices voted.

Justice Anglin stated that *Mont-Blanc*'s desperate final move across *Imo*'s bow was not made in the "agony of collision," the nautical standard for such a drastic move. Yet "the study of the whole record has left on my mind an uncomfortable impression that the case of the *Mont Blanc* . . . was, unconsciously no doubt, prejudiced in the minds of those present at the investigation and the trial"—not because they were French but because the *Mont-Blanc*'s captain and crew had abandoned ship, letting their vessel drift into the Halifax docks and "imperiling the lives of thousands of people, while seeking their own safety in hasty flight to the Dartmouth shore without taking any . . . adequate steps . . . to give warning of the imminent danger even to those in the immediate vicinity."

With this, Justice Anglin finally gave voice to what other justices had only hinted at: the sins of *Mont-Blanc*'s captain, crew, and pilot had not violated nautical laws, codes, or conventions in the *Mont-Blanc*'s dance with *Imo*. The defendants were guilty of bailing on a burning ship and rowing the long way across the Narrows to save themselves instead of warning people in Richmond of the impending disaster, compounded by their utter inactivity after the explosion. While thousands of people with no connection to the explosion were rushing to help strangers who were desperately in need, the captain, crew, and pilot never expressed the slightest concern for them—all during a week when the outpouring of compassion was everywhere. The crew's failure to warn Richmond or to help survivors, not to mention their lack of remorse and compassion, had created a deep antipathy toward them. Even if ethnicity fueled that feeling, the crew's behavior alone sparked it. But insofar as none of those actions were illegal, they were irrelevant to the laws the court was charged with judging.

Justice Anglin added that this prejudice was emphasized by *Imo* attorney Burchell, and "the license allowed [Burchell] in other respects" by Judge Drysdale "is indicative of the prevalent sentiment against the *Mont-Blanc*."

Justice Anglin added that *Imo* had "inexcusably" stayed on the wrong side of the channel until just before the collision, thereby making Anglin the first English-Canadian jurist to acknowledge this basic, crucial fact. He then concluded, "While I'm inclined to think that the *Imo* was the more blame-worthy of the two, I am not sufficiently satisfied of this to do otherwise than apportion the responsibility equally."

Based on this reasoning, Anglin would render a split decision.

With the first two justices finding for *Imo* and against *Mont-Blanc* and the swing vote splitting equally for both sides, even if the two French-Canadian justices ruled in favor of *Mont-Blanc*, the verdict would still be deadlocked at 2.5 each. According to Canadian laws, the appeal would then be dismissed, and Judge Drysdale's decision for *Mont-Blanc* would hold. This seemed to put the two French-Canadian judges in an impossible position. How to respond without dooming *Mont-Blanc* to a clearly unjust verdict?

The two French-Canadian judges, Louis-Phillipe Brodeur and Pierre-Basile Mignault, easily recognized the anti-French prejudice evident in Judge Drysdale's initial opinion and called out by Justice Anglin. With careful and copious reasoning, they concluded the fault for the collision lay wholly with *Imo*.

But if they stopped there, the court would still be deadlocked, deferring the decision back to Drysdale's ruling. So they sought to go deeper than the question before them about who was right and who was wrong and to dissect the odd legal proceedings that had occurred back in Judge Drysdale's gloomy Halifax courtroom that had led them to this juncture. While appeals courts are usually bound by the facts given to them from the lower court rulings and have to rule strictly on how the law was applied to those facts, in this unusual case, Drysdale had failed to establish what the facts of the case actually were.

This gave the Supreme Court justices the opportunity to find the facts for themselves, essentially retrying the entire case as if they were sitting in Judge Drysdale's seat in Nova Scotia. Brodeur and Mignault recognized the opportunity Drysdale's odd conduct offered them, and they seized it.

So they dived back into the evidence itself. Both decided that whether the two ships finally collided on the Dartmouth or Halifax side of the Narrows was far less important than how the ships got there in the first place. To determine that, they needed to rewind the tape to the ships' starting points. In tracking the paths of the two ships, they concluded that *Imo* had been on the wrong side at every relevant moment, and tried to get back to the correct side of the channel only after it was too late. As for *Mont-Blanc*'s last-second swing to the left, they acknowledged that it was unwise and ultimately unhelpful, but under the circumstances understandable and excusable. Taking all this in, they concluded *Imo* was solely to blame.

With the advantage of a century of hindsight, their reasoning seems sound. But that alone would still produce a deadlock, which would once again revert to Judge Drysdale's complete victory for *Imo*. They knew they had to go another step. If Justice Brodeur's and Justice Mignault's navigation through the case to that point had been impressive, it was eclipsed by their last move.

In the last paragraph of their decision, in which they found *Imo* entirely at fault, they added that they were open to adopting the reasoning of the swing vote, Justice Anglin, and find both ships equally at fault. Given the choice between a whitewash for *Imo* and a fifty-fifty split, the French-Canadian judges took what they could get for *Mont-Blanc*.

It worked. The final verdict: 3–2 for equal blame—a great outcome for *Mont-Blanc*, given the start of legal proceedings—with a wink to future readers about what the two justices really thought of the case. These judges passed away decades ago, yet we hear them clearly today.

If the French-Canadian justices' reasoning seems sound to us, it struck *Imo*'s animated attorney Charles J. Burchell much less so. As soon as the ruling came down from Canada's Supreme Court, Burchell filed an appeal with the court of last resort, the Privy Council in London, a trio of three Law Lords who would have the final say.

The fourth and final hearing of the case commenced almost a year later in January 1920, at great expense of time, effort, and money for both sides. The *Mont-Blanc* owners, who had grown progressively savvier about their defense, retained experienced English counsel for this trial, while the *Imo* team stuck with the bombastic Burchell. Five days of arguments covered the same ground all over again, without the histrionics of the Halifax hearings, after which the Lords came down with their decision a month later, on March 22, 1920.

Their ruling was also unusual, but less for the outcomes than the process employed to reach them. In assessing the work of their predecessors, the Lords clearly agreed with the two French-Canadian Supreme Court justices that Justice Drysdale had made a mess of the fact-finding process. Thus, the Lords determined that they needed to start from scratch, adjudicating not only on the law but on the facts themselves, a decision that vindicated the French-Canadian justices.

The Lords also made it clear that Burchell's shtick played a lot better in front of Judge Drysdale in Halifax, with its Anglo-French antipathies, than in the capital of the British Empire. The Lords discounted much of the testimony generated by Burchell's leading questions. The game was starting over, on a new field with new rules.

And, again like the French-Canadian judges, the Lords felt it necessary to back up the action in Halifax Harbour to the ships' starting points on the morning of December 6, 1917. They underscored the simplicity of the "collision rule," which holds that each ship, when faced with a possible collision, had only two choices: stop or reverse. Both ships, the Lords argued, should have gone full speed astern "long before they were allowed to approach so close to each other as 500 feet. Both Masters were to blame for not having prevented their respective ships from getting into it."

The Lords concluded: "It is clear that the navigators [of both ships] allowed them to approach within 400 feet of each other on practically opposite courses, thus incurring the risk of collision, and indeed practically bringing about the collision, instead of reversing their engines and going astern, as our Assessors advise us they, as a matter of good seamanship, could and should have done, long before the ships came so close together. This actually led to the collision."

In short, they ruled, *Imo* was going too fast, and *Mont-Blanc* should have known better than to come anywhere near another ship. Common sense seemed to be making a comeback.

"The manoeuvre of the *Mont-Blanc* in the agony of the collision may not have been the best manoeuvre to adopt, and yet be in the circumstances excusable. But their Lordships are clearly of the opinion that both ships are to blame for their reciprocal neglect above mentioned to have reversed and gone astern earlier than they did."

Thus, after two and a half years of litigation and enormous legal fees, the two sides came out even—a rough justice, perhaps.

Imo had committed far more violations of basic nautical conventions than did *Mont-Blanc*, but the men on *Mont-Blanc* knew they were sitting on 6 million pounds of explosives, while the men on *Imo* did not. *Imo's* leaders paid with their lives, while *Mont-Blanc's* ran for theirs—without giving a thought to mitigating the pain suffered by so many, or even expressing sympathy. While those omissions don't constitute crimes, they certainly colored how Haligonians regarded the captain and crew.

In the cosmic scheme of things, splitting the blame might be as close as anyone could get to justice. By the time the final decision came down, most Haligonians had already moved on to rebuilding their lives and their city.

Chapter 40

The Wholesome Discord
of a Thousand Saws

After the fires had been extinguished and the wounded tended to, Colonel Robert S. Low assembled an army of carpenters, masons, plumbers, and electricians to rebuild the city, which had incurred more than $35 million in damages in 1917 U.S. dollars, or $728 million today. Reconstructing Halifax would be an enormous project under the best of circumstances, but it was made far more difficult by the simple fact that the Great War was approaching its climax in 1918, and still received priority for most resources.

Lumber was hard to get, and glass almost impossible. If you could somehow get your hands on the scarce materials you needed to repair your home, finding someone to do the work was even harder. The tradesmen—carpenters, masons, and glaziers—had already been working at full capacity on the war effort before the explosion.

"For months the people of the North End lived like cavemen," Raddall recalled, "with black tarpaper in place of windows, with patched-up doors, with the heat of their stoves escaping through cracks and slashes in the walls and roofs."

But given the immense demand, more workers found their way to Halifax, and those already in town showed mercy and found time to help the needy homeowners. Some 4,000 workers completed repairs throughout the winter and spring to make homes warm and wind- and water-proof again, and repaired windows so the survivors could enjoy some much-needed sunlight.

The entire neighborhood of Richmond required a complete rebuild. But before the city broke ground, leaders knew they had to sell the neighborhood as a place people would want to live. Given the city's failed experiment erecting a "tent village" on the North Commons, where no one wanted to stay after the explosion, they learned their lesson: they would have to do more than simply replace wooden homes with wooden homes.

They decided to build the homes and apartments out of a new material called Hydrostone, manufactured across the Narrows in Dartmouth, by blasting bits of granite into cement with water. This produces a very strong, slightly sparkly variety of cinder block.

Next, they decided to eliminate a few streets, rename a large run of Gottingen to Novalea, and add a diagonal artery cutting through it. Taking advantage of the chance to remake the largely working-class neighborhood, with many unpaved roads, Colonel Low's men created parks; tree-lined, paved boulevards; and added alleyways to make it easier for milkmen to deliver and garbagemen to pick up.

They built at a furious pace "one apartment an hour" aided by the Massachusetts Temporary Relief Fund, which continued to support the project for five years. By March 1, 1918, less than three months after 325 acres of Halifax had been blown flat, Colonel Low's group had built 328 new homes and repaired 3,000 others. The neighborhood is now called the Hydrostone, a popular, up-and-coming area.

This remarkable restoration moved the normally modest Canadians to produce a poster in 1919 boasting of Halifax's rapid recovery.

"As though over night, the North End has shaken off its incubus of holocaust," the poster said. "Ruin and desolation have given place to the new order. A new city has risen out of the ashes of the old. We rub our eyes and look again—but the vision does not fade. The new city remains—and grows, building by building, street by street, amid the tumultuous music of a thousand hammers, the wholesome discord of a thousand saws."

The very renaissance movement Haligonians had struggled to start before the Great War had now occurred in less than a year.

The most anticipated federal election in Canadian history, which would decide who would be prime minister, had been scheduled for December 17, 1917. But due to the explosion, the government decided to postpone the election in Nova Scotia only, while the rest of the country cast their ballots as planned, delivering Prime Minister Borden's Conservative Party a ringing victory, and with it, securing the policy of conscription for the remainder of the war. The results rendered Nova Scotia's postponed ballot moot, but it's clear that the province would have voted overwhelmingly for its native son and supported conscription and the war it would fuel.

Wilfred Owen, the soldier-poet who wrote "Dulce et Decorum Est" while being treated for shell shock before returning to the trenches, was killed on November 4, 1918. His mother received the telegram informing her of his death exactly one week later, on

November 11, 1918—Armistice Day—while the church bells rang out, celebrating the end of the war.

The devastation, even now, is hard to grasp. The Great War cost an estimated 17 million lives and wounded another 20 million, for a total of 37 million, or more than a third of the population of the United States at the time.

While the Americans' decision to join the Allied Forces late in the war helped end a three-year stalemate, it did not give the Allies a decisive victory—but it did protect them from defeat and strengthen their position in the Versailles peace negotiations that followed.

To say that the ripples of the Great War are still with us today is to understate the case considerably. World War I created a new world order, elevated America's role in it, and remade modern warfare. Its effects are traceable in a thousand places, but perhaps most significantly, the Ottoman, German, Austro-Hungarian, and Russian empires all collapsed, creating a vacuum that the most desperate elements would fill.

When World War II arrived, the Halifax Explosion would play a central role in the war's conclusion, though it's been forgotten outside Nova Scotia since. At the time the explosion occurred, no one grasped the full significance of the event, but scientists soon caught up. Even with the low estimate of 2,000 dead, the explosion killed four times more than the San Francisco earthquake of 1906 and eight times more than the Chicago Fire of 1871. When experts rank the world's worst explosions, they generally consider five criteria: the quantity of explosives involved, the force of the blast, the area devastated, the value of property destroyed, and the number of casualties. Taking all these into account, Halifax was the biggest man-made explosion the world had ever seen until August 6, 1945, when the United States dropped the atomic bomb on Hiroshima.

President Franklin D. Roosevelt put together an all-star team of scientists to build the first atomic bomb, code-named the Manhattan Project, led by J. Robert Oppenheimer in Los Alamos, New Mexico. To estimate the effects of their bomb on Hiroshima, they had only one worthy precursor to compare: Halifax. They knew the weapon they were creating would possess unparalleled power. The trials showed them that. But they didn't know what it would do to actual buildings and people. For that, Oppenheimer and his team studied Halifax frequently and closely. In 1942, Oppenheimer set up a conference at the University of California–Berkeley, where he extrapolated the data from Halifax to estimate that the atomic bomb would create three to five times more damage, and his calculations would prove roughly correct.

It speaks to the unprecedented magnitude of the Halifax explosion that it would take a full twenty-eight years, 130,000 employees led by a team of world-class scientists, a budget of $2 billion, and the considerable advantage of atomic power to build a bomb that would prove to be only three to five times more powerful than that which a crew of stevedores in Gravesend Bay, New York, had unwittingly assembled in a few days in 1917.

Oppenheimer's work must necessarily affect how we look at Halifax. If nothing was learned from Halifax, it could be dismissed as a horrible event, on a par with the Johnstown Flood, the San Francisco earthquake, and the Galveston hurricane—still fascinating, but with little application to today's world. The Halifax explosion, in contrast, alerted generals and scientists to the potential of building the world's first weapons of mass destruction, and underscored the obvious need to take every precaution with those weapons, including preventing nuclear proliferation after the war. The need has never been greater, with nuclear security eroding at a time when nations can produce 50-megaton bombs 17,000 times more powerful than the Halifax explosion.

Another concept that World War II would popularize: attacking civilian populations to demoralize them sufficiently to end a war. This was the idea behind carpet-bombing Dresden and dropping atomic bombs on Hiroshima and Nagasaki. The irony is this: the first city wracked by the collateral damage of war—Halifax—did not bend but came back stronger and more fiercely patriotic.

But danger in various forms has always been with us, and always will be. For the vast majority of us, who stare out our windows as we sip our coffee in the morning, the bigger lesson of Halifax is how to respond if the worst occurs. The explosion should have shredded the social fabric that kept a civil society like Halifax's intact. If you wanted to walk into someone's house or business and take things, there wasn't much stopping you. But with society's infrastructure decimated, something more noble rose up to replace it: the primal instinct to take care of one another, especially the old and the young, and give them shelter, food, medical help, and simple kindness—from sending ships and trains from Boston to insisting that needier patients go first to cleaning the scalps of two kids during a haircut—with no thought of being paid back.

When the laws no longer applied, basic human decency proved even stronger.

After the Halifax explosion the survivors demonstrated the incredible human capacity for courage and compassion, reservoirs that we might be able to call upon to save a stranger's life at a moment's notice. If that day ever comes, we can only hope to respond as well as the good people of Halifax did.

PART VIII

Facing The Future

Chapter 41
New Lives

After the wounded returned from the hospitals, the families identified their relatives, and the displaced found new homes, they still struggled to build new lives.

The Reverend William Swetnam and his daughter, Dorothy, moved back from his friend's home in Dartmouth to Halifax, where they stayed for two years while the reverend served his flock. But Halifax proved too heavy with sad memories, so they decided to move to Truro. There he ministered to a new flock, remarried, and fathered another child. It was not the life they had had, and it never would be. But it was a good, full life, with a family that would sustain Dorothy into a happy adulthood.

The Pattison boys had lost their home, their father,

their little brother, Alan, and their sister, Catherine. The three remaining Pattisons—Gordon, James, and their mother—stayed with her parents in Dartmouth. But Gordon felt the need to get away from their history in Halifax, so he moved in with an uncle in the tiny town of Granville Ferry, which sits on the Annapolis River 120 miles away, for several months that spring.

Mrs. Pattison and James stayed in Dartmouth, where James attended Hawthorne School. He could handle the work, and the students were friendly enough, but he missed his friends and family. He never fully settled in at his new school, but he studied hard and excelled in mechanics and technical drawing.

Archie and Millicent Upham had lost their mother and three siblings. Their father, Charles Upham, who worked the night shift at the Richmond Railway, moved into a new house on their old block with Archie. Because it was hard enough to raise one child working the night shift, Millicent stayed with the Rasleys and their children, Reg and Annie, who had also lost an eye. Both Millicent and Annie required additional treatments before they could attend school. In the fall of 1919, the Tower Road School opened a new classroom called the Special Class for Sight Saving, which both girls attended.

The new Richmond School opened in 1919, but

Archie decided to attend the equally close and new Bloomfield School, joining his cousin Reg Rasley. With all the changes they faced, it felt good to go to school with a trusted friend.

The Driscolls moved to South Uniacke, about forty-five minutes away. Each morning, Noble and his sister walked half a mile along the railway line to go to a one-room village school in Etter's Settlement. Noble's teacher and classmates grew weary of Noble's frequent observation, "In Halifax, we didn't do it like that."

Noble got his wish in 1919 when the Driscolls moved into one of the larger houses in the new Hydro-stone neighborhood. He attended the rebuilt Richmond School, still run by Principal Huggins, despite losing his daughter Merle when the old school collapsed.

Noble was doing well enough in school, but one day Principal Huggins, who also taught the upper grades, pulled him aside. "You would be better off getting a job," Huggins said, giving odd advice for a principal. "I hardly have time to teach, and you are not learning anything new."

That night, after Noble talked it over with his father, he decided to take a job as a delivery boy for Creighton's store, the very place where Cam Creighton had warned him not to go any closer to the burning ship—advice that probably saved his life.

Shortly after Barbara Orr moved in with her cousins in Richmond, they had to rebuild the house. Even the new house was crowded, but her uncle found "a place for all of us . . . They were wonderful people, my goodness. My uncle was a wonderful man. A wonderful family to grow up with."

Her cousins felt like siblings to her, especially Gladys, who was about her age. With Richmond School being rebuilt, the girls decided to attend the Halifax Ladies' College on Pleasant Street. But the girls had been there for only one month when Gladys confessed to Barbara, "Did we ever make a mistake! I hate this place. Do you?"

"I do, too," Barbara admitted, "but we made our own choice. We agreed to come here. We'll just have to stick it out now."

If there was one thing they had mastered, it was sticking with it, and they did. They eventually grew very fond of the school and got their degrees. Their resilience had paid off again.

When the doctors at Camp Hill Hospital saw Barbara's ankle, they told her she would never play sports again, or do much of anything on that joint. She quietly set out to prove them wrong. "For a long time, I'd walk along, and zoom, I'd almost fall. [But] it got better.

"The one thing I could do was dance," she said. "I've got balance that you wouldn't believe! I've gone figure skating, played tennis—every game—soccer."

From her family's estate, Orr received $10,000. In 1920, when the Halifax Explosion Memorial Bell Tower was unveiled at Fort Needham, Orr donated her $10,000 to pay for the bells.

With all four Richmond churches destroyed, they had to make do. When the United Memorial Church opened in 1921, the Orrs, the Driscolls, the Uphams, and their cousins the Rasleys all attended, occasionally joined by the Pattisons, who took the ferry over from Dartmouth.

Barbara Orr donated a carillon for the church in memory of her family, and had their names engraved on the bell. When the church was formally dedicated in April 1921, Barbara was asked to play a hymn on the bells.

"Suppose I make a mistake?" she worried. "It will be heard as far away as Dartmouth."

She played anyway—and it was beautiful.

Chapter 42
The Accidental Doctor

A few days after the explosion, Ernest Barss returned to his parents' home in Wolfville a changed man.

After witnessing two of the greatest tragedies in human history within a year, and getting the chance to provide real help to the victims in Halifax, he knew that was what he wanted to do for the rest of his life: help those who needed it most by becoming a doctor.

It was a big decision, but doing it would be much harder.

When he shared his dream of going to medical school with his father, John Howard Barss said, "I have put you through college and do not intend to put you through medical school."

Ernest Barss had three problems: prerequisites, health, and money—not a great place for a twenty-five-year-old to start. More than a year after getting hit by a German shell, he still could not walk without a cane and a lot of pain, and he dragged his left foot behind him. His parents thought this once vibrant, confident, athletic man would be an invalid spending his days in their home, minding their grocery store, which looked the most likely outcome when he first returned.

Ernest's solution to all his physical problems was a very Canadian one: keep going anyway. The winter of 1918, his first back in Nova Scotia, he made himself go down to the rink every day, put on his old skates, and then skate "until the tears ran down his face," his mother told a friend. When the ice thawed that spring, he took up golf to force himself to walk up and down 5 miles of hills. Despite his lame leg, Barss soon achieved a golf handicap of two, just a couple of strokes from the top echelon. Barss's ability to walk improved day by day.

On March 9, 1919, almost three years after getting hit by the shell, Barss reported to Camp Hill Hospital for a checkup. On the Consultant's Report, the examining physician, Dr. Birt, wrote, "I am of the opinion that he is in fair condition. Complains of insomnia, nervousness, and discomfort . . . There is some tremor of his hands, some exaggerated knee jerks [and] ankle jerks." His spine had healed fairly well, but he still experienced numbness in his foot and leg.

Dr. Birt added this note: "Some residual 'Neurasthenia,'" a condition characterized by physical and mental exhaustion, often including headaches, insomnia, and irritability, believed to be caused by depression, emotional stress, or conflict—what we would probably call post-traumatic stress disorder—"which," Dr. Birt concluded, "resulted from being buried in explosion."

Barss's solution to his psychological problems would be the same: keep going anyway. And so he did, focusing on medical school as his next mission.

During the last year of the war he continued selling Victory Bonds, then took another government job trying to match handicapped veterans with potential employers, of which there were thousands. That group included Barss, but he was looking to help others.

For fun, he took singing lessons from a Boston woman who escaped the city's summer heat in Nova Scotia, like many Bostonians. A favorite was "I'll Sing Thee Sweet Songs of Araby," which finished with "And all my soul shall strive to wake / Sweet wonder in thine eyes." He was good enough to be invited to join the notable Chautauqua circuit, which gave concerts from town to town, but he had to decline. Because of the chlorine gas he'd inhaled during the war, he "couldn't raise a note before noon."

Barss didn't have the prerequisites to go to medical school, nor the money to pay for it. Here, Barss got lucky, as his uncle Andrew Townson, the man Barss had written about the Halifax explosion, decided to help out. Townson had arrived in the new country a poor, eleven-year-old immigrant from England and worked his way up from stockboy at Sibley, Lindsay & Curr, a major department store in Rochester, New York, to become its president by age thirty, in addition to serving as chairman of the Rochester Board of Education and as a trustee of Vassar College, while living in an impressive home he'd bought from George Eastman, of Eastman-Kodak fame.

Family lore has it that Uncle Andrew gave Ernest $100 to enroll at the University of Michigan in 1919, back when that was enough to get started. How Ernest Barss picked Michigan, however, remains a mystery.

"Darned if I know why he went to the University of Michigan," his son, Dr. Joseph Andrew Barss, told me in 1999, "but it's always been a first-class school."

Perhaps Ernest's American cousin Harold Barss, who graduated from the University of Michigan Medical School in 1914 and became an instructor in surgery, persuaded him to come.

We do know why Ernest decided to become a doctor. Having taken part in both fighting and healing, Barss chose to spend the rest of his life practicing the latter.

He threw a few things into a trunk and moved to Ann Arbor in 1919, sight unseen, where he took classes from 8:00 in the morning to 6:00 at night every weekday, and from 8:00 to 12:00 on Saturdays, just to qualify for medical school. He confessed to his aunt, "I felt pretty discouraged for a while but things are coming a little easier now and I hope to get through ok in everything."

On February 16, 1920, while Barss was working on his science prerequisites, and still trying to figure out how he would pay for it all, Uncle Andrew died, leaving Ernest the considerable sum of $10,000, or $128,000 in 2017 dollars, at a time when public university tuition cost a fraction of what it does today. His uncle's final gift was his future.

Barss knew he would lose his hard-earned progress relearning to walk if he quit pushing himself, so he made himself visit Michigan's rudimentary skating rink, a building with three sides, to limp his way around the ice. He also sang in the First Congregational Church under the leadership of Lloyd C. Douglas, who would go on to write *The Robe*, which sold 2 million copies and became a movie starring Richard Burton.

He was becoming a new man, with a new mission and a new name: Joe, because that's what his professors read off roll call. We don't know what happened to the loyal Eileen, but we do know that during his first semester at Michigan's medical school, in the fall of 1920, he went on a blind double date that "neither of us wanted to go on," recalled Helen Kolb, a Michigan undergraduate from Battle Creek. "But we had a wonderful time. I never thought anything serious would come of this date, as Joe had so far to go to become a doctor."

When Barss and a classmate, Bob Breakey, picked up their dates the next day to go to a football game, Barss brought Helen two big mums and a box of Whitman's chocolates. The man seemed to have a plan, and "worked very hard to be invited to my home for Christmas," she recalled. Although they both had other offers for the holiday, Barss won the invitation from her and dropped his others.

Shortly after that invitation, Barss asked Helen to marry him. She said yes, but asked him to keep it between them until February, "so that if either of us wanted to get out of the deal, no one would be hurt." Further, if Barss's professors found out he was getting married, which med school students were forbidden to do, he could be expelled.

"My father liked Joe & asked if he were a Republican or a Democrat," Helen wrote. "He said he was a Canadian and voted for the *man*—Father said 'If you ever live here and have anything or hope to have anything, you'll be a Republican in self defense.'"

Helen's father also worried about relations between Canada and the United States and how they might affect their future. Their plans grew more complicated when Helen's father and Joe's mother both died during their engagement, which raised the question: should they move to Battle Creek to take care of her mother, or Nova Scotia to take care of his father? Either would require one of them to live in another country.

They solved the problem by both becoming naturalized as dual citizens. If anything demonstrated the distance the two nations had traveled since the Halifax Explosion, it was the simple, small decision of Joseph Ernest Barss to become an American citizen, something he could not have conceived when he joined the British forces in 1915, grumbling about the Americans sitting it out.

Because of the medical school's strict rule against students marrying, one of Barss's classmates had gotten married secretly and had to live in the intern quarters while his wife roomed with four women in town to keep it quiet. The administrators nonetheless made an exception for Barss due to his unusual maturity. The couple wed in 1922 and had a son, Joseph Andrew, in 1923, and a daughter, Elizabeth, in 1927.

Even while Barss was busy starting a family and finishing his medical education in peaceful Ann Arbor, he was still occasionally haunted by the Great War. Like most veterans who'd seen combat, Barss was a stoic man who rarely talked of the epic battles in which he had fought. But early in their marriage, Helen was startled to discover that this otherwise poised man would get choked up whenever he heard bagpipes, as it was bagpipers who led his unit into the trenches and back out, with the soldiers carrying the writhing victims of shells, gas, and bayonets behind them. Helen noticed he would drop to the ground whenever he heard a whistle or a loud bang, a survival instinct he had learned in the awful days when enemy shells were dropping all around him.

Through the steady support of his family, his friends, and his own strong spirit, Barss was gradually able to let his memories of war recede and the simple pleasures of civilian life to take their place.

According to the box scores of Michigan's "informal team," Barss officiated many of the club's hockey games in 1922. Perhaps it was his desire to return to a normal lifestyle and have some fun again that motivated him to find time in his already overburdened schedule for such a trivial pursuit. It's easy to imagine the lightheartedness Barss must have felt as he became reacquainted with the happiness a hockey game could bring. And having gotten a taste, he wanted more.

To get more, however, Michigan needed a varsity ice hockey program—something the club players had asked for and been denied three times over the previous decade. When the Great War broke out, Michigan sponsored only five varsity teams: baseball, football, track, tennis, and basketball.

Barss paid a visit to Michigan's legendary football coach and athletic director, Fielding Yost, to ask if he could start a varsity hockey team. Yost, a native of West Virginia, didn't know much about hockey, but he knew a good coach when he saw one. Yost agreed, on one condition: Barss had to become the program's first coach.

Barss consented, but that required permission from the medical school, because the professors knew the academic burden of a medical school student was more than most could handle. Once again, the medical school made an exception for Barss, which meant he had to "rush home from classes, eat dinner, have a taxi waiting, go to the rink and coach, return by a little after nine and study for the next day's classes until midnight," Helen recalled. Because the rink lacked artificial ice—or a fourth wall—the team was at the mercy of the weather. "The tin roof [on the rink] caused him some trouble because we had to live by the weather report and temperature."

Barss attached a thermometer outside their bedroom window, which Helen Barss checked every morning. If it was too warm to skate on the Coliseum's outdoor rink, she simply rolled over and let her young husband steal a golden hour of sleep until he had to wake up for class. But if it was cold enough for the team to practice, Helen would stir her bone-tired husband out of bed to get him to the rink on time. After everything he'd seen in France and Halifax, however, Barss was not likely to complain about a little fatigue.

Barss retired after the 1927 season, his fifth, with a 26–21–4 record (.553), two league titles, and a degree from the University of Michigan School of Medicine. Dr. Barss moved his young family to Riverside, Illinois, where he eventually became chief of surgery at the Hines Veterans Hospital in Chicago before setting up a private practice in Oak Park, Illinois, Ernest Hemingway's hometown. The Michigan hockey program he started has since won an NCAA record nine national titles.

"He sure gave me a good upbringing, in terms of character and honesty," Barss's son said. "He was absolutely true-blue. He was very aware of what was right and what was wrong. My dad was a helluva guy."

In 1966, at age 74, Dr. Barss took his wife, Helen, his son, and his grandson Joe back to Nova Scotia. In Wolfville, he showed them where he had learned to skate, where he went to college, and where he sold Victory Bonds. "I remember him saying the only things that had really changed in Wolfville were a new supermarket and paved streets," his grandson Joe recalls. In Halifax, he showed them where he had recuperated, where *Mont-Blanc* had blown up, and where he'd helped victims at Camp Hill Hospital.

But he didn't tell them how he had left Acadia University a confident young man with no sense of purpose, returned from the Great War a broken man searching for one, and went to Halifax for three long days, where he found it.

Chapter 43
The Lasting Impact

The great Halifax explosion set in motion ripples we still feel today, including advances in international relations, medicine, and weaponry.

While the disaster and the Americans' response to it created no formal policy between the two nations, any talk of Americans annexing Canada stopped after the explosion. The benevolent approach of Massachusetts Governor McCall toward Canada was carried on by his lieutenant governor, a man named Calvin Coolidge, when he became president. U.S. presidents and Canadian Prime Ministers have maintained close relations ever since, with only minor trade disputes marring an otherwise perfect record of cooperation and respect, demonstrated by the world's longest undefended border.

The enduring peace between them has been mutually

beneficial, too. Although the United States entered World War II two years after Canada did, they fought side by side for four years, including storming the beaches at Normandy together—a product not just of the Americans' help after the Halifax Explosion but of the year and a half they spent fighting the Great War together.

If you asked the average American who their nation's biggest trading partner is, you might hear China, Japan, Germany, or Mexico. But the correct answer is Canada, by a long shot, and for many years.

One of the first Boston doctors to arrive in Halifax after the blast, Dr. William E. Ladd, headed a Boston Red Cross contingent of twenty-two doctors, sixty-nine nurses, and fourteen civilians, plus enough equipment and supplies to set up a temporary 560-bed hospital at Saint Mary's College. They stayed for almost a month, not leaving until January 5, 1918. Before they did, the views of the Red Cross on disaster relief and Dr. Ladd's on medicine had changed significantly. The Red Cross decided to specialize in disaster response, while Dr. Ladd's experience working with burned children in Halifax sparked insights into pediatric surgery.

Upon Dr. Ladd's return to Boston, the Boston Children's Hospital designated two beds for his practice. From this modest beginning, Dr. Ladd built North America's preeminent pediatric surgery ward. Dr.

Ladd's pioneering work is credited with elevating pediatric surgery as a separate discipline in the Western Hemisphere. When Dr. Ladd died in 1967, at eighty-six, he was considered the father of pediatric surgery, and still is.

In 1924, Canada's legislature decided the nation should stop driving on the left side of the street just because the British did. This simple change helped promote trade and tourism with the Americans. The pitch was straightforward: "We drive your way. Come North to Eat, Drink, and Drive."

It worked on Babe Ruth, who loved going to Nova Scotia to hunt, fish, drink, drive—and more. In 1919, the former Red Sox star pitcher became the New York Yankees' star hitter, drawing so many fans that Yankee Stadium, "the House that Ruth Built," was constructed to accommodate them.

The Canadian identity continued to develop, but slowly. In the 1920s, Canada opened official diplomatic relations with the United States, and replaced the Union Jack with its own Red Ensign, which featured the Union Jack in the corner. In 1946, Canadian children like my mother assembled in their school gyms to hear their principals tell them that, as of that day, they were no longer British subjects but Canadian citizens, with their own passports. In 1965, Canada officially adopted its own flag, the Maple Leaf, which was actually intended only as a rudimentary prototype but has served Canada for more than half a century. Finally, in 1982, Canada received its full independence from the United Kingdom, which had continued to make laws for Canada until then.

Since 1917, there have been two constants: an unquestioned, mutually beneficial peace between the United States and Canada, and Canadians' insistence that they're not Americans. How do you tell the difference between a Canadian and an American? You say there is none, and watch the American nod, while the Canadian objects, albeit politely.

Halifax's identity has also evolved, and largely for the better. While it has never regained its status as Canada's preeminent city, it has secured its niche as Canada's East Coast gem, the Atlantic's answer to Vancouver. In 1995, Halifax hosted the G-7 Summit, and in 2003, the World Junior Hockey Championship—a major event in every hockey-playing country but the United States.

The local economy is still dependent on shipping and tourism. Halifax remains the largest naval base in Canada, home to some twenty warships and three submarines, with a new, $30 billion contract to build more. Dozens of cruise ships visit the harbor each year,

many of them carrying American southerners following the path of Zachary Taylor Wood. They find the
old seaside town just as charming as he did.

Instead of drifting back into another long sleepwalk,
Halifax has been accelerating, spending $11.5 million
in 1955 to build its first bridge across the channel, another $31 million to build the second, right over the
Narrows, and another $207 million in 2015 to raise the
first bridge a few meters so container ships could get
all the way to a dock in Bedford Basin. The city has
spent $350 million to build a boardwalk along the bay
and $57 million for a shiny new library downtown, an
architectural centerpiece CNN judged to be the ninth
most beautiful library in the world.

If anything, Halifax is moving too quickly to hold
on to its unique history. The harbor is still home to
the HMCS *Arcadia*, which survived the explosion, the
Great War, and World War II, but in 1965, city leaders decided to bulldoze Africville, leaving a park today.
"Not our shining moment," one resident told me. Four
years later, a ship carrying thirty-two Volvos arrived so
badly damaged by the trip that the company decided
to dump them into Bedford Basin, where all thirty-two
remain on the bottom, lined up as if parked in an underwater lot.

Almost no one calls the North Halifax neighborhood "Richmond" anymore, much to the chagrin of Halifax's older citizens, but historians are trying to bring it back. Most refer to it as "the North End," one of Halifax's most desirable addresses, which now features a cute little street of markets in the middle, with cafés and restaurants named Morsels, Hamachi, and, yes, Starbucks.

The neighborhood can now boast a street named Vincent, for Vincent Coleman, who also has a building named after him. In 1985, a moving monument to the explosion, its victims, and its heroes was erected on top of Fort Needham Memorial Park, with a bell and a sightline that runs right down the street to the former location of Pier 6. But, rather incredibly, in 2007, the Halifax government permitted Irving Oil, long the most powerful corporation in the Maritimes, to build a ship-manufacturing facility directly on top of ground zero, so when you look from Fort Needham straight down Richmond street now, you see a gigantic white metal building with the Irving logo on the side.

To an outsider, this smacks not only of a soulless erasing of that monumental event but an economically ill-advised one. Purely out of fiscal self-interest, it would seem to make sense for the city to build the Irving plant elsewhere and preserve one of its most important tourist destinations—a compelling reason for the 4,000 tourists who disgorge from each of those cruise ships twice a day to head to North Halifax to learn about one of the most remarkable days in the history of North America. Instead, the tourists head to the Fairview Cemetery to see the gravestones of *Titanic* victims, to the Maritime Museum of the Atlantic to see its display of *Titanic* artifacts, and to the re-creation of *Titanic*'s grand staircase in the casino next door— skipping past the explosion casualties in the cemetery, the excellent displays about the disaster in the Maritime Museum of the Atlantic, and ground zero itself, which is now marked by the Irving colossus.

The passage of time naturally dulls memories, obscuring events that were vivid to our parents and grandparents. The Great War has been pushed aside by World War II, the Halifax Explosion has been eclipsed by Hiroshima, and 9/11 seems to obscure everything that came before it. This is not only to be expected but is in many ways healthy. To maintain a slavish devotion to the past is not merely morbid but also counterproductive, something the survivors themselves realized when it came time to focus on their futures. But it's still surprising that the Halifax schools, which used to devote a full month to the subject, have whittled that down to a few days. For their part, few Americans have heard of the explosion.

We generally spend far more time dwelling on disasters than on triumphs, on villains than on heroes. But we'd be wise not to let the example of Halifax fade so far into the past, or we'd be denying ourselves one of the greatest expressions of humanity at its finest. If it's true that our character is revealed when we think no one is watching, then December 1917 provides a monthlong case study of a people who passed that test in a thousand different ways—a ringing display of the better angels of our nature.

If the Halifax Explosion's legacy has been largely neglected by the local government and schools, let alone the world at large, its spirit can be found in the wake of 9/11, when the FAA grounded all planes for a week, and Canadians welcomed 10,000 stranded passengers from forty-two planes in Gander, Newfoundland. And it can still be found among those dedicated souls who have worked to keep the memory of Halifax alive, lest these tragic victims die twice.

In 1996, author Blair Beed was giving a tour of Halifax, with emphasis on the explosion. One of his guests, Henry Handly, was ninety-five years old. Late in the tour, the alert but quiet man finally spoke up, telling Beed that he had been a sixteen-year-old boy in Salem,

Massachusetts, when *Mont-Blanc* blew up. He remembered venturing out with his Boy Scout troop to collect money and supplies for the relief of Halifax.

Seventy-nine years later, he fulfilled his dream of visiting the city he helped save.

Chapter 44
The Reunion

In 1920, the Halifax Relief Commission started paying out pensions to 1,028 survivors. By 1994, it continued to send checks to 21 of them.

In between, on June 23, 1984, the Richmond School sent out reunion invitations to all those students who had attended the original school before *Mont-Blanc* had destroyed it sixty-seven years earlier.

Gordon and James Pattison both showed up. James's courses in drafting and mechanics had paid off when he became foreman of the Dartmouth Oil Refinery's mechanical division. His career sent him to Peru, but he had moved back to Kentville, Nova Scotia, a few minutes from Wolfville and just an hour or so away from Halifax. That night, he brought his leather school bag complete with his seventh-grade books, which might have saved his life when the ship blew up.

Noble Driscoll still lived so close that he could walk to the reunion, arriving with his brother, Al. Noble had taken Principal Huggins's advice, left school, and started working for Creighton's as a deliveryman, as did Al. Noble worked his way up to the Nova Scotia Liquor Commission, and managed the liquor store on Agricola Street for many years.

Archie Upham and his sister, Millicent, had come back, too. Like their father, Charles, Archie worked on the railway. Millicent had trained as a hairdresser in Montreal before settling in Halifax and marrying fellow survivor Bill Swindells, who had become a baker famous for his fruitcakes.

Barbara Orr joined them. She had married George Thompson, raised a family of her own, and now enjoyed her grandchildren.

Even decades after the explosion, Barbara would often dream she was at home with her family. But when she woke, she would realize all she had was a small piece of broken china, a school picture of her sister Mary and her brother Ian, and recurring dreams of being a fourteen-year-old girl in Halifax, eating breakfast with her mother and siblings in their home on Richmond Hill on Thursday morning, December 6, 1917.

"Sometimes," she said, "it seemed as if it had all happened to someone else."

A year after the Richmond reunion, on June 9, 1985, they gathered again to christen the memorial tower on top of Fort Needham, overlooking the neighborhood that used to be Richmond, and below that, the site of the explosion. Millicent Upham Swindells and her granddaughter, Anne-Louise Ihasz, inserted a time capsule in the tower, to be opened on December 6, 2017, the hundredth anniversary of the explosion.

Barbara Orr played the bells at the dedication alongside Bill Orr, her cousin, whose family took her in when she needed a home.

Against all odds, the survivors had found ways to overcome their staggering losses and lead productive, fulfilling lives—even happy ones.

In December 1918, just a few months after the Red Sox won their fifth World Series in fifteen years behind the pitching of their young lefthander, Babe Ruth, the city of Halifax sent a huge Christmas tree to Boston to thank them for their help during Halifax's darkest hour. In 1976, 200 years after the Americans broke from the British, Halifax resurrected the tradition, and has sent a fifty-foot, two-ton tree to Boston Commons every year since.

It is a testament to a time when the worst the world could inflict brought out the best in two countries. In the process, it forged a hard-earned friendship, one strong enough to overcome 141 years of distrust, subterfuge, and occasional violence, one that has stood for a century as an example to the rest of the world.

Acknowledgments

I had wanted to write this book for more than a decade for a lot of good reasons, including the chance to visit Halifax. The city is as welcoming as advertised, but the people were even better.

The former dean of Dalhousie University's business school, James McNiven, and his scholarly daughter-in-law, Lisa, gave me two thorough tours of Halifax and Dartmouth. Noted author Blair Beed followed up with a detailed exploration of the Richmond neighborhood and beyond.

After decades of neglect, the Halifax Explosion has enjoyed a quarter century of attention from dedicated scholars, starting with Janet Katz's pioneering books *Shattered City* and *Survivors*, both filled with remarkable interviews, accounts you can't find anywhere else.

Other noted authors include Alan Ruffman, who compiled the authoritative *Ground Zero*, the best investigation of the scientific aspects of the explosion. Joel Zemel's *Scapegoat* provides the most thorough research of the central figures, the ships, and the court transcripts, while Beed produced a book that is particularly helpful for my work, *1917 Halifax Explosion and American Response*.

In addition to this cabal of serious scholars, Halifax is also home to the Public Archives of Nova Scotia, where the inimitable Garry Shutlak has been helping wayward researchers find their way with good cheer for decades, and the Maritime Museum of the Atlantic (MMA), where Roger Marsters and Richard McMichael have done world-class work on *Titanic*, the explosion, and more. Author and raconteur Stephen Kimber, who updated Thomas H. Raddall's *Halifax: Warden of the North*, has become a trusted friend and guide.

All of these authors and experts agreed to meet with me on my trips to their city, giving generously of their time and knowledge during our long conversations.

In addition, Lisa McNiven was nice enough to read the manuscript and offer helpful suggestions. Several people read parts or all of the manuscript for factual accuracy, with Ashley Sutherland devoting herself to that single mission. At the MMA, Amber Laurie tracked down more than a dozen photographs for this book. Mandy O'Brien did the same at the City of Toronto archives, as did Garry Shutlak and Philip Hartling at the Archives of Nova Scotia. Chantal Allan's *Bomb Canada* and David MacKenzie's *Canada 1911* were both very helpful, as were the authors.

The grandchildren of Joseph Ernest Barss—Joe, Ted, and Bob Barrs, and John Messenger—answered my endless emails promptly and patiently, supplying the raw materials for their grandfather's story, plus lots of inside information. Ernest's son, Joe, gave me a few great interviews back in 1999, when I was writing about Barss for my first book, *Blue Ice: The Story of Michigan Hockey*. I only wish he was here to see this. Thanks also to the good people at the University of Michigan: Lora Durkee, Greg Kinney, and Matt Trevor.

I never would have had the chance to meet the experts in Halifax if my agents and publisher hadn't helped me first. Jay Mandel and Eric Lupfer at William Morris Endeavor are simply the best in the business, providing the kind of encouragement and expertise that turns inchoate ideas into great proposals. And thanks to their assistants, Lauren Shonkoff and Kitty Dulin, who kept the wheels turning with a smile.

Acclaimed editor Peter Hubbard at HarperCollins/ William Morrow helped transform that proposal and piles of research into this book. He believed in this little-known story from the start, and saw it through to completion with a calm, confident professionalism that was most welcome during many hectic weeks, as was his sense of humor. We were both backed to the hilt by HarperCollins's esteemed publisher, Liate Stehlik. Nick Amphlett and his staff of copy editors performed their vital work with care, and Maureen Cole was a champion with publicity.

As usual, I relied on many friends to help make sure my work was on track, none more important than James Tobin, an award-winning author who read several drafts of the proposal and the manuscript. He provided detailed, savvy advice, and offered much-needed empathy and advice during our many meetings. John Lofy helped shape the proposal, while a small army of smart friends read the manuscript, including Eric Adelson, Jim Carty, L. Todd Johnson, Barney Klein, Thomas Lebien, Howard Markel, Jonathan Marwill, Jim Russ, Jed Thompson, Bob Weisman, Pete Uher, and Bill Wood. They gave me excellent feedback from a variety of perspectives. The good folks at Camp Michigania served as a focus group after my first speech on the then-unfinished book, concluding that "six million pounds of high explosives" sounds better than three thousand tons. Christopher Soles, a fellow camper, dug up all the information on picric acid a writer could ever need.

My wife, Christie, not only helped with every task listed above—from research to feedback to photos to scheduling trips to Halifax—she kept our home humming with warmth and humor during my many days, weeks, and months in the "writer's cave." Our two-year-old son, Teddy, provided joy, perspective, and inspiration; you're the best reason we do all this.

While I was exploring one of the greatest tragedies in history, being with both of you reminded me on a daily basis just how fortunate I am.

Source Notes

Part I: A Forgotten Story

Chapter 1: A Century of Gratitude

4 "Why do we have to stop . . .": "Nova Scotians Learn the Christmas Tree for Boston Is Far from Free," *Boston Globe*, November 28, 2016.

Chapter 2: Under Cover of Darkness

8 "Captain Aimé Joseph Marie Le Médec . . .": Michael Bird, *The Town That Died*, Toronto: McGraw-Hill Ryerson Limited, 1962, pp. 3–4.

8 "copper nails . . .": Bird, *The Town that Died*, pp. 4–6.

10 "one of the largest caches of high explosives . . .": *Mont-Blanc* cargo contents, A. Ruffman and

C. D. Howell, *Ground Zero: A Reassessment of the 1917 Explosion in Halifax Harbour*, Halifax: Nimbus Publishing Ltd., 1994, appendix p. 296.

12 "a policy reinforced by posters . . .": Ibid., p. 10.

14 "Captain Le Médec met again . . .": Joel Zemel, *Scapegoat: The Extraordinary Legal Proceedings Following the 1917 Halifax Explosion*, Halifax: New World Publishing, 2012, p. 20.

19 "Well, some of the pebbles . . .": Ibid., *Scapegoat*, p. 19.

20 "Back at McNab's Island . . .": Laura M. MacDonald, *Curse of the Narrows*, NYC: Walker and Company, 2005, pp. 16–17.

22 "Few in Richmond were doing better . . .": All stories of the Orr family come from two of Janet Kitz's books: *Shattered City: The Halifax Explosion and the Road to Recovery*, Halifax: Nimbus Publishing Ltd., 1989, and *Survivors: Children of the Halifax Explosion*, Halifax: Nimbus Publishing Ltd. In this case, *Shattered City*, p. 17, and *Survivors*, p. 13.

23 "Not so Joseph Ernest Barss . . .": Except where noted, all of the information regarding Joseph Ernest Barss (not to be confused with Joseph Barss Jr., his great-grandfather) comes

from his and his widow's letters. When quoting specifically, the letters cited are dated.

25 "As of that night . . .": Blair Beed, *1917 Halifax Explosion and American Response*, Halifax: Self, 1988, p. 15.

25 "Nineteen-year-old Ethel Mitchell . . .": Except where noted, all information regarding Ethel Mitchell comes from Kitz, *Shattered City*, and Kitz, *Survivors*. In this case, *Shattered City*, p. 11.

Part II: O Canada
Chapter 3: "Why Aren't We Americans?"

30 "the shape of the harbour . . .": Donald Kerr, in Ruffman and Howell, *Ground Zero*, p. 365.

32 "Halifax cemented its central role . . .": Maritime Museum of the Atlantic, display.

33 "No sooner had the Rebels . . .": Mark Stein, *How the States Got Their Shapes*, Smithsonian Books: Washington, DC, 2008, p. 123.

34 "On June 18, 1812 . . .": John Boileau, *Half-Hearted Enemies: Nova Scotia, New England, and the War of 1812*, Halifax: Formac Publishing Ltd., 2005, pp. 15–16.

34 "But the British turned things around . . .": Maritime Museum of the Atlantic, various websites, Halifax: 2000.

35 "Halifax historian Thomas Akins . . .": Boileau, *Half-Hearted Enemies,* p. 24.

37 "It wasn't easy . . .": Ibid., pp. 51–58.

38 "While the American press . . .": Ibid., pp. 60–61.

41 "Haligonians also feared . . .": Thomas H. Raddall and Stephen Kimber, *Halifax: Warden of the North,* Halifax: Nimbus Publishing Ltd., updated edition, 2010, p. 194.

42 "when two Union ships . . .": Ibid., p. 196.

42 "the highly respected Dr. Almon . . .": Maritime Museum of the Atlantic, various websites, 2000.

42 "Jock Fleming . . .": from a Historical Society sign in Fisherman's Cove, Dartmouth.

43 "Captain Wood never forgot . . .": Raddall and Kimber, *Halifax: Warden of the North,* p. 197.

Chapter 4: Waking Up Just in Time

45 "This perpetual fear . . .": Ibid., pp. 193–202.

47 "Canada could claim full credit . . .": Diamond, Dan, et al., *Total Hockey: The Official Encyclopedia of the National Hockey League,* New York: Total Sports, 1998, p. 3–7.

48 "In Canada's 1911 national election . . .": David MacKenzie and Patrice Dutil, *Canada 1911: The Decisive Election that Shaped the Country,* Toronto: Dundurn, 2011, pp. 9–11.

49 "I look forward to the time . . .": Chantal Allan, *Bomb Canada and Other Unkind Remarks in the American Media*, Edmonton: Athabasca University Press, 2009, pp. 17–18.

50 "The beneficiary of this turmoil . . .": Ibid., p. 26.

51 "Reciprocity was finished off . . .": MacKenzie and Dutil, *Canada 1911*, p. 211.

52 "In 1901, Boston had . . .": Glenn Stout, *Fenway 1912: The Birth of a Ballpark, A Championship Season, and Fenway's Remarkable First Year*, New York: Houghton Mifflin Harcourt, 2011, p. 170.

52 "When Red Sox owner John I. Taylor . . .": Ibid., pp. 44–45.

54 "Harold Cottam . . .": http://www.titanicfacts. net/carpathia.html.

55 "The *Mackay-Bennett* crew . . .": Maritime Museum of the Atlantic, various websites, 2000.

56 "haunted by all they had seen . . .": Ibid.

Part III: The Great War

Chapter 5: As Near to Hell

62 "No Canadian city . . .": Raddall and Kimber, *Halifax: Warden of the North*, 2010, p. 242.

62 "Britain's enthusiasm . . .": Michael Kazin, *War*

Against War: The American Fight for Peace, 1914–1918, New York: Simon & Schuster, 2017, p. xii.

63 "forming a line of trenches . . .": Saul David, "How Germany Lost the WWI Arms Race," BBC News, February 16, 2012, http://www.bbc .com/news/magazine-17011607.

67 "It is one of the dreariest landscapes . . .": John Keegan, *The First World War*, New York: Vintage Books, 1998. p. 129.

69 "must have been as near to hell . . .": Ibid.

73 "He was sort of a stocky fella . . .": author interview with Dr. Joseph Andrew Barss, 1999.

73 "Ernest graduated . . .": Helen Kolb Barss, letter to her children, date unknown. Barss family archives.

75 "Every Saturday in warm weather . . .": Helen Kolb Barss, letter to her children, date unknown, Barss family archives.

76 "Well, this is probably the last letter . . .": Joseph Ernest Barss, letter to his parents, April 4, 1915, Barss family archives.

77 "There are only 53 left . . .": Joseph Ernest Barss, letter to his parents April 30, 1915, Barss family archives.

79 "Strange to say . . .": Joseph Ernest Barss, letter to his parents, April 4, 1915, Barss family archives.

Chapter 6: Halifax at War

80 "Halifax sent 6,000 sons . . .": Raddall and Kimber, *Halifax: Warden of the North*, pp. 247–48.

81 "Black armbands and patches . . .": Kitz, *Shattered City*, p. 10.

81 "a pioneering woman . . .": Florence J. Murray, *At The Foot of Dragon Hill*, New York: E. P. Dutton & Company, Inc., 1975, pp. vii–x.

84 "Although Halifax had always profited . . .": Raddall and Kimber, *Halifax: Warden of the North*, pp. 242–43.

84 "From just 1915 to 1916 . . .": Raddall and Kimber, *Halifax: Warden of the North*, pp. 242–43.

84 "There was a reason for that . . .": David Millichope, *Halifax in the Great War*, Barnsley, UK: Pen and Sword, 2015, pp. 149–53.

85 "The economy's sudden acceleration . . .": Raddall and Kimer, *Halifax: Warden of the North*, p. 243.

85 "Add it all up . . .": Bird, *The Town That Died*, p. 29.

85 "Neighborhoods of Italians . . .": Raddall and Kimber, *Halifax: Warden of the North*, p. 243.

86 "Four years later . . .": Ibid., p. 244.

86 "In the pubs . . .": Ibid.

87 "scores of prostitutes . . .": Kitz, *Shattered City*, p. 10.

Chapter 7: Life and Death on the Western Front

89 "I tell you it was no joke . . .": Joseph Ernest Barss, letter to his parents, September 16, 1915, Barss family archives.

90 "Nine days later . . .": Joseph Ernest Barss, letter to his parents, September 25, 1915. Barss family archives.

92 "On the lighter side . . .": Helen Kolb Barss, letter to her children, date unknown, Barss family archives.

93 "You can bet . . .": Joseph Ernest Barss, letter to his parents, October 1, 1915, Barss family archives.

96 "I am writing tonight . . .": Joseph Ernest Barss, letter to his parents, October 12, 1915, Barss family archives.

98 "he sounded much better . . .": Joseph Ernest Barss, letter to his parents, November 11, 1915, Barss family archives.

99 "After listing some of the gifts . . .": Joseph Ernest Barss, letter to his parents, January 3, 1916, Barss family archives.

100 "his commanding officer demoted him . . .": Joseph Ernest Barss, military records, Barss family archives.

Chapter 8: Halifax Harbour

102 "But many French-Canadians . . .": Maritime Museum of the Atlantic, various websites, 2000.

102 "The HMCS *Rainbow* . . .": J. G. Armstrong, *The Halifax Explosion and the Royal Canadian Navy*, Vancouver: UBC Press, 2002, p. 20.

103 "Throw in the RCN's lack of officers . . .": Maritime Museum of the Atlantic, various websites, 2000.

103 "Shortly after war broke out . . .": Wyatt's biography is drawn largely from Zemel, *Scapegoat*, pp. 16–18.

105 "Thus, during the war . . .": Armstrong, *The Halifax Explosion and the Royal Canadian Navy*, p. 20.

108 "The Royal Canadian Navy in Ottawa . . .": Zemel, *Scapegoat*, pp. 292-93.

109 "A few weeks later . . .": Ibid., p. 18.

109 "In his third letter . . ." All three of Wyatt's

letters were published in the Halifax *Morning Chronicle*, January 28, 1918.

Chapter 9: "It Can't Be Any Worse"

111 "We are going in again . . .": Joseph Ernest Barss, letter to his parents, February 15, 1916, Barss family archives.

111 "I expect to go on leave . . .": Joseph Ernest Barss, letter to his parents, February 20, 1916, Barss family archives.

112 "On February 21, 1916 . . .": Joseph Ernest Barss, official military records, Barss family archives; and Helen Kolb Barss, letter to her children, date unknown, Barss family archives.

114 "This is a very different letter . . ." Joseph Ernest Barss, letter to his parents, March 1, 1916, Barss family archives.

115 "Finally, on Sunday, May 7 . . .": Joseph Ernest Barss, letter to his parents, May 12, 1916, Barss family archives.

117 "Well, I'm back again to it all . . .": Joseph Ernest Barss, letter to his parents, May 18, 1916, Barss family archives.

118 "I think we are all heartily sick of the whole show . . .": Joseph Ernest Barss, letter to his parents, May 31, 1916, Barss family archives.

119 "The next day, Thursday, June 1, 1916, the Patricias installed four companies . . .": Most of the battle of Mont Sorrel comes from Jeffrey Williams, *First in the Field: Gault of the Patricia's*, Barnsley, UK: Pen and Sword, 1997, pp. 110–15.

122 "I have been admitted into hospital . . .": Joseph Ernest Barss, postcard to his parents, June 4, 1916, Barss family archives.

122 "and another class of men . . .": Keegan, *The First World War*, pp. 6-7.

123 "the tomb of the Unknown Soldier . . .": Ibid., pp. 5-6.

Chapter 10: "The City's Newer Part"

125 "Richmond with land to spare . . .": Blair Beed, *1917 Halifax Explosion and American Response*, Halifax: Self, 1988, p. 88.

126 "At just about any hour . . .": Kitz, *Shattered City*, p. 12.

127 "Near the turn of the century . . .": The Orr family background comes from Kitz, *Shattered City*.

129 "In 1917, most Richmond children . . .": Kitz, *Survivors*, pp. 15–17.

130 "and Grove Presbyterian . . .": Kitz, *Shattered City*, p. 13.

131 "The Driscolls' home . . .": Kitz, *Survivors*, pp. 2 and 13.

132 "With no theater in Richmond . . .": Ibid., p. 26.

133 "The Pattisons' father . . .": Ibid., pp. 6, 13, 22, and 24–25.

135 "None of the people . . .": Africville Genealogy Society, *The Spirit of Africville*, Halifax: Lorimer, 2010, p. 43.

136 "When business was humming . . .": Ibid., p. 38.

136 "By 1914, they had been reduced . . .": Ruth Holmes Whitehead, *Tracking Doctor Lonecloud: Showman to Legend Keeper*, Fredericton, New Brunswick: Goose Lane Editions, 2002.

Chapter 11: Wounded Inside and Out

139 "Just a few lines . . .": Joseph Ernest Barss, letter to his parents, June 6, 1916, Barss family archives.

139 "Barss filled in more . . .": Joseph Ernest Barss, letter to his parents, August 18, 1916, Barss family archives.

140 "His official records stated . . .": Joseph Ernest Barss, official military records, Barss family archives.

141 "In a letter to her sister . . .": Libby Barss,

letter to her sister, October 1, 1916, Barss family archives.

142 "The military doctors . . ." Helen Kolb Barss, letter to her children, Barss family archives.

143 "He looks well . . .": Howard Barss, letter to Aunt Margaret, February 17, 1917, Barss family archives.

143 "The doctors' conclusions . . .": Joseph Ernest Barss, official military records, date unknown, Barss family archives.

145 "Thus, Great Britain . . .": Kazin, *War Against War*, p. 197.

146 "Of course, the Americans would only make a difference . . .": Glenn Stout, *The Selling of The Babe: The Deal that Changed Baseball and Created a Legend*, New York: Thomas Dunn Book, 2016, pp. 19 and 28.

149 "MacNeil liked to shock . . .": Ruffman and Howell, *Ground Zero*, pp. 127–28.

150 "In the spring of 1917, Barss spent . . .": Joseph Ernest Barss, official military records, 1915–1919, Barss family archives.

150 "Barrs decided to ignore . . .": Helen Kolb Barss, letter to her children, date unknown, Barss family archives.

152 "Barss wrote to his American uncle . . .":
Joseph Ernest Barss, letter to his uncle Andrew
Townson, December 14, 1917, Barss family
archives.

Part IV: A Dangerous Dance
Chapter 12: Two Ships

156 "The vessels were equipped . . .": History
Journal, "U-Boats in World War I," https://
historyjournal.org/2012/08/28/u-boats-in-world
-war-i/.

157 "But to Noble Driscoll . . .": Kitz, *Survivors*,
pp. 2–4.

158 "Launched in 1889, the White Star Line . . .": The
background of *Imo* and Captain Haakon From
comes largely from Zemel, *Scapegoat*, pp. 21–26.

161 "In October 1917 . . .": This background of
Mont-Blanc and Captain Le Médec comes
largely from Zemel, *Scapegoat*, pp. 19–22; and
MacDonald, *Curse of the Narrows*, p. 17.

162 "What made *Mont-Blanc*'s cargo so dangerous?":
This analysis is drawn largely from Ruffman and
Howell, *Ground Zero*, pp. 275–77 and 287.

165 "She had a devil's brew aboard . . .": Raddall and
Kimber, *Halifax: Warden of the North*, p. 244.

166 "The stevedores followed orders . . .":

Armstrong, *The Halifax Explosion and the Royal Canadian Navy*, p. 30.

166 "When the crew walked past the drums . . .":
Bird, *The Town That Died*, p. 6.

167 "Instead, the ship was equipped . . .":
Armstrong, *The Halifax Explosion and the Royal Canadian Navy*, pp. 35–36.

168 "and another two hours . . .": MacDonald, *Curse of the Narrows*, p. 48.

168 "Taking all this information in . . .": Zemel, *Scapegoat*, p. 20.

Chapter 13: December 5, 1917

175 "At about 2:30 on Wednesday . . .": This exchange is derived largely from Zemel, *Scapegoat*, p. 22.

177 "What time CXO Wyatt ordered the anti-submarine gates closed . . .": MacDonald, *Curse of the Narrows*, pp. 16–17.

178 "But when he scanned . . .": Armstrong, *The Halifax Explosion and the Royal Canadian Navy*, pp. 29–30.

178 "In fact, Freeman thought *Mont-Blanc* . . .": MacDonald, *Curse of the Narrows*, p. 16.

179 "Any chance Le Médec . . .": Zemel, *Scapegoat*, p. 19.

179 "Freeman understood Le Médec and Mackey . . .": MacDonald, *Curse of the Narrows*, p. 17.

180 "Noble Driscoll was watching . . .": Kitz, *Survivors*, pp. 2–8.

182 "The Reverend William J. W. Swetnam . . .": Kitz, *Shattered City*, p. 39.

183 "Ethel Mitchell, the nineteen-year-old . . .": Ibid., p. 11.

Chapter 14: A Game of Chicken

184 "A light haze . . .": MacDonald, *Curse of the Narrows*, p. 26.

185 "Back at the Mitchells' home . . .": Kitz, *Shattered City*, pp. 17–18.

186 "Mackey read Le Médec the message . . .": Bird, *The Town That Died*, p. 15.

186 "At 7:50 a.m. . . .": Zemel, *Scapegoat*, pp. 28 and 54.

188 "The list was quite small . . .": Bird, *The Town That Died*, pp. 47–48.

190 "All ships in the harbor . . .": *Mont-Blanc* cargo contents, Ruffman and Howell, *Ground Zero*, p. 365.

192 "But all these scenarios . . .": Ibid.

188 "When the guard ship . . .": Zemel, *Scapegoat,* p. 30.

192 "After *Imo* had cleared . . .": Ibid., pp. 29–30.

196 "Nickerson saw *Imo* stirring up foam . . .": Ibid., p 31.

196 "The bloody fool!": Bird, *The Town That Died,* p. 41.

198 "Fuel oil . . .": Ibid., p. 21.

198 "At 8:27 a.m. . . .": Zemel, *Scapegoat,* pp. 28–33.

199 "At that moment . . .": MacDonald, *Curse of the Narrows,* p. 34.

201 "At the same time . . .": Zemel, *Scapegoat,* p. 34.

204 "Knowing Hayes as I do . . .": Ibid., p. 40.

205 "I knew that in the No. 2 'tween decks . . .": Ibid., p. 37.

206 "Thanks to Archie Orr's whooping cough . . .": The Orrs' story derives from Kitz, *Shattered City,* p. 17; and Kitz, *Survivors,* p. 29.

Chapter 15: "Look to Your Boats!"

209 "If the French freighter . . .": Armstrong, *The Halifax Explosion and the Royal Canadian Navy,* p. 37.

210 "could feel something like . . .": Zemel, *Scapegoat,* p. 39.

210 "The Orr children's astonishment . . .": Kitz, *Shattered City*, p. 17; and Kitz, *Survivors*, pp. 30–31.

211 "A few men . . .": MacDonald, *Curse of the Narrows*, pp. 44–48.

213 "If Le Médec heard Mackey's plan . . .": Bird, *The Town That Died*, pp. 33–36.

213 "At 8:48 . . .": Zemel, *Scapegoat*, p. 232.

214 "Le Médec went to retrieve . . .": Bird, *The Town That Died*, pp. 35–36.

214 "Jump into my boat!": Armstrong, *The Halifax Explosion and the Royal Canadian Navy*, pp. 36–37.

215 "Ralph Smith . . .": Zemel, *Scapegoat*, p. 74.

216 "The other sailors in the harbor . . .": Bird, *The Town That Died*, pp. 46–48.

219 "As Mackey later said . . .": Zemel, *Scapegoat*, p. 60.

220 "When the *Mont-Blanc* crew . . .": Ibid., pp. 59–61.

222 "Running for their lives . . .": MacDonald, *Curse of the Narrows*, p. 57.

Chapter 16: Box 83

224 "it might blow off in an instant . . .": Zemel, *Scapegoat*, p. 64.

224 "Jack Tappen, a nineteen . . .": Tappen's story comes from Kitz, *Shattered City,* p. 21.

225 "At 8:52 . . .": Most of the times cited in this section were established by Zemel, *Scapegoat,* p. 432.

229 "On the *Curaca* . . .": Ruffman and Howell, *Ground Zero,* p. 316.

229 "After the fireworks . . .": Ibid., *Shattered City,* pp. 18-22.

229 "The Burfords had emigrated . . .": Ibid., p. 22.

230 "In the harbor . . ." Maritime Museum of the Atlantic, various websites, 2000.

232 "Racing through the city streets . . .": Halifax Professional Firefighters Association website, http://www.hpff.ca/memorials/halifax -explosion/.

232 "On this day . . .": Kitz, *Shattered City,* p. 22.

233 "His friends on the truck . . .": Halifax Professional Firefighters Association website.

Chapter 17: *"Oh, Something Awful Is Going to Happen"*

235 "In the Pattisons' home . . .": Kitz, *Survivors,* p. 37.

237 "At the other end of Richmond . . .": Ibid., pp. 34–35; and Kitz, *Shattered City*, p. 22.

239 "Mr. Huggins, the principal . . .": Kitz, *Survivors*, p. 42.

240 "The owner of Richmond's general store . . .": Ibid., pp. 37–42; and Kitz, *Shattered City*, p. 37.

241 "The Orr children . . .": City of Ruins: The Halifax Explosion," CBC, 2003.

243 "Lt. Commander James Murray . . .": Bird, *The Town That Died*, pp. 46–51.

244 "William Lovett . . . immediately called . . .": Zemel, *Scapegoat*, pp. 391 and 432; and Maritime Museum of the Atlantic, various websites, 2000.

Part V: 9:04:35 a.m.

Chapter 18: One-Fifteenth of a Second

249 "To try to grasp the magnitude . . .": Robert MacNeil, *Burden of Desire*, New York: Bantam Doubleday Publishing Group, Inc., 1992, p. 22.

250 "The detonation itself . . .": Ruffman and Howell, *Ground Zero*, p. 277.

251 "with its barrel drooping . . .": Raddall and Kimber, *Halifax: Warden of the North*, p. 245.

251 "The explosion also produced . . .": Ruffman and Howell, *Ground Zero*, p. 277.

252 "This attracted the attention . . .": All these
observations come from Ruffman and Howell,
Ground Zero, p. 322.

253 "Ian Forsyth, a student . . .": Ibid., pp. 317–18.

254 "Also called shock waves . . .": Ibid., pp. 277–78
and 302.

257 "The explosion, the ground waves . . .": Ibid.,
p. 330.

257 "Phillip Mitchell, the grandfather of . . .": Kitz,
Shattered City, p. 26.

258 "George Dixon worked at a small . . .": Ruffman
and Howell, *Ground Zero*, p. 341.

259 "had been snapped . . .": Kitz, *Shattered City*,
p. 25.

259 "All told . . .": Ruffman and Howell, *Ground
Zero*, p. 245.

260 "Corpses were scattered . . .": Kitz, *Shattered
City*, p. 26.

Chapter 19: Parting the Sea

261 "Farther from Pier 6 . . .": Kitz, *Shattered City*,
pp. 26–29.

262 "*Curaca*, the American ship . . .": Ruffman and
Howell, *Ground Zero*, p. 338.

263 "McCrossan jumped onto the *Calonne* . . .":
Kitz, *Shattered City*, p. 28.

263 "The tugboat *Hilford* . . .": Ruffman and Howell, *Ground Zero*, p. 338.

264 "Just a few hundred feet . . .": Kitz, *Shattered City*, p. 30.

266 "The Dartmouth Ferry . . .": Ibid., p. 31.

268 "When the authorities arrived . . .": Maritime Museum of the Atlantic, various websites, 2000.

268 "A full half mile . . .": MacDonald, *Curse of the Narrows*, pp. 82–83.

Chapter 20: Blown Away

271 "After the fire on *Mont-Blanc* started . . .": Kitz, *Shattered City*, p. 35.

272 "Amelia Mary Griswold lived on Needham Street . . .": Ibid., pp. xvi–xvii.

274 "Jack Tappen, the nineteen-year-old apprentice . . .": Ibid., p. 50.

276 "At twenty-one, Joe Glube . . .": Ibid., p. 62.

276 "Constant's brother, Charles . . .": Ibid., pp. 37–39; and Kitz, *Survivors*, pp. 55–56.

279 "The morning after Grove Presbyterian . . .": Kitz, *Shattered*, p. 42.

281 "That morning Reverend Swetnam's wife . . .": Ibid., pp. 39–40; and Kitz, *Survivors*, p. 57.

286 "Missing school didn't improve your chances . . .": Ibid., pp. 43–44.

287 "When the Richmond School . . .": Ibid., pp. 44–45.

Chapter 21: They're All Gone

288 "The real nightmare . . .": CBC, *The Halifax Explosion: City of Ruins*, 2003.

291 "fourteen-year-old Barbara Orr . . .": Orr's account was captured by Janet Kitz in *Shattered City*, pp. 32–34, and *Survivors*, pp. 45–48.

296 "On Noble Driscoll's walk . . .": Noble Driscoll's account was retold by Janet Kitz in *Shattered City*, p. 32-33, and *Survivors*, pp. 49-50.

299 "A little after 9:00 a.m. . . .": The Pattisons' story comes from Janet Kitz's *Shattered City*, p. 34, and *Survivors*, pp. 52–54.

302 "Eileen Ryan, eleven . . .": Kitz, *Shattered City*, pp. 48–49.

303 "Across the harbor in Dartmouth . . .": Ibid., pp. 46–47.

304 "Jack Tappen, who had been shot . . .": Ibid., pp. 49–50.

Chapter 22: The Panic

306 "At 10:00 a.m., a young lieutenant . . .": Kitz, *Shattered City*, p. 54; and MacDonald, *Curse of the Narrows*, pp. 96–101.

309 "Richmond's Chebucto Road . . .": Raddall
and Kimber, *Halifax: Warden of the North*,
p. 247.

310 "When a soldier ordered Joe Glube . . .": Kitz,
Shattered City, pp. 62–63.

312 "T. J. Wallace, an optometrist . . .": Ibid., pp.
55–56.

314 "After Charles Upham had coaxed . . .": Ibid.,
p. 57; and Kitz, *Survivors*, p. 71.

315 "George Grant, the governor of Rockhead
Prison . . .": Kitz, *Shattered City*, pp. 57 and 76;
and Kitz, *Survivors*, pp. 71–72.

316 "Mrs. Rasley's son Reg . . .": Kitz, *Shattered
City*, p. 57; and Kitz, *Survivors*, p. 73.

318 "Gordon Pattison, fourteen . . .": Kitz, *Shattered
City*, pp. 56–57 and 77; and Kitz, *Survivors*, pp.
68–69.

322 "Barbara Orr was grateful . . .": Kitz, *Shattered
City*, pp. 54 and 66; and Kitz, *Survivors*, pp.
61–62.

324 "Then I realized there was something
funny . . .": CBC, *The Halifax Explosion*.

326 "No one shall leave this building . . .": Kitz,
Shattered City, p. 54.

326 "After the panic . . .": Ibid., p. 53; and Kitz,
Survivors, p. 64.

329 "With every Halifax facility . . .": Ruffman and Howell, *Ground Zero*, p. 248.

329 "At 3:30 p.m. that day . . .": Kitz, *Shattered City*, pp. 1 and 68; and Kitz, *Survivors*, pp. 65–66.

Part VI: Help

Chapter 23: No Time to Explain

335 "The Great Chicago Fire . . .": All four disasters are addressed in NPR's "An American History of Disaster and Response," http://www.npr.org/templates/story/story.php?storyId=4839530.

340 "On February 10, 1917 . . .": MacDonald., *Curse of the Narrows*, pp. 104–5.

341 "Boston was way ahead . . .": Ibid., pp. 93–95.

344 "For God's sake . . .": Ibid., p. 95.

345 "Organize a relief train . . .": Beed, *1917 Halifax Explosion and American Response*, p. 19.

345 "His message sparked a series of telegrams . . .": MacDonald, *Curse of the Narrows*, pp. 103–5.

348 "Quick decision at the risk of occasional error . . .": Ibid., p. 102.

349 "In Dartmouth, Col Ralph B. Simmonds . . .": Kitz, *Shattered City*, pp. 58–60.

351 "Colonel Thompson and his staff . . .": Beed, *1917 Halifax Explosion and American Response*, pp. 20–21.

352 "Between Halifax and Dartmouth . . .":
Ruffman and Howell, *Ground Zero*,
p. 245.

354 "Dr. Elliott immediately asked Barss . . .":
Joseph Ernest Barss, letter to his uncle Andrew
Townson, December 14, 1917, Barss family
archives.

Chapter 24: Ready to Go the Limit

357 "The telegram from Halifax . . .": MacDonald,
Curse of the Narrows, pp. 104–5.

357 "Understand your city . . .": Beed, *1917 Halifax
Explosion and American Response*, p. 19.

358 "Since sending . . .": Ibid., p. 19.

359 "On Thursday, December 6 . . .": Ibid., pp.
21–22.

360 "*Boston Post*, December 7, 1917 . . .": Ibid.,
p. 19.

361 "The most we obtained were rumors . . .":
MacDonald, *Curse of the Narrows*, p. 165.

Chapter 25: A Steady Stream of Victims

364 "Dr. Percy McGrath had graduated . . .": Kitz,
Shattered City, p. 65.

366 "Of course you have read of the terrible
disaster . . .": Joseph Ernest Barss, letter to his

uncle Andrew Townson, December 14, 1917,
Barss family archives.

368 "G. H. Cox . . .": Ruffman and Howell, *Ground Zero*, p. 249.

368 "Captain Frederick T. Tooke . . .": Ibid., p. 245.

369 "Because the records of those admitted . . .":
Kitz, *Shattered City*, p. 67.

370 "I wish I could describe . . .": Quotes of Dr.
Murphy, Dr. Kenny, and Dr. Lawlor from
Ruffman and Howell, *Ground Zero*, pp. 246–67.

371 "When Murray reported for duty . . ."
Florence J. Murray, *At The Foot of Dragon Hill*,
New York: E. P. Dutton & Company, Inc., 1975,
pp. vii–x.

372 "When a volunteer at the Armories . . .": Kitz,
Shattered City, p. 75.

373 "Murray's classmate and close friend . . .": His
stories and others from the hospital come from
Ruffman and Howell, *Ground Zero*, pp. 246–49,
except those about tetanus, the bucket, and the
C Company, which are found in Kitz, *Shattered
City*, pp. 66–67 and 77.

378 "Although Barss had no medical training . . .":
Joseph Ernest Barss, letter to his uncle Andrew
Townson, December 14, 1917, Barss family
archives.

Chapter 26: Blizzard

381 "The sunny, balmy conditions . . .": Raddall and Kimber, *Halifax: Warden of the North*, p. 247.

385 "Far worse was . . .": Raddall and Kimber, *Halifax: Warden of the North*, p. 247.

385 "the worst in a decade . . .": MacDonald, *Curse of the Narrows*, pp. 144–45.

388 "While the horse-drawn sleighs . . .": Ruffman and Howell, *Ground Zero*, p. 125.

388 "One day after workers had restored . . .": MacDonald, *Curse of the Narrows*, p. 125.

389 "The Dartmouth Relief Committee . . .": Kitz, *Shattered City*, p. 74.

390 "Since Indian days . . .": Raddall and Kimber, *Halifax: Warden of the North*, p. 247.

Chapter 27: Lost and Found

392 "For the many families . . .": Kitz, *Shattered City*, pp. 76–77.

393 "Gordon and James Pattison woke up . . .": Ibid., pp. 77 and 81; and Kitz, *Survivors*, pp. 81 and 86.

395 "Bertha's letter to her fiancé . . .": Kitz, *Shattered City*, p. 78.

396 "If this was the work of God . . .": Maritime Museum of the Atlantic, various websites, 2000.

396 "While almost everything had been

destroyed . . .": Beed, *1917 Halifax Explosion and American Response*, p. 15.

397 "Barbara Orr lay in her bed . . .": Kitz, *Survivors*, p. 75.

400 "The little girl became . . .": Kitz, *Shattered City*, p. 76.

402 "As soon as the mechanics . . .": MacDonald, *Curse of the Narrows*, pp. 174–75.

Chapter 28: The Last Stop

405 "Three lots from . . .": Kitz, *Shattered City*, pp. 106–7.

406 "A two-story house . . .": Ibid., p. 107.

408 "The *Halifax Herald* . . .": Ibid., p. 105.

408 "they still needed a burial permit . . .": Ibid.

409 "Mr. Huggins, the principal . . .": Kitz, *Survivors*, p. 74.

410 "Help. Help. Please help me.": MacDonald, *Curse of the Narrows*, pp. 163–64.

Chapter 29: The Yanks Are Coming

412 ". . . and treated an estimated 90 percent . . .": Zemel, *Scapegoat*, p. 1.

413 "Doctors and nurses arrived . . .": Raddall and Kimber, *Halifax: Warden of the North*, pp. 248–49.

414 "Ratshesky recalled . . .": MacDonald, *Curse of the Narrows*, pp. 178–79.

415 "Borden's 'answer came . . .'": Beed, *1917 Halifax Explosion and American Response*, p. 22

416 "The building was turned over to us . . .": Ibid., p. 23.

416 "Bellevue had been transformed . . .": Kitz, *Shattered City*, pp. 78 and 87.

417 "More good news from Boston . . .": Beed, *1917 Halifax Explosion and American Response*, pp. 23–24.

418 "Ernest Barss and his mentor . . .": Joseph Ernest Barss, letter to his uncle Andrew Townson, December 14, 1917, Barss family archives.

Chapter 30: A Working Sabbath

422 "From certain parts of Canada . . .": Kitz, *Shattered City*, p. 95.

423 "We would deliver . . .": Ibid.

425 "Henry B. Endicott . . .": Beed, *1917 Halifax Explosion and American Response*, pp. 23–24.

426 "This afternoon I visited the hospital . . .": Ibid., p. 23.

427 "Canada's Governor General Thanks the President . . .": Ibid., pp. 68–69.

429 "The impulse to blame someone . . .": Zemel, *Scapegoat*, p. 1.

Chapter 31: "It's Me, Barbara!"

431 "Barbara's hope waned by the hour . . .": Barbara Orr story in Kitz, *Shattered City*, pp. 79–80; and Kitz, *Survivors*, pp. 75–78.

434 "Millicent Upham was moved . . .": Kitz, *Shattered City*, p. 90; and Kitz, *Survivors*, p. 82.

434 "Frank Burford, the fifteen-year-old . . .": Kitz, *Shattered City*, pp. 56 and 81.

435 "Coleman, Vincent, funeral . . .": Beed, *1917 Halifax Explosion and American Response*, p. 35.

Chapter 32: Small Gifts

438 "The prostitutes who had come from all over Canada . . .": Ruffman and Howell, *Ground Zero*, p. 131.

439 "Six days after the explosion . . .": Kitz, *Shattered City*, pp. 79–80.

441 "There were good people . . .": Ibid., p. 91.

441 "Jean Hunter . . .": Ibid., pp. 92–94.

443 "Cliff Driscoll found the family cow . . .": Ibid., p. 94.

444 "The leaders of society . . .": Beed, *1917 Halifax Explosion and American Response*, p. 17.

445 "the Clothing Committee . . .": Kitz, *Shattered City*, p. 92.

449 "The Ford Motor Company . . .": Ibid., p. 94.

451 "Perhaps inspired by Boston's example . . .": Beed, *1917 Halifax Explosion and American Response*, pp. 66–67.

453 "A benefit concert was arranged . . .": Ibid., p. 28.

Chapter 33: A Toast to Allies

454 "The *Calvin Austin* . . .": Beed, *1917 Halifax Explosion and American Response*, p. 24.

454 "With splendid heart . . .": Raddall and Kimber, *Halifax: Warden of the North*, p. 249.

455 "The State of Maine hospital . . .": Beed, *1917 Halifax Explosion and American Response*, pp. 26 and 67.

456 "a delightful and informal dinner . . .": Ibid., p. 27.

457 "a complete warehouse of household goods . . .": Maritime Museum of the Atlantic, various websites, 2000.

457 "splendid outburst of help . . .": Kitz, *Shattered City*, p. 84.

458 " 'instant and unstinting aid . . .'": Ibid., *Shattered City*, p. 85.

458 "At Hospital you will find . . .": Beed, *1917 Halifax Explosion and American Response*, p. 30.

Part VII: Rebuilding

Chapter 34: The Missing and the Dead

464 "Walter Driscoll, 1549 Barrington Street . . .": Kitz, *Shattered City*, pp. 80–82.

467 "Some sailors could be recognized . . .": Ibid., pp. 109–12.

469 "One deceased mother . . .": Ruffman and Howell, *Ground Zero*, p. 135.

470 "It is not by the hand of the Almighty . . .": Kitz, *Shattered City*, p. 108.

471 "When they realized . . .": MacDonald, *Curse of the Narrows*, p. 250.

Chapter 35: The Inquiry

474 "Its mission was . . .": Zemel, *Scapegoat*, p. 1.

475 "An editorial in the *Truro Daily News* . . .": The discussion derives mainly from Donald A. Kerr, writing in Ruffman and Howell, *Ground Zero*, pp. 368–71.

Chapter 36: Christmas 1917

480 "But on Monday, December 17, 1917 . . .": Kitz, *Shattered City*, pp. 113–14.

482 "On December 21 . . .": Ibid., pp. 115–16.

485 "Frank Burford . . .": Ibid., pp. 116–18; and Kitz, *Survivors*, p. 87.

486 "The Overseas Club . . .": Kitz, *Shattered City*, pp. 117–18.

487 "After returning to Wolfville . . .": Joseph Ernest Barss, letter to his uncle Andrew Townson, December 14, 1917, Barss family archives.

Chapter 37: Orphans

489 "Others had lost one parent . . .": Kitz, *Shattered City*, pp. 96–102.

494 "Most correspondents were sincere . . .": Ibid., pp. 103–4; and Kitz, *Survivors*, p. 78.

Chapter 38: "Don't Stare"

498 "Of the many doctors . . .": Kitz, *Shattered City*, p. 90.

499 "The gratitude shown . . .": Ruffman and Howell, *Ground Zero*, pp. 249–50.

502 "The soldiers continued exhuming . . .": Kitz, *Shattered City*, pp. 107 and 112.

503 "In the summer of 1919 . . .": Raddall and

Kimber, *Halifax: Warden of the North,*
p. 248.

504 "Many victims never sought . . .": Ibid., p. 247.

505 "The many friends of Mrs. Vincent
Coleman . . .": Beed, *1917 Halifax Explosion and
American Response,* p. 35.

505 "Gordon Driscoll was never found . . .": Kitz,
Shattered City, pp. 81 and 112; and Kitz,
Survivors, pp. 81, 83, and 87.

508 "Not one photograph of the Orr family . . .":
Kitz, *Shattered City,* p. 82.

Chapter 39: The Trials

509 "The Wreck Commissioner's Inquiry . . .":
These legal proceeding were all covered by
Donald A. Kerr in Ruffman and Howell, *Ground
Zero,* pp. 371–75.

Chapter 40: The Wholesome Discord
of a Thousand Saws

523 "For months the people of the North End . . .":
Raddall and Kimber, *Halifax: Warden of the
North,* p. 249.

524 "The Massachusetts Temporary Relief
Fund . . .": Maritime Museum of the Atlantic,
various websites, 2000.

526 "While the Americans' decision . . ." Kazin, *War Against War*, p. xv.

527 "When experts rank . . .": Ruffman and Howell, *Ground Zero*, p. 252.

527 "Oppenheimer and his team . . .": Ibid., p. 291.

528 "It speaks to the unprecedented magnitude . . .": Ibid, p. 292.

Part VIII: Facing the Future
Chapter 41: New Lives

533 "They . . .": Kitz, *Survivors*, p. 99.

533 "The Pattison boys had lost their home . . .": Ibid., pp. 97–98 and 113–15.

533 "The Reverend William Swetnam . . .": Kitz, *Shattered City*, p. xx.

534 "Archie and Millicent Upham . . .": Kitz, *Survivors*, pp. 98, 110, and 115.

535 "The Driscolls moved to South Uniacke . . .": Ibid, pp. 97, 103, 106, and 108.

536 "Did we ever make a mistake . . .": Kitz, *Shattered City*, p. 103; and Kitz, *Survivors*, pp. 99, 101, and 113.

537 "With all four Richmond churches . . .": Kitz, *Shattered City*, p. 99; and Kitz, *Survivors*, p. 102.

Chapter 42: The Accidental Doctor

538 "I have put you through college . . .": Helen Kolb Barss, letter to her children, Barss family archives. All her letters to her children were unfortunately not dated.

539 "until the tears . . .": Helen Kolb Barss, letter to her children, Barss family archives.

539 "On March 9, 1919 . . .": Joseph Ernest Barss, official military records, Barss family archives.

540 "For fun . . .": Helen Kolb Barss, letter to her children, Barss family archives.

541 "Darned if I know . . .": Author interview with Joseph Andrew Barss, 1999.

542 "He threw a few things in a trunk . . .": Helen Kolb Barss, letter to her children, Barss family archives.

544 "Because of the medical school's strict rule . . .": Helen Kolb Barss, letter to her children, Barss family archives.

546 "Barss paid a visit . . .": Helen Kolb Barss, letter to her children, Barss family archives.

548 "He sure gave me a good upbringing . . .": Author interview with Joseph Andrew Barss, 1999.

548 "Dr. Barss took his wife . . .": Author interview with Joe Barss, 2017.

606 • Source Notes

Chapter 43: The Lasting Impact

550 "One of the first Boston doctors . . .":
MacDonald, *Curse of the Narrows*, pp. 279–80.

556 "In 1996, author Blair Beed . . .": Beed, *1917
Halifax Explosion and American Response*, p. 29.

Chapter 44: The Reunion

558 "In between, on June 23, 1984 . . .": Kitz,
Survivors, pp. 129–30.

560 "Barbara Orr played . . .": Ibid., p. 133.

560 "'Sometimes,' she said . . .": Ibid., p. 103.

Bibliography

Africville Genealogy Society, *The Spirit of Africville*, Halifax: Lorimer, 2010.

Allan, Chantal, *Bomb Canada and Other Unkind Remarks in the American Media*, Edmonton: Athabasca University Press, 2009.

Allen, Thomas B., *Tories: Fighting for the King in America's First Civil War*, New York: HarperCollins, 2010.

Armstrong, J. G., *The Halifax Explosion and the Royal Canadian Navy*, Vancouver: UBC Press, 2002.

Azzi, Stephen, *Reconcilable Differences: A History of Canada–US Relations*, Don Mills: Oxford University Press, 2015.

Beed, Blair, *1917 Halifax Explosion and American Response*, Halifax: Self, 1988.

Bird, Kai, *American Prometheus: The Triumph and Tragedy of J. Robert Oppenheimer*, New York: Vintage Books, 2006.

Bird, Michael J., *The Town That Died*, Toronto: McGraw-Hill Ryerson Limited, 1962.

Boileau, John, *Half-Hearted Enemies: Nova Scotia, New England, and the War of 1812*, Halifax: Formac Publishing Ltd, 2005.

Boyd, Michelle Hébert, *Enriched by Catastrophe: Social Work and Social Conflict after the Halifax Explosion*, Halifax: Fenwood Publishing, 2007.

Brown, G. I., *The Big Bang: A History of Explosives* Gloucestershire, UK: Sutton Publishing Limited, 2001.

Clark, Christopher, *The Sleepwalkers: How Europe Went to War in 1914*, New York: Harper Perennial, 2014.

Conant, Jennet, *109 East Palace: Robert Oppenheimer and the Secret City of Los Alamos*, New York: Simon & Schuster, 2006.

Conant, Jennet, *Tuxedo Park: A Wall Street Tycoon and the Secret Palace of Science That Changed the Course of World War II*, New York: Simon & Schuster, 2003.

Cunningham, Hilary, ed., *Insight Guides: Canada*, Boston: Houghton Mifflin, 1995.

David, Saul, "How Germany Lost the WWI Arms Race," BBC News, February 16, 2012, http://www.bbc.com/news/magazine-17011607.

Dekers Hall of Fame Biographies, located in the concourse of Yost Fieldhouse.

DeLory, Barbara, *Historic Halifax Streetscapes Then and Now, Three Walking Tours*, vol. 1, Halifax: New World Publishing, 2016.

Diamond, Dan, *Total Hockey*, New York: Total Sports, 1998.

Dupuis, Michael, *Bearing Witness: Journalists, Record Keepers and the 1917 Halifax Explosion*, Halifax: Fernwood, 2017.

Dutil, Patrice, and David MacKenzie, *Canada 1911: The Decisive Election that Shaped the Country*, Toronto: Dundurn, 2011.

Flemming, David B., *Explosion in Halifax Harbour: The Illustrated Account of a Disaster that Shook the World*, Halifax: Formac Publishing, 2004.

Fingard, J., J. Guildford, and D. Sutherland, *Halifax: The First 250 Years*, Halifax: Formac Publishing, 1999.

Fingard, J., *The Dark Side of Life in Victorian Halifax*, Nova Scotia: Pottersfield Press, 1989.

Flink, James J., *The Automobile Age*, Cambridge: MIT Press, 1990.

Flink, James J., *The Car Culture*, Cambridge: MIT Press, 1975.

Glasner, Joyce, *The Halifax Explosion: Surviving the Blast that Shook a Nation*, Canmore, Alberta: Altitude Publishing, 2003.

Goodchild, P., *J. Robert Oppenheimer: Shatterer of Worlds*, Boston: Houghton Mifflin, 1981.

Goodwin, Doris Kearns, *The Bully Pulpit: Theodore Roosevelt, William Howard Taft, and the Golden Age of Journalism*, New York: Simon & Schuster, 2014.

Gray, Charlotte, *The Promise of Canada: 150 Years—People and Ideas That Have Shaped Our Country*, New York: Simon & Schuster, 2016.

Gray, Edwin A., *The U-Boat War 1914–1918*, London: Leo Cooper, 1994.

Hadley, M. L., and R. Sarty, *Tin Pots and Pirate Ships: Canadian Naval Forces and German Sea Raiders 1880–1918*, Montreal: McGill Queens University Press, 1991.

Helen Kolb Barss letters to her children, Barss family archives.

Hemingway, Ernest, *A Farewell to Arms*, New York: Scribner's, 1957.

Hemingway, Ernest, *A Moveable Feast*, New York: Touchstone, 1996.

Hemingway, Ernest, *The Sun Also Rises*, New York: Scribner, 1954.

Hersey, John, *Hiroshima*, New York: Vintage Books, 1989.

History Journal, "U-Boats in World War I," https://historyjournal.org/2012/08/28/u-boats-in-world-war-i/

Hochschild, Adam, *To End All Wars: A Story of Loyalty and Rebellion, 1914–1918*, Boston: Mariner, 2012.

Hollander, Zander, *The Complete Encyclopedia of Hockey*, Detroit: Gale Research, 1983.

Holzman, Morey, and Joseph Nieforth, *Deceptions and Doublecross: How the NHL Conquered Hockey*, Toronto: Dundurn Press, 2002.

Jasanoff, Maya, *Liberty's Exiles: American Loyalists in the Revolutionary World*, New York: Vintage Books, 2012.

Jennings, Peter, and Todd Brewster, *The Century*, New York: Doubleday, 1998.

Jobb, D., *Crime Wave: Con Men, Rogues, and Scoundrels from Nova Scotia's Past*, Nova Scotia: Pottersfield Press, 1991.

Joseph Ernest Barrs letters, 1915–1916, Barss family archives.

Joseph Ernest Barss official military records, Barss family archives.

Kahn, Edgar A., M.D., *Journal of a Neurosurgeon*, Springfield, IL: Charles C. Thomas, 1972.

Kahn, Edgar A., M.D., "Albert Kahn: His Son Remembers," *Michigan History Magazine*, July-August, 1981, pp. 24–31.

Kazin, Michael, *War Against War: The American Fight for Peace, 1914–1918*, New York: Simon & Schuster, 2017.

Keegan, John, *The First World War*, New York: Vintage Books, 1998.

Keegan, John, *The Face of Battle: A Study of Agincourt, Waterloo and the Somme*, New York: Penguin Books, 1983.

Keegan, John, *A History of Warfare*, New York: Vintage Books, 1994.

Kelly, Cynthia C., *Manhattan Project: The Birth of the Atomic Bomb in the Words of Its Creators, Eyewitnesses, and Historians*, New York: Black Dog & Leventhal Publishers, Inc., 2007.

Kitz, Janet F., *Shattered City: The Halifax Explosion and the Road to Recovery*, Halifax: Nimbus Publishing Ltd., 1989.

Kitz, Janet F., *Survivors: Children of the Halifax Explosion*, Halifax: Nimbus Publishing Ltd., 2000.

Kitz, Janet F., and Joan Payzant, *December 1917: Re-Visiting the Halifax Explosion*, Halifax: Nimbus Publishing, 2006.

Larabee, Ann, *The Dynamite Fiend: The Chilling Tale of A Confederate Spy, Con Artist, and Mass Murderer*, New York: Palgrave Macmillan, 2005.

Larson, Erik, *Dead Wake: The Last Crossing of the Lusitania*, New York: Broadway Books, 2016.

Larson, Erik, *Isaac's Storm: A Man, A Time, and the Deadliest Hurricane in History*, New York: Crown Publishers, 1999.

Lord, Walter, *A Night to Remember: The Classic Account of the Final Hours of the Titanic*, New York: Holt Paperback, 2004.

Lord, Walter, *The Good Years: From 1900 to The First World War*, Whitefish: Kessinger Publishing, 2010.

Louder, Dean, ed., *The Heart of French Canada: From Ottawa to Quebec City*, New Brunswick, NJ: Rutgers University Press, 1992.

Lyman, George Hinckley, *The Story of the Massachusetts Committee on Public Safety*, Boston: Wright & Potter Printing Co., 1919.

MacDonald, Laura M., *Curse of the Narrows*, New York: Walker and Company, 2005.

MacKenzie, David, and Patrice Dutil, *Canada 1911: The Decisive Election that Shaped the Country*, Toronto: Dundurn, 2011.

MacKenzie, Shelagh, and Scott Robson, eds., *Halifax Street Names: An Illustrated Guide*, Halifax: Formac Publishing Company, 2002.

MacMillan, Margaret, *Paris 1919: Six Months That Changed the World*, New York, Random House Trade Paperbacks, 2003.

MacMillan, Margaret, *The War That Ended Peace: The Road to 1914*, New York: Random House Trade Paperbacks, 2014.

MacNeil, Robert, *Burden of Desire*, New York: Bantam Doubleday Publishing Group, Inc., 1992.

MacNeil, Robert, *Wordstruck*, New York: Penguin, 1990.

Madej, Bruce, et al., *Michigan: Champions of the West*, Champaign, IL: Sports Publishing, 1997.

Mahar, J., and R. Mahar, *Too Many to Mourn*, Halifax: Nimbus Publishing Ltd., 1998.

Manchester, William, *Winston Spencer Churchill: The Last Lion*, New York: Bantam, Doubleday, Dell, 1983.

March, William, *Co. K*, Tuscaloosa: University of
Alabama Press, 1933.

Maritime Museum of the Atlantic, various websites,
Halifax, 2000.

Marwil, Jonathan L., *A History of Ann Arbor*, Ann
Arbor, MI: Ann Arbor Observer Press, 1987.

Maybee, Janet, *Aftershock: The Halifax Explosion and
the Persecution of Pilot Francis Mackey*, Halifax:
Nimbus Publishing Ltd., 2016.

McCullough, David, *The Johnstown Flood*, New York:
Simon & Schuster, 1987.

Media Guides from the University of Michigan hockey
team, 1937–present, plus the 1999–2000 media
guides of the University of Minnesota, Boston
University, Boston College, and Dartmouth.

Metson, G., and A. MacMechan, *The Halifax
Explosion: December 6th, 1917*, Toronto:
McGraw-Hill Ryerson, 1978.

Meyers, Mike, *Canada*, Toronto: Doubleday Canada,
2016.

Millichope, David, *Halifax in the Great War*, South
Yorkshire: Pen & Sword Military, 2015.

Murray, Florence J., *At The Foot of Dragon Hill*, New
York: E. P. Dutton & Company, Inc., 1975, pp.
vii–x.

National Film Board of Canada, *Between Friends/Entre Amis*, Ottowa: McClelland and Stewart, 1976.

Peckham, Howard H., *The Making of the University of Michigan: 1817–1992*, Ann Arbor: Bentley Library of the University of Michigan, 1994.

Perry, Will, *The Wolverines*, Huntsville, AL: Strode Publishers, 1974.

Prince, Samuel Henry, *Catastrophe and Social Change: Based Upon a Sociological Study of the Halifax Disaster*, New York: Columbia University, 1920.

Raddall, Thomas H., *In My Time: A Memoir*, Toronto: McClelland and Stewart, 1976.

Raddall, Thomas, H., and Stephen Kimber, *Halifax: Warden of the North*, updated edition, Halifax: Nimbus Publishing Ltd., 2010.

Remarque, Erich Maria, *All Quiet on the Western Front*, New York: Ballantine, 1984.

Reynolds, Michael, *The Young Hemingway*, New York: Norton, 1998.

Rhodes, Richard, *The Making of the Atomic Bomb: 25th Anniversary Edition*, New York: Simon & Schuster, 2012.

Royal Nova Scotia Historical Society, *Collections of the Royal Nova Scotia Historical Society*, volume 41, Halifax: McCurdy Printing & Typesetting Limited, 1982.

Ruffman, A., and C. D. Howell, *Ground Zero: A Reassessment of the 1917 Explosion in Halifax Harbour*, Halifax: Nimbus Publishing Ltd., 1994.

Sanders, Sol W., James V. Capua, and William T. Alpert, eds., *The Candian Crisis: A Guide for American Media*, New York: William H. Donner Foundation, 1992.

Shackman, Grace, "Weinberg's Coliseum," *The Ann Arbor Observer*, February 1983, pp. 101–2.

Shushkewich, Val, *The Real Winnie: A One-of-a-Kind Bear*, Toronto: Natural Heritage Books, 2005.

Stager, J. K., and Harry Swain, *Canada North: Journey to the High Arctic*, New Brunswick, NJ: Rutgers University Press, 1992.

Stein, Mark, *How the States Got Their Shapes*, Washington, DC: Smithsonian Books, 2008.

Stout, Glenn, *Fenway 1912: The Birth of a Ballpark, A Championship Season, and Fenway's Remarkable First Year*, New York: Houghton Mifflin Harcourt, 2011.

Stout, Glenn, *The Selling of the Babe: The Deal that Changed Baseball and Created a Legend*, New York: Thomas Dunn Books, 2016.

Tatterie, Jon, *Black Snow: A Story of Love and Destruction*, Lawrencetown Beach: Pottersfield Press, 2009.

The University of Michigan's Bentley Historical
    Library, clip book of the *Michigan Daily,* the *Ann
    Arbor News,* the *Detroit News,* and the *Detroit
    Free Press,* 1911–present.
The University of Michigan, Minutes of the Board in
    Control of Intercollegiate Athletics, 1910–present.
The Sports Information Department of the University
    of Michigan, Media Guides for ice hockey, football,
    and basketball.
Thompson, John Herd, and Stephen J. Randall, *Canada
    and the United States: Ambivalent Allies,* fourth
    ed., Athens: University of Georgia Press, 2008.
Tuchman, Barbara W., *The Guns of August,* New York:
    Presidio Press, 1962.
Tuchman, Barbara W., *The Proud Tower: A Portrait of
    the World Before the War, 1890–1914,* New York:
    Macmillan, 1980.
Tuchman, Barbara W., *The Zimmermann Telegram,*
    New York: Random House, 1985.
Tucker, Alan, ed., *The Berlitz Travelers Guide to
    Canada,* New York: Berlitz, 1993.
Walker, Sally M., *Blizzard of Glass: The Halifax
    Explosion of 1917,* New York: Square Fish, 2014.
Walker, William, *Betrayal at Little Gibraltar: A German
    Fortress, a Treacherous American General,*

and the Battle to End World War I, New York: Scribner, 2017.

Whitehead, Ruth Holmes, *Tracking Doctor Lonecloud: Showman to Legend Keeper*, Fredericton, New Brunswick: Goose Lane Editions, 2002.

Williams, Jeffrey, *First in the Field: Gault of the Patricia's*, Barnsley, UK: Pen and Sword, 1997.

Witcover, J., *Sabotage at Black Tom: Imperial Germany's Secret War in America, 1914–17*, Chapel Hill, NC: Algonquin Books, 1989.

Zemel, Joel, *Scapegoat: The Extraordinary Legal Proceedings Following the 1917 Halifax Explosion*, Halifax: New World Publishing, 2012.

THE NEW LUXURY IN READING

We hope you enjoyed reading
our new, comfortable print size and found it
an experience you would like to repeat.

Well – you're in luck!

HarperLuxe offers the finest in fiction and
nonfiction books in this same larger print size and
paperback format. Light and easy to read, HarperLuxe
paperbacks are for book lovers who want to see
what they are reading without the strain.

For a full listing of titles and
new releases to come, please visit our website:

www.HarperLuxe.com